CLYMER®

HONDA

XL/XR 500-600 • 1979-1990

The world's finest publisher of mechanical how-to manuals

CLYMER®

P.O. Box 12901, Overland Park, Kansas 66282-2901

FIRST EDITION
First Printing May, 1989
Second Printing January, 1990

SECOND EDITION
First Printing August, 1990
Second Printing January, 1992

THIRD EDITION
First Printing January, 1993
Second Printing May, 1994

FOURTH EDITION
First Printing July, 1995
Second Printing November, 1996

FIFTH EDITION
First Printing December, 1997
Second Printing June, 1999
Third Printing January, 2001

SIXTH EDITION
First Printing April, 2002

SEVENTH EDITION
First Printing September, 2003
Second Printing December, 2004

EIGHTH EDITION
First Printing August, 2007
Second Printing February, 2011

Printed in U.S.A.

CLYMER and colophon are registered trademarks of Penton Business Media, Inc.

ISBN-10: 1-59969-142-6

ISBN-13: 978-1-59969-142-8

Library of Congress: 2007933121

TOOLS AND EQUIPMENT: K & L Supply at www.klsupply.com.

COVER: Mark Clifford Photography at www. markclifford.com.

CLYMER®

Publisher Ron Rogers

EDITORIAL

Editorial Director
James Grooms

Editor
Steven Thomas

Associate Editor
Rick Arens

Authors
Michael Morlan
George Parise
Ed Scott
Ron Wright

Technical Illustrators
Steve Amos
Errol McCarthy
Mitzi McCarthy
Bob Meyer

SALES

Sales Manager–Marine
Jay Lipton

Sales Manager–Powersport/I&T
Matt Tusken

CUSTOMER SERVICE

Customer Service Manager
Terri Cannon

Customer Service Representatives
Karen Barker
Dinah Bunnell
April LeBlond
Suzanne Myers
Sherry Rudkin

PRODUCTION

Director of Production
Dylan Goodwin

Production Manager
Greg Araujo

Production Editors
Holly McComas
Adriane Roberts

Associate Production Editor
Ashley Bally

P.O. Box 12901, Overland Park, KS 66282-2901 • 800-262-1954 • 913-967-1719

More information available at *clymer.com*

CONTENTS

QUICK REFERENCE DATA

MOTORCYCLE INFORMATION

MODEL:_____YEAR:_____

VIN NUMBER:_____

ENGINE SERIAL NUMBER:_____

CARBURETOR SERIAL NUMBER OR I.D. MARK:_____

TIRE INFLATION PRESSIRE (COLD)*

Tire size	psi	kg/cm^2
Front tire		
3.00-21 6PR	14	1.0
3.00-21 4PR	21	1.5
3.00-21 51S	22	1.55
3.00-23 6PR	15	1.03
3.00-23 4PR	21	1.5
90/80-21 6PR	15	1.03
90/90-21 6PR	14	1.0
90/100-21 51M	15	1.03
Rear tire		
4.60-17 4PR	21	1.5
5.10-17 6PR	11	0.8
5.10-17 4PR	21	1.5
4.60-18 4PR	21	1.5
4.60-18 6PR	17	1.2
4.60-18 63S	22	1.5
110/90-17 6PR	14	1.0
130/80-17 6PR	14	1.0
110/100-18 64M	15	1.03

*Recommended air pressure for factory equipped tires. Aftermarket tires may require different air pressure.

ENGINE OIL CAPACITY

	Oil drain			Rebuild	
Engine size	U.S. qt.	Liter		U.S. qt.	Liter
500 cc (1979-1982)	1.6	1.5		2.1	2.0
500 cc, 600 cc (1983-1990)	2.1	2.0		2.6	2.5

TUNE-UP SPECIFICATIONS

Item	Specification
Valve clearance	
XR600R	
Intake	0.10 mm (0.004 in.)
Exhaust	0.12 mm (0.005 in.)
All other models	
Intake	0.05 mm (0.002 in.)
Exhaust	0.10 mm (0.004 in.)
Compression pressure (at sea level)	
XR600R	
1985-1987	125.2-130.8 psi (8.8-9.2 kg/cm^2)
1988-1990	185.8-214.2 psi (13-15 kg/cm^2)
All other models	175 psi (12.5 kg/cm^2)
Spark plug type	
Standard heat range	
1978-1981	ND X24ES-U or NGK D8EA
1982	ND X24ESR-U or NGK DR8ES-L
1983-1990	ND X24EPR-U9 or NGK DPR8EA-9
Gap	0.8-0.9 mm (0.032-0.036 in.)
Ignition timing	"F" mark @ 1200 ±100 rpm
Idle speed	
1988-1990 XR600R	1300 ±100 rpm
All other models	1200 ±100 rpm

FRONT FORK OIL CAPACITY*

Model	Standard capacity		Standard distance from top of fork	
	cc	fl. oz.	mm	in.
XL500S	190	6.4	–	–
XL500R	379	12.75	163	6.42
XR500	202	6.8	–	–
XR500R				
1981-1982	345	11.7	181	7.1
1983	651	22	141	5.5
1984	651	22		
Maximum	–	–	171	6.73
Minimum	–	–	131	5.16
XL600R	455	15.4	150	5.9
XR600R				
1985-1987	631	21.3		
Maximum	–	–	147	5.8
Minimum	–	–	117	4.6
1988-1990	643	21.8		
Maximum	–	–	130	5.1
Minimum	–	–	100	3.9

*Capacity for each fork leg.

MAINTENANCE AND TUNE-UP TORQUE SPECIFICATIONS

item	N•m	ft.-lb.
Oil drain plug		
Wet sump models	30-40	22-29
Dry sump models		
Crankcase drain plug		
1988-1990 XR600R	25	18
All other models	30-40	22-29
Frame down tube		
Drain plug		
1988-1990 XR600R	40	29
All other models	25-35	18-25
Oil strainer nut		
1988-1990 XR600R	55	40
All other models	35-45	25-32
Oil strainer oil hose		
1988-1990 XR600R	40	29
All other models	35-45	25-32
Oil filter cover screws		
Models so equipped		
1988-1990 XR600R	12	9
All other models	8-10	5-7
Fork cap bolt		
1988-1990 XR600R	23	16
All other models	15-30	11-22
Rear axle nut		
Dual shock models	70-110	51-80
Pro-Link models		
1988-1990 XR600R	95	69
All other models	80-110	58-80
Balancer chain holder lockbolt	18-25	13-18
Fuel cup strainer		
Models so equipped	3-5	2-4
Wheel rim locks	9-15	7-11
Valve adjuster locknuts		
1979-1982	15-18	11-13
1983-1984 XR500R	18-22	13-16
XL600R	15-18	11-13
XR600R	23-27	17-19

DRIVE CHAIN FREE PLAY

Model	mm	in.
Dual shock models		
XL series	15-20	0.6-0.8
XR series	20	0.8
Pro-Link models		
XL series	30-40	1 1/4-1 5/8
XR series	35-45	1 3/8-1 3/4

FRONT FORK AIR PRESSURE

Model	psi	kPa
1982 XR500R	0-2.8	0-19.3
XR500R	0-14	96.5
All other models	0	0

CLYMER®

HONDA

XL/XR 500-600 • 1979-1990

CHAPTER ONE

GENERAL INFORMATION

This detailed, comprehensive manual covers the Honda XL and XR 500-600 series singles from 1979-1990.

The expert text gives complete information on maintenance, tune-up, repair and overhaul. Hundreds of photos and drawings guide you through every step. The book includes all you will need to know to keep your Honda running right. Throughout this book where differences occur among the models, they are clearly identified.

A shop manual is a reference. You want to be able to find information fast. As in all Clymer books, this one is designed with you in mind. All chapters are thumb tabbed. Important items are extensively indexed at the rear of the book. All procedures, tables, photos, etc., in this manual are for the reader who may be working on the bike for the first time or using this manual for the first time. All the most frequently used specifications and capacities are summarized in the *Quick Reference Data* pages at the front of the book.

Keep the book handy in your tool box. It will help you better understand how your bike runs, lower repair costs and generally improve your satisfaction with the bike.

Tables 1-3 are at the end of this chapter.

MANUAL ORGANIZATION

All dimensions and capacities are expressed in English units familiar to U.S. mechanics as well as in metric units.

This chapter provides general information and discusses equipment and tools useful both for preventive maintenance and troubleshooting. **Table 1** contains model designation information.

Chapter Two provides methods and suggestions for quick and accurate diagnosis and repair or problems. Troubleshooting procedures discuss typical symptoms and logical methods to pinpoint the trouble.

Chapter Three explains all periodic lubrication and routine maintenance necessary to keep your

Honda running well. Chapter Three also includes recommended tune-up procedures, eliminating the need to constantly consult chapters on the various assemblies.

Subsequent chapters describe specific systems such as the engine, clutch, transmission, fuel, exhaust, suspension and brakes. Each chapter provides disassembly, repair and assembly procedures in simple step-by-step form.

If a repair is impractical for a home mechanic, it is so indicated. It is usually faster and less expensive to take such repairs to a dealer or competent repair shop. Specifications concerning a particular system are included at the end of the appropriate chapter.

Some of the procedures in this manual specify special tools. In most cases, the tool is illustrated either in actual use or alone. Well equipped mechanics may find they can substitute similar tools already on hand or can fabricate their own.

NOTES, CAUTIONS AND WARNINGS

The terms NOTE, CAUTION and WARNING have specific meanings in this manual. A NOTE provides additional information to make a step or procedure easier or clearer. Disregarding a NOTE could cause inconvenience, but would not cause equipment damage or personal injury.

A CAUTION emphasizes areas where equipment damage could occur. Disregarding a CAUTION could cause permanent mechanical damage; however, personal injury is unlikely.

A WARNING emphasizes areas where personal injury or even death could result from negligence. Mechanical damage may also occur. WARNINGS *are to be taken seriously.* In some cases, serious injury or death has resulted from disregarding similar warnings.

Throughout this manual keep in mind 2 conventions. "Front" refers to the front of the bike. The front of any component, such as the engine, is the end which faces toward the front of the bike. The "left-" and "right-hand" sides refer to the position of the parts as viewed by a rider sitting on the seat facing forward. For example, the throttle control is on the right-hand side and the clutch lever is on the left-hand side. These rules are simple, but even experienced mechanics occasionally become disoriented.

SERVICE HINTS

Most of the service procedures covered are straightforward and can be performed by anyone reasonably handy with tools. It is suggested, however, that you consider your own capabilities carefully before attempting any operation involving major disassembly of the engine.

Some operations, for example, require the use of a press. It would be wiser to have these performed by a shop equipped for such work, rather than trying to do the job yourself with makeshift equipment. Other procedures require precise measurements. Unless you have the skills and equipment required, it would be better to have a qualified repair shop make the measurements for you.

There are many items available that can be used on your hands before and after working on your bike. A little preparation before getting "all greased up" will help when cleaning up later.

Before starting out, work Vaseline, soap or a product such as Pro-Tek Invisible Glove (**Figure 1**) onto your forearms, into your hands and under your fingernails and cuticles. This will make cleanup a lot easier.

For cleanup, use a waterless hand soap such as Sta-Lube and then finish up with powdered Boraxo and a fingernail brush.

Repairs go much faster and easier if the bike is clean before you begin work. There are special cleaners, such as Gunk or Bel-Ray Degreaser (**Figure 2**) for washing the engine and related parts. Just spray or brush on the cleaning solution, let it stand, then rinse it away with a garden hose. Clean all oily or greasy parts with cleaning solvent as you remove them.

> *WARNING*
> ***Never*** *use gasoline as a cleaning agent. It presents an extreme fire hazard. Be sure to work in a well-ventilated area when using cleaning solvent. Keep a fire extinguisher, rated for gasoline fires, handy in any case.*

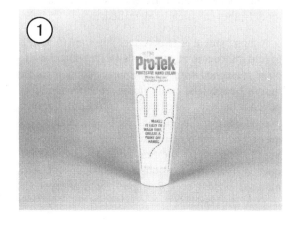

Special tools are required for some repair procedures. These may be purchased from a dealer or motorcycle shop, rented from a tool rental dealer or fabricated by a mechanic or machinist, often at a considerable savings.

Much of the expense charged by mechanics is for the labor involved in the removal and disassembly of other parts to reach the defective unit. It is usually possible to perform the preliminary operations yourself and then take the defective unit in to the dealer for repair.

Once you have decided to tackle the job yourself, read the entire section in this manual which pertains to it, making sure you have identified the proper one. Study the illustrations and text until you have a good idea of what is involved in completing the job satisfactorily. If special tools or replacement parts are required, make arrangements to get them before you start. It is frustrating and time-consuming to get partly into a job and then be unable to complete it.

Simple wiring checks can be easily made at home, but knowledge of electronics is almost a necessity for performing tests with complicated electronic testing gear.

During disassembly of parts keep a few general cautions in mind. Force is rarely needed to get things apart. If parts are a tight fit, such as a bearing in a case, there is usually a tool designed to separate them. Never use a screwdriver to pry parts with machined surfaces such as crankcase halves. You will mar the surfaces and end up with leaks.

Make diagrams or take a Polaroid picture wherever similar-appearing parts are found. For instance, crankcase bolts are often not the same length. You may think you can remember where everything came from, but mistakes are costly. There is also the possibility you may be sidetracked and not return to work for days or even weeks, in which interval carefully laid out parts may have become disturbed.

Tag all similar internal parts for location and mark all mating parts for position. Record number and thickness of any shims as they are removed. Small parts such as bolts can be identified by placing them in plastic sandwich bags. Seal and label them with masking tape.

Wiring should be tagged with masking tape and marked as each wire is removed. Again, do not rely on memory alone.

Protect finished surfaces from physical damage or corrosion. Keep gasoline and hydraulic brake fluid off plastic parts and painted and plated surfaces.

Frozen or very tight bolts and screws can often be loosened by soaking with penetrating oil, such as WD-40 or Liquid Wrench, then sharply striking the bolt head a few times with a hammer and punch (or screwdriver for screws). Avoid heat unless absolutely necessary, since it may melt, warp or remove the temper from many parts.

No parts, except those assembled with a press fit, require unusual force during assembly. If a part is hard to remove or install, find out why before proceeding.

Cover all openings after removing parts to keep dirt, small tools, etc., from falling in.

When assembling 2 parts, start all fasteners, then tighten evenly.

Wiring connections and brake components should be kept clean and free of grease and oil.

When assembling parts, be sure all shims and washers are installed exactly as they came out.

Whenever a rotating part butts against a stationary part, look for a shim or washer. Use new gaskets if there is any doubt about the condition of the old ones. A thin coat of oil on gaskets may help them seal effectively.

Heavy grease can be used to hold small parts in place if they tend to fall out during assembly. However, keep grease and oil away from electrical and brake components.

High spots may be sanded off a piston with sandpaper, but fine emery cloth and oil will do a much more professional job.

Carbon can be removed from the head, the piston crown and the exhaust port with a dull screwdriver. Do *not* scratch machined surfaces. Wipe off the surface with a clean cloth when finished.

The carburetor is best cleaned by disassembling and soaking the parts in a commercial carburetor cleaner. Never soak gaskets and rubber parts in these cleaners. Never use wire to clean out jets and air passages; they are easily damaged. Use compressed air to blow out the carburetor *after* the float has been removed.

A baby bottle makes a good measuring device for adding oil to the front forks. Get one that is graduated in fluid ounces and cubic centimeters. After it has been used for this purpose, do *not* let a small child drink out of it as there will always be an oil residue in it.

Take your time and do the job right. Do not forget that a newly rebuilt engine must be broken in the same as a new one. Keep the rpm within the limits given in your owner's manual when you get back on the road.

TORQUE SPECIFICATIONS

Torque specifications throughout this manual are given in Newton meters (N•m) and foot-pounds (ft.-lb.). Newton meters have been adopted in place of meter kilograms (mkg) in accordance with the International Modernized Metric System. Tool manufacturers offer torque wrenches calibrated in Newton meters and Sears has a Craftsman line calibrated in both values.

Existing torque wrenches calibrated in meter kilograms can be used by performing a simple conversion. All you have to do is move the decimal point one place to the right; for example, 4.7 mkg = 47 N•m. This conversion is accurate enough for mechanical work even though the exact mathematical conversion is 3.5 mkg = 34.3 N•m.

Refer to **Table 2** for standard torque specifications for various size screws, bolts and nuts that may not be covered in the various chapters.

SAFETY FIRST

Professional mechanics can work for years and never sustain a serious injury. If you observe a few rules of common sense and safety, you can enjoy many hours servicing your own machine. If you ignore these rules you can hurt yourself or damage the bike.

1. *Never* use gasoline as a cleaning solvent.
2. Never smoke or use a torch in the vicinity of flammable liquids such as cleaning solvent in open containers.
3. Never smoke or use a torch in an area where batteries are being charged. Highly explosive hydrogen gas is formed during the charging process.
4. If welding or brazing is required on the machine, remove the fuel tank to a safe distance, at least 50 feet away. Welding on gas tanks requires special safety procedures and must be performed by someone skilled in the process.

5. Use the proper sized wrenches to avoid damage to nuts and injury to yourself.
6. When loosening a tight or stuck nut, think about what would happen if the wrench should slip. Be careful; protect yourself accordingly.
7. Keep your work area clean and uncluttered.
8. Wear safety goggles during all operations involving drilling, grinding or use of a cold chisel.
9. Never use worn tools.
10. Keep a fire extinguisher handy and be sure it is rated for gasoline and electrical fires.

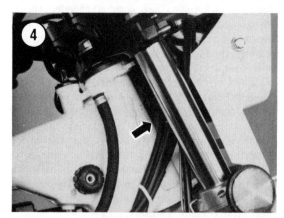

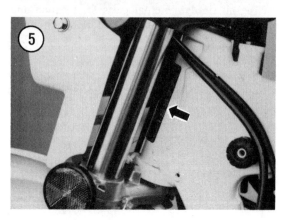

SPECIAL TIPS

Because of the extreme demands placed on a bike, several points should be kept in mind when performing service and repairs. The following items are general suggestions that may improve the overall life of the machine and help to avoid costly failures.

1. Use a locking compound such as Loctite 242 (blue Loctite) on bolts and nuts used in high-stress areas, even if they are secured with lockwashers. This type of Loctite does not harden completely and allows easy removal of the bolt or nut. A screw or bolt lost from an engine cover or bearing retainer could easily cause serious and expensive damage before its loss is noticed.

CAUTION

When applying Loctite, use a small amount. If too much is used, it can work its way down the thread and stick parts together that are not meant to be stuck.

2. Use a good quality hammer-driven impact tool to remove stubborn bolts, particlarly engine cover screws. These tools help to prevent the rounding off of bolt heads and insure tight installation.

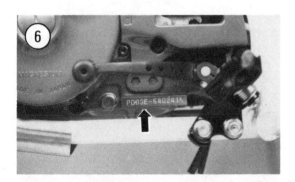

3. When replacing missing or broken fasteners (bolts, nuts and screws), especially on the engine or frame components, always use Honda replacement parts. They are specially hardened for each application. The wrong fastener could easily cause serious and expensive damage, not to mention rider injury.

4. When installing gaskets in the engine, always use Honda gaskets *without* sealer unless designated. These gaskets are designed to swell when they come in contact with oil. The head gasket has a sticky surface on each side that ensures a good seal. Gasket sealer will prevent the gaskets from swelling or sticking as intended, which can result in oil leaks. These Honda gaskets are cut from material of the precise thickness needed. Installation of a too thick or too thin gasket in a critical area could cause engine damage.

EXPENDABLE SUPPLIES

Certain expendable supplies are required during maintenance and repair work. These include grease, oil, gasket cement, wiping rags and cleaning solvent. Ask your dealer for the special locking compounds, silicone lubricants and other products (**Figure 3**) which make vehicle maintenance simpler and easier. Cleaning solvent or kerosene is available at some service stations or hardware stores.

PARTS REPLACEMENT

Honda makes frequent changes during a model year—some minor, some relatively major. When you order parts from the dealer or other parts distributor, always order by engine and frame number. Write the numbers down and carry them with you. Compare new parts to old before purchasing them. If they are not alike, have the parts manager explain the difference to you.

SERIAL NUMBERS

You must know the model serial number and VIN number for registration purposes and when ordering replacement parts.

The frame serial number is stamped on the right-hand side of the steering head (**Figure 4**). The vehicle identification number (VIN) is on the left-hand side of the steering head (**Figure 5**). The engine serial number is located on the lower left-hand side of the crankcase (**Figure 6**). The carburetor serial number is located on the carburetor body next to the float bowl (**Figure 7**).

BASIC HAND TOOLS

A number of tools are required to maintain a bike in good riding condition. You may already have some of these tools for home or automobile repairs. There are also tools made especially for motorcycle repairs; these you will have to purchase. In any case, a wide variety of quality tools will make motorcycle repairs easier and more effective.

Top quality tools are essential. They are also more economical in the long run. If you are starting to build your tool collection, stay away from the "advertised specials" featured at some parts houses, discount stores and chain drug stores. These are usually a poor grade tool that can be sold cheaply and that is exactly what they are—*cheap*. They are usually made of inferior material and are thick, heavy and clumsy. Their rough finish makes them difficult to clean and they usually don't last very long.

Quality tools are made of alloy steel and are heat treated for greater strength. They are lighter and better balanced than cheap ones. Their surface is smooth, making them a pleasure to work with and easy to clean. The initial cost of good quality tools may be more, but it is cheaper in the long run. Don't try to buy everything in all sizes in the beginning; do it a little at a time until you have the necessary tools.

Keep your tools clean and in a tool box. Keep them organized with the sockets and related drives together and the open end and box wrenches together, etc. After using a tool, wipe off dirt and grease with a clean cloth and place the tool in its correct place. Doing this will save a lot of time you would have spent trying to find a socket buried in a bunch of clutch parts.

The following tools are required to perform virtually any repair job on a bike. Each tool is described and the recommended size given for starting a tool collection. **Table 3** includes the tools that should be on hand for simple home repairs and/or major overhaul as shown in **Figure 8**. Additional tools and some duplicates may be added as you become more familiar with the bike. Almost all motorcycles and bikes, with the exception of the U.S. built Harley and some English bikes, use metric size bolts and nuts. If you are starting your collection now, buy metric sizes.

Screwdrivers

The screwdriver is a very basic tool, but if used improperly it will do more damage than good. The slot on a screw has a definite dimension and shape.

A screwdriver must be selected to conform with that shape. Use a small screwdriver for small screws and a large one for large screws or the screw head will be damaged.

Two basic types of screwdriver are required to repair the bike—a common (flat blade) screwdriver and a Phillips screwdriver.

Screwdrivers are available in sets which often include an assortment of common and Phillips blades. If you buy them individually, buy at least the following:

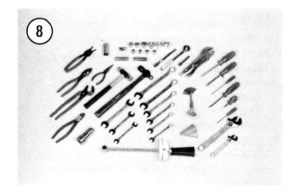

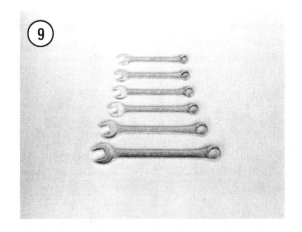

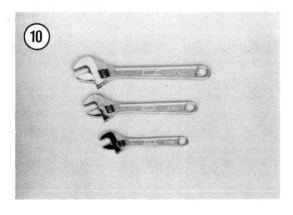

a. Common screwdriver—5/16×6 in. blade.
b. Common screwdriver—3/8×12 in. blade.
c. Phillips screwdriver—size 2 tip, 6 in. blade.

Use screwdrivers only for driving screws. Never use a screwdriver for prying or chiseling. Do not try to remove a Phillips or Allen head screw with a common screwdriver; you can damage the head so that the proper tool will be unable to remove it.

Keep screwdrivers in the proper condition and they will last longer and perform better. Always keep the tip of a common screwdriver in good condition.

Pliers

Pliers come in a wide range of types and sizes. Pliers are useful for cutting, bending and crimping. They should never be used to cut hardened objects or to turn bolts or nuts.

Each type of pliers has a specialized function. Gas pliers are general purpose pliers and are used mainly for holding things and for bending. Vise Grips are used as pliers or to hold objects very tight like a vise. Needlenose pliers are used to hold or bend small objects. Channel lock pliers can be adjusted to hold various sizes of objects; the jaws remain parallel to grip around objects such as pipe tubing. There are many other types of pliers. The ones described here are most suitable for bike repairs.

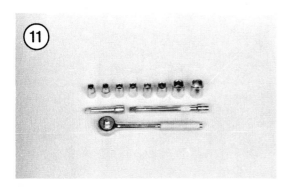

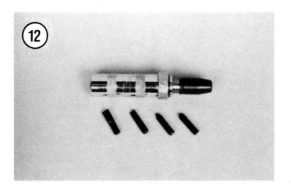

Box and Open-end Wrenches

Box and open-end wrenches are available in sets or separately in a variety of sizes. The size number stamped near the end refers to the distance between 2 parallel flats on the hex head bolt or nut.

Box wrenches are usually superior to open-end wrenches. Open-end wrenches grip the nut on only 2 flats. Unless it fits well, it may slip and round off the points on the nut. The box wrench grips all 6 flats. Both 6-point and 12-point openings on box wrenches are available. The 6-point gives superior holding power; the 12-point allows a shorter swing.

Combination wrenches (**Figure 9**) which are open on one side and boxed on the other are also available. Both ends are the same size.

Adjustable (Crescent) Wrenches

An adjustable wrench, also called crescent wrench, can be adjusted to fit nearly any nut or bolt head. See **Figure 10**. However, it can loosen and slip, causing damage to the nut and injury to your knuckles. Use an adjustable wrench only when other wrenches are not available.

Crescent wrenches come in sizes ranging from 4-18 in. overall. A 6 or 8 in. wrench is recommended as an all-purpose wrench.

Socket Wrenches

This type is undoubtedly the fastest, safest and most convenient to use. See **Figure 11**. Sockets which attach to a ratchet handle are available with 6-point or 12-point openings and 1/4, 3/8, 1/2 and 3/4 inch drives. The drive size indicates the size of the square hole which mates with the ratchet handle.

Torque Wrench

A torque wrench is used with a socket to measure how tight a nut or bolt is installed. They come in a wide price range and with either 3/8 or 1/2 in. square drive. The drive size indicates the size of the square drive which mates with the socket. Purchase one that measures 0-140 N•m (0-100 ft.-lb.).

Impact Driver

This tool makes removal of engine components easy and eliminates damage to bolts and Phillips screw heads. Good ones are available at larger hardware stores and motorcycle dealers. See **Figure 12**.

Circlip Pliers

Circlip pliers, sometimes referred to as snap-ring pliers, are necessary or remove circlips used on the transmission shaft assemblies. See **Figure 13**.

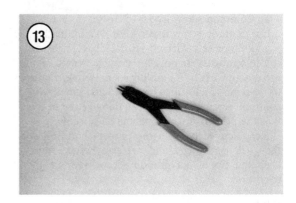

Hammers

The correct hammer is necessary for bike repairs. Use a hammer with a face (or head) of plastic or the soft-faced type that is filled with buck shot. These are sometimes necessary for engine tear-downs. *Never* use a metal-faced hammer on the bike as severe damage will result in most cases. You can always produce the same amount of force with a soft-faced hammer.

Ignition Gauge

This tool has both flat and wire measuring gauges and is used to measure the spark plug gap (**Figure 14**). This device is available at most auto or motorcycle supply stores.

Other Special Tools

A few special tools may be required for major service. These tools are described in the appropriate chapters and are available from a Honda dealer or other manufacturers as indicated.

TUNE-UP AND TROUBLESHOOTING TOOLS

Multimeter or VOM

This instrument (**Figure 15**) is invaluable for electrical system troubleshooting and service. A few of its functions may be duplicated by locally fabricated substitutes, but for the serious hobbyist it is a must. Its uses are described in the applicable sections of this book. Multimeters are available at electronic hobby stores and mail order outlets.

Strobe Timing Light

This instrument is necessary for tuning. By flashing a light at the precise instant the cylinder fires, the position of the timing mark at that instant can be seen. The timing marks are aligned with the timing mark on the engine while the engine is running.

Suitable lights range from inexpensive neon bulb types to powerful xenon strobe lights (**Figure 16**). Neon timing lights are difficult to see in dimly lit areas. Xenon strobe timing lights can be used outside in bright sunlight. Both types work on the bike. Use according to the manufacturer's instructions.

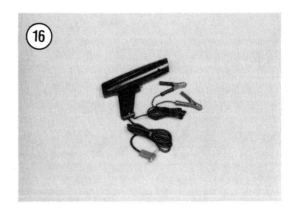

Portable Tachometer

A portable tachometer is necessary for tuning (**Figure 17**). Ignition timing and carburetor adjustments must be performed at the specified engine speed. The best instrument for this purpose is one with a low range of 0-1,000 or 0-2,000 rpm and a high range of 0-4,000 rpm. Extended range (0-6,000 or 0-8,000 rpm) instruments lack accuracy at lower speeds. The instrument should be capable of detecting changes of 25 rpm on the low range.

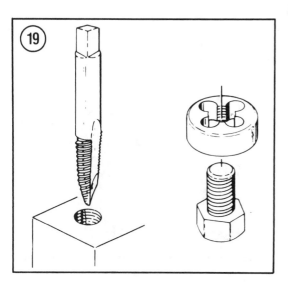

Compression Gauge

A compression gauge (**Figure 18**) measures the engine compression. The results, when properly interpreted, can indicate general ring and valve condition. They are available from motorcycle or auto supply stores and mail order outlets.

MECHANIC'S TIPS

Removing Frozen Nuts and Screws

When a fastener rusts and cannot be removed, several methods may be used to loosen it. First, apply penetrating oil such as Liquid Wrench or WD-40, available at any hardware or auto supply store. Apply it liberally and let it penetrate for 10-15 minutes. Rap the fastener several times with a small hammer; do not hit it hard enough to cause damage. Repeat the penetrating oil, if necessary.

For frozen screws, apply penetrating oil as described, then insert a screwdriver in the slot and rap the top of the screwdriver with a hammer. This will loosen the rust so the screw can be removed in the normal way. If the screw head is too chewed up to use a screwdriver, grip the head with Vise Grips and twist the screw out.

Remedying Stripped Threads

Occasionally, threads are stripped through carelessness or impact damage. Often the threads can be cleaned up by running a tap (for external threads on nuts) or die (for internal threads on bolts) through the threads. See **Figure 19**.

Removing Broken Screws or Bolts

When the head breaks off a screw or bolt, several methods are available for removing the remaining portion.

If a large portion of the remainder projects out, try gripping it with Vise Grips. If the projecting portion is too small, file it to fit a wrench or cut a slot in it to fit a screwdriver. See **Figure 20**.

If the head breaks off flush, use a screw extractor. To do this, centerpunch the remaining portion of the screw or bolt. Drill a small hole in the screw and tap the extractor into the hole. Back the screw out with a wrench on the extractor (**Figure 21**).

"OFF THE ROAD" RULES

Areas set aside by the federal government, state and local agencies for off-road riding are continuing to disappear. The loss of many of these areas is usually due to the few who really don't care and therefore ruin the sport of off-road fun for those who do. Many areas are closed off to protect wildlife habitat, vegetation and geological structures. Do not enter these areas as it can result in an expensive citation and adds to the anti-off-road sentiment that can result in further land closures. By following these basic rules, you and others will always have an open area for this type of recreational use.

1. When riding, always observe the basic practice of good sportsmanship and recognize that other people will judge all off-road vehicle owners by your actions.

2. Don't litter the trails or camping areas. Leave the area cleaner than it was before you came.

3. Don't pollute lakes, streams or the ocean.

4. Be careful not to damage living trees, shrubs or other natural terrain.

5. Respect other people's rights and property.

6. Help anyone in distress.

7. Make yourself and your bike available for assistance in any search and rescue parties.

8. Don't harass other people using the same area as you are. Respect the rights of others enjoying the recreation area.

9. Be sure to obey all federal, state, provincial and other local rules regulating the operation of the bike.

10. Inform public officials when using public lands.

11. Don't harass wildlife and stay out of areas posted for the protection and feeding of wildlife.

12. Keep your exhaust noise to a minimum.

SAFETY

General Tips

1. Read your owner's manual and know your machine.

2. Check the throttle and brake controls before starting the engine.

3. Know how to make an emergency stop.

4. Know all state, federal and local laws concerning off-road riding. Respect private property.

5. Never add fuel while anyone is smoking in the area or when the engine is running.

6. Never wear loose scarves, belts or boot laces that could catch on moving parts or tree limbs.

7. Always wear protective clothing to protect your *entire* body. **Figure 22** shows a well equipped off road rider who is ready for almost any riding condition. Today's riding apparel is very stylish

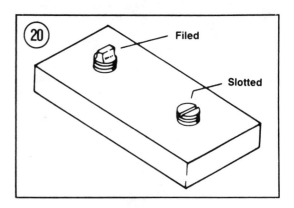

Filed

Slotted

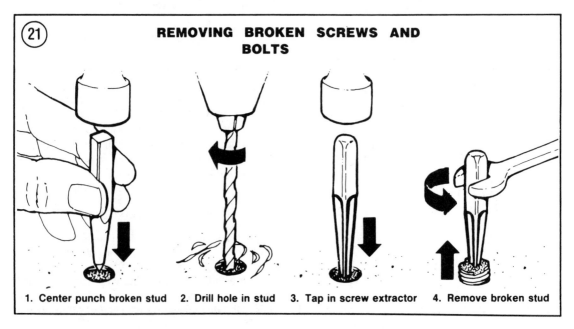

REMOVING BROKEN SCREWS AND BOLTS

1. Center punch broken stud   2. Drill hole in stud   3. Tap in screw extractor   4. Remove broken stud

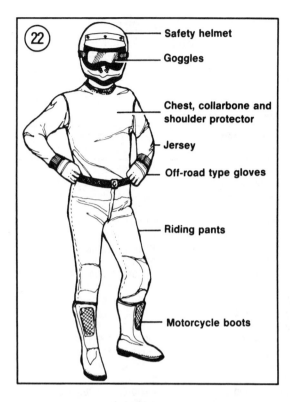

(22)
- Safety helmet
- Goggles
- Chest, collarbone and shoulder protector
- Jersey
- Off-road type gloves
- Riding pants
- Motorcycle boots

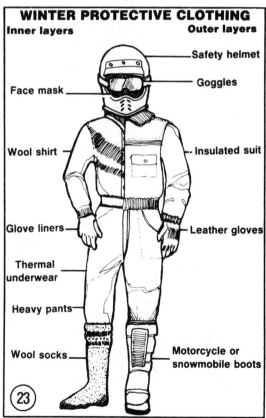

WINTER PROTECTIVE CLOTHING

Inner layers   **Outer layers**

- Safety helmet
- Goggles
- Face mask
- Wool shirt
- Insulated suit
- Glove liners
- Leather gloves
- Thermal underwear
- Heavy pants
- Wool socks
- Motorcycle or snowmobile boots

(23)

and you will be ready for action as well as being well protected.

8. Riding in the winter months requires a good set of clothes to keep your body dry and warm, otherwise your entire trip may be miserable. If you dress properly, moisture will evaporate from your body properly. If you become too hot and if your clothes trap the moisture, you will become cold. **Figure 23** shows some recommended inner and outer layers of cold weather clothing. Even mild temperatures can be very uncomfortable and dangerous when combined with a strong wind or high-speed riding. Always dress according to what the wind chill factor is, not the ambient temperature.

9. Never allow anyone to operate the bike without proper instruction. This is for their bodily protection and to keep the machine from damage or destruction.

10. Use the "buddy system" for long trips, just in case you have a problem or run out of gas.

11. Never attempt to repair your bike with the engine running except when necessary for certain tune-up procedures.

12. Check all of the bike's components and hardware frequently, especially the wheels and the steering.

13. Push the bike onto the trailer or truck bed –never ride it on. Secure the bike firmly to the truck or trailer with tie-downs. If towing a trailer, make sure the taillights and brake lights operate correctly.

Operating Tips

1. Never operate the bike in crowded areas or steer toward people.

2. Avoid dangerous terrain.

3. Cross highways (where permitted) at a 90°angle after looking in both directions. Post traffic guards if crossing in groups.

4. Do not ride the bike on or near railroad tracks. The bike's engine and exhaust noise can drown out the sound of an approaching train.

5. Keep the headlight free of dirt and never ride at night without the headlight on.

6. Always steer with both hands.

7. Do not panic if the throttle sticks. Turn the engine stop switch to the OFF position.

8. Do not speed through wooded areas. Hidden obstructions, hanging tree limbs, unseen ditches and even wild animals and hikers can cause injury and damage to the bike.

9. Do not tailgate. Rear end collisions can cause injury and machine damage.

10. Do not mix alcoholic beverages or drugs with riding.

11. Check your fuel supply regularly. Do not travel farther than your fuel supply will permit you to return.

WARNING
Do not use an open flame to check in the fuel tank. A serious explosion is certain to result.

Table 1 MODEL, YEAR AND FRAME NUMBER

Model	Year	Engine beginning serial number	Frame beginning serial number
XL500S	1979	PD01E-5000057-on	PD01-5000054-on
	1980	PD01E-5100001-on	PD01-5100001-on
	1981*	PD01E-5200001-on	PD01-BM200004-on
XL500R	1982*	PD02E-5000006-on	PD020-CM500006-on
XR500	1979	PE01E-5000001-on	PE01-5000001-on
	1980*	PE01E-5100001-on	PE01-5100001-on
XR500R	1981	PE01E-5200014-on	PE010-BM2000009-on
	1982	PE01E-5300001-on	PE010-CM3000001-on
	1983	PE03E-5000034-on	PE030-DM0000022-on
	1984*	PE03E-5100006-on	PE030-EM1000006-on
XL600R	1983	PD03E-5000053-on	PD030-DM0000027-on
Cal	1984	PD03E-5100214-on	PD031-EM1000007-on
49-state	1984	PD03E-5100007-on	PD030-EM1000006-on
Cal	1985	PD03E-5200008-on	PD030-FK2000002-on
49-state	1985	PD03E-5200004-on	PD030-FK2000003-on
Cal	1986	PD03E5300002-5304613	PD031-GK300001-GK301422
49-state	1986	PD03E-5300000-5304451	PD030-GK3000002-GK303182
Cal	1987*	PD03E-5400008-on	PD031-HK4000001-on
49-state	1987*	PD03E-5400003-on	PD030-HK4000002-on
XR600R	1985	PE04E-5000038-5004145	PE040-FK000024-FK003185
	1986	PD04E-5100003-5104912	PD040-GK1000003-GK104177
	1987	PD04E-5200003-5204824	PD040-HK2000003-HK203930
	1988	PD04E-5300014-5302505	PE040-JK3000009-JK301886
	1989	PE04E-5400001-5403801	PE040-KK400001-KK402027
	1990	PE04E-550001-on	PE040-LK500001-on
*Last year of production for this model.			

Table 2 MISCELLANEOUS TORQUE SPECIFICATIONS

Item	N•m	ft.-lb.
5 mm bolt and nut	4.5-6	3-4
6 mm bolt and nut	8-12	6-9
8 mm bolt and nut	18-25	13-18
10 mm bolt and nut	30-40	22-29
12 mm bolt and nit	50-60	36-43
5 mm screw	3.5-5	2-4
6 mm screw and 6 mm bolt with 8 mm head	7-11	5-8
6 mm flange bolt and nut	10-14	7-10
8 mm flange bolt and nut	24-30	17-22
10 mm flange bolt and nut	35-45	25-33

Table 3 WORKSHOP TOOLS

Tool	Size or specification
Screwdrivers	
Slot	5/16 × 8 in. blade
Slot	3/8 × 12 in. blade
Phillips	Size 2 tip, 6 in. blade
Pliers	
Gas pliers	6 in. overall
Vise grips®	10 in. overall
Needlenose	6 in. overall
Channel lock	12 in. overall
Snap ring	–
Wrenches	
Box-end set	10-17, 20, 32 mm
Open-end set	10-17, 20, 32 mm
Crescent (adjustable)	6 and 12 in. overall
Socket set	1/2 in. drive ratchet with 10-17, 20, 32 mm sockets
Allen set	2-10 mm
Cone wrenches	–
Spoke wrenches	–
Other special tools	
Impact driver	1/2 in. drive with ass't tips
Torque wrench	1/2 in. drive–0-100 ft.-lb.
Tire levers	For moped or motorcycle tires

CHAPTER TWO

TROUBLESHOOTING

Diagnosing mechanical problems is relatively simple if you use orderly procedures and keep a few basic principles in mind.

The troubleshooting procedures in this chapter analyze typical symptoms and show logical methods of isolating causes. These are not the only methods. There may be several ways to solve a problem, but only a systematic, methodical approach can guarantee success.

Never assume anything. Do not overlook the obvious. If you are riding along and the engine suddenly quits, check the easiest, most accessible problems first. Is there gasoline in the tank? Is the fuel shutoff valve in the ON position? Has a spark plug wire fallen off? On models so equipped, check the ignition switch and key. Sometimes the weight of the key ring may turn the ignition off suddenly.

If nothing obvious turns up in a quick check, look a little further. Learning to recognize and describe symptoms will make repairs easier for you or a mechanic at the shop. Describe problems accurately and fully. Saying that "it won't run" isn't the same as saying "it quit at high speed and won't start" or that "it sat in my garage for 3 months and then wouldn't start."

Gather as many symptoms together as possible to aid in diagnosis. Note whether the engine lost power gradually or all at once. Remember that the more complicated a machine is, the easier it is to troubleshoot because symptoms point to specific problems.

After the symptoms are defined, areas which could cause the problems are tested and analyzed. Guessing at the cause of a problem may provide the solution, but it can easily lead to frustration, wasted time and a series of expensive, unnecessary parts replacements.

You do not need fancy equipment or complicated test gear to determine whether repairs

can be attempted at home. A few simple checks could save a large repair bill and time lost while the bike sits in a dealer's service department. On the other hand, be realistic and don't attempt repairs beyond your abilities. Service departments tend to charge a lot for putting together a disassembled

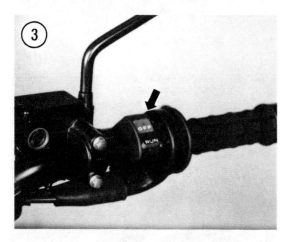

engine that may have been abused. Some dealers won't even take on such a job—so use common sense and don't get in over your head.

OPERATING REQUIREMENTS

An engine needs 3 basics to run properly: correct fuel-air mixture, compression and a spark at the correct time. If one or more are missing, the engine just won't run. The electrical system is the weakest link of the 3 basics. More problems result from electrical breakdowns than from any other source. Keep that in mind before you begin tampering with carburetor adjustments and the like.

If the bike has been sitting for any length of time and refuses to start, check and clean the spark plugs and then look to the gasoline delivery system. This includes the fuel tank, fuel shutoff valve and the fuel line to the carburetor. Gasoline deposits may have formed and gummed up the carburetor's jets and air passages. Gasoline tends to lose its potency after standing for long periods. Condensation may contaminate the fuel with water. Drain the old fuel and try starting with a fresh tankful.

EMERGENCY TROUBLESHOOTING

When the bike is difficult to start or won't start at all, it does not help to wear out your leg on the kickstarter. Check for obvious problems even before getting out your tools. Go down the following list step by step. Do each one; you may be embarrassed to find your kill switch is stuck in the OFF position, but that is better than wearing out your leg. If it still will not start, refer to the appropriate troubleshooting procedure which follows in this chapter.

1. Is there fuel in the tank? Open the filler cap (**Figure 1**) and rock the bike. Listen for fuel sloshing around.

> *WARNING*
> *Do not use an open flame to check in the tank. A serious explosion is certain to result.*

2. Is the fuel shutoff valve (**Figure 2**) in the ON position?
3. Make sure the kill switch (**Figure 3**) is not stuck in the OFF position.
4. Is the spark plug wire (**Figure 4**) on tight? Push all of them on and slightly rotate them to clean the electrical connection between the plug and the connector.

5. Is the choke in the right position?
  a. On XL500S and XL500R models, the knob should be pulled *up* (**Figure 5**) for a cold engine and pushed *down* for a warm engine.
  b. On XL600R models, the lever should be pulled *toward* the hand grip for a cold engine and pushed *away* for a warm engine (**Figure 6**).
  c. On XR600R models, the lever should be pulled *up* at the carburetor for a cold engine and pushed *down* for a warm engine.
6. Is the vent tube (**Figure 7**) from the fuel filler cap blocked?
7. On models so equipped, has the main fuse blown (**Figure 8**)? Replace with a new one.

ENGINE STARTING

An engine that refuses to start or is difficult to start is very frustrating. More often than not, the problem is very minor and can be found with a simple and logical troubleshooting approach.

The following items show a beginning point from which to isolate engine starting problems.

Engine Fails to Start

Perform the following spark test to determine if the ignition system is operating properly.
1. Remove one of the spark plugs from the cylinder.
2. Connect the spark plug wire and connector to the spark plug and touch the spark plug's base to a good ground such as the engine cylinder head (**Figure 9**). Position the spark plug so you can see the electrodes.

> *WARNING*
> *If it is necessary to hold the high voltage lead, do so with an insulated pair of pliers. The high voltage generated by the ignition pulse generator and CDI unit could produce a serious or fatal shock.*

3. Crank the engine over with the kickstarter. A fat blue spark should be evident across the plug's electrodes.

4. If the spark is good, check for one or more of the following possible malfunctions.
  a. Obstructed fuel line.
  b. Low compression.
  c. Leaking head gasket.
  d. Choke not operating properly.
  e. Throttle not operating properly.
5. If spark is not good, check for one or more of the following.

  a. Weak ignition coil.
  b. Weak CDI pulse generator.
  c. Broken or shorted high tension lead to the spark plug.
  d. Loose electrical connections.
  e. Loose or broken ignition coil ground wire.

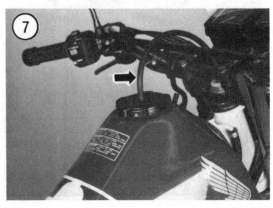

Engine Is Difficult to Start

Check for one or more of the following possible malfunctions.

a. Fouled spark plug.
b. Improperly adjusted choke.
c. Contaminated fuel system.
d. Improperly adjusted carburetor.
e. Weak ignition coil.
f. Weak CDI pulse generator.
g. Incorrect type ignition coil.
h. Poor compression.

Engine Will Not Crank

Check for one or more of the following possible malfunctions.

a. Discharged battery (models so equipped).
b. Defective or broken kickstarter mechanism.
c. Seized piston.
d. Seized crankshaft bearings.
e. Broken connecting rod.
f. Locked-up transmission or clutch assembly.

ENGINE PERFORMANCE

In the following check list, it is assumed that the engine runs, but is not operating at peak performance. This will serve as a starting point from which to isolate a performance malfunction.

The possible causes for each malfunction are listed in a logical sequence and in order of probability.

Engine Will Not Start Or Is Hard To Start

a. Empty fuel tank.
b. Obstructed fuel line or fuel shutoff valve.
c. Sticking float valve in carburetor(s).
d. Carburetor incorrectly adjusted.
e. Improper choke operation.
f. Fouled or improperly gapped spark plug.
g. Weak CDI pulse generator.
h. Ignition timing incorrect (faulty component in system).
i. Broken or shorted ignition coil.
j. Weak or faulty spark unit or pulse generator.
k. Improper valve timing.
l. Clogged air filter element.
m. Contaminated fuel.

Engine Will Not Idle or Idles Erratically

a. Carburetor(s) incorrectly adjusted.
b. Fouled or improperly gapped spark plug.
c. Leaking head gasket or vacuum leak.
d. Weak CDI pulse generator.
e. Ignition timing incorrect (faulty component in system).
f. Improper valve timing.
g. Obstructed fuel line or fuel shutoff valve.

Engine Misses at High Speed

a. Fouled or improperly gapped spark plug.
b. Improper ignition timing (faulty component in system).
c. Improper carburetor main jet selection.
d. Clogged jets in the carburetor(s).
e. Weak ignition coil.
f. Weak CDI pulse generator.
g. Improper valve timing.
h. Obstructed fuel line or fuel shutoff valve.

**Engine Continues to
Run with Ignition Off**

  a. Excessive carbon build-up in engine.
  b. Vacuum leak in intake system.
  c. Contaminated or incorrect fuel octane rating.

Engine Overheating

  a. Obstructed cooling fins on the cylinder and cylinder head.
  b. Improper ignition timing (faulty component in system).
  c. Improper spark plug heat range.

Engine Misses at Idle

  a. Fouled or improperly gapped spark plug.
  b. Spark plug cap faulty.
  c. Ignition cable insulation deteriorated (shorting out).
  d. Dirty or clogged air filter element.
  e. Carburetor(s) incorrectly adjusted (too lean or too rich).
  f. Choke valve stuck.
  g. Clogged jet(s) in the carburetor.
  h. Carburetor float height incorrect.

Engine Backfires—Explosions in Mufflers

  a. Fouled or improperly gapped spark plug.
  b. Spark plug cap faulty.
  c. Ignition cable insulation deteriorated (shorting out).
  d. Ignition timing incorrect.
  e. Improper valve timing.
  f. Contaminated fuel.
  g. Burned or damaged intake and/or exhaust valves.
  h. Weak or broken intake and/or exhaust valve springs.

**Pre-ignition (Fuel Mixture
Ignites Before Spark Plug Fires)**

  a. Hot spot in combustion chamber (piece of carbon).
  b. Valve(s) stuck in guide.
  c. Overheating engine.

Smoky Exhaust and Engine Runs Roughly

  a. Too rich carburetor mixture.
  b. Choke not operating correctly.
  c. Water or other contaminants in fuel.
  d. Clogged fuel line.
  e. Clogged air filter element.

**Engine Loses Power at
Normal Riding Speed**

  a. Carburetor incorrectly adjusted.
  b. Engine overheating.
  c. Improper ignition timing (faulty component in system).
  d. Weak CDI pulse generator.
  e. Incorrectly gapped spark plug.
  f. Weak ignition coil.
  g. Weak CDI pulse generator.
  h. Obstructed mufflers.
  i. Dragging brake(s).

Engine Lacks Acceleration

  a. Carburetor mixture too lean.
  b. Clogged fuel line.
  c. Improper ignition timing (faulty component in system).
  d. Improper valve clearance.
  e. Dragging brake(s).

ENGINE NOISES

1. *Knocking or pinging during acceleration—* Caused by using a lower octane fuel than recommended. May also be caused by poor fuel. Pinging can also be caused by spark plugs of the wrong heat range. Refer to *Spark Plug Selection* in Chapter Three.

2. *Slapping or rattling noises at low speed or during acceleration—* May be caused by piston slap (excessive piston to cylinder wall clearance).

3. *Knocking or rapping while decelerating—* Usually caused by excessive rod bearing clearance.

4. *Persistent knocking and vibration—* Usually caused by excessive main bearing clearance.

5. *Rapid on-off squeal—* Compression leak around cylinder head gasket or spark plug.

EXCESSIVE VIBRATION

Usually this is caused by loose engine mounting hardware. Otherwise, this can be difficult to find without disassembling the engine.

FRONT SUSPENSION AND STEERING

Poor handling may be caused by improper tire pressure, a damaged or bent frame or front steering components, a worn front fork assembly, worn wheel bearings or dragging brakes.

BRAKE PROBLEMS

Sticking disc brakes may be caused by a stuck piston in a caliper assembly or a warped pad shim.

A sticking drum brake may be caused by worn or weak return springs, dry pivot and cam bushings or improper adjustment. Grabbing brakes may be caused by greasy linings which must be replaced. Brake grab may also be due to an out-of-round drum. Glazed linings will cause loss of stopping power.

2

CHAPTER THREE

LUBRICATION, MAINTENANCE AND TUNE-UP

A motorcycle, even in normal use, is subjected to tremendous heat, stress and vibration. When neglected, any bike becomes unreliable and actually dangerous to ride.

To gain the utmost in safety, performance and useful life from the Honda it is necessary to make periodic inspections and adjustments. Frequently, minor problems are found during these inspections that are simple and inexpensive to correct at the time. If they are not found and corrected at this time they could lead to major and more expensive problems later on.

Start out by doing simple tune-up, lubrication and maintenance. Tackle more involved jobs as you become more acquainted with the bike.

Tables 1-12 are located at the end of this chapter.

ROUTINE CHECKS

The following simple checks should be performed at each fuel stop.

Engine Oil Level

Refer to *Periodic Lubrication* in this chapter.

General Inspection

1. Quickly inspect the engine for signs of oil or fuel leakage.
2. Check the tires for embedded stones. Pry them out with your ignition key.
3. Make sure all lights work.

NOTE
At least check the brake light. It can burn out at any time. Motorists cannot stop as quickly as you and need all the warning you can give.

Tire Pressure

Tire pressure must be checked with the tires cold. Correct tire pressure varies with the load you are carrying. See **Table 1**.

Battery (XL Series)

On XL series models, remove the right-hand side cover and check the battery electrolyte level. The level must be between the upper and lower level marks on the case (**Figure 1**). For complete details see *Battery Removal, Installation and Electrolyte Level Check* in this chapter.

Check the level more frequently in hot weather; electrolyte will evaporate rapidly as heat increases.

Crankcase Breather Hose

Inspect the hoses for cracks and deterioration and make sure that all hose clamps are tight (**Figure 2**).

Evaporative Emission Control System (California XL Series)

Inspect the hoses (**Figure 3**) to make sure they are not kinked or bent and that they are securely connected to their respective parts.

Lights and Horn

With the engine running, check the following.

NOTE
XR series bikes are equipped with only
a headlight and taillight. The headlight
is controlled by a dimmer switch.

1. Pull the front brake lever on and check that the brake light comes on.

2. Push the rear brake pedal down and check that the brake light comes on soon after you have begun depressing the pedal.

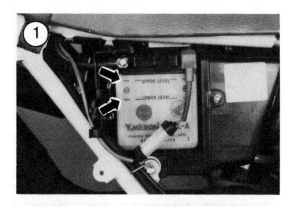

3A. On XL series, perform the following:
   a. Turn the headlight switch to the ON position. Check that both the headlight and taillight are on.
   b. Press the headlight dimmer switch to both the HI and LO positions and check to see that both headlight elements are working.

3B. On XR series, press the headlight dimmer switch to both the HI and LO positions and check to see that both headlight elements are working.

4. On XL series, turn the turn signal switch to the left and right positions and check that all 4 turn signals are working.

5. On XL series, push the horn button and make sure that the horn blows loudly.

6. If during the test, the rear brake pedal traveled too far before the brakelight came on, adjust the rear brakelight switch as described in Chapter Eight.

7. If the horn or any of the lights failed to operate properly, refer to Chapter Eight.

PRE-CHECKS

The following checks should be performed before the first ride of the day.

1. Inspect all fuel lines and fittings for wetness.

2. Make sure the fuel tank is full of fresh gasoline.

3. Make sure the engine oil level is correct.

4. Check the operation of the front brake. On disc brake models, add hydraulic fluid to the brake master cylinder if necessary.

5. Check the throttle and the rear brake pedal. Make sure they operate properly with no binding.

6. Inspect the front and rear suspension; make sure it has a good solid feel with no looseness.

7. Check tire pressure. Refer to **Table 1**.

8. Check the exhaust system for damage.

9. Check the tightness of all fasteners, especially engine mounting hardware.

SERVICE INTERVALS

The services and intervals shown in **Table 2** are recommended by the factory. Strict adherence to these recommendations will ensure long service from the Honda. If the bike is run in an area of high humidity, the lubrication services must be done more frequently to prevent possible rust damage.

Service intervals differ between the XL and XR series because the XR will be most likely be ridden harder and in dirtier areas. If your bike is an XL but is used off-road frequently you should follow the service recommended for the XR.

If you are riding your bike in competition events, refer to **Table 3** for suggested pre-race inspection areas and items.

For convenience when maintaining your motorcycle, most of the services shown in these tables are described in this chapter. However, some procedures which require more than minor disassembly or adjustment are covered elsewhere in the appropriate chapter.

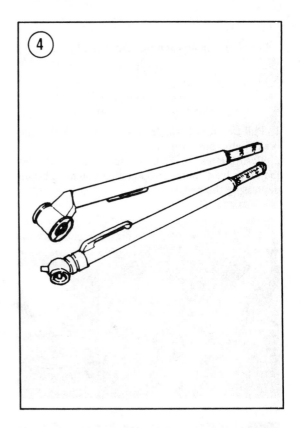

TIRES AND WHEELS

Tire Pressure

Tire pressure should be checked and adjusted to maintain the smoothness of the tire, good traction and handling and to get the maximum life out of the tire. A simple, accurate gauge (**Figure 4**) can be purchased for a few dollars and should be carried in your motorcycle tool kit. The appropriate tire pressures are shown in **Table 1**.

Tire Inspection

The tires take a lot of punishment so inspect them periodically for excessive wear, cuts, abrasions, etc. If you find a nail or other object in the tire, mark its location with a light crayon before removing it. This will help locate the hole for repair. Refer to Chapter Nine for tire changing and repair information.

Check local traffic regulations concerning minimum tread depth. Measure the tread depth at the center of the tire tread using a tread depth gauge (**Figure 5**) or small ruler. Honda recommends that original equipment tires be replaced when the depth is 8 mm (0.30 in.) or less.

Rim Inspection

Frequently inspect the wheel rims. If a rim has been damaged it might have been enough to knock it out of alignment. Improper wheel alignment can cause severe vibration and result in an unsafe riding condition.

Wheel Spoke Tension

1. Tap each spoke with a wrench. The higher the pitch of sound it makes, the tighter the spoke. The lower the sound frequency, the looser the spoke. A "ping" is good; a "clunk" says the spoke is too loose.
2. If one or more of the spokes are loose, tighten them as described under *Wheels* in Chapter Nine.

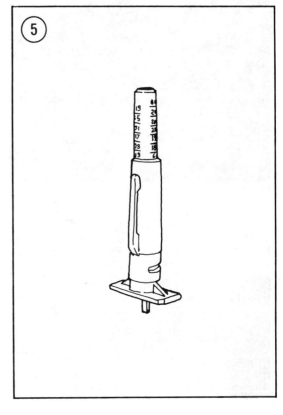

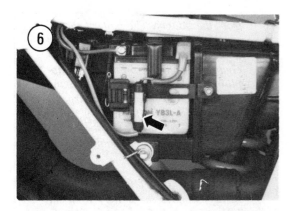

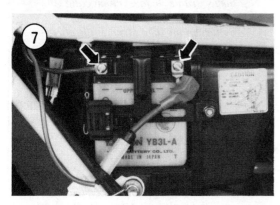

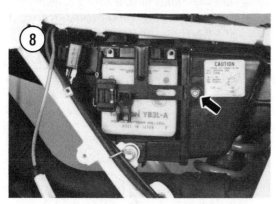

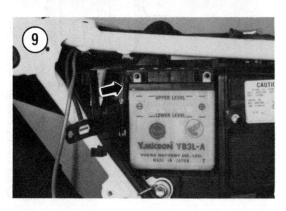

BATTERY (XL SERIES)

**Removal, Installation and
Electrolyte Level Check**

The battery is the heart of the electrical system. Check and service the battery at the interval indicated in **Table 2**. The majority of electrical system troubles can be attributed to neglect of this vital component.

The electrolyte level may be checked with the battery in the frame. However, it is necessary to remove the right-hand side panel and the battery bracket. The electrolyte level should be maintained between the 2 marks on the battery case (**Figure 1**). If the electrolyte level is low, it's a good idea to remove the battery from the frame so it can be thoroughly serviced and checked.

NOTE
Battery removal and installation varies slightly among the different models. This procedure shows a typical removal and installation procedure.

1. Remove the right-hand side cover.
2. Pull the main fuse holder (**Figure 6**) out of the battery bracket.
3. First disconnect the battery negative lead and then the positive lead from the terminals (**Figure 7**).
4. Remove the nut (**Figure 8**) securing the bracket and hinge it out of the way.
5. Pull the battery part way out of the compartment.
6. Disconnect the breather tube (**Figure 9**).
7. Slide the battery out the rest of the way and remove it from the bike's frame.

WARNING
Protect your eyes, skin and clothing. If electrolyte gets into your eyes, flush your eyes thoroughly with clean water and get prompt medical attention.

CAUTION
Be careful not to spill battery electrolyte on plastic, painted or plated surfaces. The liquid is highly corrosive and will damage the finish. If it is spilled, wash it off immediately with soapy water and thoroughly rinse with clean water.

8. Remove the cap from the battery cells and add distilled water to correct the level. Never add electrolyte (acid) to correct the level.

NOTE
*If distilled water has been added, re-install the battery caps and **gently** shake the battery for several minutes to mix the existing electrolyte with the new water.*

9. After the fluid level has been corrected and the battery allowed to stand for a few minutes, remove the battery caps and check the specific gravity of the electrolyte with a hydrometer (**Figure 10**). See *Battery Testing* in this chapter.
10. After the battery has been refilled, recharged or replaced, install it by reversing these removal steps.

CAUTION
If you removed the breather tube from the frame, be sure to route it so that residue will not drain onto any part of the bike's frame. The tube must be free of bends or twists as any restrictions may pressurize the battery and damage it.

Testing

Hydrometer testing is the best way to check battery condition. Use a hydrometer with number graduations from 1.100 to 1.300 rather than one with just color-coded bands. To use the hydrometer, squeeze the rubber ball, insert the tip into the cell and release the pressure on the ball.

Draw enough electrolyte to float the weighted float inside the hydrometer. Note the number in line with the surface of the electrolyte; this is the specific gravity for this cell. Squeeze the rubber ball again and return the electrolyte to the cell from which it came.

The specific gravity of the electrolyte in each battery cell is an excellent indication of that cell's condition. A fully charged cell will read from 1.260-1.280, while a cell in good condition reads from 1.230-1.250 and anything below 1.140 is discharged.

If the cells test in the poor range, the battery requires recharging. The hydrometer is useful for checking the progress of the charging operation. **Table 4** shows approximate state of charge.

Charging

WARNING
During the charging process, highly explosive hydrogen gas is released

from the battery. The battery should be charged only in a well-ventilated area away from any open flames (including pilot lights on home gas appliances). Do not allow any smoking in the area. Never check the charge by arcing (connecting pliers or other metal objects) across the terminals; the resulting spark can ignite the hydrogen gas.

CAUTION
Always remove the battery from the bike's frame before connecting the battery charger. Never recharge a battery in the bike's frame; the corrosive mist that is emitted during the charging process will corrode all surrounding surfaces.

1. Connect the positive (+) charger lead to the positive (+) battery terminal and the negative (–) charger lead to the negative (–) battery terminal.

CAUTION
Some models have a 6-volt battery (3 battery vent caps) and electrical system while other models have a 12-volt battery (6 battery vent caps) and electrical system. Use the proper charger voltage.

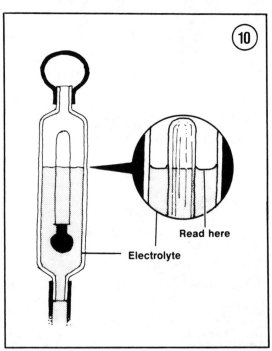

Read here

Electrolyte

2. Remove all vent caps from the battery, set the charger to either 6 or 12 volts (depending on the bike's electrical system) and switch the charge on. If the output of the charger is variable, it is best to select a low setting—1 1/2 to 2 amps.

CAUTION
The electrolyte level must be maintained at the upper level during the charging cycle; check and refill as necessary.

3. After the battery has been charged for about 8 hours, turn the charger off, disconnect the leads and check the specific gravity of each cell. It should be within the limits specified in **Table 4**. If it is, and remains stable for 1 hour, the battery is considered charged.

4. Clean the battery terminals, electrical cable connectors and surrounding case and reinstall the battery in the frame, reversing the removal steps. Coat the battery terminals with Vaseline or silicone spray to retard corrosion and decomposition of the terminals.

CAUTION
Route the breather tube so that it does not drain onto any part of the frame. The tube must be free of bends or twists as any restriction may pressurize the battery and damage it.

New Battery Installation

When replacing the old battery with a new one, be sure to charge it completely (specific gravity 1.260-1.280) before installing it in the bike. Failure to do so, or using the battery with a low electrolyte level, will permanently damage the new battery.

PERIODIC LUBRICATION

Oil

Oil is graded according to its viscosity, which is an indication of how thick it is. The Society of Automotive Engineers (SAE) system distinguishes oil viscosity by numbers. Thick oils have higher viscosity numbers than thin oils. For example, an SAE 5 oil is a thin oil while an SAE 90 oil is relatively thick.

Grease

A good quality grease, preferably waterproof, should be used. Water does not wash grease off parts as easily as it washes oil off. In addition, grease maintains its lubricating qualities better than oil on long and strenuous rides. In a pinch, though, the wrong lubricant is better than none at all. Correct the situation as soon as possible.

Engine Oil Level Check
(Wet-sump Models)

Engine oil level is checked with the dipstick/oil filler cap, located at the front of the crankcase on the right-hand side (**Figure 11**).

1. Place the bike on level ground.
2. Start the engine and let it idle for 2-3 minutes.
3. Shut off the engine and let the oil settle.
4. Unscrew the dipstick and wipe it clean. Reinsert the dipstick onto the threads in the hole; do not screw it in.
5. Remove the dipstick and check the oil level. The level should be between the 2 lines and not above the upper one (**Figure 12**). If the level is below the lower line, add the recommended type engine oil (**Figure 13**) to correct the level.

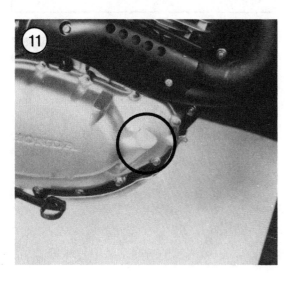

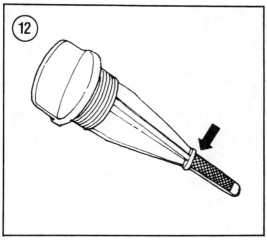

Engine Oil Level Check
(Dry-sump Models)

On models equipped with a dry-sump type engine, the major portion of the engine oil is stored in a closed-off section of the engine bike's frame while some of the oil is carried in the crankcase.

Engine oil level is checked in 2 places—the dipstick on the frame and the oil level check bolt on the crankcase.

1. Place wood blocks under the skid plate to support the bike securely in a vertical position.
2. Start the engine and let it idle for 2-3 minutes.
3. Shut off the engine and let the oil settle.
4. Unscrew the dipstick (**Figure 14**) from the frame between the steering head and the fuel tank.
5. Wipe the dipstick clean and reinsert the dipstick onto the threads in the hole; do *not* screw it in.
6. Remove the dipstick and check the oil level. The level should be between the 2 lines and not above the upper one. If the level is below the lower line, add the recommended type engine oil (**Figure 13**) to correct the level.
7. Install the dipstick and tighten securely.
8. Restart the engine and allow it to run for a couple of minutes.
9. Shut off the engine and allow the oil to settle.
10. Unscrew the crankcase oil level check bolt (**Figure 15**).
11. The crankcase oil level is correct if the oil is up to the bottom surface of the threads in the hole.
12. If the oil level is correct on the dipstick but the crankcase oil level is incorrect, some part of the oil system is not operating properly. Do not operate the bike until you have found and fixed the problem. Perform the following:
   a. Recheck the oil level on the dipstick.
   b. Inspect the oil lines and fittings from the engine to the bike's frame.
   c. Inspect the oil pump as described in Chapter Five.
13. Reinstall the oil level check bolt and tighten securely.

Engine Oil Change

Change the engine oil at the factory-recommended oil change interval indicated in **Table 2**. This assumes that the motorcycle is operated in moderate climates. In extreme climates, oil should be changed every 30 days. The time interval is more important than the mileage interval because acids formed by combustion blowby will contaminate the oil even if the motorcycle is not run for several months. If the motorcycle is operated under dusty conditions, the

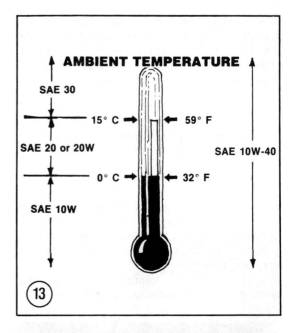

AMBIENT TEMPERATURE

SAE 30

15° C → ← 59° F

SAE 20 or 20W

SAE 10W-40

0° C → ← 32° F

SAE 10W

(13)

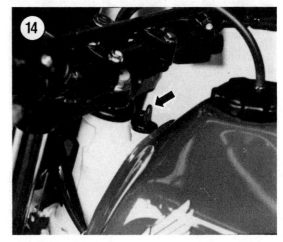

(14)

(15)

oil will get dirty more quickly and should be changed more frequently than recommended.

Use only a high-quality detergent motor oil with an API classification of SE or SF. The classification is stamped on top of the can or printed on the label on the plastic bottle (**Figure 16**). Try to use the same brand of oil at each change. Use of oil additives is not recommended as it may cause clutch slippage. Refer to **Figure 13** for correct oil viscosity to use under anticipated ambient temperatures—not engine oil temperature.

3

NOTE
*Never dispose of motor oil in the trash, on the ground, or down a storm drain. Many service stations accept used motor oil and waste haulers provide curbside used motor oil collection. Do not combine other fluids with motor oil to be recycled. To locate a recycler, contact the American Petroleum Institute (API) at **www.recycleoil.org**.*

To change the engine oil and filter you will need the following:

   a. Drain pan.
   b. Funnel.
   c. Can opener or pour spout (oil in cans).
   d 17 mm wrench (drain plug).
   e. Oil (refer to **Table 5** for quantity).

There are a number of ways to discard the old oil safely. Some service stations and oil retailers will accept your used oil for recycling; some may even give you money for it. Never drain the oil onto the ground.

1. Start the engine and let it reach operating temperature; 15-20 minutes of stop-and-go riding is usually sufficient.

2. Turn the engine off and place the bike on level ground.

3A. On dry-sump models, place a drain pan under the crankcase and remove the drain plug (**Figure 17**). Remove the dipstick/oil filler cap. This will speed up the flow of oil.

3B. On wet-sump models, place a drain pan under the left-hand crankcase and remove the drain plug (**Figure 18**). Remove the dipstick/oil filler cap. This will speed up the flow of oil.

CAUTION
Make sure the ignition switch is in the OFF position. Do not let the engine start and run without oil in the crankcase.

4. Let the oil drain for at least 15-20 minutes. During this time, kick the kickstarter a couple of times to help drain any remaining oil.

5. Inspect the sealing washer on the crankcase drain plug. Replace it if its condition is in doubt.

6. Install the drain plug and washer and tighten to the torque specification listed in **Table 6**.

7. On dry-sump models, perform the following:

  a. Remove the bolts securing the skid plate and remove the skid plate (**Figure 19**).

  b. Move the drain pan under the frame down tube and remove the drain plug (**Figure 20**) from the frame.

  c. Let the oil drain for at least 15-20 minutes.

  d. Inspect the sealing washer on the drain plug; replace it if necessary.

  e. Install the drain plug and tighten to the torque specification listed in **Table 6**.

8. If the oil filter screen is to be cleaned, clean as described in this chapter.

9. On wet-sump models, if the oil filter is going to be replaced, replace as described in this chapter.

10. Insert a funnel into the oil fill hole and fill the engine with the correct viscosity and quantity of oil. Refer to **Table 5**.

11. Install the dipstick/oil filler cap.

12. Start the engine, let it run at idle speed and check for leaks.

13. Turn the engine off and check for correct oil level; adjust as necessary.

Oil Filter Screen Cleaning
(Wet-sump Models)

The oil filter screen should be cleaned at the interval indicated in **Table 2**.

1. Drain the engine oil as described in this chapter.

2. Remove the bolts (**Figure 21**) securing the skid plate and remove the skid plate.

3. Remove the clamping bolt and remove the kickstarter arm.

4. Disconnect the clutch and decompression release cables from the right-hand crankcase cover.

5. Remove the bolts securing the right-hand footpeg and remove the footpeg assembly.

6. Remove the rear brake pedal.

7. Remove the bolts (**Figure 22**) securing the right-hand crankcase cover and remove the cover and gasket.

8. Remove the oil filter screen (**Figure 23**).

9. Clean the screen in solvent with a medium soft toothbrush and carefully dry with compressed air.

10. Inspect the screen. Replace it if there are any breaks or holes in the screen.

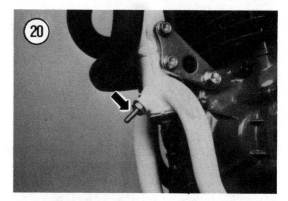

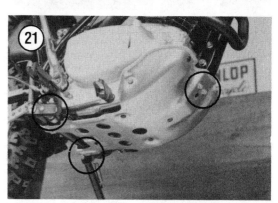

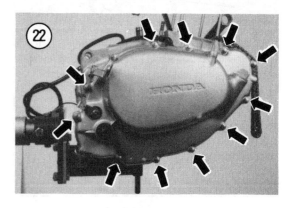

11. Position the screen with the thick end facing toward the outside and install the screen into the crankcase.

NOTE
On models with a chain-driven balancer system, it is a good idea to

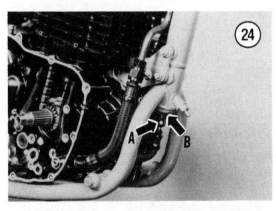

adjust the balancer chain while the crankcase cover is removed. Refer to **Balancer Chain Adjustment** *in this chapter.*

12. Install a new crankcase cover gasket.
13. Hold the compression release follower lever in the raised position and install the crankcase cover and bolts. Tighten the bolts securely.
14. Install the following items:
   a. Rear brake pedal.
   b. Front right-hand footpeg.
   c. Clutch and compression release cables.
   d. Kickstarter arm.
   e. Skid plate.
15. Refill the crankcase with the recommended type and quantity of engine oil as described in this chapter.
16. Adjust the clutch, compression release and rear brake as described in this chapter.

Oil Strainer Cleaning

1. Drain the engine oil as described in this chapter.
2. Loosen the oil hose nut (A, **Figure 24**) and disconnect the oil line from the oil strainer nut.
3. Remove the oil strainer nut and O-ring (B, **Figure 24**) from the frame down-tube.
4. Clean the oil strainer in solvent with a medium soft toothbrush and carefully dry with compressed air.
5. Inspect the screen; replace if there are any breaks or holes in it.
6. Inspect the O-ring seal; replace if damaged or deteriorated.
7. Install the oil strainer nut and O-ring. Tighten the nut to the torque specification listed in **Table 6**.
8. Install the oil hose. Hold onto the oil strainer nut with a wrench and tighten the oil hose to the torque specification listed in **Table 6**.
9. Make sure the oil hose curves naturally from the frame down-tube to the engine and is not kinked.

**Oil Filter Replacement
(600 cc Models)**

1. Drain the engine oil as described in this chapter.
2. Place the drain pan under the right-hand crankcase cover.
3. Remove the bolts (**Figure 25**) securing the oil filter cover and remove the cover.
4. Remove the oil filter and spring. Discard the oil filter.
5. Wipe out the oil filter cavity with a shop rag and cleaning solvent. Remove any sludge.

6. Install the spring (**Figure 26**) and the filter element (**Figure 27**).

7. Inspect the O-ring seal (**Figure 28**) on the cover and replace it if necessary.

8. Install the cover and make sure the index marks align (**Figure 29**) between the cover and the crankcase cover.

9. Tighten the bolts to the torque specification listed in **Table 6**.

Front Fork Oil Change
(Without Air Assist)

It is a good practice to change the fork oil at the interval listed in **Table 2** or once a year. If it becomes contaminated with dirt or water, change it immediately.

1. Remove the plastic protective cap and remove the upper fork cap bolt (**Figure 30**). Use the 17 mm male socket provided in the factory tool kit or a 17 mm bolt head held with Vise-Grips.

2. Place a drip pan under the fork and remove the drain screw (**Figure 31**). Allow the fork oil to drain for at least 5 minutes. Never reuse fork oil.

> *CAUTION*
> *Do not allow the fork oil to come in contact with any of the brake components.*

3. With both of the bike's wheels on the ground and with the front brake applied, push down on the handlebar grips to work the forks up and down. Continue until all fork oil is expelled.

4. Install the drain screw and washer.

5. Fill the fork with DEXRON automatic transmission fluid or 10W fork oil. Refer to **Table 7** for fork oil capacities.

> *NOTE*
> *To measure the correct amount of fluid, use a plastic baby bottle. These have measurements in fluid ounces (oz.) and cubic centimeters (cc) on the side.*

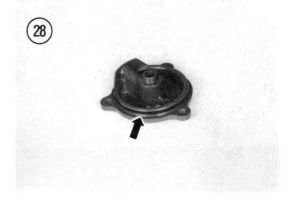

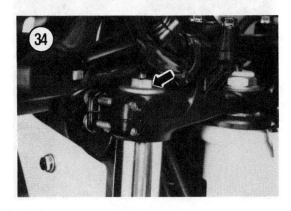

6. After filling the fork tube, slowly pump the forks several times to expel air from the upper and lower fork chambers.

7. Install the fork cap bolt while pushing down on the spring. Start the bolt slowly; don't cross thread it. Tighten to the torque specifications listed in **Table 6**.

8. Repeat Steps 1-7 for the other fork.

9. Road test the bike and check for leaks.

3

Front Fork Oil Change
(With Air-assist)

There is no factory recommended oil change interval but it's a good practice to change it at the interval indicated in **Table 2** or when it becomes contaminated.

1. Place the bike on wood blocks with the front wheel off the ground.

> *WARNING*
> *Release the air pressure gradually. If it is released too fast, oil will spurt out with the air. Protect your eyes and clothing accordingly.*

2. Unscrew the dust cap (**Figure 32**) and *bleed off all air pressure* by depressing the valve stem (**Figure 33**).

3. Slowly unscrew the fork cap bolt/air valve assembly (**Figure 34**); it is under pressure from the fork spring.

4. Place a drain pan under the fork and remove the drain screw (**Figure 35**). Allow the oil to drain for at least 5 minutes. *Never* reuse the oil.

> *CAUTION*
> *Do not allow the fork oil to come in contact with any of the brake components.*

5. Inspect the gasket on the drain screw; replace it if necessary. Install the drain screw and tighten securely.

6. Repeat for the other fork.

7. Place a shop cloth around the top of the fork tube to catch any residual fork oil. Withdraw the fork spring from each fork tube.

8. Fill the fork with DEXRON automatic transmission fluid or 10W fork oil. Refer to **Table 7** for fork oil capacities.

> *NOTE*
> *To measure the correct amount of fluid, use a plastic baby bottle. These have measurements in fluid ounces (oz.) and cubic centimeters (cc) on the side.*

9. After filling the fork tube, remove the wood blocks from under the engine and let the front wheel down onto the ground.

10. With both of the bike's wheels on the ground and with the front brake applied, push down on the handlebar grips to bottom out the forks. Hold the handlebar in this position with the forks totally compressed. Have an assistant measure the distance from the top of the fork tube to the top of the fork oil (**Figure 36**). Different fork damping characteristics will result, even with the standard air inflation pressure, from varying the amount of fork oil in the fork tube. Refer to **Table 7**.

11. Inspect the O-ring seal on the fork cap bolt; replace it if necessary. Install the fork cap bolt while pushing down on the spring. Start the bolt slowly; don't cross thread it. Tighten to the torque specifications listed in **Table 6**.

12. Inflate the forks to the recommended air pressure listed in **Table 8**. Do not use compressed air; use only a small hand-held air pump like the one shown in **Figure 37**.

13. Road test the bike and check for leaks.

Drive Chain Lubrication

Oil the drive chain at the interval indicated in **Table 2** or sooner if it becomes dry.

1. Place wood blocks under the engine or frame to support the bike securely.

2. Oil the bottom run with a good grade of commercial chain lubricant. Concentrate on getting the oil down between the side plates of the chain links, into the pins, bushings and rollers.

3. Rotate the rear wheel to bring the unoiled portion of the chain within reach. Continue until all the chain is lubricated.

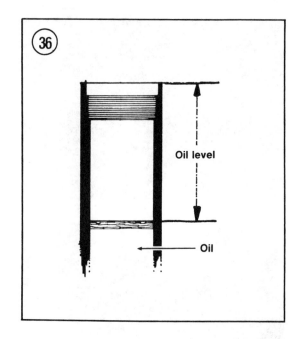

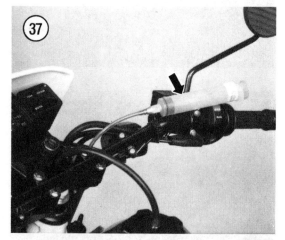

Swing Arm Bearing Lubrication

Lubricate the swing arm bushings at the interval indicated in **Table 2**. Apply lubricant with a small hand-held grease gun. On dual-shock models, use a good grade multipurpose grease. On Pro-Link models, use molybdenum disulfide grease (NLGI No. 2).

1. Wipe the grease fittings clean of all dirt and grease residue. Force the grease into the fitting until the grease runs out of both ends of the swing arm.
2. Clean off all excessive grease.
3. If the grease will not run out of the ends of the swing arm, unscrew the grease fitting from the swing arm. Clean it out with solvent; make sure the ball check valve is free. Reinstall the fitting or replace with a new one.
4. Apply the grease gun again. If the grease still does not run out of both ends of the swing arm, remove the swing arm as described in Chapter Ten. Disassemble the swing arm and thoroughly clean and regrease.

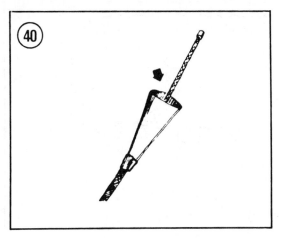

Pro-Link Suspension Lubrication

Lubricate the Pro-Link suspension at the interval listed in **Table 2**. Apply molybdenum disulfide grease (NLGI No. 2) with a small hand-held grease gun.

1. Wipe the grease fittings clean of all dirt and grease residue.
2. Force the grease into the fitting until the grease runs out past the dust seals on each of the links. The number of fittings varies among the different models. There is a fitting on the shock arm (**Figure 38**) and on most models there are 2 fittings on the shock link (**Figure 39**).
3. Clean off all excessive grease from all parts.
4. If the grease will not run out of the ends of the joints, unscrew the grease fitting from the arm or link. Clean it out with solvent and make sure the ball check valve is free. Reinstall the fitting or replace with a new one.
5. Apply the grease gun again. If the grease still does not run out of both ends, remove the suspension components as described in Chapter Ten.

Control Cables

The control cables should be lubricated at the interval listed in **Table 2**. They should also be inspected at this time for fraying and the cable sheath checked for chafing. The cables are relatively inexpensive and should be replaced when found to be faulty.

The control cables can be lubricated either with oil or any popular cable lubricant and a cable lubricator. The first method requires more time and the complete lubrication of the entire cable is less certain.

On the throttle cable(s) it is necessary to remove the screws securing the right-hand switch assembly together to gain access to the throttle cable(s) ends.

1. Disconnect the cable from the clutch, decompression levers and the throttle grip assembly.
2. Make a cone of stiff paper and tape it to the end of the cable sheath (**Figure 40**).
3. Hold the cable upright and pour a small amount of thin oil (SAE 10W-30) into the cone. Work the cable in and out of the sheath for several minutes to help the oil work its way down to the end of the cable.

NOTE
To avoid a mess, place a shop cloth at the end of the cable to catch the oil as it runs out.

4. Remove the cone, reconnect the cable and adjust the cable(s) as described in this chapter.

NOTE
While the throttle cable is removed and the switch assembly disassembled, apply a light coat of grease to the metal surfaces of the throttle grip assembly.

Lubricator method

1. Disconnect the cable from the lever.
2. Attach a lubricator following the manufacturer's instructions.
3. Insert the nozzle of the lubricant can in the lubricator, press the button on the can and hold down until the lubricant begins to flow out of the other end of the cable.
4. Remove the lubricator, reconnect the cable and adjust the cable as described in this chapter.

Miscellaneous Lubrication Points

Lubricate the clutch lever, front brake lever, sidestand pivot point and the footpeg pivot points. Use SAE 10W-40 engine oil.

PERIODIC MAINTENANCE

Drive Chain Adjustment (Dual-shock Models)

The drive chain should be checked, lubricated and adjusted at the interval listed in **Table 2** or more often if ridden in wet or dusty conditions. It should be removed and cleaned at the interval listed in **Table 2**.
1. Place the transmission in NEUTRAL.

2. Remove the rear axle cotter pin. Loosen the axle nut (A, **Figure 41**) and the axle adjuster locknuts (B, **Figure 41**).
3A. On XL500S models, perform the following:
  a. Place the motorcycle on a support block.
  b. Measure the free play of the chain when it is pushed up midway between the sprockets (**Figure 42**). Specifications for free play are listed in **Table 9**.
  c. Rotate the rear wheel to move the chain to another position and recheck the free play; chains rarely wear or stretch evenly. As a result, the free play will not remain constant over the entire chain.

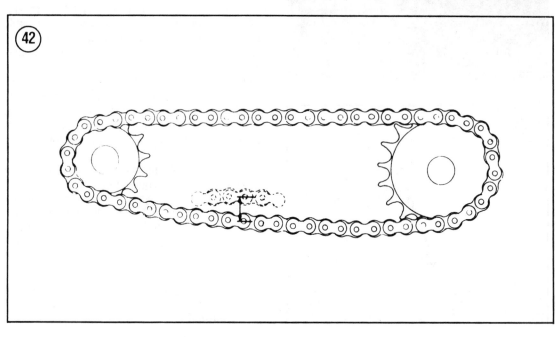

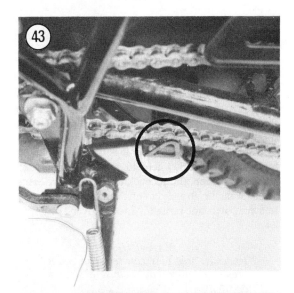

d. To adjust free play, turn the adjuster bolts (C, **Figure 41**) either in or out, as required, in equal amounts.

> *WARNING*
> *Excessive free play can result in chain breakage which could cause a serious accident.*

e. If the chain cannot be adjusted within the limits in **Table 9**, it is excessively worn and stretched and should be replaced.

f. After adjustment, tighten the axle adjuster locknuts securely.

3B. On XR500 models, perform the following:

a. Inspect the drive chain tensioner slider (**Figure 43**). If it is worn to the wear line, remove the screw and replace the slider before adjusting the drive chain.

b. Measure the distance between the bottom of the swing arm and top of the drive chain (**Figure 44**). Adjust if the distance is 20 mm (3/4 in.) or less.

c. Turn the adjuster bolt (C, **Figure 41**) until the distance shown in **Figure 44** is the same as listed in **Table 9**.

d. Rotate the rear wheel to move the chain to another position and recheck the adjustment; chains rarely wear or stretch evenly. As a result, the free play will not remain constant over the entire chain. If the chain cannot be adjusted within these limits, it is excessively worn and stretched and must be replaced as described in Chapter Ten. Always replace both sprockets when replacing the drive chain; never install a new drive chain over worn sprockets. The replacement numbers are listed in **Table 10**.

> *WARNING*
> *Excessive free play can result in chain breakage which could cause a serious accident.*

e. If the drive chain cannot be adjusted within the limits in **Table 9**, it is excessively worn and stretched and should be replaced.

f. After adjustment, tighten the axle adjuster locknuts securely.

4. On all models, make sure the index marks on the swing arm align with the same reference mark on both the right and left-hand side (**Figure 45**).

5. When the adjustment is correct, sight along the chain from the rear sprocket to see that it is correctly aligned. It should leave the top of the rear sprocket in a straight line (A, **Figure 46**). If it is cocked to one side or the other (B or C, **Figure 46**), the rear wheel is incorrectly aligned and must be corrected by turning the adjusters counter to one another until the chain and sprocket are correctly aligned.

6. Tighten the rear axle nut to the torque specification listed in **Table 6**. Install a new cotter pin and bend the ends over completely.

7. Adjust the rear brake pedal free play as described in this chapter.

Drive Chain Adjustment (Pro-Link Models)

The drive chain should be checked, lubricated and adjusted at the interval listed in **Table 2** or more often if ridden in wet or dusty conditions. It should be removed and cleaned at the interval listed in **Table 2**. The correct amount of chain free play when pushed up midway between the sprockets on the upper chain run is listed in **Table 9**. See A, **Figure 47**. If adjustment is necessary, perform the following.

1. Place wood blocks under the engine to support the bike securely with the rear wheel off the ground.

2. Place the transmission in NEUTRAL.

3. Loosen the axle nut (A, **Figure 48**).

4. On models so equipped, loosen the holder nut (**Figure 49**) on the snail adjuster.

5. Turn both snail adjusters (B, **Figure 48**) in equal amounts to either increase or decrease drive chain tension. After adjustment is complete, make sure that the same adjustment mark number on both snail adjusters aligns with the stopper pin on both sides of the swing arm (**Figure 50**).

6. Rotate the rear wheel to move the chain to another position and recheck the free play. Chains rarely wear or stretch evenly and, as a result, the free play will not remain constant over the entire length.

> *WARNING*
> *Excessive free play can result in chain breakage which could cause a serious accident.*

7. If the chain cannot be adjusted within the limits in **Table 9**, it is excessively worn and should be replaced. Always replace both sprockets when replacing the drive chain; never install a new chain over worn sprockets. The replacement numbers are listed in **Table 10**.

8. When the adjustment is correct, sight along the chain from the rear sprocket to see that it is correctly aligned. It should leave the top of the rear

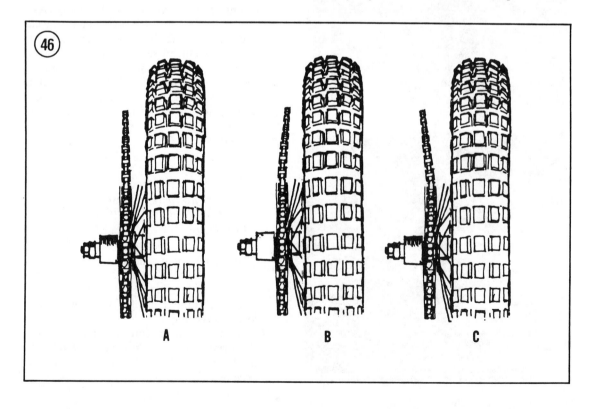

(46)

A   B   C

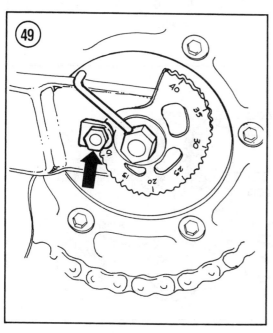

sprocket in a straight line (A, **Figure 46**). If it is cocked to one side or the other (B or C, **Figure 46**), the rear wheel is incorrectly aligned and must be corrected by turning the adjusters counter to one another until the chain and sprocket are correctly aligned.

9. Tighten the self-locking rear axle nut to the torque specification listed in **Table 6**.

10. After the drive chain has been adjusted to the correct amount of free play, drill a small hole in the drive chain guard (B, **Figure 47**) directly above the top of the chain. This can be used as a reference mark for future checks.

11. Adjust the rear brake pedal free play as described in this chapter.

Drive Chain Cleaning, Inspection and Lubrication (XR500R and XL600R Pro-Link Models)

Clean and lubricate the drive chain at the interval indicated in **Table 2**, or more frequently if ridden in dusty or muddy terrain.

NOTE
These models are equipped with an O-ring type drive chain.

1. Remove the drive chain as described under *Rear Wheel Removal/Installation* in Chapter Ten.

2. Immerse the drive chain in a pan of kerosene or non-flammable solvent that will not destroy the rubber O-rings.

3. Allow it to soak for about 10-15 minutes. Move it around and flex it during this period so that the dirt between the links, pins and plates may work its way out.

4. Scrub the rollers and side plates with a soft brush and rinse away loosened grit. Rinse it a couple of times to make sure all dirt is washed out. Wipe the drive chain dry with a shop cloth. Hang up the chain and allow it to dry thoroughly.

5. After cleaning the chain, examine it carefully for wear or damage. If any signs are visible, replace the chain.

6. Lay the chain alongside a ruler (**Figure 51**) and pull the chain taut. Measure the distance between the number of pins listed in **Table 11**. If the chain has stretched to the service limit it must be replaced. Replacement chain numbers are listed in **Table 10**.

CAUTION
*Always check both sprockets (**Figure 52**) every time the drive chain is removed. If any wear is visible on the teeth, replace the sprocket. Never install a new chain over worn sprockets or a worn chain over new sprockets.*

7. Check the inner faces of the inner plates. They should be lightly polished on both sides. If they show considerable wear on both sides, the sprockets are not aligned. Adjust alignment as described in this chapter.

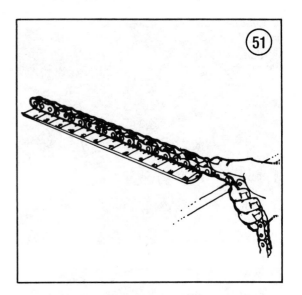

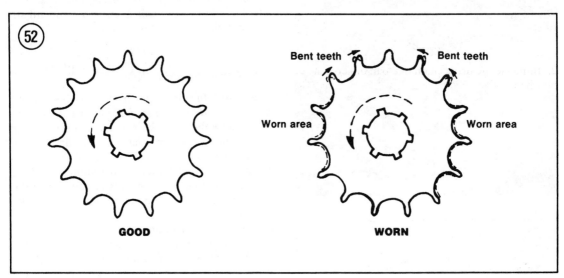

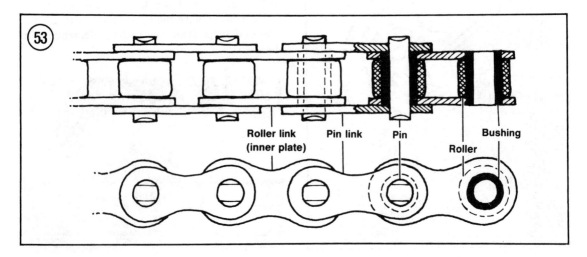

8. Lubricate the drive chain with SAE 80 or 90 gear oil or a good grade of chain lubricant (formulated for O-ring chains) carefully following the manufacturer's instructions.

CAUTION
Do not use engine oil as a lubricant as it will damage the O-rings. Use a chain lubricant specifically formulated for use with this type of chain or specified gear oil.

9. Reinstall the drive chain as described in Chapter Ten.
10. Adjust the drive chain tension as described in this chapter.

Drive Chain Cleaning, Inspection and Lubrication (All Except XR500R and XL600R Pro-Link Models)

Clean and lubricate the drive chain at the interval indicated in **Table 2**, or more frequently if ridden in dusty or muddy terrain.
1. Remove the drive chain as described under *Rear Wheel Removal/Installation* in Chapter Ten.
2. Immerse the drive chain in a pan of kerosene or non-flammable solvent.
3. Allow it to soak for about a half hour. Move it around and flex it during this period so that the dirt between the links, pins and plates may work its way out.

4. Scrub the rollers and side plates with a soft brush and rinse away loosened grit. Rinse it a couple of times to make sure all dirt is washed out. Wipe the drive chain dry with a shop cloth. Hang up the chain and allow it to dry thoroughly.
5. After cleaning the chain, examine it carefully for wear or damage. If any signs are visible, replace the chain.
6. Lay the chain alongside a ruler (**Figure 51**) and pull the chain taut. Measure the distance between the number of pins listed in **Table 11**. If the chain has stretched to the service limit it must be replaced. The replacement chain numbers are listed in **Table 10**.

CAUTION
*Always check both sprockets (**Figure 52**) every time the drive chain is removed. If any wear is visible on the teeth, replace the sprocket. Never install a new chain over worn sprockets or a worn chain over new sprockets.*

7. Check the inner faces of the inner plates (**Figure 53**). They should be lightly polished on both sides. If they show considerable wear on both sides, the sprockets are not aligned. Adjust alignment as described in this chapter.
8. Lubricate the drive chain with a good grade of chain lubricant carefully following the manufacturer's instructions.
9. Reinstall the drive chain as described in Chapter Ten.
10. Adjust the drive chain tension as described in this chapter.

Drive Chain Tensioners (Pro-Link Models)

On Pro-Link models there are either rollers or a slider on the chain tensioner arm (**Figure 54**). There is also a drive chain guide (A, **Figure 55**) and a flat slider (B, **Figure 55**) attached to the left-hand side of the swing arm near the pivot point.

There are no factory-specified wear limit dimensions for the rollers. If they are worn unevenly or worn close to the attachment bolt, they should be replaced. Remove the bolt and nut securing the roller and replace with a new roller.

Inspect the slider attached to the swing arm. If the wear groove is worn more than halfway through the material, replace the slider as follows:
  a. Remove the screws and washers securing the slider to the swing arm.
  b. Remove the slider and install a new slider.
  c. Tighten the screws securely.

Drum Brake Lining

Check the front and rear brake linings for wear. If the arrow on the brake arm aligns with the raised index mark on the brake backing plate (**Figure 56**) when the brake is applied, the brake linings require replacement.

If replacement is necessary, refer to Chapter Eleven.

Disc Brake Fluid Level

The fluid level in the front brake reservoir should be up to the upper mark within the reservoir. This upper level mark is only visible when the master cylinder top cover is removed. If the brake fluid level reaches the lower level mark, visible through the viewing port on the side of the master cylinder reservoir, the fluid level must be corrected by adding fresh brake fluid.

1. Place the bike on level ground and position the handlebars so the master cylinder reservoir is level.
2. Clean any dirt from the area around the top cover before removing the cover.
3. Remove the screws securing the top cover (**Figure 57**). Remove the top cover, diaphragm plate (models so equipped) and the diaphragm. Add brake fluid until the level is to the upper level line within the master cylinder body. Use fresh brake fluid from a sealed brake fluid container.

> *WARNING*
> *Use brake fluid from a sealed container clearly marked DOT 3 or DOT 4 only (specified for disc brakes). Others may vaporize and cause brake failure. Do not intermix different brands or types of brake fluid as they may not be compatible. Do not intermix a silicone based (DOT 5) brake fluid as it can cause brake component damage leading to brake system failure.*

> *CAUTION*
> *Be careful when handling brake fluid. Do not spill it on painted or plated surfaces or plastic parts as it will destroy the surface. Wash the area immediately with soapy water and rinse it off thoroughly.*

4. Reinstall the diaphragm, diaphragm plate (models so equipped) and the top cover. Tighten the screws securely.

Disc Brake Lines

Check brake lines between the master cylinder and the brake caliper. If there is any leakage, tighten the connections and bleed the brakes as described in Chapter Eleven. If this does not stop the leak or if a brake line is obviously damaged, cracked or chafed, replace the brake line and bleed the system.

Disc Brake Pad Wear

Inspect the brake pads for excessive or uneven wear, scoring and oil or grease on the friction surface. Look up at the bottom of the caliper assembly and check the wear lines on the brake pads. Replace both pads if the wear line on the pads reaches the brake disc.

If any of these conditions exist, replace the pads as described in Chapter Eleven.

Disc Brake Fluid Change

Every time the reservoir cap is removed, a small amount of dirt and moisture enters the brake fluid. The same thing happens if a leak occurs or any part of the hydraulic system is loosened or disconnected. Dirt can clog the system and cause unnecessary wear. Water in the brake fluid vaporizes at high temperature, impairing the hydraulic action and reducing the brake's stopping ability.

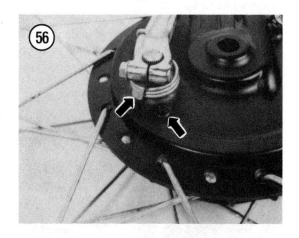

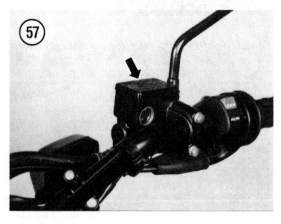

To maintain peak performance, change the brake fluid as indicated in **Table 2**. To change brake fluid, follow the *Bleeding the Brake System* procedure in Chapter Eleven. Continue adding new fluid to the master cylinder and bleeding out at the caliper until the fluid leaving the caliper is clean and free of contaminates.

WARNING
Use brake fluid from a sealed container and clearly marked DOT 3 or DOT 4 only (specified for disc brakes). Others may vaporize and cause brake failure. Do not intermix different brands or types of brake fluid as they may not be compatible. Do not intermix a silicone based (DOT 5) brake fluid as it can cause brake component damage leading to brake system failure.

Front Brake Lever Adjustment (Drum Brake Models)

The front brake cable should be adjusted so there will be 25-30-mm (1-1 1/4 in.) of brake lever movement require to actuate the brake, but it must not be

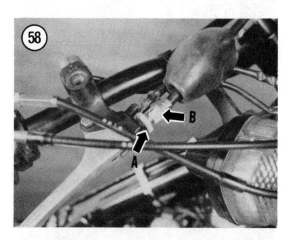

so closely adjusted that the brake shoes contact the brake drum with the lever in the released position.

Minor adjustments should be made at the hand lever, but major adjustments should be made at the brake lever at the brake mechanism.

1. Loosen the locknut (A, **Figure 58**) and turn the adjusting barrel (B, **Figure 58**) in order to obtain the correct amount of free play. Tighten the locknut (A, **Figure 58**).

2. Because of the normal brake wear, this adjustment will eventually be "used up." It is then necessary to loosen the locknut (A, **Figure 58**) and screw the adjusting barrel (B) all the way in toward the hand grip. Tighten the locknut (A, **Figure 58**).

3A. On XL500S and XR500 models, at the lower adjustment on the front fork, loosen the locknut (C, **Figure 59**) and turn the adjuster nut (D), until the brake lever can once again be used for fine adjustment. Tighten the locknut (C, **Figure 59**).

3B. On all other models, at the lower adjustment on the brake panel, loosen the locknut and turn the adjuster nut, until the brake lever can once again be used for fine adjustment. Tighten the locknut (C, **Figure 59**).

4. When the 2 arrows on the brake arm and brake panel align (**Figure 56**) the brake shoes must be replaced as described in Chapter Eleven.

Front Brake Lever Free Play (Disc Brake Models–1985-1990 XR600R)

A free play adjustment has been added to the brake lever. There should be 1-8 mm (0.04-0.31 in.) of travel at the tip of the lever (A, **Figure 60**).

To increase or decrease brake lever free play, loosen the locknut (B, **Figure 60**) and turn the adjuster (C) in the desired direction until the free play is correct. Tighten the locknut securely.

If the brake lever free play exceeds 8 mm (0.31 in.) and the clearance between the front master cylinder piston and the adjuster (D, **Figure 60**) is less than 1.4 mm (0.06 in.) there is probably air in the brake system and the system must be bled as described under *Bleeding The System* in Chapter Eleven.

Front Brake Lever Free Play (All Disc Brake Models– Except 1985-1990 XR600R)

The front disc brake lever has 2 free play positions.

1. Slide back the rubber protective boot from the brake lever pivot point area.

2. To increase free play, use a flat-bladed screwdriver and rotate the eccentric screw (**Figure 61**) until the single dot on the screw aligns with the index mark on the brake lever.

3. To decrease free play, use a flat-bladed screwdriver and rotate the eccentric screw (**Figure 61**) until the double dot on the screw aligns with the index mark on the brake lever.

CAUTION
Do not leave the eccentric screw between the 2 positions. It must always be aligned with one of the marks or the brake lever will not operate properly.

Rear Brake Pedal Height Adjustment

The rear brake pedal height should be adjusted at the interval listed in **Table 2**.

1. Make sure the brake pedal is in the at-rest position.

2A. *Cable-operated brake*—To change height, loosen the locknut (A, **Figure 62**) and turn the adjuster bolt (B, **Figure 62**). Tighten the locknut (A).

2B. *Rod-operated brake*—To change height, loosen the locknut (A, **Figure 63**) and turn the adjuster bolt (B, **Figure 63**). Tighten the locknut (A).

3. Adjust the pedal free play as described in this chapter.

Rear Brake Pedal Free Play Adjustment

Free play is the distance the rear brake pedal travels from the at-rest position to the applied position when the pedal is depressed by hand.

1. Adjust the rear brake to the correct height as described in this chapter.

2. Turn the adjust nut on the end of the brake rod until the pedal has 10-15 mm (3/8-5/8 in.) free play. Refer to **Figure 64** or **Figure 65**.

3. Rotate the rear wheel and check for brake drag.

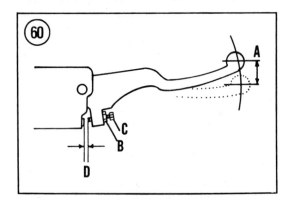

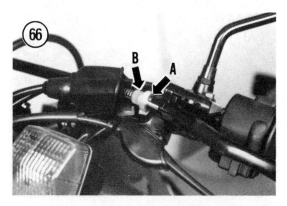

4. Operate the brake pedal several times to make sure the pedal returns to the at-rest position immediately after release.

5. On XL series models, adjust the rear brake light switch as described in Chapter Eight.

Clutch Adjustment

Adjust the clutch at the interval indicated in **Table 2**. For the clutch to fully engage and disengage, there must be the following amount of free play.

    a. XL500S, XR500, 1981-1982 XR500R: 15-25 mm (5/8-1 in.).

    b. All other models: 10-20 mm (3/8-3/4 in.).

1. Minor adjustments can be made at the upper adjuster at the hand lever as follows:

    a. Pull back the rubber protective boot.

    b. Loosen the locknut (A, **Figure 66**) and turn the adjuster (B, **Figure 66**) in or out to obtain the correct amount of free play. Tighten the locknut.

NOTE
If the proper amount of free play cannot be achieved at the hand lever, additional adjustment can be made at the clutch actuating lever on the engine or in-line adjuster on the clutch cable.

2. At the clutch lever, loosen the locknut (A, **Figure 66**) and turn the adjuster (B, **Figure 66**) in all the way toward the hand grip. Tighten the locknut (A).

3A. On XL500S, XR500 and 1981-1982 XR500R models, perform the following:

    a. Near the right-hand crankcase cover, loosen the locknut (A, **Figure 67**) and turn the adjuster (B, **Figure 67**) until the correct amount of free play can be achieved.

    b. Tighten the locknut (A).

3B. On all other models, perform the following:

    a. On the left-hand crankcase cover, loosen the locknut and turn the adjuster (**Figure 68**) until the correct amount of free play can be achieved.

    b. Tighten the locknut.

4. If necessary, do some final adjusting at the clutch lever as described in Step 1.

5. After adjustment is complete, check that the locknuts are tight at the hand lever, at the clutch actuating lever on the crankcase and at the cable in-line adjuster.

sure the clutch fully engages; if it does not, the clutch will slip, particularly when accelerating in high gear.

7. If the proper amount of adjustment cannot be achieved using this procedure, the cable has stretched to the point where it needs replacing. Refer to Chapter Six for replacement.

Throttle Adjustment and Operation

The throttle grip should have 2-6 mm (1/8-1/4 in.) rotational free play (**Figure 69**). If adjustment is necessary, make minor adjustments at the throttle grip and the major adjustments at the top of the carburetor.

NOTE
There are 2 throttle cables, but only the "pull" cable is adjustable.

1A. On XL500S and XR500 models, perform the following:
   a. Loosen the locknut and turn the adjuster (**Figure 70**) on the rear throttle cable at the throttle grip in or out to achieve proper free play rotation. Tighten the locknut.
   b. If additional adjustment is necessary, remove the fuel tank as described in Chapter Seven.
   c. Loosen the locknut and turn the adjuster (**Figure 71**) on the upper throttle cable at the carburetor assembly in or out to achieve proper free play rotation. Tighten the locknut and install the fuel tank.

1B. On all other models, perform the following:

NOTE
The throttle assembly on 1988-1990 XR600R models is different in appearance than prior XR600R models but the adjustment procedure is exactly the same.

   a. Slide back the rubber protective boot.
   b. Loosened the locknut and turn the adjuster (**Figure 72**) on the lower throttle cable at the throttle grip in or out to achieve proper free play rotation. Tighten the lock nut.
   c. If additional adjustment is necessary, remove the fuel tank as described in Chapter Seven.
   d. Loosen the locknut and turn the adjuster (**Figure 73**) on the lower throttle cable at the carburetor assembly in or out to achieve proper free play rotation. Tighten the locknut and install the fuel tank.

2. Check the throttle cables from the grip to the carburetor. Make sure they are not kinked or chafed; replace as necessary.

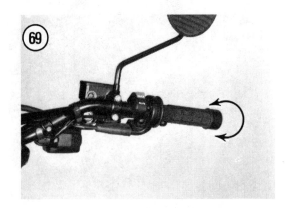

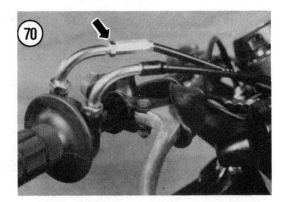

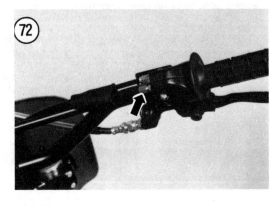

3. Make sure the throttle grip rotates freely from a fully closed to fully open position. Check with the handlebar at center, at full right and at full left. If necessary, remove the throttle grip and apply a lithium base grease to it.

WARNING
With the engine idling, move the handlebar from side-to-side. If idle speed

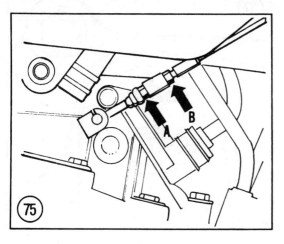

*increases during this movement, the throttle cable(s) may need adjusting or may be incorrectly routed through the frame. Correct this problem immediately. Do **not** ride the bike in this unsafe condition.*

Cam Chain Tensioner Adjustment (RFC Engine Models)

There is no provision for cam chain tensioner adjustment on these models. Chain tension is maintained automatically.

Cam Chain Tensioner Adjustment (All Except RFVC Engine Models)

In time the camshaft chain and guide will wear and develop slack. This will cause engine noise and if neglected too long will cause engine damage. Adjust the camshaft chain tensioner at the interval indicated in **Table 2**.

1. Start the engine and let it reach normal operating temperature.

CAUTION
*Do **not** loosen the upper tensioner bolt or lower locknut more than 2 turns or the tensioner assembly within the engine may work loose and cause severe engine damage.*

2. Let the engine idle. Loosen the tensioner upper bolt (A, **Figure 74**) and the lower locknut (B) 1 1/2-2 turns.
3. When the tensioner bolt and locknut are loosened as described in Step 2, the tensioner will automatically adjust to the correct tension.
4. Tighten the tensioner bolt and locknut securely.

Starter Decompression Adjustment (Single-cable–1998-1990 XR600R Models)

NOTE
*Valve clearance must be correctly adjusted before adjusting the decompression. Refer to **Valve Clearance Adjustment** in this chapter.*

1. Measure the free play clearance at the tip of the manual decompression lever on the left-hand handlebar. The correct amount of free play is 5-8 mm (3/16–5/16 in.).
2. To adjust the free play, loosen the locknut (A, **Figure 75**) and turn the adjuster (B) until the correct amount of free play is achieved.
3. Tighten the locknut securely.

Starter Decompression Adjustment
(Single-cable – All Other Models)

NOTE
Valve clearance must be correctly adjusted before adjusting the decompressor. Refer to Valve Clearance Adjustment in this chapter.

1. Remove the 2 inspection covers on the left-hand crankcase cover (**Figure 76**).
2. Remove the spark plug. This will make it easier to rotate the engine by hand.
3. Rotate the crankshaft with the nut on the alternator rotor. Turn it counterclockwise until the piston is at top dead center (TDC) on the compression stroke.

NOTE
A cylinder at TDC will have both its rocker arms loose, indicating that the exhaust and intake valves are closed. Remove the valve adjusting covers and make this test. If the rocker arms are tight, the cylinder is on its exhaust stroke. Rotate the crankshaft one full turn and check again to make sure the rocker arms are loose.

4. Make sure the "T" timing mark on the alternator rotor aligns with the fixed notch in the case (**Figure 77**).
5. Measure the free play at the top of the decompressor valve lifter (A, **Figure 78**). The correct amount of free play is 1-2 mm (0.04-0.08 in.).
6. To adjust the free play, loosen the locknut (B, **Figure 78**) and turn the adjuster (C, **Figure 78**) until the correct amount of free play is achieved.

CAUTION
Excessive free play will result in hard starting. Insufficient free play will cause erratic engine idle and a burned exhaust valve.

7. Tighten the locknut (B, **Figure 78**), install the valve adjusting covers, the spark plug and the 2 inspection covers.

Starter Decompressor Adjustment
(Dual-cable Models)

NOTE
Valve clearance must be correctly adjusted before adjusting the decompressor. Refer to Valve Clearance Adjustment in this chapter.

The dual-cable models have a manual starter decompressor located on the left-hand handlebar

and a decompressor that works directly with the kickstarter lever. Both the manual and kickstarter decompressor cables must be adjusted correctly or neither will work.

1. Place the bike on the sidestand.
2. Remove the fuel tank as described in Chapter Seven.
3. Remove the 2 inspection covers on the left-hand crankcase cover (**Figure 79**).
4. Remove the spark plug. This will make it easier to rotate the engine by hand.
5. Rotate the crankshaft with the nut on the alternator rotor. Turn it *counterclockwise* until the piston is at top dead center (TDC) on the compression stroke.

NOTE
A cylinder at TDC will have both its rocker arms loose, indicating that the exhaust and intake valves are closed. Remove the valve adjusting covers and make this test. If the rocker arms are tight, the cylinder is on its exhaust stroke. Rotate the crankshaft one full turn and check again to make sure the rocker arms are loose.

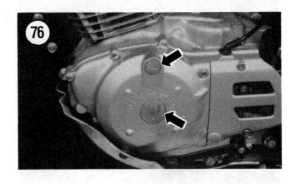

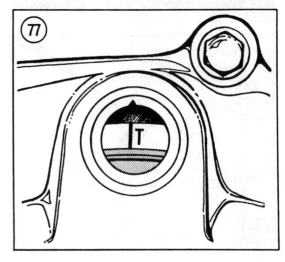

6. Make sure the "T" timing mark on the alternator rotor aligns with the fixed notch in the case (**Figure 77**).

7. The correct amount of free play is as follows:
   a. At the tip of the kickstarter decompressor lever: 1-2 mm (1/32-1/16 in.).
   b. At the tip of the manual decompressor lever: 5-8 mm (3/16-5/16 in.).

8. If adjustment is necessary, perform the following:
   a. Loosen the manual cable locknut and adjust nut to gain slack in the cable.
   b. Disconnect the manual cable from the decompressor starter valve lifter lever on the cylinder head cover.
   c. Loosen the locknut on the kickstarter cable and turn the adjust nut until the correct amount of free play is achieved.
   d. Tighten the locknut and operate the kickstarter several times and check the operation of the decompressor mechanism.
   e. Reconnect the manual cable to the lever.

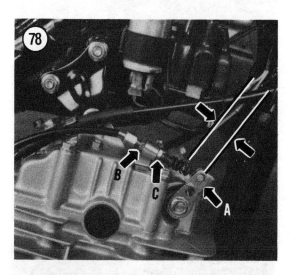

f. Loosen the locknut on the manual cable and turn the adjusting nut until the correct amount of free play is achieved. Tighten the locknut.

> *CAUTION*
> *Excessive free play will result in hard starting. Insufficient free play will cause erratic engine idle and a burned exhaust valve.*

9. Install the valve adjusting covers, the spark plug and the 2 inspection covers.

**Balancer Chain Adjustment
(XL500S, 1981-1982 XR500R
and 1982 XL500R)**

The balancer chain should be adjusted at the interval listed in **Table 2**.

> *NOTE*
> *All other models have a gear-driven balancer system that does not require routine adjustment.*

1. Drain the engine oil as described in this chapter.
2. Remove the bolts securing the skid plate and remove the skid plate.
3. Remove the kickstarter arm.
4. Disconnect the clutch and starter decompressor lever cables from the right-hand crankcase cover.
5. Remove the bolts securing the right-hand footpeg assembly and remove the assembly.
6. Remove the brake pedal.
7. Remove the bolts securing the right-hand crankcase cover and remove it and the gasket.
8. Loosen the bolt (A, **Figure 80**) securing the balancer holder flange.
9. When the bolt is loosened, the spring (B, **Figure 80**) will pull the holder flange counterclockwise.

> *NOTE*
> *If the holder flange bottoms out on the bolt, it will have to be repositioned. Refer to Steps 12-18.*

10. Move the holder flange *clockwise* one graduation from where it stops (C, **Figure 80**).

> *NOTE*
> *Align the graduations on the holder flange with the arrow on the crankcase.*

11. Tighten the bolt to the torque specification listed in **Table 6**.
12. To reposition the holder flange, remove the small circlip (D, **Figure 80**) and slide off the balancer weight and thrust washer (E, **Figure 80**).

13. Remove the spring (A, **Figure 81**) and bolt (B, **Figure 81**).

14A. On 500 cc models, remove the circlip and washer (C, **Figure 81**).

14B. On all other models, note the original position of the holder flange on the shaft. Slide the holder flange off the shaft splines and reposition it one graduation to the left of the original position.

15. On 500 cc models, install the washer and circlip.

16. Install the thrust washer, balancer weight and circlip. Make sure the circlip is properly seated in the shaft groove.

> *CAUTION*
> *The index mark on the balancer weight must align with the punch mark on the end of the shaft (E, **Figure 80**).*

17. Install the spring (B, **Figure 80**) and bolt—do *not* tighten the bolt at this time.

18. Repeat Step 10 and Step 11.

19. Complete by reversing Steps 1-7. Tighten the holder bolt to the torque specification listed in **Table 6**.

20. Fill the crankcase with the recommended type and quantity of engine oil as described in this chapter.

Air Filter Element

The air filter removes dust and abrasive particles from the air before the air enters the carburetor and engine. Without the air filter, very fine particles could enter into the engine and cause rapid wear of the piston rings, cylinder and bearings and might clog small passages in the carburetor(s). Never run the bike without the air filter element installed.

Proper air filter servicing can do more to ensure long service from your engine than almost any other single item. The air filter element should be removed and cleaned at the interval listed in **Table 2**.

Air Filter Element
Removal/Installation
(XL500S, XR500, 1982 XL500R)

1. Place the bike on the sidestand.

2A. On XL500S and XR500 models, perform the following:

    a. Remove the screws securing the left-hand side cover and remove the cover.

    b. Unscrew the wing nut (**Figure 82**) and withdraw the element holder and element from the air box.

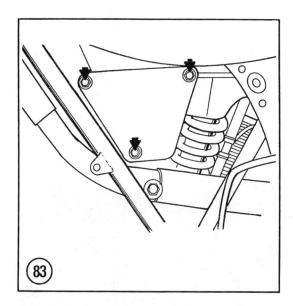

(83)

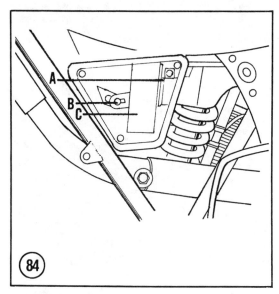

(84)

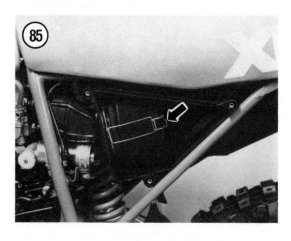

(85)

2B. On 1982 XL500R models, perform the following:

   a. Remove the left-hand side cover.

   b. Remove the screws securing the air filter cover and remove the cover.

   c. Unscrew the wing nut and withdraw the element holder and element from the air box.

3. Separate the air filter element from the holder.

4. Wipe out the interior of the air box with a shop rag dampened with cleaning solvent. Remove any foreign matter that may have passed through a broken element.

5. Clean and re-oil the element as described in this chapter.

6. Install by reversing these removal steps, noting the following.

7. Make sure the element is correctly seated into the air box so there is no air leak. Be sure to tighten the wing nut securely.

8. On XL500S and XR500 models, inspect the raised sealing ridge that fits into the perimeter gasket on the air box. If the ridge is cracked or broken, the side cover must be replaced.

Air Filter Element
Removal/Installation
(1981-1982 XR500R)

1. Place the bike on the sidestand.

2. Remove the right-hand side cover.

3. Remove the screws securing the air filter cover and remove the cover (**Figure 83**).

4. Loosen the clamping screw (A, **Figure 84**) on the band at the front of the element.

5. Unscrew the wing nut (B, **Figure 84**) and withdraw the element assembly (C) from the air box.

6. Separate the air filter element from the holder.

7. Wipe out the interior of the air box with a shop rag dampened with cleaning solvent. Remove any foreign matter that may have passed through a broken element.

8. Clean and re-oil the element as described in this chapter.

9. Install by reversing these removal steps, noting the following.

10. Make sure the element is correctly seated into the air box so there is no air leak.

Air Filter Element Removal/Installation
(1983-1984 XR500R, 1985-1990 XR600R)

1. Place the bike on the sidestand.

2. Remove the bolts securing the left-hand side cover and remove the side cover.

3. Unhook the element retaining strap (**Figure 85**).

4. Withdraw the element assembly from the air box.

5. Separate the air filter element from the holder (**Figure 86**).

6. Wipe out the interior of the air box with a shop rag dampened with cleaning solvent. Remove any foreign matter that may have passed through a broken element.

7. Clean and re-oil the element as described in this chapter.

8. Install by reversing these removal steps, noting the following.

9. Make sure the element is correctly seated into the air box so there is no air leak.

Air Filter Element
Removal/Installation
(XL600R)

1. Place the bike on the sidestand.
2. Remove the left-hand side cover.
3. Remove the screws securing the air filter cover and remove the cover (**Figure 87**).
4. Pull the element assembly (**Figure 88**) from the air box.
5. Separate the air filter element from the holder.
6. Wipe out the interior of the air box with a shop rag dampened with cleaning solvent. Remove any foreign matter that may have passed through a broken element.
7. Clean and re-oil the element as described in this chapter.
8. Install by reversing these removal steps, noting the following.
9. Make sure the element is correctly seated into the air box so there is no air leak.

Air Filter Element Cleaning
and Re-oiling (All Models)

1. Clean the element gently in a non-flammable or high flash point cleaning solvent until all dirt is removed. Thoroughly dry with a clean shop cloth until all residue is removed. Let dry for about one hour.

> *CAUTION*
> *Inspect the element; if it is torn or broken in any area it should be replaced. Do not run the engine with a damaged element as it may allow dirt to enter the engine.*

2. Pour a small amount of SAE 80-90 gear oil or foam air filter oil onto the element and work it into the porous foam material. Do not oversaturate as too much oil will restrict air flow. The element should be discolored by the oil and should have an even color indicating that the oil is distributed evenly.

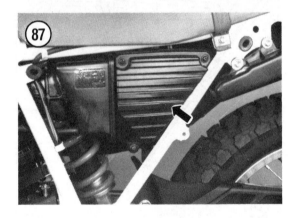

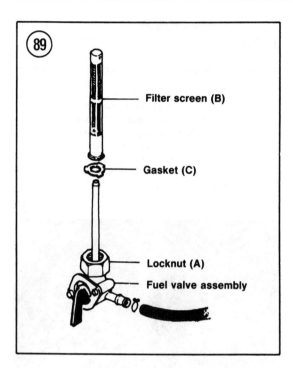

(89)

Filter screen (B)

Gasket (C)

Locknut (A)

Fuel valve assembly

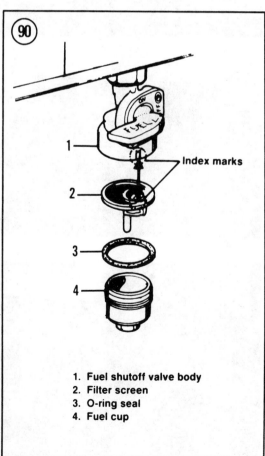

(90)

1 —

Index marks

2 —

3 —

4 —

1. Fuel shutoff valve body
2. Filter screen
3. O-ring seal
4. Fuel cup

3. If foam air filter oil was used, let the element dry for another hour before installation. If installed too soon, the chemical carrier in the foam air filter oil will be drawn into the engine and may cause damage.

Fuel Shutoff Filter and Valve Removal/Installation

The fuel filter is built into the shutoff valve and removes particles which might otherwise clog the carburetor.

1. Turn the shutoff valve to the OFF position and remove the fuel line to the carburetor.

2. Place the loose end in a clean, sealable metal container. This fuel can be reused if it is kept clean.

3. Open the valve to the RESERVE position and remove the fuel filler cap. This will allow air to enter the fuel tank and speed up the flow of fuel. Drain the fuel tank completely.

4A. On metal fuel tanks, unscrew the locknut (A, **Figure 89**) securing the fuel shutoff valve to the fuel tank. Remove the valve.

4B. On plastic fuel tanks, remove the screw securing the fuel shutoff valve to the fuel tank. Remove the metal collars that surround the screws and remove the valve.

5. After removing the valve from the fuel tank, insert a corner of a shop cloth into the opening in the tank to stop the dribbling of fuel onto the engine and frame.

6. Remove the fuel filter (B, **Figure 89**) from the shutoff valve. Clean the filter with a medium soft toothbrush and blow out with compressed air. Replace the filter if it is broken in any area.

7. Install by reversing these removal steps, noting the following.

8A. On metal fuel tanks, be sure to install a gasket (C, **Figure 89**) between the shutoff valve and the fuel tank. Tighten the locknut securely.

8B. On plastic fuel tanks, be sure to install the O-ring seal onto the valve. Do not forget to install the collars that surround the screws. Tighten the screws securely.

9. Turn the fuel shutoff valve to the ON position and check for leaks.

Fuel Strainer Cleaning (XL600R)

The fuel strainer is built into the shutoff valve and removes particles which might otherwise clog the carburetor.

Refer to **Figure 90** for this procedure.

1. Turn the shutoff valve to the OFF position.

2. Unscrew the fuel cup (**Figure 91**), O-ring and screen from the shutoff valve. Dispose of fuel remaining in the fuel cup properly.

3. Clean the screen with a medium soft toothbrush and blow out with compressed air. Replace the screen if it is broken in any area.

4. Align the index marks on the screen and shutoff valve body.

5. Install the O-ring seal and screw on the fuel cup.

6. Hand tighten the fuel cup to the torque specification listed in **Table 6**. Do *not* overtighten the fuel cup as it may be damaged.

7. Turn the fuel shutoff valve to the ON position and check for leaks.

Fuel Line Inspection

Inspect the fuel line (**Figure 92**) from the fuel shutoff valve to the carburetor. If it is cracked or starting to deteriorate it must be replaced. Make sure the hose clamps are in place and holding securely.

> *WARNING*
> *A damaged or deteriorated fuel line presents a very dangerous fire hazard to both the rider and the vehicle if fuel should spill onto a hot engine or exhaust pipe.*

Crankcase Breather (U.S. Only)

At the interval listed in **Table 2**, or sooner if a considerable amount of riding is done at full throttle or in the rain, remove the drain plug (**Figure 93**) and drain out all residue. Install the cap.

Refer to Chapter Seven for detailed information on the breather system.

Evaporative Emission Control System (1983-on XL Series Only)

Fuel vapor from the fuel tank is routed into a charcoal canister when the engine is stopped. When the engine is started these vapors are drawn into the air filter, through the carburetor and into the engine to be burned. Make sure all vacuum hoses are correctly routed and attached. Inspect the hoses (**Figure 94**) and canister for damage. Replace damaged items.

Refer to Chapter Seven for detailed information on the evaporative emission control system and for vacuum hose routing.

Spark Arrester Cleaning (U.S. Only)

The spark arrestor should be periodically cleaned.

> *WARNING*
> *To avoid burning your hands do not perform this cleaning operation with the exhaust system hot. Work in a well-ventilated area (outside your garage) that is free from fire hazards. Be sure to protect your eyes with safety goggles or glasses.*

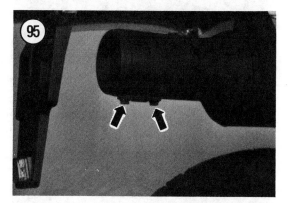

1. Remove the bolts (**Figure 95**) securing the muffler rear port cover. Remove the cover and the gasket.

> *WARNING*
> *Wear heavy gloves to protect your hands in the next step.*

2. Wad up a couple of heavy shop cloths or rags and plug the end of the muffler to create back pressure. This will force the exhaust and carbon deposits out of the rear port.
3. Start the engine and rev it up a couple of times.
4. Continue revving the engine until carbon stops coming out.
5. Install a new gasket onto the port cover and install the port cover. Tighten the bolts securely.

Wheel Bearings

There is no factory-recommended mileage interval for cleaning and repacking the wheel bearings. They should be inspected and serviced, if necessary, every time the wheel is removed or whenever there is a likelihood of water contamination. The correct service procedures are covered in Chapter Nine and Chapter Ten.

Wheel Hubs, Rims and Spokes

Check the wheel hubs and rims for bends and other signs of damage. Check both wheels for broken or bent spokes. Replace damaged or broken spokes as described in Chapter Nine. Plunk each spoke with your finger like a guitar string or tap each one lightly with a small metal tool. All spokes should emit the same sound. A spoke that is too tight will have a higher pitch than others; one that is too loose will have a lower pitch. If only one or two spokes are slightly out of adjustment, adjust with a spoke wrench made for this purpose. If more are affected, the wheel should be removed and trued as described in Chapter Nine.

On models so equipped, make sure the rim locks are tight. If necessary, tighten to the torque specification listed in **Table 6**.

Front Suspension Check

1. Apply the front brake and pump the forks up and down as vigorously as possible. Check for smooth operation and check for any oil leaks.
2. Make sure the upper and lower fork bridge bolts are tight (**Figure 96**).
3. Make sure the bolts securing the handlebar holders (**Figure 97**) are tight and that the handlebar is secure.

4. Make sure the front axle, or axle nut is tight and on models so equipped, make sure the cotter pin is in place.

5. On models so equipped, make sure the axle pinch bolt and the nuts securing the axle holder nuts are tight.

CAUTION
If any of the previously mentioned bolts and nuts are loose, refer to Chapter Nine for correct procedures and torque specifications.

Rear Suspension Check

1. Place wood blocks under the engine to support it securely with the rear wheel off the ground.

2. Push hard on the rear wheel (sideways) to check for side play in the rear swing arm bushings. Remove the wood blocks.

3A. On dual-shock models, check the tightness of the upper and lower mounting nuts on each shock absorber (**Figure 98**).

3B. On Pro-Link models, check the tightness of the upper and lower mounting bolts and nuts (**Figure 99**) on the shock absorber.

4. Make sure the swing arm pivot bolt and nut (**Figure 100**) are tight.

5. On Pro-Link models, check the tightness of the suspension pivot arm assembly bolts and nuts (**Figure 101**).

6. Make sure the rear axle nut (**Figure 102**) is tight and that on models so equipped the cotter pin is in place.

7. On models so equipped, check the tightness of the rear brake torque arm bolt. Make sure the cotter pin is in place.

CAUTION
If any of the previously mentioned bolts and nuts are loose, refer to Chapter Ten for correct procedures and torque specifications.

Nuts, Bolts and Other Fasteners

Constant vibration can loosen many of the fasteners on the motorcycle. Check the tightness of all fasteners, especially those on:
 a. Engine mounting hardware.
 b. Engine crankcase covers.
 c. Handlebar and front forks.
 d. Gearshift lever.
 e. Brake pedal and lever.
 f. Exhaust system.
 g. Lighting equipment (XL series only).

Sidestand Rubber (XL Series Only)

The rubber pad on the sidestand kicks the sidestand up if you should forget. If it wears down to the molded line, replace the rubber as it will no longer be effective and must be replaced.

Steering Head Adjustment Check

Check the steering head ball bearings for looseness at the interval listed in **Table 2**.

Place wood blocks under the engine to support it securely with the front wheel off the ground.

Hold onto the front fork tube and gently rock the fork assembly back and forth. If you feel looseness, refer to Steering Head Adjustment in Chapter Nine.

TUNE-UP

Perform a complete tune-up at the interval listed in **Table 2** for normal riding. More frequent tune-ups may be required if the bike is ridden in stop-and go traffic. If the bike is used for racing, it should be tuned up before each race. The purpose of the tune-up is to restore the performance lost due to normal wear and deterioration of parts.

The spark plugs should be routinely replaced at every other tune-up or if the electrodes show signs of erosion. In addition, this is a good time to clean the air filter element. Have the new parts on hand before you begin.

Because the different systems in an engine interact, the procedures should be done in the following order.

a. Tighten the cylinder head nuts (except Radial Four Valve Combustion engines).
b. Adjust valve clearances.
c. Run a compression test.
d. Check and adjust the ignition components and timing.
e. Set the idle speed.

Table 12 summarizes tune-up specifications. To perform a tune-up on your Honda, you will need the following tools and equipment.

a. 18 mm (5/8 in.) spark plug wrench.
b. Socket wrench and assorted sockets.
c. Flat feeler gauge.
d. Compression gauge.
e. Spark plug wire feeler gauge and gapper tool.
f. Ignition timing light.

Cylinder Head Nuts
(Except Radial Four Valve Combustion Engines)

The cylinder head (not the cylinder head cover) is held in place with 4 acorn nuts. The 2 on the left-hand side are exposed but the 2 on the right-hand side are within the cylinder head cavity.

The nuts should only be tightened on the first tune-up after purchase of a new bike or after the cylinder head has been removed for service. If you wish to tighten the 4 nuts, remove the cylinder head cover and tighten the nuts as described in Chapter Four.

Valve Clearance Adjustment (All Models Except 1988-1990 XR600R)

Valve clearance measurement and adjustment must be performed with the engine cool, at room temperature (below 35° C/95° F). The correct valve clearance for all models is listed in **Table 12**. The exhaust valves are located at the front of the engine and the intake valves are located at the rear of the engine.

NOTE
Make sure there is free play in the starter compressor lever. If not, it will hold down the exhaust valves and make the exhaust valve clearance incorrect. If necessary, adjust the starter decompressor as described in this chapter to allow sufficient slack. Readjust the starter decompressor clearance after the valve clearance is correctly adjusted.

1. Place the bike on the sidestand.
2. Remove the seat.
3. Remove the fuel tank as described in Chapter Seven.

4. Remove the 2 inspection covers (**Figure 103**) on the left-hand crankcase cover.

5A. On RFVC engine models, unscrew each valve adjustment cover (**Figure 104**).

5B. On all other models, remove the bolts (**Figure 105**) securing the front and rear valve adjustment covers and remove the covers and gaskets.

6. Remove the spark plug. This will make it easier to rotate the engine.

7. Rotate the engine with the bolt or nut on the alternator rotor. Rotate the engine *counterclockwise* until the engine is at top dead center (TDC) on the compression stroke.

> *NOTE*
> *A cylinder at TDC on its compression stroke will have free play in all of its rocker arms, indicating that all intake and exhaust valves are closed.*

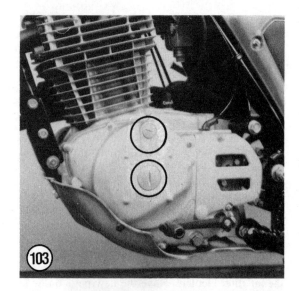

8. Make sure the ignition timing mark "T" aligns with the index mark on the crankcase (**Figure 106**).

9. With the engine timing mark on the "T," if all rocker arms are not loose, rotate the engine *counterclockwise* an additional 360° until all rocker arms have free play.

10. Again make sure the ignition timing mark "T" aligns with the index mark on the crankcase (**Figure 106**).

11. Check the clearance of both intake and exhaust valves by inserting a flat feeler gauge between the adjusting screw and the valve stem (**Figure 107**). When the clearance is correct, there will be a slight drag on the feeler gauge when it is inserted and withdrawn.

12. To correct the clearance, perform the following:
    a. Loosen the adjuster locknut.
    b. Screw the adjuster in or out so there is a slight resistance felt on the feeler gauge (**Figure 108**).
    c. Hold the adjuster to prevent it from turning further and tighten the locknut (**Figure 109**) to the torque specification listed in **Table 6**.
    d. Recheck the clearance to make sure the adjuster did not turn after the correct clearance was achieved; readjust if necessary.
    e. Repeat for all 4 valves.

13. Inspect the rubber gaskets on all valve adjusting covers. Replace any that are starting to deteriorate or harden; replace as a set even if only one is bad. Install all covers.

14. Install all items removed.

15. Adjust the starter decompressor as described in this chapter.

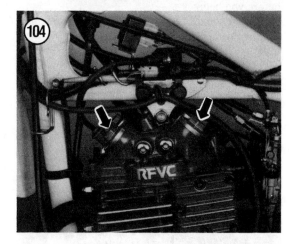

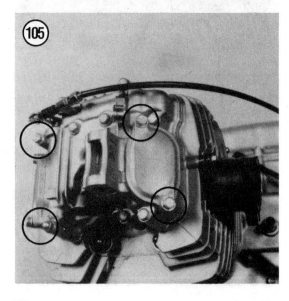

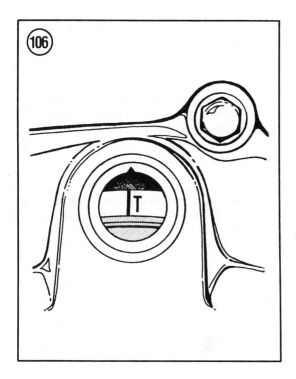

Valve Clearance Adjustment
(1988-1990 XR600R Models)

Due to the automatic decompression system built into the camshaft on these models, it is necessary to follow this procedure carefully. Adjustment of the right-hand exhaust valve is very critical and must be followed exactly.

Valve clearance measurements and adjustments must be performed with the engine cool, at room temperature (below 35° C/ 95° F). The correct valve clearance is listed in **Table 12**. The exhaust valves are located at the front of the engine and the intake valves are located at the rear of the engine.

> *NOTE*
> *Make sure there is free play in the starter decompression lever. If not, it will hold down the right-hand exhaust valve and make the exhaust valve and make the exhaust valve clearance incorrect. If necessary, adjust the starter decompressor, as described in this chapter to allow sufficient slack.*

1. Place the bike on the sidestand.

2. Remove the seat.

3. Remove the fuel tank as described in Chapter Seven.

4. Remove the 2 inspection covers (**Figure 103**) on the left-hand crankcase cover.

5. Unscrew each valve adjustment cover (**Figure 104**).

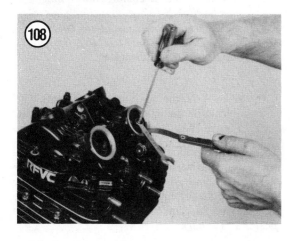

6. Remove the spark plug. This will make it easier to rotate the engine.

7. Rotate the engine with the bolt on the alternator rotor. Rotate the engine counterclockwise until the engine is at top dead center (TDC) on the compression stroke.

NOTE
A cylinder at TDC on its compression stroke will have free play in all of its rocker arms, indicating that the intake valves and exhaust valves are closed.

8. Make sure the ignition timing mark "T" aligns with the index mark on the crankcase (**Figure 106**).

9. With the ignition timing mark on the "T", if all rocker arms are not loose, rotate the engine an additional 360° until all rockers have free play.

NOTE
Do not check the clearance of the right-hand exhaust valve in Step 10. It will be checked later.

10. At this point, check the clearances of the *left-hand* exhaust valve and both intake valves. Insert a flat feeler gauge between the adjusting screw and the valve stem (**Figure 107**). When the clearance is correct, there will be a slight drag on the feeler gauge when it is inserted and withdrawn.

11. To correct the clearance, perform the following:
   a. Loosen the adjuster locknut.
   b. Screw the adjuster in or out so there is a slight resistance felt on the feeler gauge (**Figure 108**).
   c. Hold the adjuster to prevent it from turning any further and tighten the locknut to the torque specification listed in **Table 6**.
   d. Recheck the clearance to make sure the adjuster did not turn after the correct clearance was achieved; readjust if necessary.
   e. Repeat for the remaining *2 valves*.

12. Adjust the starter decompression as described for 1988-1990 XR600R models, in this chapter.

NOTE
*Prior to checking the clearance of the right-hand exhaust valve, the engine's TDC position must be **accurately** checked. The decompressor cam on the right-hand end of the camshaft slightly opens the right-hand exhaust valve when the engine is **slightly before TDC on the compression stroke**. Therefore the en-*

gine must be exactly aligned at the TDC position.

NOTE
A cylinder at TDC on its compression stroke will have free play in all of its rocker arms, indicating that the intake valves and exhaust valves are closed.

13. Make sure the ignition timing mark "T" is still aligned with the index mark on the crankcase (**Figure 106**). If the "T" mark has passed by the index mark, even the slightest amount, it must be realigned as indicated in Step 14.

14. If the "T" timing mark must be realigned, perform the following:
   a. Rotate the engine with the bolt on the alternator rotor. Rotate the engine *counterclockwise* until the engine is at top dead center (TDC) on the compression stroke.

NOTE
A cylinder at TDC on its compression stroke will have free play in all of its rocker arms, indicating that the intake valves and exhaust valves are closed.

CAUTION
*Never rotate the engine **clockwise**. Due to the design of the decompression system, the engine must always be rotated **counterclockwise** for this procedure. If the engine is rotated clockwise the decompression cam may be slightly raised, thus lifting the rocker arm and decreasing any valve clearance, This would lead to a false valve clearance indication.*

   b. Make sure the ignition timing mark "T" aligns with the index mark on the crankcase (**Figure 106**). *Do not go past the "T" mark.*

15. With the ignition timing mark on the "T", if all rocker arms are not loose, rotate the engine an additional 360° until all rocker have free play. Make sure the ignition timing mark "T" aligns with the index mark on the crankcase (**Figure 106**). *Do not go past the "T" mark.*

16. At this point, check the clearance of the *right-hand exhaust valve*. Insert a flat feeler gauge between the adjusting screw and the valve stem. When the clearance is correct, there will be a slight drag on the feeler gauge when it is inserted and withdrawn.

17. To correct the clearance, perform the following:
   a. Loosen the adjuster locknut.
   b. Screw the adjuster in or out so there is a slight resistance felt on the feeler gauge (**Figure 108**).
   c. Hold the adjuster to prevent it from turning any further and tighten the locknut to the torque specification listed in **Table 6.**
   d. Recheck the clearance to make sure the adjuster did not turn after the correct clearance was achieved; readjust if necessary.

18. Adjust the starter decompression for the 1988-on XR600R models, as described in this chapter.

19. Inspect the rubber gaskets on each valve adjuster covers. Replace any that are starting to deteriorate or harden; replace as a set even if only one is bad. Install the covers and tighten securely.

20. Install all items removed.

Compression Test

Check the cylinder compression at the interval indicated in **Table 2**. Record the results and compare them to the results at the next interval. A running record will show trends in deterioration so that corrective action can be taken before complete failure.

The results when properly interpreted, can indicate general cylinder, piston ring and valve condition.

1. Warm the engine to normal operating temperature, then shut it off. Make sure the choke valve and throttle valve are completely open.

2. Remove the spark plug.

3. Connect the compression tester following the manufacturer's instructions.

4. Have an assistant crank the engine over until there is no further rise in pressure.

5. Remove the tester and record the reading. When interpreting the results, actual readings are not as important as the difference between readings over time. Readings substantially different from those listed in **Table 12** indicate broken rings, leaky or sticking valves, a blown head gasket or a combination of all.

If a low reading is obtained, it indicates valve or ring trouble. To determine which, pour about a tespoon of engine oil through the spark plug hole onto the top of the piston. Turn the engine over once to clear the oil, then take another compression test and record the reading. If the compression increases significantly, the valves are good but the rings are defective. If the compression does not increase, the valves require servicing. A valve could be hanging open or a piece of carbon could be on a valve seat.

Spark Plug Selection

Spark plugs are available in various heat ranges, hotter or colder than plugs originally installed at the factory.

Select plugs of a heat range designed for the loads and temperature conditions under which the bike will be run. The use of incorrect heat ranges can cause a seized piston, scored cylinder wall or damaged piston crown.

In general, use a hot plug for low speeds, low engine loads and low temperatures. Use a cold plug for high speeds, high engine loads and high temperatures. The plug should operate hot enough to burn off unwanted deposits, but not so hot that it is damaged or causes preignition. A spark plug of the correct heat range will show a light tan color on the portion of the insulator within the cylinder after the plug has been in service.

In areas where seasonal temperature variations are great, the factory recommends a "2-plug system"—cold plugs for hard summer riding and hot plugs for slower winter operation.

The reach (length) of a plug is also important (**Figure 110**). A longer than normal plug could interfere with the valves and pistons, causing permanent and severe damage. The recommended spark plugs are listed in **Table 12**.

Spark Plug Removal/Cleaning

1. Grasp the spark plug lead (**Figure 111**) as near to the plug as possible and pull it off the plug. If the boot is stuck to the plug, twist it slightly to break it loose.

2. Blow away any dirt that has accumulated in the spark plug well.

CAUTION
The dirt could fall into the cylinder when the plug is removed, causing serious engine damage.

3. Remove spark plug with an 18 mm spark plug wrench.

NOTE
If the plug is difficult to remove, apply penetrating oil around base of plugs and let it soak in about 10-20 minutes.

4. Inspect the spark plug carefully. Look for a broken center porcelain, excessively eroded electrodes and excessive carbon or oil fouling. Replace such a plug. If deposits are light, the plug

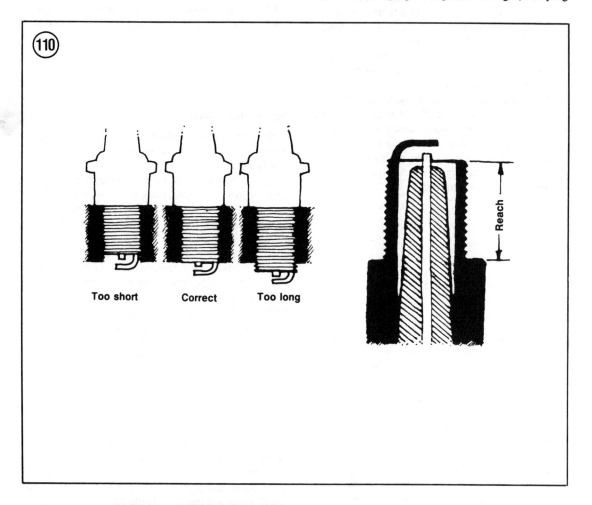

Too short   Correct   Too long

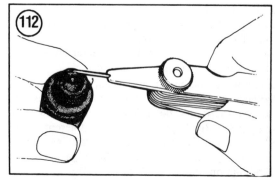

may be cleaned in solvent with a wire brush or in a special spark plug sandblast cleaner. Regap the plug as explained in this chapter.

Spark Plug Gapping and Installation

A new plug should be carefully gapped to ensure a reliable, consistent spark. You must use a special spark plug gapping tool with a wire feeler gauge.

1. Remove the new plug from the box.

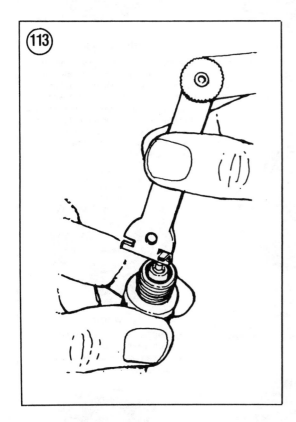

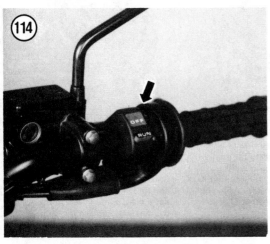

2. Insert a wire feeler gauge between the center and the side electrode of each plug (**Figure 112**). The correct gap is listed in **Table 12**. If the gap is correct, you will feel a slight drag as you pull the wire through. If there is no drag or the gauge won't pass through, bend the side electrode *with the gapping tool* (**Figure 113**) to set the proper gap.

3. Put a *small* drop of oil or aluminum anti-seize compound on the threads of the spark plug.

4. Screw the spark plug in by hand until it seats. Very little effort is required. If force is necessary, you have the plug cross threaded; unscrew it and try again.

5. Tighten the spark plug an additional 1/2 turn after the gasket has made contact with the head. If you are reinstalling an old, regapped plug and are reusing the old gasket, only tighten an additional 1/4 turn.

> *CAUTION*
> *Do not overtighten. This will only squash the gasket and destroy its sealing ability.*

6. Install the spark plug lead. Make sure the lead is on tight.

Reading Spark Plugs

Much information about engine and spark plug performance can be determined by careful examination of the spark plug. This information is more valid after performing the following steps.

1. Ride the bike a short distance at full throttle in any gear.

2. Turn the engine kill switch (**Figure 114**) to the OFF position before closing the throttle and simultaneously pull in the clutch or shift to NEUTRAL; coast and brake to a stop.

3. Remove the spark plug and examine it. Compare it to **Figure 115**. If the insulator is white or burned, the plug is too hot and should be replaced with a colder one.

A too-cold plug will have sooty or oily deposits ranging in color from dark brown to black. Replace with a hotter plug and check for too-rich carburetion or evidence of oil blowby at the piston rings.

If the plug has a light tan or gray colored deposit and no abnormal gap wear or electrode erosion is evident, the plug and the engine are running properly.

If the plug exhibits a black insulator tip, a damp and oily film over the firing end and a carbon layer over the entire nose, it is oil fouled. An oil fouled plug can be cleaned, but it is better to replace it.

SPARK PLUG CONDITION

(115)

NORMAL

- Identified by light tan or gray deposits on the firing tip.
- Can be cleaned.

GAP BRIDGED

- Identified by deposit buildup closing gap between electrodes.
- Caused by oil or carbon fouling. If deposits are not excessive, the plug can be cleaned.

OIL FOULED

- Identified by wet black deposits on the insulator shell bore and electrodes.
- Caused by excessive oil entering combustion chamber through worn rings and pistons, excessive clearance between valve guides and stems, or worn or loose bearings. Can be cleaned. If engine is not repaired, use a hotter plug.

CARBON FOULED

- Identified by black, dry fluffy carbon deposits on insulator tips, exposed shell surfaces and electrodes.
- Caused by too cold a plug, weak ignition, dirty air cleaner, too rich a fuel mixture, or excessive idling. Can be cleaned.

LEAD FOULED

- Identified by dark gray, black, yellow, or tan deposits or a fused glazed coating on the insulator tip.
- Caused by highly leaded gasoline. Can be cleaned.

WORN

- Identified by severely eroded or worn electrodes.
- Caused by normal wear. Should be replaced.

FUSED SPOT DEPOSIT

- Identified by melted or spotty deposits resembling bubbles or blisters.
- Caused by sudden acceleration. Can be cleaned.

OVERHEATING

- Identified by a white or light gray insulator with small black or gray brown spots and with bluish-burnt appearance of electrodes.
- Caused by engine overheating, wrong type of fuel, loose spark plugs, too hot a plug, or incorrect ignition timing. Replace the plug.

PREIGNITION

- Identified by melted electrodes and possibly blistered insulator. Metallic deposits on insulator indicate engine damage.
- Caused by wrong type of fuel, incorrect ignition timing or advance, too hot a plug, burned valves, or engine overheating. Replace the plug.

CDI Ignition Timing

All models are equipped with a capacitor discharge ignition (CDI) system. This system uses no breaker points and is non-adjustable. The ignition timing should be checked to make sure all ignition components are operating correctly.

Incorrect ignition timing can cause a drastic loss of engine performance and efficiency. It may also cause overheating.

Before starting on this procedure, check all electrical connections related to the ignition system. Make sure all connections are tight and free of corrosion and that all ground connections are tight.

1. Start the engine and let it reach normal operating temperature. Shut the engine off.
2. Place the bike on the sidestand or center stand.
3. Remove the ignition timing cap (**Figure 116**).
4. Connect a portable tachometer following the manufacturer's instructions.
5. Connect a timing light following the manufacturer's instructions.
6. Fill in the timing marks on the pulse generator rotor or alternator rotor with white grease pencil or typewriter white correction fluid. This will make the marks more visible.
7. Start the engine and let it idle at the idle speed listed in **Table 12**. If necessary, readjust the idle speed as described in this chapter.
8. Aim the timing light at the timing hole and pull the trigger. If the timing mark "F" aligns with the fixed pointer on the crankcase cover (**Figure 117**), the timing is correct.
9. Increase engine speed to slightly above 3,500 rpm.
10. Aim the timing light at the timing hole and pull the trigger. If the fixed pointer aligns between the full advance timing marks (**Figure 118**) the timing is correct.
11. If timing at either idle or full advance is not correct, refer to Chapter Eight and check the pulse generator and CDI unit.
12. There is no method for adjusting ignition timing.
13. Shut off the engine and disconnect the timing light and portable tachometer.
14. Make sure the O-ring seal is in place and install the ignition timing cap.

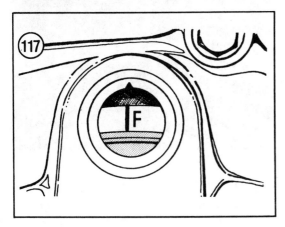

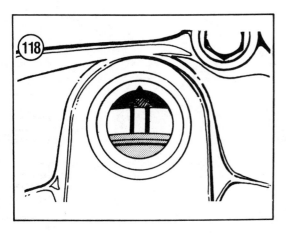

Carburetor Idle Speed Adjustment

Before making this adjustment, the air filter element must be clean and the engine must have adequate compression. See *Compression Test* in this chapter. Otherwise this procedure cannot be done properly.

1. Start the engine and let it reach normal operating temperature. Make sure the choke knob or lever is in the open position for a warm engine.
2. Connect a portable tachometer following the manufacturer's instructions.

3A. On 1988-1990 XR600R RFVC engines, turn the black knob on the idle adjust screw (on the left-hand side of the carburetor) in or out to adjust idle speed.

3B. On all other RFVC engines, turn the idle adjust screw (**Figure 119**) in or out to adjust idle speed.

3C. On all other models, turn the idle adjust screw (**Figure 120**) in or out to adjust idle speed.

4. The correct idle speed is listed in **Table 12**.

5. Open and close the throttle a couple of times. Check for variations in speed; readjust if necessary.

> *WARNING*
> *With the engine running at idle speed, move the handlebars from side-to-side. If the idle speed increased during this movement, the throttle cable may need adjusting or it may be incorrectly routed through the frame. Correct this problem immediately. Do not ride the bike in this unsafe condition.*

6. Shut the engine off and disconnect the portable tachometer.

Carburetor Idle Mixture

The idle mixture (pilot screw) is preset at the factory and *is not to be reset*. Do not adjust the pilot screw unless the carburetor(s) has been overhauled. If so, refer to Chapter Seven for service procedures.

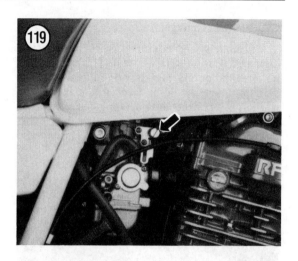

Table 1 TIRE INFLATION PRESSURE*

Tire size	Air pressure	
	psi	kg/cm²
Front tire		
3.00-21 6PR	14	1.0
3.00-21 4PR	21	1.5
3.00-23 6PR	15	1.03
3.00-23 4PR	21	1.5
90/80-21 6PR	15	1.03
90/90-21 6PR	14	1.0
80/100-21 51M	15	1.03
Rear tire		
4.60-17 4PR	21	1.5
5.10-17 6PR	11	0.8
5.10-17 4PR	21	1.5
4.60-18 4PR	21	1.5
4.60-18 6PR	17	1.2
110/90-17 6PR	14	1.0
130/80-17 6PR	14	1.0
110/100-18 64M	15	1.03

* Tire inflation pressure for factory equipped tires. Aftermarket tire inflation pressure may vary according to manufacturer's instructions.

Table 2 MAINTENANCE SCHEDULE

XL SERIES MODELS

Every 300 miles (500 km) or when dry	• Lubricate and adjust the drive chain
Every 500 miles (800 km) or 6 months	• Clean air filter element
	• Check engine oil level
	• Lubricate all control cables
	• Lubricate rear brake pedal and shift lever
	• Lubricate side stand pivot point
	• Inspect front steering for looseness
	• Check wheel bearings for smooth operation
	• Check battery electrolyte level and condition
	• Check ignition timing
	• Check and adjust idle speed
	• Check clutch lever free play
	• Check fuel shutoff valve and filter
	• Check wheel spoke condition
	• Check wheel runout
Every 1,000 miles (1,600 km)	• Lubricate swing arm bushings
Every 1,800 miles (3,000 km)	• Change engine oil
Every 4,000 miles (6,400 km)	• Clean air filter element
	• Replace engine oil filter
	• Inspect spark plug, regap if necessary
	• Check and adjust valve clearance
	• Adjust cam chain tension (models so equipped)
	• Adjust balancer chain tension (models so equipped)

(continued)

Table 2 MAINTENANCE SCHEDULE (continued)

XL SERIES MODELS	
	• Inspect decompressor free play, adjust if necessary • Inspect fuel lines for chafed, cracked or swollen ends • Inspect and repack wheel bearings • Inspect crankcase ventilation hoses for cracks or loose hose clamps—drain out all residue • Check engine mounting bolts for tightness • Check steering for free play • Check all suspension components • Adjust front and rear brake levers
Every 6,000 miles (10,000 km)	• Complete engine tune-up • Check and adjust valve clearance • Adjust the cam chain tension (models so equipped) • Check and adjust ignition timing • Check and adjust the carburetor(s) • Replace spark plug • Dismantle and clean carburetor(s) • Change front fork oil • Inspect and repack swing arm bushings • Replace air filter element • Lubricate speedometer cable • Inspect brake shoes (or pads) for wear • Check engine mounting bolts for tightness • Check all suspension components • Inspect all drive chain, roller tensioners and sliders • Lubricate control cables • Inspect and repack steering head bearings
Every 8,000 miles (12,800 km)	• Remove and clean engine oil screen • Replace the spark plug • Inspect the evaporative emission control system hoses and canister for damage (Calif. models only)
XR SERIES MODELS	
Every 300 miles (500 km) or when dry	• Lubricate and adjust the drive chain • Clean air filter element
Every 30 operating days, 1,000 miles, (1,600 km)	• Check engine oil level • Lubricate all control cables • Lubricate rear brake pedal and shift lever • Lubricate side stand pivot point • Inspect front steering for looseness • Check wheel bearings for smooth operation • Check ignition timing • Check and adjust idle speed • Check clutch lever free play • Check fuel shutoff valve and filter • Check wheel spoke condition • Check wheel runout

(continued)

Table 2 MAINTENANCE SCHEDULE (continued)

XR SERIES MODELS

Every 1,000 miles (1,600 km)
- Change engine oil
- Lubricate swing arm bushings
- Clean engine oil screen (models so equipped)
- Clean engine oil screen in frame down tube
- Replace engine oil filter (models so equipped)
- Inspect spark plug, regap if necessary
- Check and adjust valve clearance
- Check and adjust carburetor idle speed
- Adjust cam chain tension (models so equipped)
- Adjust balancer chain tension (models so equipped)
- Check and adjust clutch free play
- Inspect decompressor free play, adjust if necessary
- Inspect fuel lines for chafed, cracked or swollen ends
- Inspect throttle operation
- Clean and inspect fuel filter screen
- Inspect and repack wheel bearings
- Inspect crankcase ventilation hoses for cracks or loose hose clamps—drain out all residue
- Check engine mounting bolts for tightness
- Check steering for free play
- Check all suspension components
- Adjust front and rear brake levers
- Inspect brake shoes (or pads) for wear
- Inspect entire brake system
- Check engine mounting bolts for tightness
- Check all suspension components
- Check and adjust headlight aim
- Inspect all drive chain, roller tensioners and sliders
- Adjust drive chain tension
- Lubricate Pro-Link linkage assembly (models so equipped)
- Lubricate swing arm bearings

Every 2,000 miles (3,200 km)
- Complete engine tune-up
- Check and adjust valve clearance
- Adjust the cam chain tension (models so equipped)
- Check and adjust ignition timing
- Check and adjust the carburetor(s)
- Replace spark plug
- Dismantle and clean carburetor(s)
- Change front fork oil
- Replace air filter element
- Lubricate speedometer cable
- Lubricate control cables
- Inspect and repack steering head bearings

Every 2 years
- Replace hydraulic brake fluid (models so equipped)

*This Honda factory maintenance schedule should be considered as a guide to general maintenance and lubrication intervals. Harder than normal use and exposure to mud, water, sand, high humidity, etc. will naturally dictate more frequent attention to most maintenance items.

Table 3 COMPETITION PRE-RACE INSPECTION

Item	Inspection
Engine oil	Check for contamination, change if dirty
Fuel line	Check for leaks and deterioration, replace
Air cleaner	Check for tears and contamination, replace or clean
Cam chain tension	Adjust if necessary to correct clearance
Carburetor idle speed	Check and adjust if necessary
Balancer chain tension	Adjust if necessary (check while inspecting the clutch disc)
Starter decompressor	Check for correct free play, adjust if necessary
Clutch disc wear	Check for abnormal wear and/or discoloration
Spark plug	Check for proper heat range, gap, tightness and plug cap tightness
Steering head	Check for free rotation of handlebar, check tightness of steering stem nut, adjust and or tighten if necessary
Front suspension	Check for oil leaks, tight boot clamps and smooth action of forks
Rear suspension	Check for oil leaks and smooth operation
Swing arm bushings	Check for abnormal side play, replace if necessary
Brake shoes	Check wear indicators for wear beyond limits, replace brake shoes
Drive chain	Inspect for damage and chain stretch, replace if necessary
Sprockets (both)	Inspect for wear and tightness of installation
Seat	Check for tightness of mounting hardware
Control cables	Check for smooth operation and frayed outer sheath; lubricate or replace
Engine mounting bolts	Check for tightness and fractures on mounting hardware
Headlight	Proper headlight adjustment
Instrument lights	Check for proper operation
Tires	Check for proper inflation and inspect for cuts and deep abrasions; replace if necessary
Exterior of engine	Clean the entire engine and frame prior to a race

Table 4 BATTERY STATE OF CHARGE

Specific gravity	State of charge
1.110-1.130	Discharged
1.140-1.160	Almost discharged
1.170-1.190	One-quarter charged
1.200-1.220	One-half charged
1.230-1.250	Three-quarters charged
1.260-1.280	Fully charged

Table 5 ENGINE OIL CAPACITY

| Engine size | Oil drain | | Rebuild | |
	U.S. qt.	Liter	U.S. qt.	Liter
500 cc (1979-1982)	1.6	1.5	2.1	2.0
500, 600 cc (1983-1990)	2.1	2.0	2.6	2.5

Table 6 MAINTENANCE AND TUNE-UP TORQUE SPECIFICATIONS

Item	N•m	ft.-lb.
Oil drain plug		
Wet sump models	30-40	22-29
Dry sump models		
Crankcase drain plug		
1998-1990 XR600R	25	18
All other models	30-40	22-29
Frame down tube		
Drain plug		
1988-1990 XR600R	40	29
All other models	25-35	18-25
Oil strainer nut		
1988-1990 XR600R	55	40
All other models	35-45	25-32
Oil strainer oil hose		
1988-1990 XR600R	40	29
All other models	35-45	25-32
Oil filter cover screws		
Models so equipped		
1988-1990 XR600R	12	9
All other models	8-10	5-7
Fork cap bolt		
1988-1990 XR600R	23	16
All other models	15-30	11-22
Rear axle nut		
Dual-shock models	70-110	51-80
Pro-Link models		
1988-1990	95	69
All other models	80-110	58-80
Balancer chain holder lockbolt	18-25	13-18
Fuel cup strainer		
Models so equipped	3-5	2-4
Wheel rim locks	9-15	7-11
Valve adjuster locknuts		
1979-1982	15-18	11-13
1983-1984 XR500R	18-22	13-16
XL600R	15-18	11-13
XR600R	23-27	17-19

Table 7 FRONT FORK OIL CAPACITY*

Model	Standard capacity		Standard distance from top of fork	
	cc	fl. oz.	mm	in.
XL500S	190	6.4	–	–
XL500R	379	12.75	163	6.42
XR500	202	6.8	–	–
XR500R				
1981-1982	345	11.7	181	7.1
1983	651	22	141	5.5
1984	651	22		
Maximum	–	–	171	6.73
Mininum	–	–	131	5.16
XL600R	455	15.4	150	5.9
(continued)				

Table 7 FRONT FORK OIL CAPACITY* (continued)

| Model | Standard capacity | | Standard distance from top of fork | |
	cc	fl. oz.	mm	in.
XR600R				
1985-1987	631	21.3		
Maximum	–	–	147	5.8
Minimum	–	–	117	4.6
1988-1990	643	21.8		
Maximum	–	–	130	5.1
Minimum	–	–	100	3.9
*Capacity for each fork leg.				

Table 8 FRONT FORK AIR PRESSURE

Model	psi	kg/cm^2
1982 XL500R	0-2.87	0-0.2
XR500R	0-14	0-0.98
All other models	0	0

Table 9 DRIVE CHAIN FREE PLAY

Model	mm	in.
Dual shock models		
XL series	15-20	0.6-0.8
XR series	20	0.8
Pro-Link models		
XL series	30-40	1 1/4-1 5/8
XR series	35-45	1 3/8-1 3/4

Table 10 DRIVE CHAIN REPLACEMENT NUMBERS

Model	Standard
XL500S	520KD-96
XL500R	520VS-100L
XR500	DID520KD-100L or DID520KD-102L
XR500R	520KO-104FJ
XL600R	520VS-104CD or 520SO-104LE
XR600R	520SMO-110RJ

Table 11 DRIVE CHAIN SERVICE SPECIFICATIONS

| Model | Number of pins | Dimension | |
		mm	in.
XL500S	41	648	25.4
XL500R	NA		
XR500	100	1944	76.5
		(continued)	

Table 11 DRIVE CHAIN SERVICE SPECIFICATIONS (continued)

Model	Number of pins	Dimension mm	in.
XR500R			
1981-1982	105	1645	64.75
1983-1984	107	1716	67.55
XL600R	NA		
XR600R			
1985-1987	109	1765	69.5
1988-1990	111	1780	70.0

NA. Honda does not provide service information for all models.

Table 12 TUNE-UP SPECIFICATIONS

Item	Specification
Valve clearance	
XR600R	
Intake	0.10 mm (0.004 in.)
Exhaust	0.12 mm (0.005 in.)
All other models	
Intake	0.05 mm (0.002 in.)
Exhaust	0.10 mm (0.004 in.)
Compression pressure (at sea level)	
XR600R	
1985-1987	125.2-130.8 psi (8.8-9.2 kg/cm^2)
1988-1990	185.8-214.2 psi (13-15 kg/cm^2)
All other models	175 psi (12.5 kg/cm^2)
Spark plug type	
Standard heat range	
1978-1981	ND X24ES-U or NGK D8EA
1982	ND X24ESR-U or NGK DR8ES-L
1983-1990	ND X24EOR-U9 or NGK DPR8EA-9
Gap	0.900.9 mm (0.032-0.036 in.)
Ignition timing	"F" mark @1200 100 ±rpm
Idle speed	
1988-1990 XR600R	1300 ±100 rpm
All other models	1200 ±100 rpm

CHAPTER FOUR

1979-1982 500 CC ENGINES

All models covered in this chapter are equipped with an air-cooled, 4-stroke, single cylinder engine with a single overhead camshaft. The cylinder head incorporates a pair of dual valves with each set having its own rocker arm. Each valve has its own adjuster.

The crankshaft is supported by 2 large ball bearings and engine vibration is minimized by 2 counter-rotating balancers that are driven off the crankshaft by either a chain or gears.

To ease starting the engine, it has a starter decompressor. As the kickstarter pedal is depressed, a cam on the pedal operates a lever that transmits movement via a cable to the decompressor valve lifter on the cylinder head. This lifter opens the exhaust valves momentarily and then allows them to close as the pedal continues its downward travel.

Engine lubrication is by wet sump with the oil pump located on the right-hand side of the engine and driven by the kickstarter idle gear.

The camshaft is chain-driven from the sprocket on the right-hand side of the crankshaft.

This chapter contains information for removal, inspection, service and reassembly of the engine. Although the clutch and transmission are located within the engine, they are covered in Chapter Six to simplify this material.

Table 1 provides complete specifications for the engine and **Table 2** lists all of the engine torque

specifications. **Table 1** and **Table 2** are located at the end of this chapter.

Before beginning work, re-read Chapter One of this book. You will do a better job with this information fresh in your mind.

Throughout the text there is frequent mention of the right-hand and left-hand side of the engine. This refers to the engine as it sits in the bike's frame, *not* as it sits on your workbench. The right- and left-hand refers to a rider sitting on the seat facing forward.

ENGINE PRINCIPLES

Figure 1 explains how the engine works. This will be helpful when troubleshooting or repairing the engine.

ENGINE COOLING

Cooling is provided by air passing over the cooling fins on the engine cylinder head and cylinder. It is very important to keep these fins free from build-up of dirt, oil, grease and other foreign matter. Brush out the fins with a whisk broom or small stiff paint brush.

CAUTION
Remember, these fins are thin in order to dissipate heat and may be damaged if struck too hard.

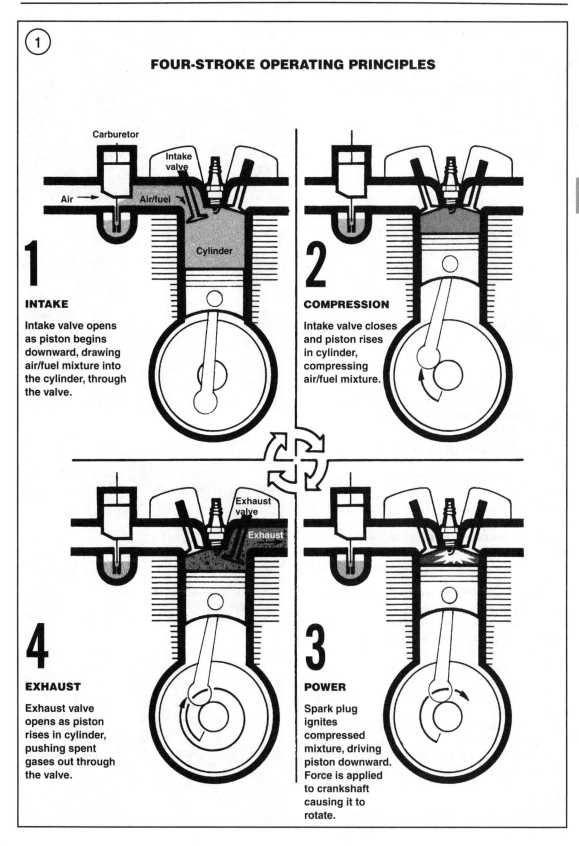

FOUR-STROKE OPERATING PRINCIPLES

1

INTAKE

Intake valve opens as piston begins downward, drawing air/fuel mixture into the cylinder, through the valve.

2

COMPRESSION

Intake valve closes and piston rises in cylinder, compressing air/fuel mixture.

4

EXHAUST

Exhaust valve opens as piston rises in cylinder, pushing spent gases out through the valve.

3

POWER

Spark plug ignites compressed mixture, driving piston downward. Force is applied to crankshaft causing it to rotate.

SERVICING ENGINE IN FRAME

The following components can be serviced while the engine is mounted in the frame. The bike's frame is a great holding fixture for breaking loose stubborn bolts and nuts.

   a. Carburetor
   b. Kickstarter
   c. Alternator
   d. Clutch assembly
   e. External shift mechanism

ENGINE
REMOVAL/INSTALLATION

> *WARNING*
> *Because of the engine's weight, 2 people are required to remove the engine safely.*

1. Remove the right- and left-hand side covers and the seat.

> *NOTE*
> *On XL500S models, reinstall the seat strap bolts as they also hold the upper portion of the shock absorbers in place (**Figure 2**). Remove and install one bolt at a time.*

2. Drain the engine oil as described in Chapter Three.
3. Remove the fuel tank as described in Chapter Seven.
4. Remove the exhaust system as described in Chapter Seven.
5. Remove the carburetor as described in Chapter Seven.
6. Disconnect the spark plug lead and tie it up out of the way.
7. Remove the bolts (**Figure 3**) securing the skid plate and remove the skid plate.
8. On models so equipped, disconnect the battery negative lead or the main fuse (**Figure 4**).
9. Remove the kickstarter pedal.
10. Disconnect the rear brake light switch return spring and cable.
11. Remove the left-hand front footpeg and the gearshift lever.
12. Slacken the clutch cable at the hand lever. Disconnect the clutch cable at the crankcase cover.
13. Disconnect the alternator electrical connector.
14. Disconnect the ignition pulse generator wires at the electrical connector. Refer to **Figure 5** or **Figure 6**.
15. Remove the screws (**Figure 7**) securing the drive sprocket cover and remove the cover.

16. Remove the bolts and kee securing the drive sprocket and remove sprocket and drive chain.

NOTE
If you are just removing the engine and are not planning to disassemble it, do not perform Step 17. The engine assembly is small enough that external components can be left on during engine removal.

17. If the engine is going to be disassembled, remove the following parts.
   a. Remove the alternator as described in Chapter Eight.
   b. Remove the clutch assembly as described in Chapter Six.
   c. Remove the external shift mechanism as described in Chapter Six.

18. Disconnect the crankcase breather hose from the engine.

19. Take a final look all over the engine to make sure everything has been disconnected.

20. Place a suitable size jack, with a piece of wood to protect the crankcase, under the engine (A, **Figure 9**). Apply a small amount of jack pressure up on the engine.

21. Remove the engine front hanger bolts (B, **Figure 9**) and nuts and remove the hanger.

22. Remove the upper rear mounting bolt and nut (**Figure 10**).

NOTE
*Don't lose the spacers (**Figure 10**) between the frame and the engine. Be sure to reinstall them.*

23. Remove the lower rear mounting bolt and nut (C, **Figure 9**).

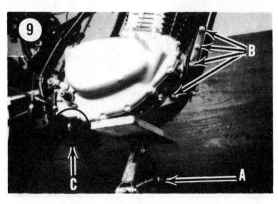

24. Remove the upper bolts, nuts and plates
(**Figure 11**).

> *CAUTION*
> *Continually adjust jack pressure during engine removal and installation to prevent damage to the mounting bolt threads and hardware.*

> *WARNING*
> *The following steps require the aid of a helper to safely remove the engine assembly from the frame.*

25. Lower the engine assembly to clear the frame mounting brackets and pull the engine out through the right-hand side of the frame. Take it to a workbench for further disassembly.

26. Install by reversing these removal steps, noting the following.

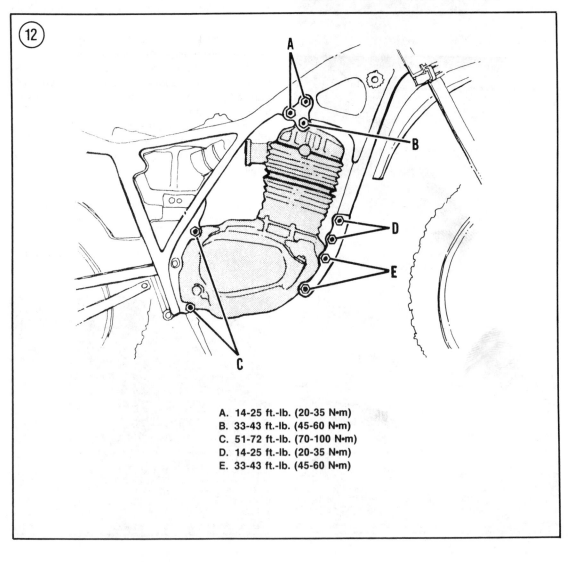

A. 14-25 ft.-lb. (20-35 N•m)
B. 33-43 ft.-lb. (45-60 N•m)
C. 51-72 ft.-lb. (70-100 N•m)
D. 14-25 ft.-lb. (20-35 N•m)
E. 33-43 ft.-lb. (45-60 N•m)

27. Tighten the mounting bolts to the torque specifications in **Table 2** and **Figure 12**.

28. Fill the engine with the recommended type and quantity of oil; refer to Chapter Three.

29. Adjust the starter decompressor lever free play, the clutch, drive chain and rear brake pedal as described in Chapter Three.

30. Start the engine and check for leaks.

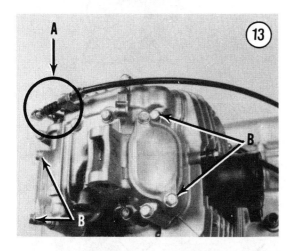

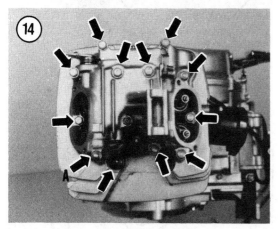

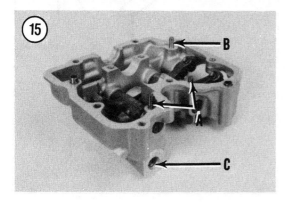

CYLINDER HEAD COVER

Removal

CAUTION
To prevent any warpage and damage, remove the cylinder head cover only when the engine is at room temperature.

1. Remove the engine as described in this chapter.

2. Remove the fuel tank as described in Chapter Seven.

3. Loosen the starter decompressor cable locknut and remove the cable from the lifter lever (A, **Figure 13**).

4. Remove the bolts (B, **Figure 13**) securing each valve adjuster cover and remove both covers.

5. Remove the bolts (**Figure 14**) and one acorn nut (A, **Figure 14**) securing the cylinder head cover. Remove the cover and gasket. Don't lose the locating dowels.

Disassembly/Inspection/Assembly

1. To remove the dowel pins (A, **Figure 15**) securing the rocker arm shaft, perform the following:

    a. Cut a 2 mm notch (**Figure 16**) in each dowel pin with a small rotary grinder.

CAUTION
*In the following step, do **not** overtighten the vise holding the cylinder head cover. Use the vise only as a holding fixture.*

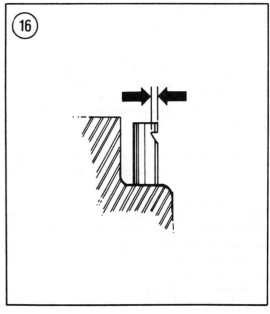

b. Very carefully place the cylinder head cover in a vise with soft jaws.

c. Insert a drift or chisel in through the valve adjustment cover opening in the cylinder head cover and tap out the dowel pins. Remove the dowel pins and discard them.

CAUTION
Be careful not to damage the cylinder head cover or rocker arms during the removal procedure.

NOTE
If these pins are difficult to remove, apply Liquid Wrench to the base of the pins and let sit for 10-15 minutes. This may help to loosen them.

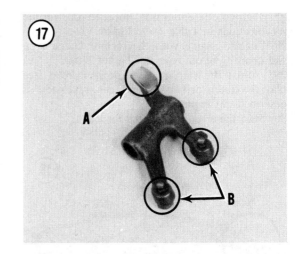

2. Remove the dowel pin securing the valve lifter lever (B, **Figure 15**).

CAUTION
Do not use a metal hammer in Step 3 as the cover will be damaged.

3. Hold the cover upside down in your hand and tap on the engine mounting boss (C, **Figure 15**) with a plastic mallet several times. Tap on the side where the rocker shaft ends are exposed. This tapping will cause the rocker arm shafts to work their way out enough to grip it with your fingers. Do not use pliers as there is an O-ring seal on each shaft end.

4. Pull the rocker arm shaft out and remove the rocker arm and spring washer. Repeat for the other shaft.

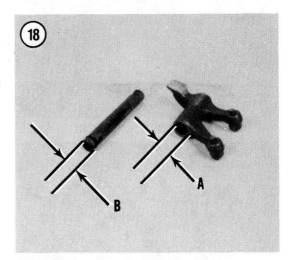

NOTE
*Mark the shafts with an "I" (intake) or "E" (exhaust) as they must be reinstalled into their original position. The rocker arms are **not** identical and must be identified.*

5. Pull the valve lifter lever out with the spring.

6. Wash all parts in solvent and dry thoroughly with compressed air.

7. Inspect the rocker arm pad where it rides on the cam lobe (A, **Figure 17**) and where the adjuster rides on the valve stem (B, **Figure 17**). If the pad is scratched or unevenly worn, inspect the cam lobe for scoring, chipping or flat spots. Replace the rocker arm if defective.

8. Measure the inside diameter of the rocker arm bore (A, **Figure 18**) with an inside micrometer and

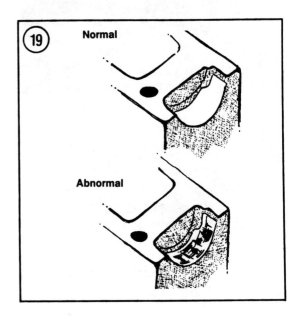

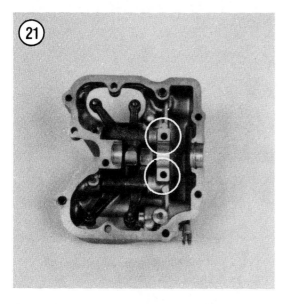

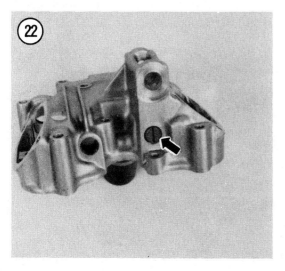

check against the dimensions in **Table 1**; replace if worn to the service limit or greater.

9. Inspect the rocker arm shaft for signs of wear or scoring. Measure the outside diameter (B, **Figure 18**) with a micrometer and check against the dimensions in **Table 1**; replace if worn to the service limit or less.

10. Inspect the camshaft bearing surfaces (**Figure 19**) for excessive wear.

11. Check the spring washers for breakage or distortion; replace if necessary.

12. Inspect the O-ring seals on the rocker arm shafts and valve lifter lever shaft; replace if they have lost their resiliency.

13. Inspect the valve lifter lever shaft and the bearing surface in which it rides in the cover. Replace the valve lifter shaft if necessary.

14. Coat the rocker arm shaft, rocker arm bore and the shaft receptacles in the cover with assembly oil or clean engine oil.

15. Make sure the O-ring seal is in place on each rocker arm shaft.

16. Refer to marks made in Step 4, and be sure to install the rocker arm shafts into their original location.

17. Install the rocker arm shaft with the O-ring end facing out. Partially insert the rocker arm shaft into the cylinder head.

18. Install the spring washer (**Figure 20**) on the left-hand side of the rocker arm. Push the rocker arm shaft through the spring washer and the rocker arm.

19. After the shaft is installed, rotate it to align the locating notch with the bolt hole (**Figure 21**) in the cover. Rotate the shaft using the slot (**Figure 22**) in the exposed end of the shaft.

20. Install new dowel pins (**Figure 23**). Tap them into place with a hammer. *Never* reuse a dowel pin that has a removal notch ground into it.

21. Repeat Steps 15-20 for the other rocker arm assembly.

22. Coat the decompressor valve lifter shaft with assembly oil and install the lever and spring as shown in **Figure 24**. Install the locating dowel (B, **Figure 15**) to secure it in place.

Installation

1. Make sure all sealant residue is removed from the sealing surfaces of the cylinder head and cylinder head cover. Spray both sealing surfaces with contact cleaner and wipe dry with a clean cloth.

> *CAUTION*
> *Do not apply sealant to the areas surrounding the camshaft bearing surfaces (**Figure 25**).*

2. Apply a thin even coat of Three Bond, or equivalent to the cylinder head sealing surface.
3. If removed, install the camshaft plug (**Figure 25**).
4. Add fresh engine oil into the camshaft pocket in the cylinder head. The camshaft lobes must be submerged in oil or they will be damaged when the engine is first started up. Also lubricate the camshaft bearing journals and bearing surfaces in the cylinder head cover.
5. Make sure the locating dowels are in place.
6. Install the cylinder head cover and press it into position.
7. Install the cylinder head cover bolts and acorn nut. Don't forget to install the cable clips on the right-hand side along with the 2 longest bolts (**Figure 26**).
8. Tighten the cylinder head bolts and nut in 2-3 stages in the torque pattern indicated in **Figure 27**. Tighten to the torque specification listed in **Table 2**.
9. Install the engine upper mounting plates, bolts and nuts. Tighten the bolts and nuts to the torque specification listed in **Table 2**.
10. Attach the starter decompressor cable to the lever on the cylinder head cover.
11. Adjust the valves as described in Chapter Three.
12. Install the fuel tank, valve adjuster covers, seat and side covers.

CYLINDER HEAD

> *NOTE*
> *Cylinder head removal and inspection are the same for all engines. Installation differs because of a different camshaft chain tensioner design. Be sure to use the correct installation procedure for your particular bike.*

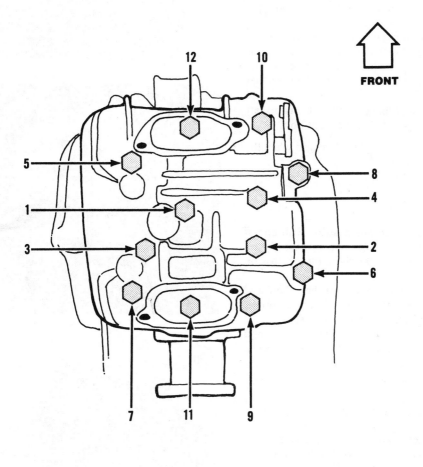

**CYLINDER HEAD COVER
TIGHTENING SEQUENCE
(1979-1982 500 CC ENGINES)**

FRONT

4

Removal (All Models)

> *CAUTION*
> *To prevent any warpage and damage, remove the cylinder head only when the engine is at room temperature.*

1. Remove the cylinder head cover as described in this chapter.
2. Remove the carburetor as described in Chapter Seven.
3. Remove the exhaust system as described in Chapter Seven.
4. If still installed, remove the camshaft plug (A, **Figure 28**).
5. Remove both timing hole caps (**Figure 29**).
6. Rotate the engine with the bolt on the alternator rotor (bottom timing hole) until one of the camshaft sprocket bolts is exposed. Remove that bolt (B, **Figure 28**).
7. Again rotate the engine until the other camshaft sprocket bolt is exposed. Remove that bolt.

> *NOTE*
> *Don't drop these bolts in the camshaft cavity as they will fall into the crankcase.*

8. Leave the sprocket in this position with one of the bolt holes at the 12 o'clock position. Gently pry the camshaft sprocket to the right, off the boss on the camshaft.
9. Attach a piece of wire to the camshaft chain and tie it to the exterior of the engine. This will prevent the chain from falling into the crankcase.
10. Disengage the chain from the sprocket and place the chain to the left, behind the sprocket. Remove the sprocket.
11. Remove the camshaft.

> *CAUTION*
> *If the crankshaft must be rotated when the camshaft is removed, pull up on the camshaft chain and keep it taut while rotating the crankshaft. Make certain that the drive chain is positioned correctly on the crankshaft timing sprocket. If this is not done, the drive chain may become kinked and may damage both the chain and the timing sprocket on the crankshaft.*

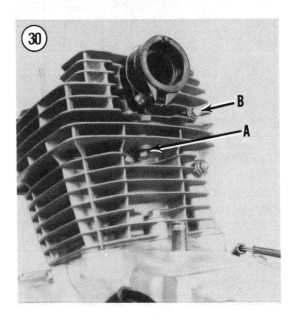

12. Remove the lower nuts and washers (A, **Figure 30**), one at the front and one at the rear.
13. Remove the camshaft chain tensioner upper lockbolt and washer (B, **Figure 30**).

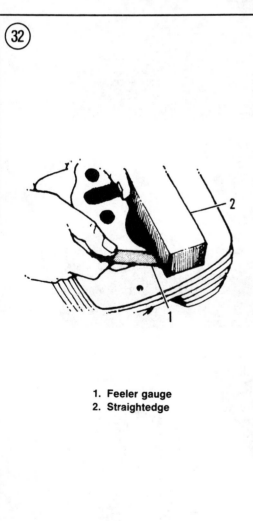

1. Feeler gauge
2. Straightedge

14. Loosen the cylinder head acorn nuts (**Figure 31**) in a crisscross pattern in 2-3 stages. Remove the nuts and washers.

15. Loosen the cylinder head by tapping around the perimeter with a rubber or soft faced mallet. If necessary, *gently* pry the head loose with a broad-tipped screwdriver.

> *CAUTION*
> *Remember the cooling fins are fragile and may be damaged if tapped or pried on too hard. Never use a metal hammer.*

16. Lift the cylinder head straight up and off the cylinder and crankcase studs. Guide the camshaft chain through the opening in the cylinder head and retie the wire to the exterior of the engine. This will prevent the drive chain from falling down into the crankcase.

17. Remove the cylinder head gasket and discard it. Don't lose the locating dowels.

18. Place a clean shop cloth into the camshaft chain opening in the cylinder to prevent the entry of foreign matter.

Inspection (All Models)

Because the cylinder head and cylinder head cover are machined as a set during manufacture, they must be replaced as a set if either is damaged or defective.

1. Remove all traces of gasket material from the cylinder head mating surfaces.

2. *Without removing the valves,* remove all carbon deposits from the combustion chamber and valve ports with a wire brush. A blunt screwdriver or chisel may be used if care is taken not to damage the head, valves and spark plug threads.

3. After the carbon is removed from the combustion chamber and the valve intake and exhaust ports, clean the entire head in cleaning solvent. Blow dry with compressed air.

4. Clean away all carbon from the piston crown. Do not remove the carbon ridge at the top of the cylinder bore.

5. Check for cracks in the combustion chamber and exhaust ports. A cracked head must be replaced.

6. After the head has been cleaned thoroughly, place a straightedge across the cylinder head/cylinder gasket surface at several points (**Figure 32**). Measure the warp by inserting a flat feeler gauge between the straightedge and the cylinder head at each location. There should be no warpage; if a small amount is present, it can be resurfaced by a dealer or qualified machine shop.

Replace the cylinder head and cylinder head cover as a set if the gasket surface is warped to or beyond the limit listed in **Table 1**.

7. Check the cylinder head cover mating surface using the procedure in Step 6. There should be no warpage.

8. Check the valves and valve guides as described in this chapter.

9. Check the end seal plug (A, **Figure 28**). Make sure it fits tightly; if not, replace it.

10. Inspect the camshaft bearing surfaces in the cylinder head and cylinder head cover for wear or scoring. Replace the cylinder head and cylinder head cover as a set if the bearing surfaces are worn or scored.

11. Inspect the oil grooves (**Figure 33**) in the camshaft bearing surfaces. Make sure they are clean.

Installation (1982 XL500R, 1982 XR500R)

1. Install the dowel pins (**Figure 34**). Install the O-ring seal on the dowel pin adjacent to the camshaft chain tensioner.

2. Install a new cylinder head gasket. Make sure the holes align exactly.

3. Push the camshaft chain tensioner wedge "B" (**Figure 35**) down and pull up on wedge "A." Pull wedge "A" (A, **Figure 36**) up enough to expose the 2 mm hole in the wedge.

4. Insert a piece of wire (approximately 2 mm in diameter) into the hole to hold wedge "A" in the up position. Refer to B, **Figure 36**. A straightened No. 2 paper clip will work.

> *NOTE*
> *Be careful that the piece of wire holding the camshaft tensioner wedge does not work loose while installing the cylinder head. If the wire jumps out of place it will fall down into the crankcase.*

5. Remove the shop rag from the opening in the cylinder.

6. Carefully slide the cylinder head onto the cylinder. Feed the camshaft chain through the chain cavity in the cylinder head and secure the other end of the wire again.

7. Apply oil to the threads of the crankcase studs.

8. Install the cylinder head washers and acorn nuts. Tighten in a crisscross pattern, in 2-3 stages. Tighten to the torque specification listed in **Table 2**.

9. Install the lower washers and nuts (A, **Figure 30**) and tighten to the torque specifications listed in **Table 2**.

10. Install the camshaft chain tensioner set bolt and sealing washer (**Figure 37**).

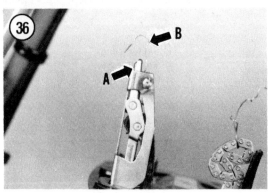

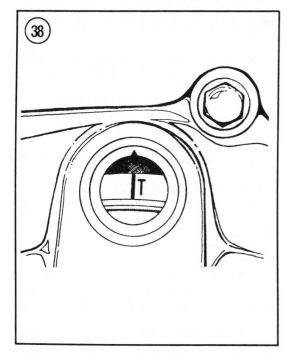

11. Lubricate all camshaft lobes and bearing journals with assembly oil. Also coat the camshaft bearing surfaces in the cylinder head and cylinder head cover.

CAUTION
When rotating the crankshaft, keep the camshaft chain taut and engaged with the timing sprocket on the crankshaft.

12. The engine must be at top dead center (TDC) for the following steps for correct valve timing. Hold the camshaft chain out and taut while rotating the crankshaft to avoid damage to the chain and/or the crankcase.

13. Pull up on the chain, making sure it is properly engaged on the crankshaft sprocket. Rotate the engine until the "T" timing mark on the alternator rotor aligns with the fixed notch on the crankcase cover (**Figure 38**).

14. Position the camshaft sprocket so the 2 timing marks face toward the center of the engine and with the elongated notch up toward the top (**Figure 39**).

15. Hold the camshaft sprocket and chain in this position and feed the camshaft through both parts. Rest the camshaft on the bearing surfaces in the cylinder head.

16. Rotate the camshaft sprocket until the 2 timing marks on the backside align with the top surface of the cylinder head (**Figure 40**).

17. Rotate the camshaft until the bolt mounting holes align with the camshaft sprocket—do *not* place the sprocket up on the camshaft boss at this time.

NOTE
*The camshaft can be installed with the lobes up or down as long as the bolt holes align with the camshaft sprocket and the timing marks on the sprocket align with the cylinder head (**Figure 40**). It is easier if the lobes are facing down*

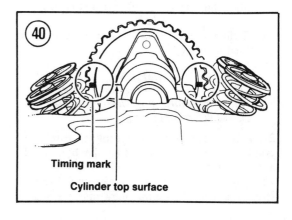

Timing mark

Cylinder top surface

as this will place less of a load on the rocker arms during cylinder head cover installation.

NOTE
If the engine is relatively new or a new camshaft chain has been installed, Step 18 may be difficult. Carefully insert a long, broad-tipped screwdriver down into the camshaft chain cavity and depress the tensioner from the inside. This will give you additional chain slack enabling the camshaft sprocket and chain to slide up onto the camshaft boss. Be careful not to damage anything in the camshaft cavity with the screwdriver.

18. Install the chain onto the sprocket without rotating the sprocket. Slide the sprocket and chain up and onto the camshaft boss. Recheck the following:
   a. Refer to Step 13 and make sure the "T" mark is still properly aligned (**Figure 38**); readjust if necessary.
   b. Make sure the index marks on the camshaft sprocket are perfectly aligned with the top surface of the cylinder head (**Figure 40**).
19. If alignment is incorrect, reposition the camshaft chain on the sprocket and recheck the alignment. Refer to **Figure 38** and **Figure 40**.

CAUTION
Very expensive damage could result from improper camshaft and camshaft chain alignment. Recheck your work several times to be sure alignment is correct.

20. When alignment is correct, perform the following:
   a. Install the bolt into the exposed bolt hole. Tighten only finger-tight at this time.
   b. Rotate the engine to expose the other bolt hole and install the other bolt.
   c. Make sure the camshaft sprocket is correctly seated on the camshaft boss.
   d. Tighten both bolts to the torque specification listed in **Table 2**.

CAUTION
*If there is any binding while rotating the crankshaft, **stop**. Determine the cause before proceeding.*

21. After installation is complete, rotate the crankshaft several times using the bolt on the alternator rotor.
22. Make one final check to make sure alignment is correct. The "T" timing mark must be aligned with the mark and the timing marks on the camshaft sprocket must be perfectly aligned with the top surface of the cylinder head.
23. Remove the piece of 2 mm wire from the hole in wedge "A." Make sure the camshaft chain tensioner wedge "A" slides down into the released position (**Figure 41**).
24. Fill the oil pocket in the cylinder head with new engine oil so the cam lobes are submerged in the oil.
25. Install the cylinder head cover as described in this chapter.
26. Install the carburetor and exhaust system as described in Chapter Seven.
27. Adjust the valves and camshaft chain tension as described in Chapter Three.

Installation (All Except 1982 XL500R and 1982 XR500R)

1. Install the camshaft chain tensioner locknut; pull the tensioner assembly all the way up and tighten the locknut.
2. Install the dowel pins. Install the O-ring seal on the rear right-hand side.
3. Install a new cylinder head gasket. Make sure the holes align exactly.
4. Remove the shop rag from the opening in the cylinder.
5. Carefully slide the cylinder head onto the cylinder. Feed the camshaft chain through the chain cavity in the cylinder head and secure the other end of the wire again.
6. Apply oil to the threads of the crankcase threaded studs.
7. Install the cylinder washers and acorn nuts. Tighten in a crisscross pattern, in 2-3 stages. Tighten to the torque specification listed in **Table 2**.
8. Install the lower washers and nuts (A, **Figure 30**) and tighten to the torque specifications listed in **Table 2**.

NOTE
Make sure the O-ring seal is installed on the lockbolt.

9. Install the camshaft chain tensioner lockbolt and washer (B, **Figure 30**).
10. Lubricate all camshaft lobes and bearing journals with assembly oil. Also coat the camshaft bearing surfaces in the cylinder head and cylinder head cover.

CAUTION
When rotating the crankshaft, keep the camshaft chain taut and engaged with the timing sprocket on the crankshaft.

11. The engine must be at top dead center (TDC) for the following steps for correct valve timing. Hold the camshaft chain out and taut while rotating the crankshaft to avoid damage to the chain and/or the crankcase.

12. Pull up on the chain, making sure it is properly engaged on the crankshaft sprocket. Rotate the engine until the "T" timing mark on the alternator rotor aligns with the fixed notch on the crankcase cover (**Figure 38**).

13. Position the camshaft sprocket so the 2 timing marks face toward the center of the engine.

14. Hold the camshaft sprocket and chain in this position and feed the camshaft through both parts. Rest the camshaft on the bearing surfaces in the cylinder head.

15. Rotate the camshaft sprocket until the 2 timing marks on the backside align with the top surface of the cylinder head (**Figure 40**).

16. Rotate the camshaft until the bolt mounting holes align with the camshaft sprocket—do *not* place the sprocket up on the camshaft boss at this time.

NOTE
*The camshaft can be installed with the lobes up or down as long as the bolt holes align with the camshaft sprocket and the timing marks on the sprocket align with the cylinder head (**Figure 40**). It is easier if the lobes are facing down as this will place less of a load on the rocker arms during cylinder head cover installation.*

NOTE
If the engine is relatively new or a new camshaft chain has been installed, Step 17 may be difficult. Carefully insert a long, broad tipped screwdriver down into the camshaft chain cavity and depress the tensioner from the inside. This will give you additional chain slack enabling the camshaft sprocket and chain to slide up onto the camshaft

boss. Be careful not to damage anything in the camshaft cavity with the screwdriver.

17. Install the chain onto the sprocket without rotating the sprocket. Slide the sprocket and chain up and onto the camshaft boss. Recheck the following:
   a. Refer to Step 12 and make sure the "T" mark is still properly aligned (**Figure 38**). Readjust if necessary.
   b. Make sure the index marks on the camshaft sprocket are perfectly aligned with the top surface of the cylinder head (**Figure 40**).

18. If alignment is incorrect, reposition the camshaft chain on the sprocket and recheck the alignment. Refer to **Figure 38** and **Figure 40**.

CAUTION
Very expensive damage could result from improper camshaft and camshaft chain alignment. Recheck your work several times to be sure alignment is correct.

19. When alignment is correct, perform the following:
   a. Install the bolt into the exposed bolt hole. Tighten only finger-tight at this time.
   b. Rotate the engine to expose the other bolt hole and install the other bolt.
   c. Make sure the camshaft sprocket is correctly seated on the camshaft boss.
   d. Tighten both bolts to the torque specification listed in **Table 2**.

CAUTION
*If there is any binding while rotating the crankshaft, **stop**. Determine the cause before proceeding.*

20. After installation is complete, rotate the crankshaft several times using the bolt on the alternator rotor.

21. Make one final check to make sure alignment is correct. The "T" timing mark must be aligned with the mark and the timing marks on the camshaft sprocket must be perfectly aligned with the top surface of the cylinder head.

22. Fill the oil pocket in the cylinder head with new engine oil so the cam lobes are submerged in the oil.

23. Install the cylinder head cover as described in this chapter.

24. Install the carburetor and exhaust system as described in Chapter Seven.

25. Adjust the valves and camshaft chain tension as described in Chapter Three.

REED VALVE ASSEMBLY
(XR500R)

The XR500R has a power reed valve assembly in the intake port of the cylinder head. The reed valve helps the engine achieve higher torque in the low to medium engine speed range. On a 4-stroke engine, part of the fuel/air mixture from the carburetor is forced back into the intake port and manifold during low to medium engine speed. This occurs because the fuel/air mixture enters the cylinder at a low velocity and the piston is trying to push it back before the intake valve has closed completely.

The reed valve is a one-way valve. It allows the fuel/air mixture to go past the reed valve and into the combustion chamber. The reed valve prevents the fuel/air mixture from reversing its flow, thus keeping more of the fuel/air mixture in the combustion chamber to be burned.

Removal/Installation

Particular care must be taken when handling the reed valve assembly.

Refer to **Figure 42** for this procedure.

1. Remove the carburetor as described in Chapter Seven.

> *NOTE*
> *Make sure that all parts are clean and free of small dirt particles or lint from a shop cloth as they may cause distortion in the reed valve.*

2. Remove the bolts securing the rubber intake manifold and reed valve assembly to the cylinder head.
3. Carefully remove the reed valve assembly and gaskets from the cylinder head. If the assembly is difficult to remove, use a drift or broad-tipped screwdriver and gently tap on the side of the assembly to help break it loose from the gasket and the cylinder head.
4. Inspect as described in this chapter.
5. Install a new gasket, the heat insulator, another new gasket and the reed valve assembly onto the cylinder head.
6. Inspect the O-ring seal on the rubber intake manifold; replace if necessary.
7. Install the rubber intake manifold with the carburetor locating notch facing up. Install the bolts and tighten securely.
8. Install the carburetor.

Inspection

Refer to **Figure 43** for basic reed valve construction.

Carefully examine the reed plate, reed stop and gasket. Check for signs of cracks, metal fatigue, distortion or damage from foreign matter. Pay particular attention to the rubber gasket seal. If any part of the Honda reed valve assembly is defective the entire assembly must be replaced. Replacement parts are not available.

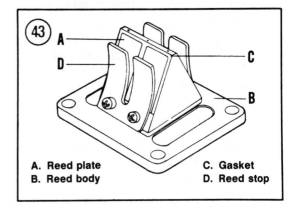

A. Reed plate   C. Gasket
B. Reed body   D. Reed stop

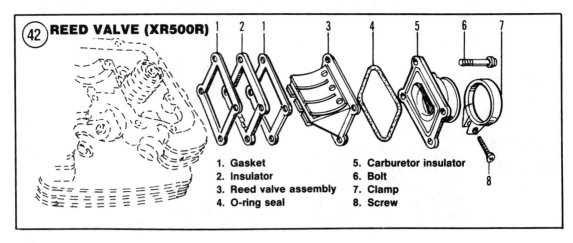

REED VALVE (XR500R)

1. Gasket
2. Insulator
3. Reed valve assembly
4. O-ring seal
5. Carburetor insulator
6. Bolt
7. Clamp
8. Screw

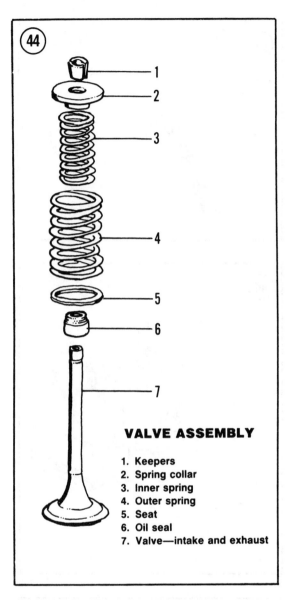

VALVE ASSEMBLY

1. Keepers
2. Spring collar
3. Inner spring
4. Outer spring
5. Seat
6. Oil seal
7. Valve—intake and exhaust

VALVES AND VALVE COMPONENTS

NOTE
General practice among those who do their own service is to remove the cylinder head and take it to a machine shop or dealer for inspection and service. Since the cost is low relative to the required effort and equipment, this is the best approach, even for experienced mechanics. The following procedures are included if you choose to perform these tasks yourself.

Removal

Refer to **Figure 44** for this procedure.
1. Remove the cylinder head as described in this chapter.

CAUTION
To avoid loss of spring tension, do not compress the springs any more than necessary to remove the keepers.

2. Compress the valve springs with a valve compressor tool (**Figure 45**). Remove the valve keepers and release the compression. Remove the valve compressor tool.
3. Remove the valve spring collar and valve springs.
4. Before removing the valve, remove any burrs from the valve stem (**Figure 46**). Otherwise the valve guide will be damaged.
5. Remove the valve.
6. Mark all parts as they are disassembled so that they will be installed in their same locations.

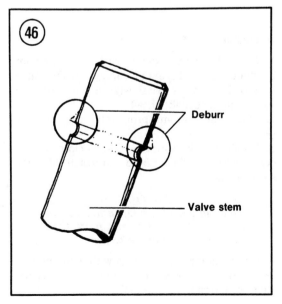

Deburr

Valve stem

Inspection

1. Clean the valves with a wire brush and solvent.
2. Inspect the contact surface of each valve for burning or pitting (**Figure 47**). Unevenness of the contact surface is an indication that the valve is not serviceable. The valve contact surface can *not* be ground and must be replaced if defective.
3. Inspect the valve stem for wear and roughness and measure the vertical runout of the valve stem as shown in **Figure 48**. The runout should not exceed the service limit listed in **Table 1**.
4. Measure the valve stem for wear (**Figure 49**). If worn to the wear limit listed in **Table 1** or less, the valve must be replaced.
5. Remove all carbon and varnish from the valve guide with a stiff spiral wire brush.
6. Insert each valve in its guide. Hold the valve with the head just slightly off the valve seat and rock it sideways. If it rocks more than slightly, the guide is probably worn and should be replaced. As a final check, take the cylinder to a dealer and have the valve guides measured.
7. Measure each valve spring free length with a vernier caliper (**Figure 50**). All should be within the length specified in **Table 1** with no signs of bends or distortion. Replace defective springs in pairs (inner and outer).
8. Check the valve spring retainer and valve keepers. If they are in good condition they may be reused; replace as necessary.
9. Inspect the valve seats. If worn or burned, they must be reconditioned. This should be performed by a dealer or qualified machine shop.

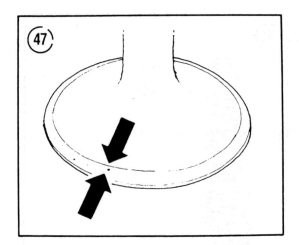

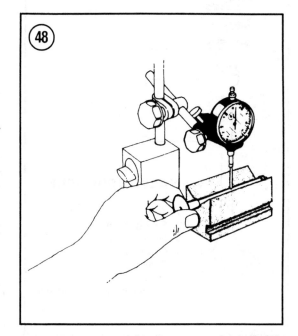

Installation

1. Coat the valve stems with molybdenum disulfide grease. To avoid damage to the valve stem seal, turn the valve slowly while inserting the valve into the cylinder head.
2. Install the bottom spring retainers and new seals.
3. Install the valve springs with their closer wound coils facing the cylinder head and install the valve spring retainer.

> *CAUTION*
> *To avoid loss of spring tension, do not compress the springs any more than necessary to install the keepers.*

4. Compress the valve springs with a compressor tool (**Figure 45**) and install the valve keepers. Remove the compression tool.

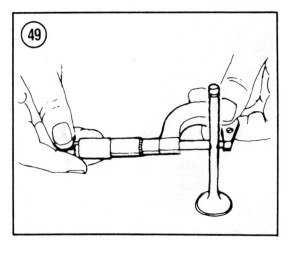

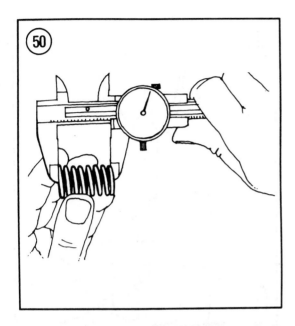

5. After all springs have been installed, gently tap the end of the valve stem with a soft aluminum or brass drift and hammer. This will ensure that the keepers are properly seated.

6. Install the cylinder head as described in this chapter.

Valve Guide Replacement

When valve guides are worn so that there is excessive stem-to-guide clearance or valve tipping, the guides must be replaced. Replace all, even if only one is worn. This job should only be done by a dealer as special tools are required. If the valve guides are replaced; replace the valves also.

Valve Seat Reconditioning

This job is best left to a dealer or qualified machine shop. They have special equipment and knowledge for this exacting job. You can still save considerable money by removing the cylinder head and taking the head to the shop for repairs.

CAMSHAFT

Removal

1. Remove the cylinder head cover as described in this chapter.

2. Remove the carburetor as described in Chapter Seven.

3. Remove the exhaust system as described in Chapter Seven.

4. If still installed, remove the camshaft plug (A, **Figure 51**).

5. Remove both timing hole caps (**Figure 52**).

6. Rotate the engine with the bolt on the alternator rotor (bottom timing hole) until one of the camshaft sprocket bolts is exposed. Remove that bolt (B, **Figure 51**).

7. Again rotate the engine until the other camshaft sprocket bolts is exposed. Remove that bolt.

> *CAUTION*
> *Don't drop these bolts in the camshaft cavity as they will fall into the crankcase.*

8. Leave the sprocket in this position with one of the bolt holes at the 12 o'clock position. Gently pry the camshaft sprocket to the right, off the boss on the camshaft.

9. Attach a piece of wire to the camshaft chain and tie it to the exterior of the engine. This will prevent the chain from falling into the crankcase.

10. Disengage the chain from the sprocket and place the chain to the left, behind the sprocket. Remove the sprocket.

11. Remove the camshaft.

Inspection

1. Measure both the right- and left-hand camshaft bearing journals (**Figure 53**) for wear and scoring. Compare to the dimensions given in **Table 1**. If worn to the service limit or less the camshaft must be replaced.

> *NOTE*
> *Don't confuse the sprocket boss area (**Figure 54**) for the right-hand bearing journal.*

2. Check the camshaft lobes for wear. The lobes should show no signs of scoring and the edges should be square. Slight damage may be removed with a silicon carbide oilstone. Use No. 100-120 grit stone initially, then polish with a No. 280-320 grit stone.

> *NOTE*
> *The cam is dark in color due to the manufacturing heat treating process. It is not due to lack of oil pressure or excessive engine heat.*

3. Even though the camshaft lobe surface appears to be satisfactory, with no visible signs of wear, the camshaft lobes must be measured with a micrometer (**Figure 55**). Compare to the dimensions given in **Table 1**.

4. Inspect the camshaft bearing surfaces in the cylinder head and cylinder head cover. They should not be scored or excessively worn (**Figure 56**). Replace the cylinder head and cylinder head cover as a set if the bearing surfaces are worn or scored.

5. Remove the camshaft plug from the cylinder head. Install the cylinder head cover and tighten the bolts in the torque sequence shown in **Figure 57**. Tighten to the torque specification listed in **Table 2**.

6. Measure the inside diameter of the bearing surfaces, both the right- and left-hand side. Compare to dimensions listed in **Table 1**. If either dimension exceeds the wear limit in **Table 1**, the cylinder head and cylinder head cover must be replaced as a set. Remove the cylinder head cover.

7. Inspect the camshaft sprocket for wear; replace if necessary.

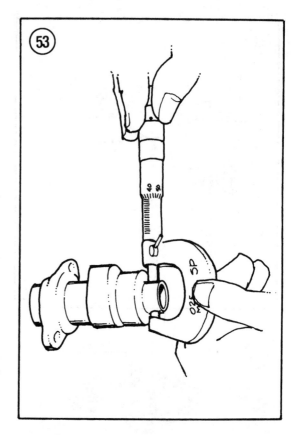

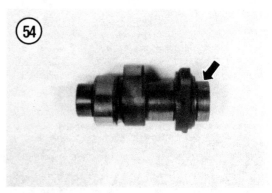

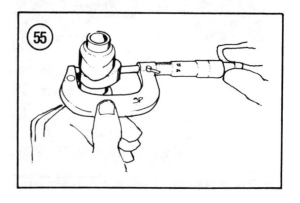

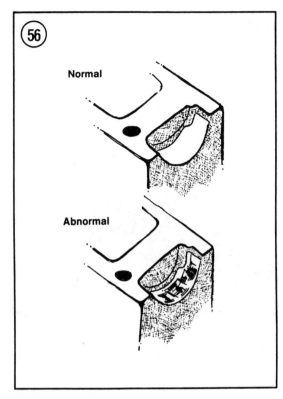

Installation

1. Lubricate all camshaft lobes and bearing journals with assembly oil. Also coat the camshaft bearing surfaces in the cylinder head and cylinder head cover.

CAUTION
When rotating the crankshaft, keep the camshaft chain taut and engaged with the timing sprocket on the crankshaft.

2. The engine must be at top dead center (TDC) for the following steps for correct valve timing. Hold the camshaft chain out and taut while rotating the crankshaft to avoid damage to the chain and/or the crankcase.

3. Pull up on the chain, making sure it is properly engaged on the crankshaft sprocket. Rotate the engine until the "T" timing mark on the alternator rotor aligns with the fixed notch on the crankcase cover (**Figure 38**).

4. Position the camshaft sprocket so the 2 timing marks face toward the center of the engine.

5. Hold the camshaft sprocket and chain in this position and feed the camshaft through both parts. Rest the camshaft on the bearing surfaces in the cylinder head.

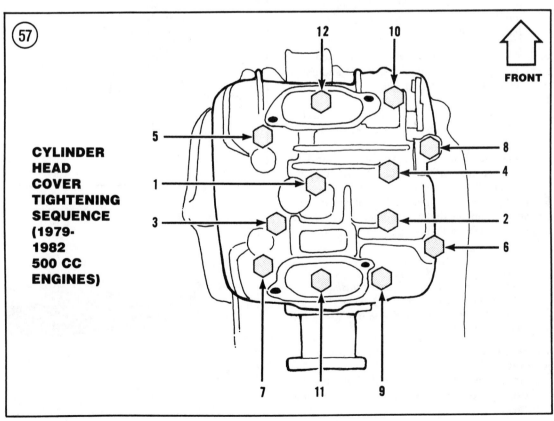

6. Rotate the camshaft sprocket until the 2 timing marks on the backside align with the top surface of the cylinder head (**Figure 40**).

7. Rotate the camshaft until the bolt mounting holes align with the camshaft sprocket—do *not* place the sprocket up on the camshaft boss at this time.

> *NOTE*
> *The camshaft can be installed with the lobes up or down as long as the bolt holes align with the camshaft sprocket and the timing marks on the sprocket align with the cylinder head (**Figure 40**). It is easier if the lobes are facing down as this will place less of a load on the rocker arms during cylinder head cover installation.*

> *NOTE*
> *If the engine is relatively new or a new camshaft chain has been installed, Step 8 may be difficult. Carefully insert a long, broad-tipped screwdriver down into the camshaft chain cavity and depress the tensioner from the inside. This will give you additional chain slack enabling the camshaft sprocket and chain to slide up onto the camshaft boss. Be careful not to damage anything in the camshaft cavity with the screwdriver.*

8. Install the chain onto the sprocket without rotating the sprocket. Slide the sprocket and chain up and onto the camshaft boss. Recheck the following:

    a. Refer to Step 3 and make sure the "T" mark is still properly aligned (**Figure 38**); readjust if necessary.

    b. Make sure the index marks on the camshaft sprocket are perfectly aligned with the top surface of the cylinder head (**Figure 40**).

9. If alignment is incorrect, reposition the camshaft chain on the sprocket and recheck the alignment. Refer to **Figure 38** and **Figure 40**.

> *CAUTION*
> *Very expensive damage could result from improper camshaft and camshaft chain alignment. Recheck your work several times to be sure alignment is correct.*

10. When alignment is correct, perform the following:

    a. Install the camshaft sprocket bolt into the exposed bolt hole. Tighten only finger-tight at this time.

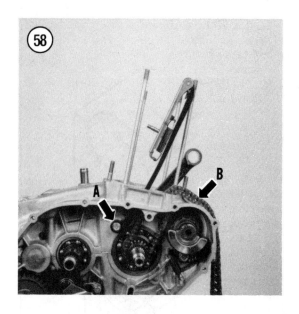

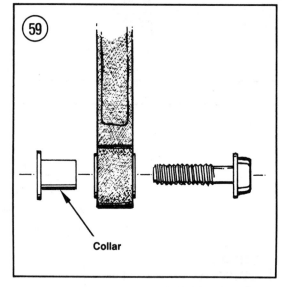

Collar

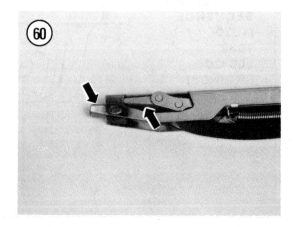

b. Rotate the engine to expose the other bolt hole and install the other bolt.

c. Make sure the camshaft sprocket is correctly seated on the camshaft boss.

d. Tighten both bolts to the torque specification listed in **Table 2**.

> *CAUTION*
> *If there is any binding while rotating the crankshaft, **stop**. Determine the cause before proceeding.*

11. After installation is complete, rotate the crankshaft several times using the bolt on the alternator rotor.

12. Make one final check to make sure alignment is correct. The "T" timing mark must be aligned with the mark and the timing marks on the camshaft sprocket must be perfectly aligned with the top surface of the cylinder head.

13. Fill the oil pocket in the cylinder head with new engine oil so the cam lobes are submerged in the oil.

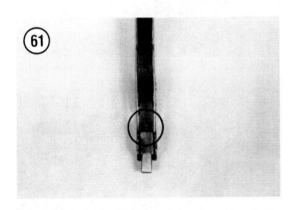

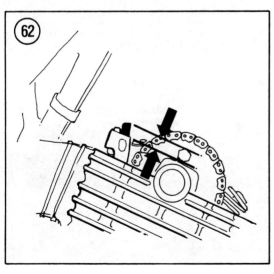

14. Install the cylinder head cover as described in this chapter.

CAMSHAFT CHAIN AND DAMPERS
Removal/Installation

1. Remove the cylinder head cover, cylinder head and cylinder as described in this chapter.

2. Remove the clutch assembly as described in Chapter Six.

3. Remove the ignition advance assembly as described in this chapter.

4. Remove the bolt (A, **Figure 58**) securing the cam chain tensioner and remove it.

> *NOTE*
> *The cam chain guide was removed in the cylinder removal sequence.*

5. Disengage the cam chain from the crankshaft sprocket and remove it (B, **Figure 58**).

6. Install by reversing these removal steps. Tighten the cam chain tensioner bolt to the torque specifications listed in **Table 2**.

> *CAUTION*
> *Make sure the collar (**Figure 59**) is in place in the tensioner assembly before installation.*

Cam Chain Tensioner Assembly Inspection (1982 XL500R, 1982 XR500R)

The upper end of the cam chain tensioner assembly is a set of sliding wedges that work together to maintain the correct tension on the cam chain, eliminating the need for periodic adjustment.

1. Inspect the mating surfaces of both wedges (**Figure 60**) for uneven wear or damage. If either is damaged to the extent that they do not slide smoothly against each other, the tensioner must be replaced.

2. Check the small spring (**Figure 61**) that holds the upper wedge up. If it is weak or broken, the tensioner must be replaced.

Camshaft Chain Inspection (1982 XL500R, 1982 XR500R)

The camshaft chain is a Hy-Vo type and rarely wears out, but will stretch with prolonged use. To check for chain wear remove the cylinder head cover as described in this chapter. Measure the distance that the upper wedge (wedge "B") protrudes above the upper surface of the tensioner assembly bracket (**Figure 62**). The chain must be replaced if the dimension is 9.0 mm (0.35 in.) or more.

If the chain is worn, check the drive and driven sprockets for wear also; they may also require replacement.

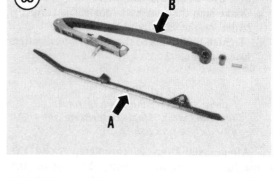

Cam Chain Tensioner Assembly and Camshaft Chain Inspection (All Other Models)

Check the top surface of the guide (A, **Figure 63**) and the tensioner assembly (B, **Figure 63**). If either is worn or damaged it must be replaced. This may indicate a worn chain or improper chain adjustment.

Check all of the components of the tensioner assembly (B, **Figure 63**). If any part is defective, replace the assembly.

The camshaft chain is a Hy-Vo type and rarely wears out, but will stretch with prolonged use. Check it thoroughly and if damaged, replace it. If it needs replacing, also check the drive sprocket on the crankshaft and the cam sprocket. They also may be defective.

CYLINDER

Removal

1. Remove the cylinder head cover and cylinder head as described in this chapter.
2. Remove the cylinder head gasket, locating dowels and O-ring seal.
3A. On 1982 XL500R and 1982 XR500R models, perform the following:
    a. Remove the camshaft chain guide (**Figure 64**).
    b. Remove the camshaft chain tensioner set bolt and copper washer (**Figure 65**) and push the tensioner assembly forward.
    c. Remove the bolts (**Figure 66**) securing the cylinder on the right-hand side.

3B. On all other models, perform the following:
    a. Remove the camshaft chain tensioner locknut and sealing washer. Remove the O-ring seal from the threaded stud on the tensioner assembly.
    b. Push the tensioner assembly forward to move the threaded stud out of the hole in the cylinder.
    c. Remove the bolts securing the cylinder on the right-hand side.
4. Loosen the cylinder by tapping around the perimeter with a rubber or plastic mallet. If

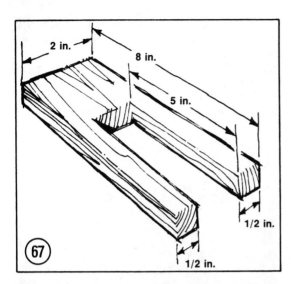

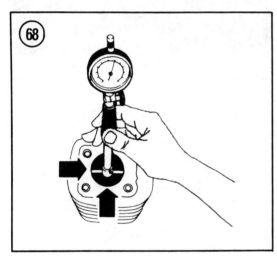

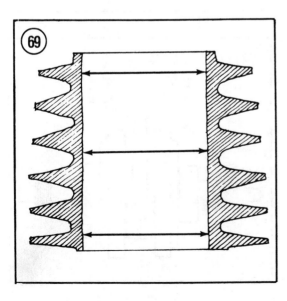

necessary, *gently* pry the cylinder loose with a broad-tipped screwdriver.

CAUTION
Remember the cooling fins are fragile and may be damaged if tapped or pried too hard. Never use a metal hammer.

5. Pull the cylinder straight out and off of the piston and crankcase studs. Work the camshaft chain wire through the opening in the cylinder. Reattach the wire to the exterior of the crankcase.

6. Remove the cylinder base gasket and discard it. Remove the dowel pins from the crankcase receptacles.

7. Install a piston holding fixture under the piston to protect the piston skirt from damage. This fixture may be purchased or may be a homemade unit of wood. See **Figure 67** for dimensions.

Inspection

The following procedure requires the use of highly specialized and expensive measuring instruments. If such equipment is not readily available, have the measurements performed by a dealer or qualified machine shop.

1. Soak with solvent any old cylinder head gasket material on the cylinder. Use a broad-tipped, *dull* chisel and gently scrape off all gasket residue. Do not gouge the sealing surface as oil and air leaks will result.

2. Measure the cylinder bore with a cylinder gauge (**Figure 68**) or inside micrometer at the points shown in **Figure 69**. Measure in 2 axes—in line with the piston pin and at 90° to the pin. If the taper or out-of-round is 0.05 mm (0.002 in.) or greater, the cylinder must be rebored to the next oversize and a new piston installed.

NOTE
The new piston should be obtained before the cylinder is rebored so that the piston can be measured; slight manufacturing tolerances must be taken into account to determine the actual size and working clearance.

3. Check the cylinder wall for scratches; if evident, the cylinder should be rebored.

NOTE
*The maximum wear limit on the cylinder is listed in **Table 1**. If the cylinder is worn to this limit, it must be replaced. Never rebore a cylinder if the finished rebore diameter will be this dimension or greater.*

NOTE
After having the cylinder rebored, wash it thoroughly in hot soapy water. This is the best way to clean the cylinder of all fine grit material left from the bore job. After washing the cylinder, run a clean white cloth through it. The cloth should show no traces of dirt or other debris. If the rag is dirty, the cylinder is not clean enough and must be rewashed. When the cylinder is thoroughly clean, dry and lubricate the cylinder wall with clean engine oil to prevent the cylinder liner from rusting.

Installation

1. Check that the top surface of the crankcase and the bottom surface of the cylinder are clean before installing a new base gasket.
2. Install a new cylinder base gasket and dowel pins.
3. Make sure the oil control orifice (**Figure 70**) is clean (not clogged) and is in place in the receptacle in the crankcase.
4. Install a piston holding fixture under the piston.
5. Make sure the end gaps of the piston rings are *not* lined up with each other—they must be staggered. Lightly oil the piston rings and the inside of the cylinder bore with assembly oil.
6. Carefully feed the camshaft chain and wire up through the opening in the cylinder and tie it to the engine.
7. Start the cylinder down over the piston and crankcase studs. Compress each piston ring with your fingers as it enters the cylinder.
8. Slide the cylinder down until it bottoms on the piston holding fixture.
9. Remove the piston holding fixture and slide the cylinder down into place on the crankcase.
10. Install the bolts securing the cylinder to the crankcase on the right-hand side and tighten to the torque specification listed in **Table 2**.
11A. On 1982 XL500R and 1982 XR500R models, pull the camshaft chain tensioner to the rear and up. Then install the tensioner set bolt and copper washer (**Figure 65**).
11B. On all other models, perform the following:
   a. Pull the camshaft chain tensioner to the rear until the threaded stud comes through the hole in the cylinder.
   b. Install the O-ring seal, sealing washer and locknut onto the threaded stud.
12. Install the camshaft chain guide. Make sure the lower end of the guide is properly indexed into

the receptacle in the crankcase. If improperly installed, it will interfere and bind with the camshaft chain.
13. Install the cylinder head and cylinder head cover as described in this chapter.
14. Adjust the valves and the camshaft chain tensioner as described in Chapter Three.

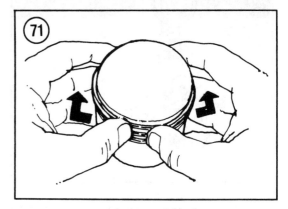

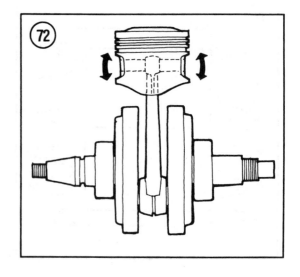

15. Follow the *Break-in Procedure* in this chapter if the cylinder was rebored, honed or a new piston or piston rings were installed.

PISTON, PISTON PIN AND PISTON RINGS

The piston is made of an aluminum alloy. The piston pin is made of steel and is a precision fit. The piston pin is held in place by a clip at each end.

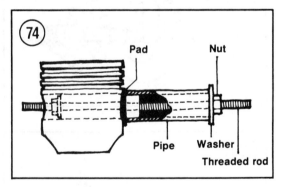

Pad   Nut

Pipe   Washer

Threaded rod

Piston Removal

1. Remove the cylinder head cover, cylinder head and cylinder as described in this chapter.

> *WARNING*
> *The edges of all piston rings are very sharp. Be careful when handling them to avoid cutting fingers.*

2. Remove the top ring with a ring expander tool or by spreading the ends with your thumbs just enough to slide the ring up over the piston (**Figure 71**). Repeat for the remaining rings.

3. Before removing the piston, hold the rod tightly and rock the piston as shown in **Figure 72**. Any rocking motion indicates wear on the piston pin, piston pin bore or connecting rod small-end bore; or, more likely, a combination of these. The normal sliding motion is not to be confused with a rocking motion.

> *NOTE*
> *Wrap a clean shop cloth under the piston so that the piston pin clip will not fall into the crankcase.*

4. Remove the clips from each side of the piston pin bore (**Figure 73**) with a small screwdriver or scribe. Hold your thumb over one edge of the clip when removing it to prevent the clip from springing out.

5. Use a proper size wooden dowel or socket extension and push out the piston pin.

> *CAUTION*
> *Be careful when removing the pin to avoid damaging the connecting rod. If it is necessary to gently tap the pin to remove it, be sure that the piston is properly supported so that lateral shock is not transmitted to the lower connecting rod bearing.*

6. If the piston pin is difficult to remove, heat the piston and pin with a hair dryer. The pin will probably push right out. Heat the piston to only about 140° F (60° C), i.e., until it is too warm to touch, but not excessively hot. If the pin is still difficult to push out, use a homemade tool as shown in **Figure 74**.

7. Lift the piston off the connecting rod.

8. If the piston is going to be left off for some time, place a piece of foam insulation tube over the end of the rod to protect it.

Inspection

1. Carefully clean the carbon from the piston crown with a chemical remover or with a soft scraper (**Figure 75**). Do not remove or damage the

carbon ridge around the circumference of the piston above the top ring. If the piston, rings and cylinder are found to be dimensionally correct and can be reused, removal of the carbon ring from the top of the piston or the carbon ridge from the top of the cylinder will promote excessive oil consumption.

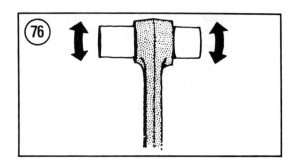

CAUTION
Do not wire brush the piston skirts.

2. Examine each ring groove for burrs, dented edges and wide wear. Pay particular attention to the top compression ring groove as it usually wears more than the others.
3. If damage or wear indicates piston replacement, select a new piston as described under *Piston Clearance* in this chapter.
4. Oil the piston pin and install it in the connecting rod. Slowly rotate the piston pin and check for radial play (**Figure 76**). If any play exists, the piston pin should be replaced, providing the rod bore is in good condition.
5. Measure the inside diameter of the piston pin bore with a snap gauge (**Figure 77**) and measure the outside diameter of the piston pin with a micrometer (**Figure 78**). Compare with dimensions given in **Table 1**. Replace the piston and piston pin as a set if either or both are worn.
6. Check the piston skirt for galling and abrasion which may have been caused by piston seizure. If light galling is present, smooth the affected area with No. 400 emery paper and oil or a fine oilstone. However, if galling is severe or if the piston is deeply scored, replace it.

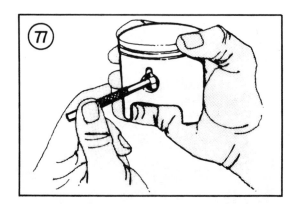

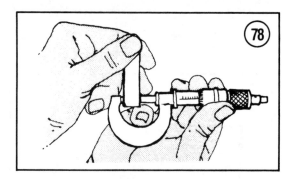

Piston Clearance

1. Make sure the piston and cylinder walls are clean and dry.
2. Measure the inside diameter of the cylinder bore at a point 13 mm (1/2 in.) from the upper edge with a bore gauge.
3. Measure the outside diameter of the piston across the skirt (**Figure 79**) at right angles to the piston pin. Measure at a distance 18 mm (0.70 in.) up from the bottom of the piston skirt.
4. Piston clearance is the difference between the maximum piston diameter and the minimum cylinder diameter. Subtract the dimension of the piston from the cylinder dimension and compare to the dimension listed in **Table 1**. If the clearance exceeds that specified, the cylinder should be rebored to the next oversize and a new piston installed.

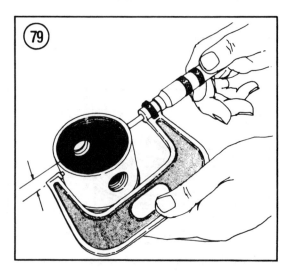

5. To establish a final overbore dimension with a new piston, add the piston skirt measurement to the specified clearance. This will determine the dimension for the cylinder overbore size. Remember, do not exceed the cylinder maximum service limit inside diameter indicated in **Table 1**.

Piston Installation

1. Apply molybdenum disulfide grease to the inside surface of the connecting rod.

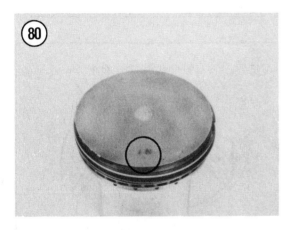

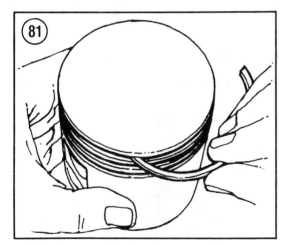

2. Oil the piston pin with assembly oil and install it in the piston until its end extends slightly beyond the inside of the boss.

3. Place the piston over the connecting rod with the IN mark (**Figure 80**) on the piston crown directed toward the rear of the engine.

4. Line up the piston pin with the hole in the connecting rod. Push the piston pin through the connecting rod and into the other side of the piston until it is even with the piston pin clip grooves.

> *CAUTION*
> *If it is necessary to tap the piston pin into the connecting rod, do so gently with a block of wood or a soft-faced hammer. Make sure you support the piston to prevent the lateral shock from being transmitted to the connecting rod bearing.*

> *NOTE*
> *In the next step, install the clips with the gap away from the cutout in the piston.*

5. Install new piston pin clips in both ends of the pin boss. Make sure they are seated in the grooves in the piston.

6. Check the installation by rocking the piston back and forth around the pin axis and from side to side along the axis. It should rotate freely back and forth but not from side to side.

7. Install the piston rings as described in this chapter.

8. Install the cylinder, cylinder head and cylinder head cover as described in this chapter.

Piston Ring
Removal/Inspection/Installation

> *WARNING*
> *The edges of all piston rings are very sharp. Be careful when handling them to avoid cutting fingers.*

1. Remove the top ring by spreading the ends with your thumbs just enough to slide the ring up over the piston (**Figure 71**); repeat for the remaining rings.

2. Carefully remove all carbon build-up from the ring grooves with a broken piston ring (**Figure 81**). Inspect the grooves carefully for burrs, nicks or broken and cracked lands. Recondition or replace the piston if necessary.

3. Roll each ring around its piston groove, as shown in **Figure 82**, to check for binding. Minor binding may be cleaned up with a fine-cut file.

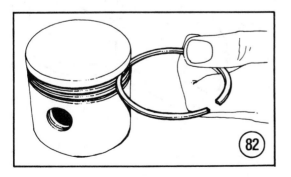

4. Measure the side clearance of each ring in its groove with a flat feeler gauge (**Figure 83**) and compare to dimensions given in **Table 1**. If the clearance is greater than specified, the rings must be replaced. If the clearance is still excessive with the new rings, the piston must also be replaced.

5. Measure each ring for wear. Place each ring, one at a time, into the cylinder and push it in about 20 mm (3/4 in.) with the crown of the piston to ensure that the ring is square in the cylinder bore. Measure the gap with a flat feeler gauge (**Figure 84**) and compare to dimensions in **Table 1**. If the gap is greater than specified, the rings should be replaced. When installing new rings, measure their end gap in the same manner as for old ones. If the gap is less than specified, recheck to make sure you have the correct rings. If ring size is correct for the bore, carefully file the ends (**Figure 85**) with a fine-cut file until the gap is correct.

6. Install the piston rings in the order shown in **Figure 86**.

7. Install the oil ring spacer first, then the side rails. New oil ring side rails do not have top and bottom designations. If reassembling used parts, install the side rails as they were removed.

8. Install the second compression ring, then the top—by carefully spreading the ends of the ring with your thumbs and slipping the ring over the top of the piston. Remember that the marks on the piston rings are toward the top of the piston.

9. Make sure the rings are seated completely in their grooves all the way around the piston and that the ends are distributed around the piston. The important thing is that the ring gaps are not aligned with each other when installed.

10. If new rings were installed, measure the side clearance of each ring in its groove with a flat feeler gauge (**Figure 83**) and compare to dimensions given in **Table 1**.

11. Follow the *Break-in Procedure* in this chapter if a new piston or piston rings have been installed or the cylinder was rebored or honed.

IGNITION ADVANCE MECHANISM

Removal

1. Remove both side covers and the seat.

> *NOTE*
> *On XL500S models, reinstall the seat strap bolts as they also hold the upper portion of the shock absorber to the frame (**Figure 87**). Remove and reinstall one bolt at a time.*

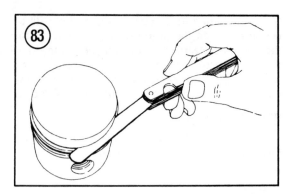

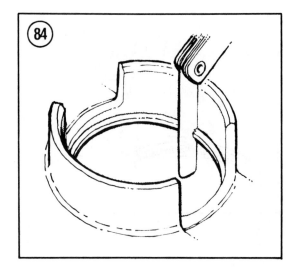

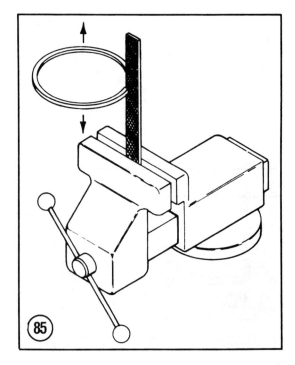

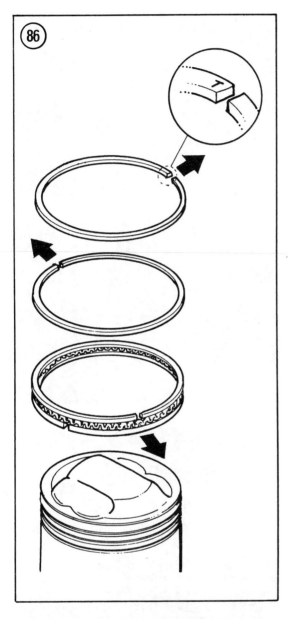

2. Remove the bolts securing the skid plate and remove the skid plate.

3. Drain the engine oil as described in Chapter Three.

4. Place wood blocks under the frame to support the bike securely.

5. On XL models, disconnect the battery negative lead or disconnect the main fuse (**Figure 88**).

6. Remove the fuel tank as described in Chapter Seven.

7. Remove the kickstarter pedal (A, **Figure 89**).

8. Disconnect the rear brake light switch return spring and cable (B, **Figure 89**), the right-hand footpeg (C, **Figure 89**) and the rear brake pedal (D, **Figure 89**).

9. Slacken the clutch cable at the hand lever and disconnect the clutch cable at the crankcase cover (E, **Figure 89**).

10. Disconnect the starter decompressor cable at the crankcase cover (F, **Figure 89**).

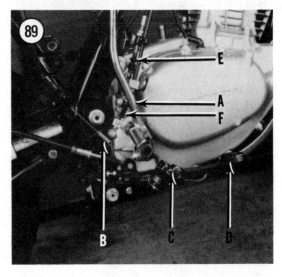

11. Disconnect the ignition pulse generator electrical connector. Refer to **Figure 90** for XL series models or **Figure 91** for XR series models.

12. Remove the bolts securing the right-hand crankcase cover and remove the cover and gasket. Don't lose the locating dowels.

13. Place a copper washer (or penny) between the primary drive gear and the clutch outer housing gear. This will prevent the primary drive gear from turning while removing the locknut in Step 14.

14. Remove the 14 mm locknut (**Figure 92**).

15. Remove the stopper pin securing the oil pressure pad (**Figure 93**).

16. Remove the oil pressure pad and spring (A, **Figure 94**) and washer (B, **Figure 94**).

17. Slide the pulse generator rotor off of the crankshaft.

18. Remove the copper washer (or penny) from the gears.

19. Inspect all components as described in Chapter Eight.

Installation

> *NOTE*
> *If either the advance rotor or pulse generator have been replaced with new units, they must have the same identification mark (**Figure 95**). Failure to do so will result in poor engine performance.*

1. Align the cutout notch on the rotor with the dowel pin on the crankshaft and slide on the rotor.

2. Install the washer and the locknut. Tighten the locknut to the torque specification listed in **Table 2**.

3. Make sure the locating dowels are in place and install a new gasket.

4. Hold the starter decompressor lever in the raised position and install the right-hand crankcase cover. Tighten the screws securely.

> *CAUTION*
> *After the crankcase cover is installed, check the operation of the clutch and the starter decompressor levers. They should operate without binding. If they do bind, remove the cover and correct the problem.*

5. Connect the ignition pulse generator electrical connector. Make sure it is pushed together tightly.
6. On XL series models, connect the battery negative lead or reconnect the main fuse.
7. Connect the clutch and starter decompressor cables.
8. Install the rear brake pedal, right-hand footpeg and kickstarter arm.
9. Connect the rear brake switch return spring and cable.
10. Install the skid plate, seat and side covers.
11. Install the fuel tank as described in Chapter Seven.
12. Fill the crankcase with the recommended type and quantity of engine oil as described in Chapter Three.
13. Adjust the clutch cable, starter decompressor and rear brake as described in Chapter Three.

OIL PUMP AND OIL FILTER SCREEN

The oil pump is located on the right-hand side of the engine. The oil pump can be removed with the engine in the frame. This procedure is shown with the engine removed for clarity.

Removal/Installation

1. Remove the clutch assembly as described in Chapter Six.
2. Remove the bolts (**Figure 96**) securing the set plate and remove it.
3. Remove the kickstarter idle gear (A, **Figure 97**) from the shift fork shaft (B, **Figure 97**).

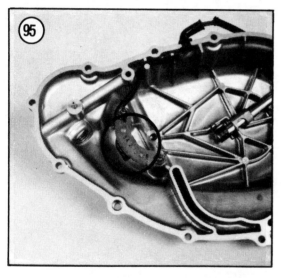

4. Slide the oil pump assembly off the shaft and remove the O-ring seals (A, **Figure 98**).

5. Slide out the oil filter screen (B, **Figure 98**) and clean it with a medium soft toothbrush. Dry it carefully with compressed air. Inspect the screen; replace it if there are any breaks or holes in it.

6. Thoroughly clean out the oil filter screen cavity (**Figure 99**) in the crankcase. Wipe it clean with a cloth saturated in solvent and dry with compressed air.

7. Install the oil filter screen with the thick side facing out (**Figure 100**).

8. Install the O-ring seals (A, **Figure 98**) and make sure the locating dowel (**Figure 101**) is in place in the oil pump assembly.

9. Install the oil pump assembly and kickstarter idle gear.

10. Rotate the shift fork shaft (B, **Figure 97**) so that it aligns with the oil pump set plate. Install the set plate and bolts (**Figure 102**). Tighten the bolts securely.

> *CAUTION*
> *The set plate must align with the shift fork shaft as shown in **Figure 102**. Set it flush against the shaft so there is no clearance. If the shift fork shaft rotates, the lubrication passages within it will be blocked causing oil starvation to the transmission, resulting in transmission damage.*

11. Install the clutch assembly as described in Chapter Six.

Disassembly/Inspection/Assembly

Refer to **Figure 103** for this procedure.

1. Inspect the outer housing and cover for cracks.

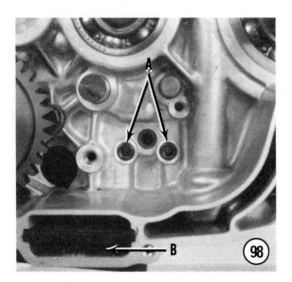

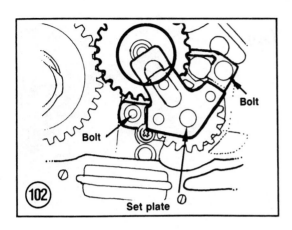

(102)

Bolt

Bolt

Set plate

2. Remove the locating dowel (A, **Figure 104**) and screw (B, **Figure 104**) securing the cover to the body and separate the two parts.

3. Remove the inner and outer rotors. Inspect both parts for scratches and abrasions. Replace both parts if evidence of this is found.

4. Clean all parts in solvent and dry thoroughly. Coat all parts with fresh engine oil before assembly.

5. Install the outer rotor into the pump body and measure the clearance between the outer rotor and the oil pump body with a flat feeler gauge (**Figure 105**). If worn to the wear limit listed in **Table 1** or greater, replace the worn part.

4

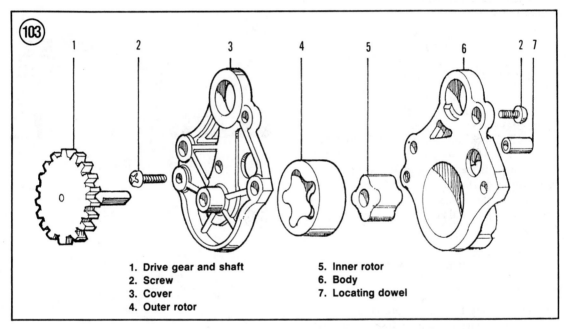

(103)

1. Drive gear and shaft
2. Screw
3. Cover
4. Outer rotor
5. Inner rotor
6. Body
7. Locating dowel

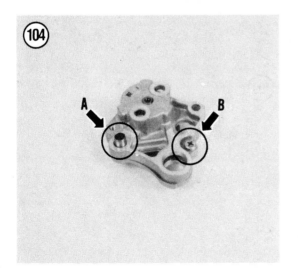

(104)

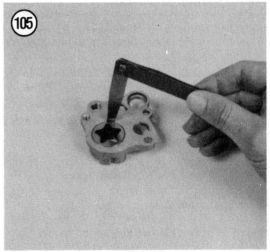

(105)

6. Install the inner rotor and measure the clearance between the inner rotor tip and the outer rotor with a flat feeler gauge (**Figure 106**). If worn to the wear limit listed in **Table 1** or greater, replace the worn part.

7. Measure the clearance between the rotor end and the pump body with a straightedge and a flat feeler gauge (**Figure 107**). If worn to the wear limit listed in **Table 1** or greater, replace either the rotors or the oil pump assembly.

8. Remove the inner and outer rotor from the pump body.

9. Install pump drive gear and shaft into the pump cover (**Figure 108**).

10. Install the inner and outer rotors onto it (**Figure 109**).

> *NOTE*
> *Align the flat side on the pump shaft with the flat within the inner rotor.*

11. Install the pump housing, locating dowel (A, **Figure 104**) and screw. Tighten the screw securely.

12. Measure the inside diameter of the kickstarter idle gear. Replace if worn to the wear limit in **Table 1**, or greater. Inspect the gear for excessive wear, burrs, pitting or chipped teeth; replace if necessary.

13. Inspect the O-ring seals (A, **Figure 98**). Replace as a set if either has lost its resiliency or is deteriorated.

KICKSTARTER

Removal

Refer to **Figure 110** for this procedure.

1. Remove the engine from the frame as described in this chapter.

2. Remove the thrust washer, kickstarter cam, spring and spring seat (**Figure 111**).

3. Split the crankcase as described in this chapter.

4. From within the crankcase, disconnect the kickstarter return spring from the spring hook pin.

5. Remove the kickstarter assembly from the crankcase.

Disassembly/Inspection/Assembly

Refer to **Figure 110** for this procedure.

1. Remove the kickstarter return spring.

2. Remove the 16 mm circlip, thrust washer and collar from the shaft.

3. Slide off the return spring, thrust washer, springs, (**Figure 112**) and kickstarter ratchet from the shaft.

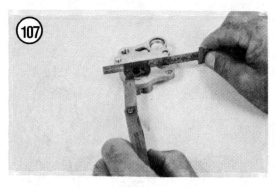

4. Remove the 22 mm circlip, thrust washer, kickstarter gear, thrust washer and 24 mm circlip.

5. Measure the inside diameter of the kickstarter gear. If worn to the wear limit listed in **Table 1**, or greater, replace the gear.

6. Measure the outside diameter of the kickstarter shaft where the gear rides. If worn to the wear limit listed in **Table 1**, or less, replace the shaft.

7. Check for chipped or missing te

8. Inspect the internal splines on a

9. Check all parts for uneven wear; replace as necessary.

10. Inspect the splines on the kickstarter shaft.

11. Check the ratchet surfaces on both the kickstarter ratchet and the kickstarter gear for wear; replace if necessary.

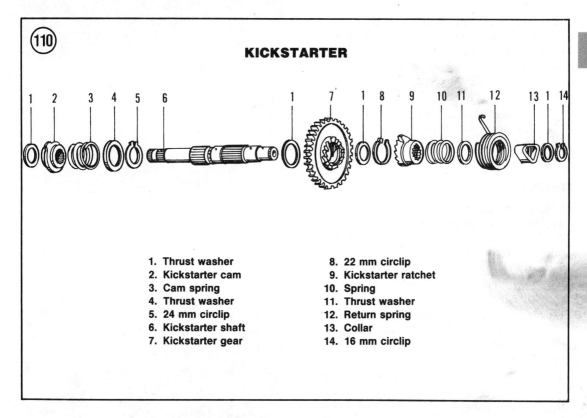

KICKSTARTER

1. Thrust washer	8. 22 mm circlip
2. Kickstarter cam	9. Kickstarter ratchet
3. Cam spring	10. Spring
4. Thrust washer	11. Thrust washer
5. 24 mm circlip	12. Return spring
6. Kickstarter shaft	13. Collar
7. Kickstarter gear	14. 16 mm circlip

12. Apply clean engine oil to all sliding surfaces of all parts before assembly and installation.

13. Install the 24 mm circlip on the right-hand side where the kickstarter gear rides. Slide on the thrust washer.

14. Position the kickstarter gear with the ratchet side going on last and slide on the gear.

15. Slide on the thrust washer and the 22 mm circlip.

16. Align the punch mark on the ratchet and shaft and slide on the kickstarter ratchet (**Figure 113**).

17. Install the thrust washer and ratchet spring.

18. Slide on the collar.

> *NOTE*
> *Before installing the shaft assembly into the crankcase, check with **Figure 114** for correct placement of all components.*

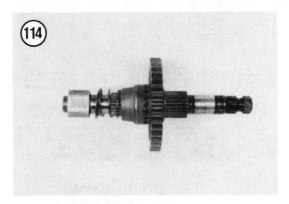

Installation

1. Install the assembled shaft into the crankcase with the oil and spring holes facing up.

2. Pour a small amount of clean engine oil into the oil hole (**Figure 115**).

3. Install the return spring (**Figure 116**) and hook the end into the hole in the shaft.

> *NOTE*
> *Install the circlip with the chamfered edge toward the end of the shaft. Make sure the circlip is completely seated in the groove in the shaft.*

4. Install the thrust washer and 16 mm circlip.

5. Pull the spring into position using a motorcycle muffler spring hook (**Figure 117**) or use Vise Grips.

6. Install the spring seat and spring.

7. Align the punch mark on the shaft with the mark on the kickstarter cam (**Figure 118**), then slide the cam down onto the shaft splines.

8. Install the thrust washer (**Figure 119**).

9. Assemble the crankcase and install the engine in the frame as described in this chapter.

CRANKCASE

Disassembly of the crankcase (splitting the cases) requires that the engine be removed from the frame.

The thin-walled crankcase is made in 2 halves of precision diecast aluminum alloy. To avoid damage, do not hammer or pry on any of the interior or exterior projected walls. These areas are

easily damaged. The cases are split horizontally down the centerline of the crankshaft. The cases are assembled *without* a gasket between the 2 halves. Dowel pins align the halves when they are bolted together.

The procedure which follows is presented as a complete, step-by-step, major lower end rebuild that should be followed if an engine is to be completely reconditioned. However, if you're replacing a part that you know is defective, the disassembly should be carried out only until the failed part is accessible. There is no need to disassemble the engine beyond that point so long as you know the remaining components are in good condition and that they were not affected by the failed part.

Crankcase Disassembly

1. Remove all exterior engine assemblies as described in this chapter and other related chapters.
   a. Cylinder head cover and cylinder head
   b. Cylinder and piston
   c. Alternator
   d. External shift mechanism
   e. Oil pump
   f. External portion of the kickstarter assembly
2. Remove the engine as described in this chapter.
3. Remove the ignition advance mechanism (A, **Figure 120**), clutch assembly (B, **Figure 120**) and small oil pipe (C, **Figure 120**). Refer to Chapter Six for clutch removal.
4. Remove the bolt (**Figure 121**) securing the camshaft chain tensioner and remove the tensioner assembly.

5. Remove the camshaft drive chain (A, **Figure 122**), the front balancer holder lockbolt (B, **Figure 122**) and spring (C, **Figure 122**).

6. Remove the bolts (**Figure 123**) securing the balancer chain guide and remove it.

7. Turn the engine upside down on the work bench on blocks of wood to protect the connecting rod and the crankcase studs.

8. Loosen the lower crankcase bolts in 2-3 stages in a crisscross pattern to avoid warpage. Remove all bolts.

9. Turn the crankcase right side up and set it on wood blocks.

10. Loosen the upper crankcase bolts in 2-3 stages in a crisscross pattern to avoid warpage. Remove all bolts.

11. Tap around the perimeter of the crankcase halves with a plastic or soft-faced mallet. Do *not* use a metal hammer as it will cause damage.

CAUTION
*Honda's thin-walled crankcase castings are just that—**thin**. To avoid damage to the cases do not hammer on the projected walls that surround the clutch and alternator. These areas are easily damaged if stressed.*

CAUTION
If it is necessary to pry the crankcase halves apart, do it very carefully so that you do not mar the gasket sealing surfaces. If you do, they will leak and the crankcase halves must be replaced.

12. Lift up on the upper crankcase half and move it toward the rear (**Figure 124**).

13. Remove the balancer chain from the rear balancer on the transmission mainshaft.

14. Remove the crankshaft assembly and both transmission shaft assemblies from the lower crankcase half.

15. Remove the shift drum and shift forks as described in Chapter Six.

16. Remove the internal portion of the kickstarter assembly as described in this chapter.

17. Remove the bolts (**Figure 125**) securing the crankcase breather separator baffle plate and remove the plate.

18. Don't lose the locating dowels if they came out of the case. They do not have to be removed from the case if they are secure.

19. Inspect the crankcase halves and crankshaft as described in this chapter.

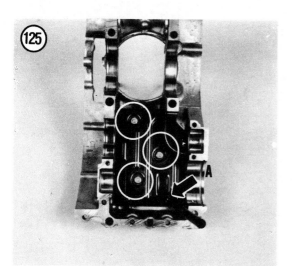

Crankcase Assembly

1. Before the installation of parts, coat all surfaces with assembly oil or clean engine oil. Do not get any oil on the sealing surfaces of the case halves.

2. Install the crankcase breather separator baffle plate and tighten the screws securely.

3. Apply assembly oil to the crankshaft bearings.

4. Install the inner portion of the kickstarter assembly and crankshaft assembly into the lower crankcase half.

5. Install the transmission assemblies as described in Chapter Six.

6. If the factory-painted marks on the balancer chain have come off, refer to **Figure 126** and re-mark as follows:

    a. Lay the chain out flat in a loop.

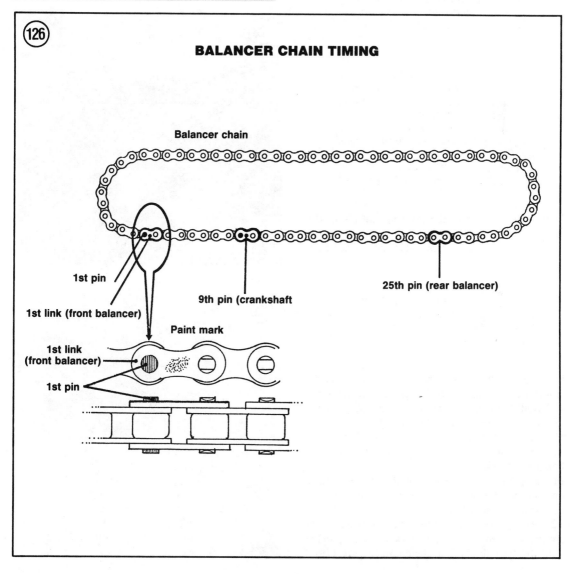

BALANCER CHAIN TIMING

b. Make all marks on the lower loop of the chain.

c. Place a spot of quick-drying paint on a link plate (it makes no difference which one you start with).

d. The pin on the *left-hand side* of this link plate will be pin No. 1.

e. Count to the right until you reach pin No. 9 and mark that link plate with a spot of paint.

f. Continue to count to the right until you reach the 25th pin. Mark that link plate with a spot of paint. The pin on the left-hand side of that link plate will be pin No. 25.

> *CAUTION*
> *This is very important for balancer timing; each mark must be accurate or extreme engine vibration will occur.*

> *CAUTION*
> *Do **not** disconnect or remove the balancer system from your motorcycle. The engine is designed to operate with it to reduce engine vibration. If the balancers are removed or disconnected an excessive amount of vibration could result in cracks or damage to the frame and/or engine. Also any applicable manufacturer's warranty will be voided.*

7. If removed, install the locating dowels in the lower crankcase half (**Figure 127**). Make sure the transmission bearing set rings are also in position.

> *NOTE*
> *Make sure the mating surfaces are clean and free of all old sealant material. Make sure you get a leak-free seal.*

8. Install the front balancer assembly in the upper crankcase. Do not install the sprocket at this time.

9. Install the balancer chain with the marks made in Step 6 on the lower half of the chain.

10. Partially lift the transmission mainshaft out of the crankcase and install the chain over the rear balancer sprocket.

11. Align the 25th pin's plate with the punch mark on the sprocket (**Figure 128**). Reinstall the transmission mainshaft.

12. Install the chain onto the front balancer sprocket. Align the punch mark on the sprocket with the 1st link plate on the chain (**Figure 129**).

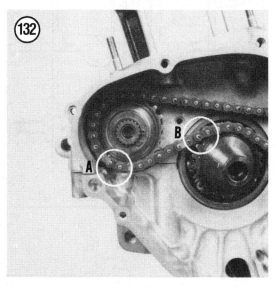

4

13. Pull the front balancer sprocket and chain forward and align the punch mark on the crankshaft sprocket with the 9th pin's link plate on the chain (**Figure 130**). Let the front balancer sprocket and chain hang from the crankshaft sprocket.

14. Thoroughly clean the sealing surfaces of both crankcase halves with contact cleaner and wipe dry with a lint-free cloth.

15. Apply a light coat of Three Bond, or equivalent, to the sealing surfaces of the upper crankcase half. Coat only flat surfaces, not the curved bearing surfaces. Apply the coating as thin as possible, but well covered, or the case can shift and hammer out the bearings. Use only a non-hardening sealant.

16. Make sure all alignments made in Steps 11-13 are still correct. If not, repeat Steps 11-13 until all are correct. Position the upper crankcase onto the rear of the lower crankcase.

17. Align the punch mark on the front balancer shaft with the punch mark on the sprocket and install the front balancer sprocket onto the balancer unit (A, **Figure 131**).

18. Install the circlip securing the sprocket to the balancer unit. Make sure the circlip is properly seated in the groove.

19. Completely join the 2 crankcase halves together. Again check the alignment of the punch marks and chain pins on the front balancer (A, **Figure 132**) and crankshaft (B, **Figure 132**). If alignment is incorrect, correct it before proceeding.

20. Make sure that the transmission bearing races are engaged into the dowel pins and set rings. If not seated correctly this will keep the crankcase from completely seating.

CAUTION
*Do **not** install any crankcase bolts until the sealing surface around the entire crankcase perimeter has seated completely.*

21. Lightly tap the case halves together with a plastic or rubber mallet until they seat.

CAUTION
Crankcase halves should fit together without force. If the crankcase halves do not fit together completely, do not attempt to pull them together with the crankcase bolts. Separate the crankcase halves and investigate the cause of the interference. If the transmission shafts were disassembled, recheck to make sure that a gear is not installed backwards. Do not risk damage by trying to force the cases together.

22. Before installing the bolts, slowly spin the transmission shafts and shift through all gears. Also spin the crankshaft to make sure there is no binding.

23. Apply oil to all crankcase bolt threads.

24. Install the upper crankcase bolts and tighten only finger-tight.

25. Tighten the upper crankcase bolts in 2-3 stages in the sequence shown in **Figure 133**. Tighten the bolts to the torque specification listed in **Table 2**. There are 2 different size bolts, 6 mm and 8 mm. Be sure to tighten them to their correct torque specification.

26. Turn the engine over and install the lower crankcase bolts and tighten only finger-tight.

27. Tighten the lower crankcase bolts in 2-3 stages in the sequence shown in **Figure 134**. Tighten the bolts to the torque specification listed in **Table 2**.

28. After the crankcase halves are completely assembled, and the bolts tightened, again rotate the crankshaft and transmission shafts to make sure there is no binding. If any is present, disassemble the crankcase and correct the problem.

29. Install the balancer chain guide (B, **Figure 131**).

30. Install the camshaft drive chain, front balancer holder lockbolt and spring (**Figure 122**). Tighten the bolt to the torque specification listed in **Table 2**.

31. Be sure to install the small oil pipe (C, **Figure 120**) before installing the right-hand crankcase cover.

32. Install all exterior engine assemblies as described in this chapter and other related chapters.

    a. Cylinder head cover and cylinder head.

    b. Cylinder and piston.

    c. Clutch assembly.

    d. Alternator.

    e. External shift mechanism.

    f. Oil pump.

    g. External portion of the kickstarter mechanism.

33. Install the engine as described in this chapter.

34. Refill the crankcase with the recommended type and quantity of engine oil as described in Chapter Three.

Crankcase Inspection

1. Clean both crankcase halves inside and out with cleaning solvent. Thoroughly dry with compressed air and wipe off with a clean shop cloth. Be sure to remove all traces of old gasket material from all mating surfaces.

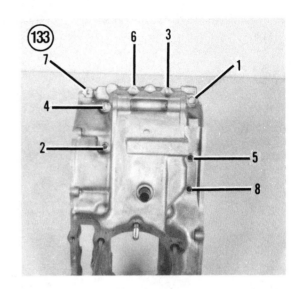

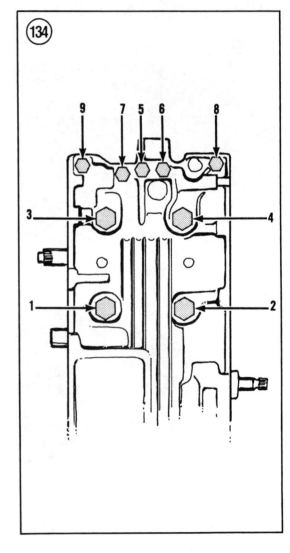

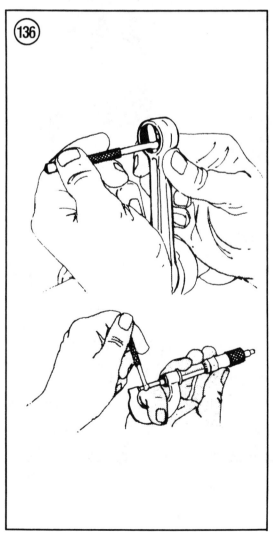

2. Make sure all oil passages are clean; be sure to blow them out with compressed air.

3. Carefully inspect the cases for cracks and fractures, especially in the lower areas; they are vulnerable to rock damage. Inspect the mating surfaces of both halves. They must be free of gouges, burrs or any damage that could cause an oil leak.

4. If damage is found, have them repaired by a shop specializing in the repair of precision aluminum castings or replace them.

5. Make sure the cylinder studs are not bent and that threads are in good condition. Make sure they are screwed into the crankcase tightly.

6. Inspect the balancer system as described in this chapter.

CRANKSHAFT
AND CONNECTING ROD

The crankshaft assembly is made up of 2 full-circle flywheels pressed together on a hollow crankpin. The connecting rod big end bearing on the crankpin is a needle bearing assembly. The crankshaft assembly is supported in 2 ball bearings in the crankcase. Service to the crankshaft assembly is limited to removal and replacement.

Removal/Installation

1. Disassemble the crankcase as described in this chapter.

2. Remove the crankshaft assembly from the lower crankcase half.

3. Before installing the crankshaft, lubricate the large ball bearings and connecting rod large end bearing with assembly oil.

4. Make sure the crankshaft bearing set ring (**Figure 135**) is in place in the lower crankcase half.

5. Install the crankshaft assembly into the lower crankcase half. Make sure the set ring is properly seated into the bearing outer race.

6. Assemble the crankcase as described in this chapter.

Crankshaft Inspection

1. Measure the inside diameter of the connecting rod small end with a snap gauge and an inside micrometer (**Figure 136**). Compare to dimensions given in **Table 1**. If worn to the service limit or greater the crankshaft assembly must be replaced.

2. Check the connecting rod-to-crankshaft side clearance with a flat feeler gauge (**Figure 137**). Compare to dimensions given in **Table 1**. If the clearance is greater than specified the crankshaft assembly must be replaced.

3. Check the crankshaft main bearings (**Figure 138**) for roughness, pitting, galling and play by rotating them slowly by hand. If any roughness or play can be felt in the bearing it must be replaced. This must be entrusted to a dealer as special tools are required.

4. Check the connecting rod big end bearing by grasping the rod in one hand and lifting up on it. With the heel of your other hand, rap sharply on the top of the rod. A sharp metallic sound, such as a click, is an indication that the bearing or crankpin or both are worn and the crankshaft assembly should be replaced.

5. Mount the crankshaft assembly in a pair of V-blocks and use a dial indicator as shown in **Figure 139**. Rotate the crankshaft slowly several complete revolutions. Measure the runout, using the dial indicator, at each end. Replace the crankshaft assembly if the runout exceeds 0.1 mm (0.0004 in.) at either end.

6. Mount the crankshaft assembly as in Step 5 and measure the clearance between the connecting rod and crankpin (**Figure 140**). Replace the crankshaft assembly if the clearance exceeds the wear limit dimension listed in **Table 1**.

7. Inspect the balancer drive sprocket or gear (**Figure 141**) for wear or missing teeth. If the sprocket or gear is damaged, it must be replaced. This must be entrusted to a dealer as special tools are required.

8. Inspect the camshaft drive sprocket for wear or missing teeth. If the sprocket is damaged, it must be replaced. This must be entrusted to a dealer as special tools are required.

BALANCER SYSTEM

The balancer system eliminates the vibration normally associated with a large displacement single cylinder engine. The engine and motorcycle frame are designed for use with this balancer system. If the balancers are disconnected or eliminated it will result in an excessive amount of engine vibration. This vibration will result in major fatigue to engine and frame components. Do *not* eliminate this feature by disconnecting it.

CAUTION
Any applicable manufacturer's warranty will be voided if the balancer system is modified, disconnected or removed.

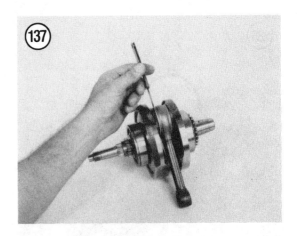

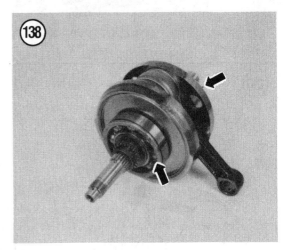

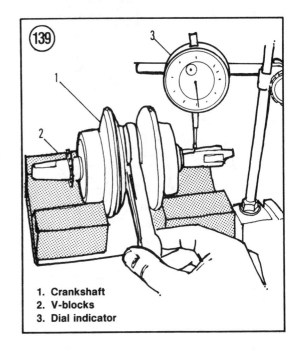

1. Crankshaft
2. V-blocks
3. Dial indicator

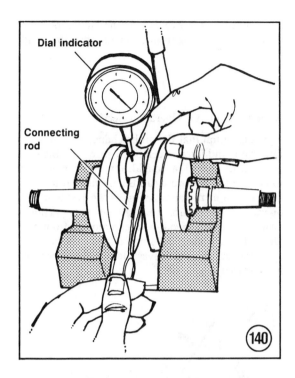

Dial indicator

Connecting rod

(140)

(141)

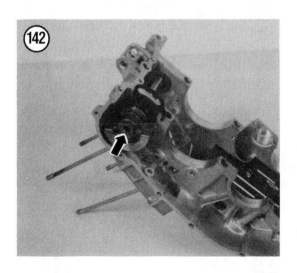

(142)

Front Balancer
Removal/installation

1. Remove the engine and disassemble the crankcase as described in this chapter.

NOTE
The right- and left-hand side refers to the engine as it sits in the bike's frame—not as it sits on your workbench.

2. Remove the 20 mm circlip from the balancer shaft on the left-hand side of the engine. Remove the chain sprocket.
3. Slide the balancer shaft (**Figure 142**) out the right-hand side.
4. Slide the balancer shaft holder (**Figure 143**) out the right-hand side.
5. Install by reversing these removal steps, noting the following.
6. Apply assembly oil to all needle bearings and rotating surfaces before installation.

Front Balancer Inspection

1. Inspect the needle bearings. Make sure they rotate smoothly with no signs of wear or damage; replace as necessary.
2. Measure the inside diameter (A, **Figure 144**) of the balancer shaft holder. Replace if the diameter is worn to the wear limit in **Table 1**, or greater.

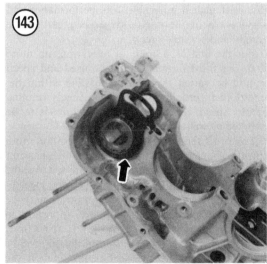

(143)

3. Measure the outside diameter (B, **Figure 144**) of the bearing surfaces at each end of the balancer shaft holder. Replace if the diameter is worn the wear limit in **Table 1** or less.

4. Inspect the sprocket teeth for wear or damage; replace if necessary.

Rear Balancer
Removal/Installation

1. Remove the engine from the frame and disassemble the crankcase as described in this chapter.

2. Remove the transmission mainshaft as described in Chapter Six.

3. Slide off the outer race and needle bearing (A, **Figure 145**) and thrust washer.

4. Slide off the rear balancer assembly (B, **Figure 145**).

5. Remove the collar that is outside of the needle bearing.

6. Install by reversing these removal steps, noting the following.

7. Install the parts in this exact order: thrust washer, needle bearing, needle bearing, rear balancer, thrust washer, needle bearing and outer race.

BREAK-IN PROCEDURE

If the rings were replaced, a new piston installed, the cylinder rebored or honed or major lower end work performed, the engine should be broken in just as though it were new. The performance and service life of the engine depends greatly on a careful and sensible break-in.

For the first 5-10 hours of operation, no more than one-third throttle should be used and speed should be varied as much as possible within the one-third throttle limit. Prolonged steady running at one speed, no matter how moderate, is to be avoided as well as hard acceleration.

Following the first 5-10 hours of operation more throttle should not be used until the bike has run for 100 hours and then it should be limited to short bursts of speed until 150 hours have been logged.

During this period, oil consumption may be higher than normal. It is therefore important to frequently check and correct oil level. At no time, during the break-in or later, should the oil level be allowed to drop below the bottom line on the dipstick. If the oil level is low, the oil will become overheated resulting in insufficient lubrication and increased wear.

After 10 Hours Of Operation Service

It is essential that the oil be changed and the oil filter rotor and filter screen be cleaned after the first 10 hours of operation. In addition, it is a good idea to change the oil and clean the oil filter rotor and filter screen at the completion of the 100 hours of operation to ensure that all of the particles produced during break-in are removed from the lubrication system. The small added expense may be considered a smart investment that will pay off in increased engine life.

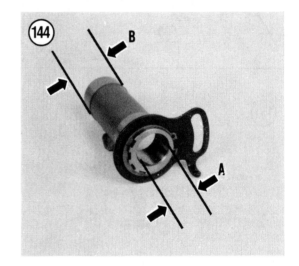

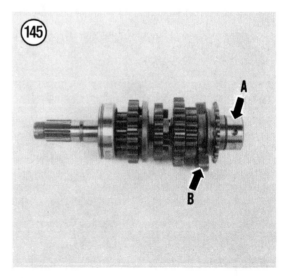

Table 1 500 cc ENGINE SPECIFICATIONS

Item	Specifications	Wear limit
General		
Type	4-Stroke, air-cooled, SOHC	
Number of cylinder	1	
Bore and stroke	89.0 × 80.0 mm (3.50 × 3.15 in.)	
Displacement	498 cc (30.37 cu. In.)	
Compression ratio	8.6 to 1	
Compression pressure	175 psi (12.5 kg.cm^2)	
Cylinder head warpage		0.1 mm (0.004 in.)
Cylinder		
Bore	89.00-89.01 mm (3.5039-3.5043 in.)	89.11 mm (3.508 in.)
Out of round	–	0.05 mm (0.002 in.)
Piston/cylinder clearance	0.01-0.04 mm (0.0004-0.0016 in.)	0.1 mm (0.004 in.)
Warpage across top	–	0.1 mm (0.004 in.)
Piston		
Diameter	88.97-88.99 mm (3.503-3.504 in.)	88.88 mm (3.499 in.)
Clearance in bore	0.01-0.04 mm (0.0004-0.0016 in.)	0.10 mm (0.004 in.)
Piston pin bore	21.002-21.008 mm (0.8268-0.8271 in.)	21.08 mm (0.830 in.)
Piston pin outer diameter	20.994-21.000 mm (0.8265-0.8268 in.)	20.96 mm (0.825 in.)
Piston rings		
Number of rings		
Compression	2	
Oil control	1	
Ring end gap		
Top and second	0.30-0.50 mm (0.0118 -0.0197 in.)	0.65 mm (0.026 in.)
Oil (side rail)	0.2-0.9 mm (0.007-0.035 in.)	NA
Ride side clearance		
Top ring	0.030-0.065 mm (0.0012-0.0026 in.)	0.12 mm (0.006 in.)
Second ring	0.015-0.045 mm (0.0006-0.0018 in.)	0.12 mm (0.006 in.)
Oil control	NA	
Crankshaft/connecting rod		
Small end inner diameter	21.020-21.041 mm (0.8276-0.8284 in.)	21.07 mm (0.830 in.)
Connecting rod big end side clearance	0.05-0.65 mm (0.002-0.0256 in.)	0.80 mm (0.031 in.)
Connecting rod big radial clearance	0.006-0.018 mm (0.0002-0.0007 in.)	0.05 mm (0.002 in.)

(continued)

Table 1 500 cc ENGINE SPECIFICATIONS

Item	Specifications	Wear limit
Camshaft		
Cam lobe height		
Intake	36.431 mm	36.23 mm (1.426 in.)
	(1.4343 in.)	
Exhaust	36.466 mm	36.27 mm (1.428 in.)
	(1.4357 in.)	
Cam journal O.D.		
Left-hand end	19.954-19.975 mm	19.9 mm (0.78 in.)
	(0.7856-0.7864 in.)	
Right-hand end	23.954-23.975 mm	23.9 mm (0.94 in.)
	(0.9431-0.9439 in.)	
Cam bearing surface in cylinder		
head and cylinder head cover		
Left-hand side	20.000-20.021 mm	20.05 mm (0.789 in.)
	(0.7874-0.7882 in.)	
Right-hand side	24.000-24.021 mm	24.05 mm (0.947 in.)
	(0.9449-0.9457 in.)	
Valves		
Valves stem outer diameter		
Intake	6.575-6.590 mm	6.565 mm (0.258 in.)
	(0.2589-0.2594 in.)	
Exhaust	6.560-6.570 mm	6.55 mm (0.2579 in.)
	(0.2583-0.2587 in.)	
Valves guide inner diameter		
Intake and exhaust	6.600-6.615 mm	6.63 mm (0.261 in.)
	(0.2598-0.2604 in.)	
Stem to guide clearance		
Intake	0.010-0.040 mm	0.065 mm (0.0026 in.)
	(0.0004-0.0016 in.)	
Exhaust	0.030-0.055 mm	0.080 mm (0.0031 in.)
Valve face width		
Intake and exhaust	1.2-1.4 mm	2.0 mm (0.08 in.)
	(0.048-0.055 in.)	
Valve springs free length		
Intake and exhaust		
Inner	38.1 mm (1.50 in.)	37.0 mm (1.46 in.)
Outer	36.24 mm (1.43 in.)	35.3 mm (1.39 in.)
Rocker arm assembly		
Rocker arm bore ID	12.000-12.018 mm	12.05 mm (0.474 in.)
	(0.4724-0.4731 in.)	
Rocker arm shaft ID	11.966-11.984 mm	11.91 mm(0.469 in.)
	(0.4711-0.4718 in.)	
Oil pump		
Inner to outer	0.15 mm (0.006 in.)	0.20 mm (0.08 in.)
rotor tip clearance		
Outer rotor to	0.15-0.21 mm	0.25 mm (0.010 in.)
body clarance	(0.006-0.008 in.)	
Rotor end to body	0.02-0.08 mm	0.12 mm (0.005 in.)
clearance	(0.0008-0.003 in.)	
(continued)		

Table 1 500 cc ENGINE SPECIFICATIONS (continued)

Item	Specifications	Wear limit
Counter balancer system		
Front		
Shaft holder ID	26.007-26.020 mm (1.0239-1.0244 in.)	26.05 mm (1.026 in.)
Shaft holder OD	39.964-39.980 mm (1.5734-1.5740 in.)	39.91 mm (1.571 in.)
Rear		
Balancer ID	26.007-26.020 mm (1.0239-1.0244 in.)	26.05 mm (1.026 in.)
Kickstarter		
Gear ID	22.000-22.021 mm (0.8661-0.8670 in.)	22.10 mm (0.870 in.)
Shaft OD (where gear rides)	21.959-21.980 mm (0.8645-0.8653 in.)	21.91 mm (0.863 in.)
NA. Honda does not provide service information for all items nor all models		

4

Table 2 ENGINE TORQUE SPECIFICATIONS

Item	N•m	ft.-lb
Engine mounting bolts (upper 3)		
8 mm bolts–all models	20-35	14-25
10 mm bolts		
XL series	30-50	22-36
XR series	45-60	33-44
Engine hanger bolts (front 4)		
Upper 8 mm bolts–all models	30-50	22-36
Lower 10 mm bolts		
XL series	30-50	22-36
XR series	45-60	33-44
Engine mounting bolts		
10 mm–XL series	30-50	22-36
12 mm–XR series	70-100	51-74
Valve adjuster cover volts	10-14	7-10
Cylinder head nuts	22-28	16-20
Cylinder head cover bolts		
and acorn nut	10-14	7-10
Cylinder front, rear and		
side bolts	22-28	16-20
Cylinder nut (XR500R)	22-28	16-20
Cam sprocket bolts	17-23	12-17
Cam chain tensioner bolt	10-14	7-10
Ignition advance mechanism nut	45-60	33-44
Right- and left-hand crankcase	8-12	6-9
cover bolts		
Alternator rotor bolt	100-120	74-87
Upper crankcase bolts		
6 mm bolts	10-14	7-10
8 mm bolts	22-28	16-20
Lower crankcase bolts		
6 mm bolts	10-14	7-10
8 mm bolts	22-28	16-20
9 mm bolts	27-32	20-23
10 mm bolts	33-37	24-27
Balancer holder lockbolt	22-28	16-20

CHAPTER FIVE

RFVC ENGINES

All models covered in this chapter are equipped with a rather unique 4-valve, air-cooled, 4-stroke, single cylinder engine with a single overhead camshaft. The engine is called the Radial Four Valve Combustion (RFVC) engine. The cylinder head incorporates 2 intake and 2 exhaust valves arranged radially. This design allows the largest possible valves to maximize the intake and exhaust efficiency. Each pair of dual valves has its own set of rocker arms and each valve has it own adjuster.

The crankshaft is supported by 2 large ball bearings and engine vibration is minimized by a counter-rotating balancer that is driven off the crankshaft.

To ease starting the engine, it has a starter decompressor. As the kickstarter pedal is depressed, a cam on the pedal operates a lever that transmits movement via a cable to the decompressor valve lifter on the cylinder head. This lifter opens the exhaust valves momentarily and then allows them to close as the pedal continues its downward travel.

Engine lubrication is by wet sump with the oil pump located on the right-hand side of the engine and is gear driven by the crankshaft.

This chapter contains information for removal, inspection, service and reassembly of the engine. Although the clutch and transmission are located within the engine, they are covered in Chapter Six to simplify this material.

Table 1 provides complete specifications for the engine and **Table 2** lists all of the engine torque specifications. **Table 1** and **Table 2** are located at the end of this chapter.

Before beginning work, re-read Chapter One of this book. You will do a better job with this information fresh in your mind.

Throughout the text there is frequent mention of the right-hand and left-hand side of the engine. This refers to the engine as it sits in the bike's frame, *not* as it sits on your workbench. The right- and left-hand refers to a rider sitting on the seat facing forward.

ENGINE PRINCIPLES

Figure 1 explains how the engine works. This will be helpful when troubleshooting or repairing the engine.

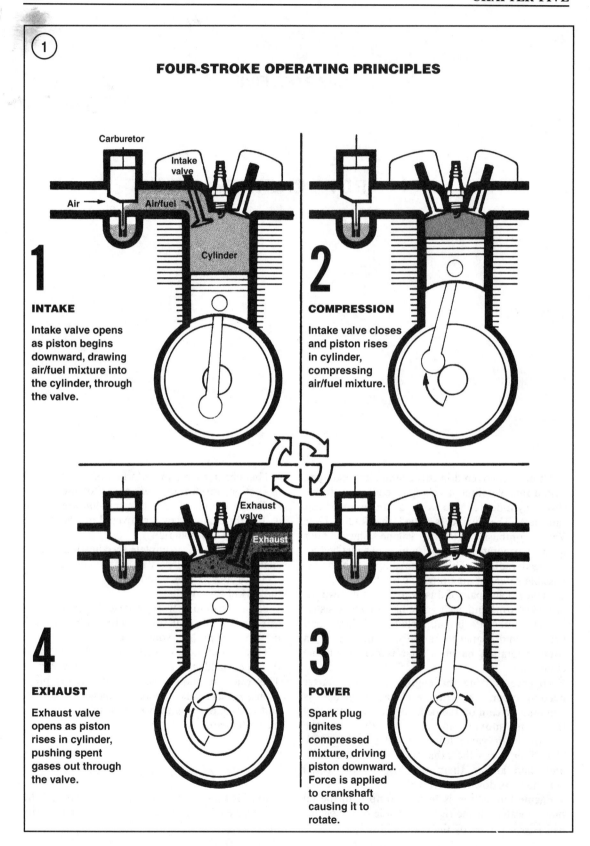

① FOUR-STROKE OPERATING PRINCIPLES

1

INTAKE

Intake valve opens
as piston begins
downward, drawing
air/fuel mixture into
the cylinder, through
the valve.

2

COMPRESSION

Intake valve closes
and piston rises
in cylinder,
compressing
air/fuel mixture.

4

EXHAUST

Exhaust valve
opens as piston
rises in cylinder,
pushing spent
gases out through
the valve.

3

POWER

Spark plug
ignites
compressed
mixture, driving
piston downward.
Force is applied
to crankshaft
causing it to
rotate.

ENGINE COOLING

Cooling is provided by air passing over the cooling fins on the engine cylinder head and cylinder. It is very important to keep these fins free from build-up of dirt, oil, grease and other foreign matter. Brush out the fins with a whisk broom or small stiff paint brush.

CAUTION
Remember, these fins are thin in order to dissipate heat and may be damaged if struck too hard.

SERVICING
ENGINE IN FRAME

The following components can be serviced while the engine is mounted in the frame. The bike's frame is a great holding fixture for breaking loose stubborn bolts and nuts.

  a. Carburetor.
  b. Kickstarter.
  c. Alternator.
  d. Clutch assembly.
  e. External shift mechanism.

ENGINE
REMOVAL/INSTALLATION

WARNING
Because of the engine's weight, 2 people are required to remove the engine safely.

1. Drain the engine oil as described in Chapter Three.
2. Remove the bolts securing the skid plate (**Figure 2**) and remove the skid plate.
3. Remove both side covers and the seat.
4. Remove the bolts securing the right-hand footpeg and remove the footpeg.
5. Remove the pivot bolt on the rear brake pedal. Move the brake pedal assembly to the rear. It is not necessary to completely remove the assembly.
6. Place wood blocks under the frame to support the bike securely.
7. Remove the fuel tank as described in Chapter Seven.
8. Remove the exhaust system as described in Chapter Seven.
9. Remove the carburetor as described in Chapter Seven.
10. Disconnect the spark plug lead and tie it up out of the way.
11. Remove the bolts (**Figure 3**) securing the external oil pipe and remove the oil pipe from the engine. Don't lose the sealing washers on each side of the fittings on the oil pipe.
12. Disconnect the starter decompressor cable(s) (A, **Figure 4**) from the cylinder head cover.
13. Disconnect the oil tank breather tube (B, **Figure 4**) from the cylinder head cover.
14. Remove the bolt securing the gear shift lever and remove the gear shift lever.
15. Slacken the clutch cable at the hand lever. Disconnect the clutch cable from at the crankcase cover.
16. Disconnect the alternator electrical connector.
17. Disconnect the ignition pulse generator wires at the electrical connector.

5

18. Remove the bolts securing the drive sprocket cover and remove the cover.

19. Remove the bolts (A, **Figure 5**) securing the drive sprocket.

20. Rotate the drive sprocket holder (B, **Figure 5**) in either direction and slide it off the shaft.

21. Loosen the rear axle nut and move the snail adjusters to loosen the drive chain.

22. Push the rear wheel forward and remove the drive sprocket and drive chain from the shaft.

23. Disconnect the crankcase breather tube from the crankcase.

24. To disconnect the oil lines, perform the following:

    a. Hold onto the fittings either on the metal oil line or the frame and unscrew the flexible oil lines from the frame (**Figure 6**).

    b. Remove the bolts securing the oil line assemblies to the engine (**Figure 7**) and remove the oil lines. Don't lose the O-ring seals on the oil lines.

NOTE
If you are just removing the engine and are not planning to disassemble it, do not perform Step 25. The engine assembly is small enough that external components can be left on during engine removal.

25. If the engine is going to be disassembled, remove the following parts.

    a. Remove the alternator as described in Chapter Eight.

    b. Remove the clutch assembly as described in Chapter Six.

    c. Remove the external shift mechanism as described in Chapter Six.

    d. Remove the oil pump assembly as described in this chapter.

26. Take a final look all over the engine to make sure everything has been disconnected.

27. Place a suitable size jack, with a piece of wood to protect the crankcase, under the engine. Apply a small amount of jack pressure up on the engine.

28. Remove the engine upper hanger bolts (**Figure 8**) and nuts and remove the hanger plates.

29. Remove the bolts (A, **Figure 9**) securing the front hanger plates to the frame on each side.

30. Remove the front through-bolt and nut (B, **Figure 9**). Remove the hanger plates.

31. Remove the bolts securing the upper rear hanger plates on the right-hand side.

32. Remove the upper rear through-bolt and nut from the left-hand side. Remove the hanger plate on the right-hand side.

33. Remove the lower front through-bolt (A, **Figure 10**) from the right-hand side. Don't lose the spacer (B, **Figure 10**) on the right-hand side.

CAUTION
Continually adjust jack pressure during engine removal and installation to prevent damage to the mounting bolts threads and hardware.

WARNING
The following steps require the aid of a helper to safely remove the engine assembly from the frame.

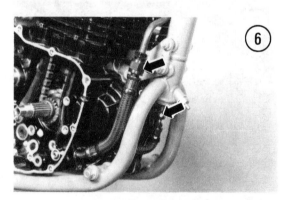

34. Pull the engine assembly up and slightly forward. Remove the engine from the right-hand side. Take it to a workbench for further disassembly.

35. Install by reversing these removal steps, noting the following.

36. Be sure to install the spacer (B, **Figure 10**) on the right-hand side of the lower front through-bolt.

37. Tighten the mounting bolts and nuts to the torque specifications in **Table 2**.

38. Be sure to install a sealing washer on each side of the fittings on the external oil pipe. Tighten the union bolt securely.

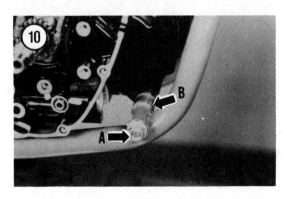

39. Fill the engine with the recommended type and quantity of oil; refer to Chapter Three.

40. Refer to Chapter Three and adjust the following:
   a. Clutch.
   b. Starter decompressor.
   c. Throttle grip free play.
   d. Drive chain slack.
   e. Rear brake pedal free play.

41. Start the engine and check for leaks.

CYLINDER HEAD COVER AND CAMSHAFT

The cylinder head cover carries the rocker arm assemblies and the starter decompression lever.

The camshaft is held in place between the cylinder head cover and the cylinder head.

The camshaft is driven by a chain off the sprocket on the crankshaft.

The camshaft on the 1988-2000 XR600R and XR650L models, also incorporates the starter decompression mechanism on the right-hand or driven sprocket end of the camshaft. Camshaft removal and installation is the same for all models and years covered in this chapter.

Removal

> *CAUTION*
> *To prevent any warpage and damage, remove the cylinder head cover only when the engine is at room temperature.*

1. Remove the engine from the frame as described in this chapter.

2. Remove the side covers and the seat.

3. Remove the fuel tank as described in Chapter Seven.

4. Remove the valve adjuster covers.

5. If removed, reinstall the alternator rotor and the left-hand crankcase cover. Remove the inspection covers on the left-hand crankcase cover.

6. Using the bolt on the alternator rotor, rotate the crankshaft counterclockwise until the piston is at top dead center (TDC) on the compression stroke. Check that the "T" mark on the alternator rotor aligns with the stationary pointer on the crankcase cover (**Figure 11**).

> *NOTE*
> *A cylinder at TDC on its compression stroke will have free play in all of its*

rocker arms, indicating that both the intake and exhaust valves are closed. If the rocker arms are tight, the cylinder is on its exhaust stroke. Rotate the crankshaft one full turn and check again to make sure the rocker arms are loose.

7. Using a crisscross pattern, loosen the bolts (**Figure 12**) securing the cylinder head cover. Remove the bolts.

8. Remove the cylinder head cover and gasket. Don't lose the locating dowel.

9. Remove the camshaft chain tensioner as described in this chapter.

10. Using the alternator rotor, rotate the engine until one of the camshaft sprocket bolts is visible. Remove that bolt.

11. Again rotate the engine until the other camshaft sprocket bolt is visible. Remove that bolt.

12. Pull the camshaft chain sprocket and camshaft chain toward the center of the engine and off of the shoulder on the camshaft.

13. Tie a piece of wire to the camshaft chain and secure the loose end to the exterior of the engine. This will prevent the camshaft chain from falling into the crankcase.

14. Remove the camshaft and sprocket from the cylinder head.

> *CAUTION*
> *If the crankshaft must be rotated when the camshaft is removed, pull up on the camshaft chain and keep it taut while rotating the crankshaft. Make certain that the chain is positioned correctly on the crankshaft sprocket. If this is not done, the chain may become kinked and may damage both the chain and the sprocket on the crankshaft.*

Camshaft Inspection

1. Check the camshaft bearings (A, **Figure 13**) for roughness, pitting, galling and play by rotating them by hand. If any roughness or play can be felt in a bearing, it must be replaced.

2. Check the camshaft lobes for wear. The lobes should show no signs of scoring and the edges should be square. Slight damage may be removed with a silicon carbide oilstone. Use No. 100-120 grit stone initially, then polish with a No. 280-320 grit stone.

> *NOTE*
> *The cam is dark in color due to the manufacturing heat treating process. It*

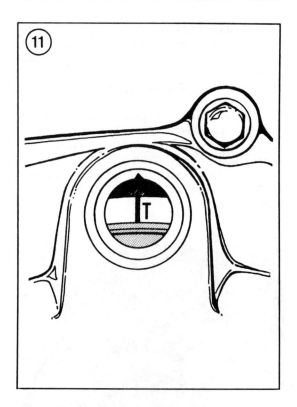

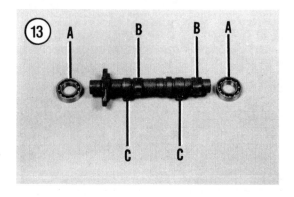

is not due to lack of oil pressure or excessive engine heat.

3. Even though the camshaft lobe surface appears to be satisfactory, with no visible signs of wear, the camshaft lobes must be measured with a micrometer or vernier caliper.

NOTE
Position the camshaft with the camshaft sprocket boss on the right-hand side. The camshaft lobe locations from left to right are as follows: exhaust, intake exhaust, intake.

4. Measure both the intake (B, **Figure 13**) and exhaust (C) lobes of the camshaft. Compare to the dimensions given in **Table 1**. If any of the lobes are worn to the wear limit or less the camshaft must be replaced.

5. Inspect the camshaft sprocket for wear, replace if necessary.

6. On 1988-1990 XR600R models, inspect the starter decompression mechanism for wear or damage. Disassemble it if necessary as described in this chapter.

Starter Decompression Mechanism
Disassembly/Inspection/Assembly
(1988-1990 XR600R Models)

Refer to **Figure 14** for this procedure.

This procedure requires the use of a hydraulic press and insert to remove the decompression components

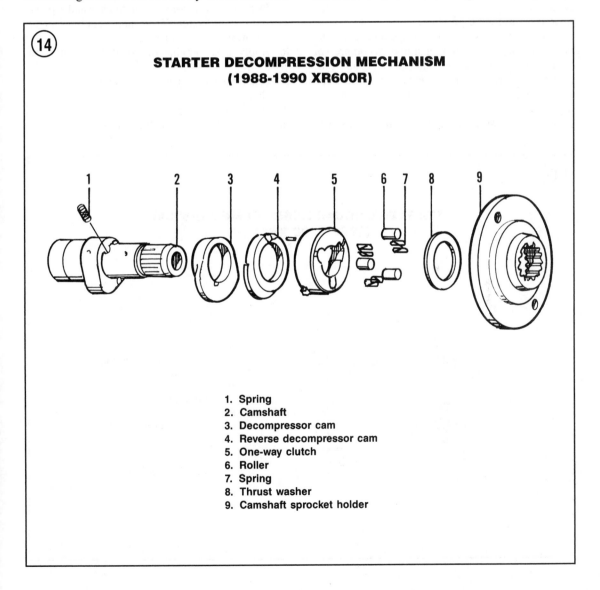

STARTER DECOMPRESSION MECHANISM
(1988-1990 XR600R)

1. Spring
2. Camshaft
3. Decompressor cam
4. Reverse decompressor cam
5. One-way clutch
6. Roller
7. Spring
8. Thrust washer
9. Camshaft sprocket holder

from the right-hand end of the camshaft. If you don't have the equipment or feel unqualified to carry out this procedure correctly, have a dealer perform this operation for you.

1. Remove the bearing from each end of the camshaft.

2. Install the insert under the camshaft sprocket holder on the right-hand end of the camshaft.

3. Install the camshaft and insert in the hydraulic press.

4. Place a suitable size rod or socket extension onto the end of the camshaft. The extension must be small enough to pass through the inner diameter of the camshaft sprocket holder being pressed off of the camshaft.

5. While holding onto the camshaft, slowly press the camshaft sprocket holder off of the end of the camshaft.

6. Release hydraulic pressure.

7. Remove the camshaft from the hydraulic press and hold the camshaft and the remaining decompressor components with the right-hand end facing up. If the camshaft is turned over, the remainder of the parts will slide off of the camshaft and could be lost or damaged.

8. Take the camshaft assembly to the workbench.

9. Slide off the thrust washer.

10. Perform this step close down to the surface of the work bench to prevent losing the small parts.

NOTE
When the one-way clutch is removed from the end of the camshaft, the small rollers and springs will "pop" out of the one-way clutch. Don't lose them.

11. Slide off the one-way clutch along with its rollers and springs. Don't lose the small pin in the backside of the one-way clutch.

12. Slide off the reverse decompressor cam.

13. Slide off the decompressor cam and remove the small spring from its receptacle in the camshaft.

14. Clean all parts in solvent and thoroughly dry with compressed air.

15. Inspect all parts for wear or damage and replace if necessary. Honda does not supply service specifications for any of these parts.

16. Apply clean engine oil to all parts prior to installation.

17. Install the small spring into its receptacle in the camshaft.

18. Position the decompressor cam with the cam lobe side going on last and install the decompressor cam

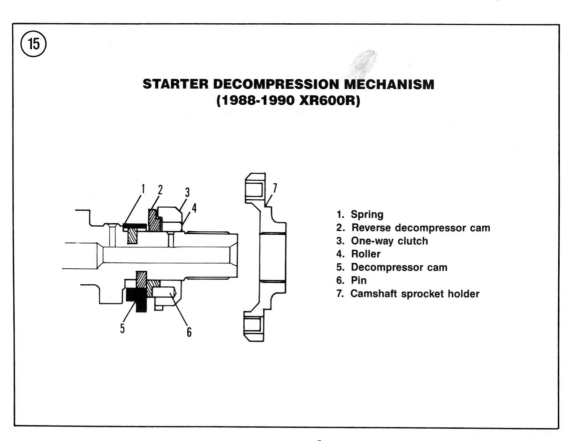

⑮

STARTER DECOMPRESSION MECHANISM
(1988-1990 XR600R)

1. Spring
2. Reverse decompressor cam
3. One-way clutch
4. Roller
5. Decompressor cam
6. Pin
7. Camshaft sprocket holder

onto the camshaft. Carefully index the receptacles in the decompressor cam onto the spring in the camshaft and the locating pins. Make sure they are properly meshed.

19. Position the reverse decompressor cam with the cam lobe side going on first and install the reverse decompressor cam onto the camshaft.

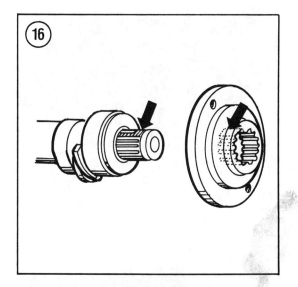

20. Install the springs and rollers into the one-way clutch and slide the one-way clutch assembly onto the camshaft. Align the pin on the backside of the one-way clutch with the receptacle in the reverse decompressor and push the one-way clutch all the way on until it bottoms out.

21. Install the thrust washer.

22. Refer to **Figure 15** to make sure all parts have been installed correctly. Reassemble if necessary.

23. Hold the thrust washer up against the one-way clutch and rotate the one-way clutch *counterclockwise* as viewed from the right-hand end of the camshaft. The one-way clutch should *only* be able to rotate *counterclockwise* and *not* in the other direction. If it can rotate in both directions the springs or rollers within the one-way clutch are either installed incorrectly or are faulty and must be replaced.

24. The sprocket holder can be installed onto the camshaft in only one position. Align the wide spline on the sprocket holder with the lug on the camshaft splines as shown in **Figure 16**.

25. Place the camshaft assembly into the hydraulic press and set the left-hand end on the press plates. Have an assistant hold the camshaft in place.

26. Place a suitable size socket onto the end of the cam sprocket holder and slowly press the cam sprocket holder onto the camshaft until it bottoms out on the camshaft shoulder.

27. Release the hydraulic pressure and remove the socket and camshaft.

28. Install the bearing onto each end of the camshaft.

Cylinder Head Cover
Disassembly/Inspection/Assembly

It is recommended that one rocker arm assembly be disassembled, inspected and then assembled to avoid the intermixing of parts. This is especially true of a well run-in engine as different sets of parts have taken a set and wear pattern.

1. To remove the starter decompressor valve lifter lever, perform the following:
   a. Remove the dowel pin (**Figure 17**) securing the lever.
   b. Remove the lifter lever and return spring from the cylinder head cover.

2. Unscrew the valve adjuster covers.

3. To remove the sub-rocker arm assembly, perform the following:
   a. Unscrew the exhaust valve sub-rocker arm shaft (**Figure 18**).
   b. Remove the rocker arm shaft, copper sealing washer and wave washer.

c. Remove the sub-rocker arm (A, **Figure 19**).

d. Repeat Steps a-c for the intake valve sub-rocker arm shaft and sub-rocker arm.

4. To remove the main rocker arm assemblies, perform the following:

    a. Unscrew the main rocker arm shaft (**Figure 20**).

    b. Remove the main rocker arm shaft, copper sealing washer and wave washers.

    c. Remove the main rocker arms.

5. Wash all parts in cleaning solvent and dry thoroughly.

6. Inspect the sub-rocker arm components as follows:

    a. Inspect the sub-rocker arm pad where it rides on the main rocker arm adjuster. If the pad is scratched or unevenly worn, inspect the main rocker arm where the sub-rocker arm rides for scoring, chipping or flat spots. Replace the rocker arm if defective.

    b. Measure the inside diameter of the sub-rocker arm bore with a snap gauge and check against the dimensions in **Table 1**. Replace if worn to the service limit or greater.

    c. Inspect the rocker arm shaft for signs of wear or scoring. Measure the outside diameter with a micrometer and check against the dimensions in **Table 1**. Replace if worn to the service limit or less.

7. Inspect the main rocker arm components as follows:

    a. Inspect the main rocker arm pad where it rides on the cam lobe and where the adjuster rides on the sub-rocker arm. If the pad is scratched or unevenly worn, inspect the cam lobe for scoring, chipping or flat spots. Replace the rocker arm if defective.

    b. Measure the inside diameter of the main rocker arm bore with a snap gauge and check against the dimensions in **Table 1**. Replace if worn to the service limit or greater.

    c. Inspect the rocker arm shaft for signs of wear or scoring. Measure the outside diameter with a micrometer and check against the dimensions in **Table 1**. Replace if worn to the service limit or less.

8. Coat the rocker arm shaft and rocker arm bores with assembly oil.

9. To install the main rocker arm assemblies, perform the following:

    a. Position the main rocker arms as shown in **Figure 21**. Each main rocker arm has its own identifying mark. The exhaust valves are identified as "A" (A, **Figure 21**) and the intake valves are marked "B" (B, **Figure 21**).

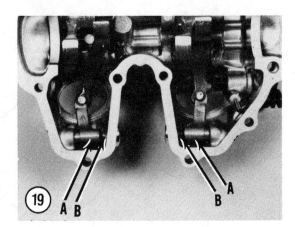

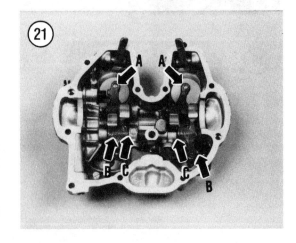

b. Place a wave washer on the inboard side of each rocker arm (C, **Figure 21**).

c. Place a copper sealing washer on each rocker arm shaft.

d. Push the main rocker arm shaft through the cylinder head cover, rocker arm, wave washer (models so equipped), cover boss, wave washer and rocker arm.

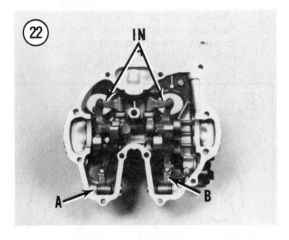

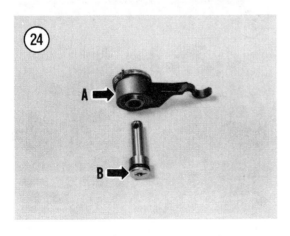

e. Screw in the main rocker arm shaft and tighten to the torque specification listed in **Table 2**.

10. To install the sub-rocker arm assemblies, perform the following:

a. Position the main rocker arms as shown in **Figure 22**. Each sub-rocker arm has its own identifying mark. The exhaust valves are identified "A" (A, **Figure 22**) (left-hand side) or "B" (B, **Figure 22**) (right-hand side). The intake valves are marked with an "IN".

b. Place a wave washer on the intake valve sub-rocker arm as shown in **Figure 23** and on the exhaust valve sub-rocker arm as shown in B, **Figure 19**.

c. Place a copper sealing washer on each rocker arm shaft.

d. On the intake valve sub-rocker arm, push the sub-rocker arm shafts through the cylinder head cover, rocker arm, wave washer and cover boss.

e. On the exhaust valve sub-rocker arm, push the sub-rocker arm shafts through the cylinder head cover, wave washer, rocker arm and cover boss.

f. Screw in each sub-rocker arm shaft and tighten to the torque specification listed in **Table 2**.

11. Perform Steps 3-10 for each rocker arm or sub-rocker arm assembly.

12. Inspect the cam chain tensioner lifter assembly (A, **Figure 24**) for wear or damage. Replace the O-ring seal (B, **Figure 24**) if it is starting to harden or deteriorate.

13. To install the starter decompressor lever, perform the following:

a. Install the spring into the lifter lever.

b. Install the lifter lever into the cylinder head cover and position the spring onto the boss.

c. Align the cutout in the lifter lever shaft with the dowel pin hole in the cylinder head cover.

d. Apply a light coat of grease to the dowel pin. This will hold the dowel in place when the cylinder head cover is turned upside down during installation.

e. Install the dowel pin (**Figure 17**) into the cylinder head cover and past the lifter lever shaft.

Installation

1. Lubricate all camshaft lobes with molybdenum disulfide grease. Apply assembly oil or clean engine oil to the camshaft bearings.

2. If removed, install the bearings onto the camshaft. The sealed bearing goes onto the sprocket boss end of the cam with the sealed side facing out.

> *CAUTION*
> *When rotating the crankshaft, keep the camshaft chain taut and engaged with the timing sprocket on the crankshaft.*

3. If removed, temporarily install the alternator cover and remove the timing mark hole cap.
4. The engine must be at top dead center (TDC) for the following steps for correct valve timing. Hold the camshaft chain out and taut while rotating the crankshaft to avoid damage to the chain and/or the crankcase.
5. Pull up on the chain, making sure it is properly engaged on the crankshaft sprocket. Rotate the engine until the "T" timing mark on the alternator rotor aligns with the fixed notch on the crankcase cover (**Figure 13**).
6. If removed, install the camshaft bearing stopper pins (**Figure 25**) into the cylinder head. They *must* be installed as they control camshaft bearing end-float.
7. Position the camshaft with the sprocket boss toward the left-hand side. Install the camshaft through the camshaft chain and into position in the cylinder head.
8. Position the camshaft sprocket with the flush side toward the left-hand side and install the camshaft sprocket onto the camshaft.
9. Position the camshaft sprocket so the alignment marks are aligned with the top surface of the cylinder head.
10. Make sure the camshaft chain is meshed properly with the drive sprocket on the crankshaft.
11. Hold the camshaft sprocket in this position and install the chain onto the camshaft sprocket.

> *NOTE*
> *The camshaft can be positioned with the lobes up or down as long as the bolt holes align with the camshaft sprocket and the timing marks on the sprocket align with the cylinder head (**Figure 26**). It is easier if the lobes are facing down as this will place less of a load on the rocker arms during cylinder head cover installation.*

12. Pull the camshaft chain and sprocket assembly up onto the shoulder on the camshaft. Check that the alignment marks are still aligned with the top surface of the cylinder head (**Figure 26**) and that the alternator rotor "T" mark is still aligned (**Figure 13**).
13. If alignment is incorrect, reposition the camshaft chain on the sprocket and recheck the alignment.

> *CAUTION*
> *Very expensive damage could result from improper camshaft and camshaft chain alignment. Recheck your work several times to be sure alignment is correct.*

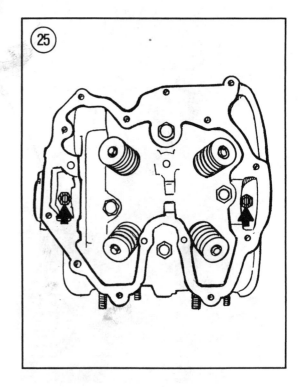

14. Rotate the camshaft until the sprocket boss bolt hole aligns with the exposed bolt in the camshaft sprocket.

15. When alignment is correct, perform the following:

    a. Install the bolt into the exposed bolt hole. Tighten only finger-tight at this time.

    b. Rotate the engine to expose the other bolt hole and install the other bolt.

    c. Make sure the camshaft sprocket is correctly seated on the camshaft boss.

    d. Tighten both bolts to the torque specification listed in **Table 2**.

> *CAUTION*
> *If there is any binding while rotating the crankshaft,* **stop**. *Determine the cause before proceeding.*

16. After installation is complete, rotate the crankshaft several times using the bolt on the alternator rotor.

17. Make one final check to make sure alignment is correct. The "T" timing mark must be aligned with the mark and the timing marks on the camshaft sprocket must be perfectly aligned with the top surface of the cylinder head.

18. Install the camshaft chain tensioner as described in this chapter.

19. Fill the oil pocket in the cylinder head with new engine oil so the cam lobes are submerged in the oil for the initial start up.

20. Make sure all locating dowel are in place in the cylinder head.

21. Loosen the valve adjusters fully. This is to relieve strain on the rocker arms and cylinder head cover during installation.

22. Wrap a small rubber band (**Figure 27**) around each sub-rocker arm and then attach it to the exterior of the cylinder head cover. This is to hold the main and sub-rocker arms up during cylinder head cover installation.

23. Make sure all sealing surfaces of the cylinder head and the cylinder head cover are completely clean. Spray both sealing surfaces with contact cleaner and wipe dry with a clean lint-free cloth.

> *CAUTION*
> *Do not destroy the silicone surface on the cylinder head cover gasket as it will destroy its sealing ability.*

24. Install a new cylinder head cover gasket.

25. Preload the starter decompressor lever and install the cylinder head cover.

26. Remove the rubber bands.

27. Install the 6 mm and 8 mm bolts and tighten in a crisscross pattern in 2-3 steps to the torque specification listed in **Table 2**.

28. Adjust the valves and starter decompressor as described in Chapter Three.

CAMSHAFT CHAIN TENSIONER

Removal

1A. On 1983-1986 models, remove the dowel pin (**Figure 28**) securing the camshaft chain tensioner.

1B. On 1987 models, unscrew the bolt securing the camshaft chain tensioner.

2. Screw a 6 mm bolt into the threaded hole (**Figure 29**) in the camshaft chain tensioner.
3. Withdraw the camshaft chain tensioner shaft.

> *WARNING*
> *In the next step, the camshaft chain tensioner is under spring tension. As the tensioner is removed from the cylinder head the spring will snap but will **not** fly out. It is captured in the tensioner. Do **not** put your fingers down into the cylinder cavity during this procedure as they may get cut by the spring.*

4. Carefully withdraw the camshaft chain tensioner from the cylinder head.

> *NOTE*
> *Do not drop the camshaft sprocket bolts as they may become lodged in the camshaft tensioner slippers. If this happens; further engine disassembly will be necessary to retrieve them.*

Installation

The camshaft chain tensioner can be installed with or without special tools. Both ways are included in this procedure.

If removed, install the camshaft chain tensioner spring onto the tensioner lifter as shown in **Figure 30**.

With special tool

1. Partially install the tensioner lifter assembly into the cylinder head with the curved surface on the arm facing toward the camshaft chain.
2. Insert Honda special tool (tensioner setting holder, part No. 07973-MG3001) onto the tensioner as shown in **Figure 31**.
3. Push the tensioner lifter assembly down until the hole aligns with the hole in the cylinder head.
4. Apply clean engine oil to the O-ring seal on the tensioner shaft and install the tensioner shaft. Use a wide-bladed screwdriver and rotate the shaft until the shaft hole aligns with the hole in the cylinder head cover.
5A. On 1983-1986 models, install the dowel pin (**Figure 32**) securing the camshaft chain tensioner. Push it down all the way.
5B. On 1987 models, install the bolt securing the camshaft chain and tighten securely.
6. Remove the special tool.

Without special tool

1. Wrap a piece of wire around the tensioner lifter and the spring and compress the spring (**Figure 33**).

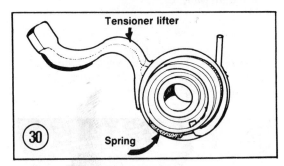

Tensioner lifter

Spring

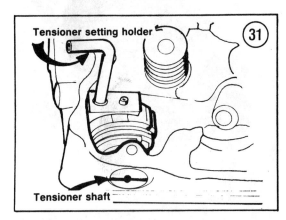

Tensioner setting holder

Tensioner shaft

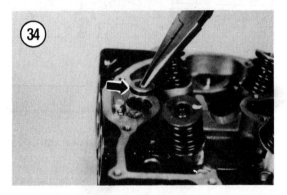

2. Partially install the tensioner lifter assembly into the cylinder head with the curved surface on the arm facing toward the camshaft chain.

3. Push the tensioner lifter assembly down until the hole aligns with the hole in the cylinder head. You may have to use a long narrow-bladed screwdriver to help push the spring down into position onto the flat surface within the cylinder head.

4. Apply clean engine oil to the O-ring seal on the tensioner shaft and install the tensioner shaft. Use a wide-bladed screwdriver and rotate the shaft until the shaft hole aligns with the hole in the cylinder head cover.

5A. On 1983-1986 models, install the dowel pin (**Figure 32**) securing the camshaft chain tensioner. Push it down all the way.

5B. On 1987 models, install the bolt securing the camshaft chain and tighten securely.

6. Cut the wire and pull it out. Make sure that all pieces of wire are removed from the engine.

CYLINDER HEAD

Removal/Installation

CAUTION
To prevent any warpage and damage, remove the cylinder head only when the engine is at room temperature.

1. Remove the cylinder head cover and camshaft as described in this chapter.

2. Remove the cylinder head bolt hole plug and O-ring (**Figure 34**).

3. Remove the nuts (**Figure 35**) on the right-hand side.

4. Loosen the cylinder head bolts (**Figure 36**) in a crisscross pattern in 2-3 stages. Remove the bolts and nuts. The washers may stay in the bolt receptacles in the cylinder head. After the cylinder head is removed, turn the cylinder head upside down and remove the washers.

5. If the camshaft bearing stopper pins are loose, remove them. If they are secure in the cylinder head, do not remove them.

6. Loosen the cylinder head by tapping around the perimeter with a rubber or soft faced mallet. If necessary, *gently* pry the head loose with a broad-tipped screwdriver.

CAUTION
Remember the cooling fins are fragile and may be damaged if tapped or pried too hard. Never use a metal hammer.

7. Untie the wire securing the camshaft chain and retie it to the cylinder head.

8. Lift the cylinder head straight up and off the cylinder. Guide the camshaft chain through the opening in the cylinder head and retie the wire to the exterior of the engine. This will prevent the drive chain from falling down into the crankcase.

9. Remove the cylinder head gasket and discard it. Don't lose the locating dowels.

10. Place a clean shop cloth into the camshaft chain opening in the cylinder to prevent the entry of foreign matter.

NOTE
In the following step, removal of the sub-chamber cover is necessary so that any solvent and grinding residue can be removed from the chamber. Nothing mechanical is contained within the chamber.

11. If the valve seats are going to be ground, perform the following:
   a. Remove the bolts securing the sub-chamber cover and remove the cover on the left-hand side.
   b. Remove the cover and gasket.

12. Install by reversing these removal steps, noting the following.

13. Clean the mating surface of the cylinder and cylinder head of any old gasket material.

14. If removed, install the locating dowels in the cylinder.

15. Install a new cylinder head gasket. Make sure the holes align exactly.

16. Apply oil to the threads of the cylinder head bolts and/or nuts.

17. Install the cylinder head bolts and washers and/or nuts and tighten in a crisscross pattern, in 2-3 stages. Tighten to the torque specification listed in **Table 2**.

18. Make sure the O-ring seal is in good condition and install the cylinder head plug and O-ring seal (**Figure 37**).

19. If removed, install the camshaft bearing stopper pins. They *must* be installed as they control the end float of both camshaft bearings.

20. Install the cylinder head cover as described in this chapter.

Inspection

1. Remove all traces of gasket material from the cylinder head mating surfaces.

2. *Without* removing the valves, remove all carbon deposits from the combustion chamber and valve ports with a wire brush. A blunt screwdriver or chisel may be used if care is taken not to damage the head, valves and spark plug threads.

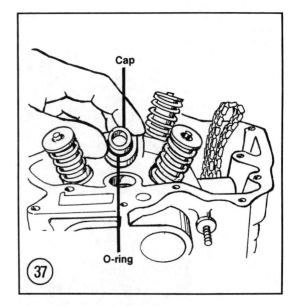

Cap

O-ring

37

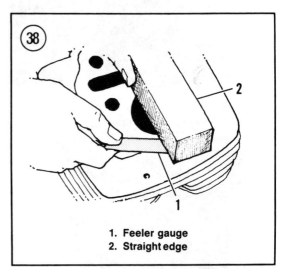

38

1. Feeler gauge
2. Straight edge

39

3. After the carbon is removed from the combustion chamber and the valve intake and exhaust ports, clean the entire head in cleaning solvent. Blow dry with compressed air.

4. Clean away all carbon from the piston crown. Do not remove the carbon ridge at the top of the cylinder bore.

5. Check for cracks in the combustion chamber and exhaust ports. A cracked head must be replaced.

6. After the head has been cleaned thoroughly, place a straightedge across the cylinder head/cylinder gasket surface at several points (**Figure 38**). Measure the warp by inserting a flat feeler gauge between the straightedge and the cylinder head at each location. There should be no warpage; if a small amount is present, it can be resurfaced by a dealer or qualified machine shop. Replace the cylinder head and cylinder head cover as a set if the gasket surface is warped to or beyond the limit listed in **Table 1**.

7. Check the cylinder head cover mating surface using the procedure in Step 6. There should be no warpage.

8. Check the valves and valve guides as described in this chapter.

9. On XR500R and 1983 XL600R models, perform the following:

   a. Inspect the reed valve (A, **Figure 39**) for wear, burning or distortion.

   b. If necessary, remove the screw (B, **Figure 39**) securing the reed valve and reed stopper.

   c. Do not bend or distort the reed stopper.

   d. Install a new reed valve and stopper. Tighten the screw securely.

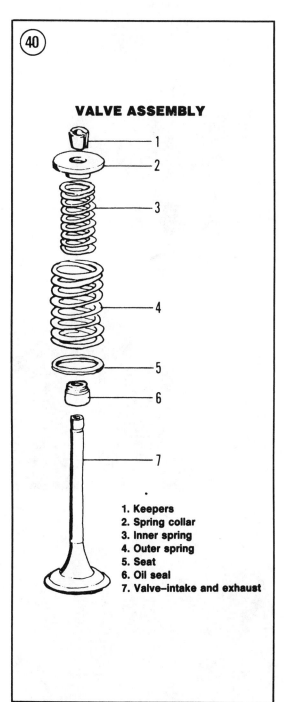

VALVE ASSEMBLY

1. Keepers
2. Spring collar
3. Inner spring
4. Outer spring
5. Seat
6. Oil seal
7. Valve—intake and exhaust

VALVES AND VALVE COMPONENTS

NOTE
General practice among those who do their own service is to remove the cylinder head and take it to a machine shop or dealer for inspection and service. Since the cost is low relative to the required effort and equipment, this is the best approach, even for experienced mechanics. The following procedures are included if you choose to perform these tasks yourself.

Removal

Refer to **Figure 40** for this procedure.

1. Remove the cylinder head as described in this chapter.

CAUTION
To avoid loss of spring tension, do not compress the springs any more than necessary to remove the keepers.

2. Compress the valve springs with a valve compressor tool (**Figure 41**). Remove the valve keepers and release the compression. Remove the valve compressor tool.

3. Remove the valve spring collar and valve springs (**Figure 42**).

4. The spring seat (**Figure 43**) and the valve stem seal (**Figure 44**) may stay in the cylinder head.

5. Before removing the valve, remove any burrs from the valve stem (**Figure 45**). Otherwise the valve guide will be damaged.

6. Remove the valve.

7. On 600 cc models, perform the following to remove the decompressor valve located at the rear of the cylinder head between the 2 intake valves.

    a. Hold onto the valve face with your hand and compress the valve spring with the fingers of your other hand.

    b. Slide the valve retainer from the groove in the valve.

    c. Remove the valve spring.

    d. Before removing the valve, remove any burrs from the valve stem (**Figure 45**). Otherwise the valve guide will be damaged.

8. Mark all parts as they are disassembled so that they will be installed in their same locations.

Inspection

1. Clean the valves with a wire brush and solvent.

2. Inspect the contact surface of each valve for burning or pitting (**Figure 46**). Unevenness of the contact surface is an indication that the valve is not serviceable. The valve contact surface can *not* be ground and must be replaced if defective.

3. Inspect the valve stem for wear and roughness. Pay particular attention to the valve keeper groove and keepers (**Figure 47**).

4. Measure the valve stem for wear (**Figure 48**). If worn to the wear limit listed in **Table 1**, or less the valve must be replaced.

5. Remove all carbon and varnish from the valve guide with a stiff spiral wire brush.

6. Insert each valve in its guide. Hold the valve with the head just slightly off the valve seat and rock it sideways. If it rocks more than slightly, the guide is probably worn and should be replaced. As a final check, take the cylinder to a dealer and have the valve guides measured.

7. Measure each valve spring free length with a vernier caliper (**Figure 49**). All should be within the length specified in **Table 1** with no signs of bends or distortion. Replace defective springs in pairs (inner and outer).

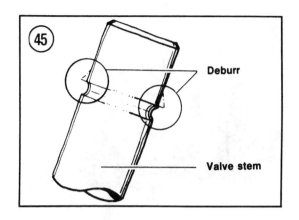

Deburr

Valve stem

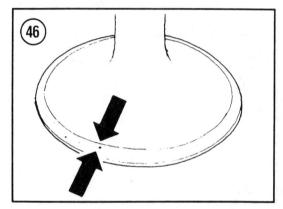

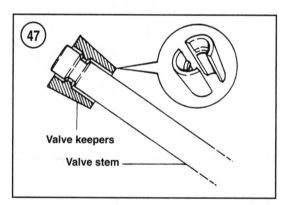

Valve keepers

Valve stem

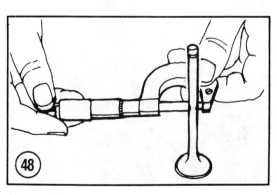

8. Check the valve spring retainer and valve keepers. If they are in good condition they may be reused; replace as necessary.

9. Inspect the valve seats. If worn or burned, they must be reconditioned. This should be performed by a dealer or qualified machine shop.

Installation

1. Coat the valve stems with molybdenum disulfide grease. To avoid damage to the valve stem seal, turn the valve slowly while inserting the valve into the cylinder head.

2. Install the bottom spring retainers and new seals.

3. Install the valve springs with their closer wound coils facing the cylinder head and install the valve spring retainer.

CAUTION
To avoid loss of spring tension, do not compress the springs any more than necessary to install the keepers.

4. Compress the valve springs with a compressor tool (**Figure 41**) and install the valve keepers. Remove the compressor tool.

5. After all springs have been installed, gently tap the end of the valve stem with a soft aluminum or brass drift and hammer. This will ensure that the keepers are properly seated.

6. Install the cylinder head as described in this chapter.

Valve Guide Replacement

When valve guides are worn so that there is excessive stem-to-guide clearance or valve tipping, the guides must be replaced. Replace all, even if only one is worn. This job should only be done by a dealer as special tools are required. If the valve guides are replaced, replace the valves also.

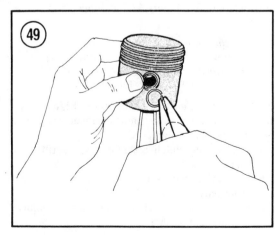

Valve Seat Reconditioning

This job is best left to a dealer or qualified machine shop. They have special equipment and knowledge for this exacting job. You can still save considerable money by removing the cylinder head and taking the head to the shop for repairs.

CYLINDER

Removal

1. Remove the cylinder head cover and cylinder head as described in this chapter.
2. Remove the bolts securing the cylinder base to the crankcase on the right-hand side.
3. Loosen the cylinder bolts (**Figure 50**) in a crisscross pattern in 2-3 stages.
4. Remove the cylinder bolts and washers.
5. Loosen the cylinder by tapping around the perimeter with a rubber or plastic mallet. If necessary, *gently* pry the cylinder loose with a broad-tipped screwdriver.

> *CAUTION*
> *Remember the cooling fins are fragile and may be damaged if tapped or pried too hard. Never use a metal hammer.*

6. Pull the cylinder straight out and off of the piston. Work the camshaft chain wire through the opening in the cylinder. Reattach the wire to the exterior of the crankcase.
7. Remove the cylinder base gasket and discard it. Remove the dowel pins from the crankcase receptacles.
8. Install a piston holding fixture under the piston to protect the piston skirt from damage. This fixture may be purchased or may be a homemade unit of wood. See **Figure 51** for dimensions.

> *NOTE*
> *If the following 2 items are to be removed, remove the clutch as described in Chapter Six and the oil pump as described in this chapter.*

9. Remove the camshaft chain guide (**Figure 52**).
10. To remove the cam chain tensioner assembly, perform the following:
   a. Remove the clutch assembly as described in Chapter Six.
   b. Remove the bolt (**Figure 53**) securing the cam chain tensioner assembly.
   c. Remove the cam chain tensioner assembly, bushing and washer.

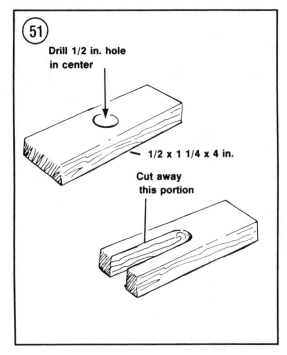

Drill 1/2 in. hole in center

1/2 x 1 1/4 x 4 in.

Cut away this portion

Inspection

The following procedure requires the use of highly specialized and expensive measuring instruments. If such equipment is not readily available, have the measurements performed by a dealer or qualified machine shop.

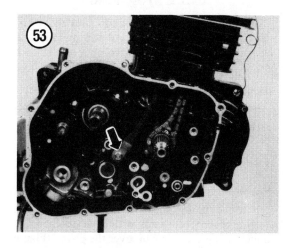

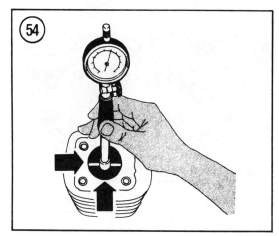

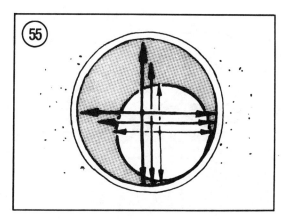

1. Soak with solvent any old cylinder head gasket material on the cylinder. Use a broad-tipped, *dull* chisel and gently scrape off all gasket residue. Do not gouge the sealing surface as oil and air leaks will result.

2. Measure the cylinder bore with a cylinder gauge (**Figure 54**) or inside micrometer at the points shown in **Figure 55**. Measure in 2 axes—in line with the piston-pin and at 90° to the pin. If the taper or out-of-round is 0.10 mm (0.004 in.) or greater, the cylinder must be rebored to the next oversize and a new piston installed.

NOTE
The new piston should be obtained before the cylinder is rebored so that the piston can be measured; slight manufacturing tolerances must be taken into account to determine the actual size and working clearance.

3. Check the cylinder wall for scratches; if evident, the cylinder should be rebored.

NOTE
*The maximum wear limit on the cylinder is listed in **Table 1**. If the cylinder is worn to this limit, it must be replaced. Never rebore a cylinder if the finished rebore diameter will be this dimension or greater.*

NOTE
After having the cylinder rebored, wash it thoroughly in hot soapy water. This is the best way to clean the cylinder of all fine grit material left from the bore job. After washing the cylinder, run a clean white cloth through it. The cloth should show no traces of dirt or other debris. If the rag is dirty, the cylinder is not clean enough and must be rewashed. After the cylinder is thoroughly clean, dry and lubricate the cylinder wall with clean engine oil to prevent the cylinder liner from rusting.

Installation

1. Check that the top surface of the crankcase and the bottom surface of the cylinder are clean before installing a new base gasket.

2. If removed, install the following:
   a. Install the washer, bushing and the camshaft chain tensioner assembly. Install the bolt (**Figure 53**) and tighten securely.

b. Install the camshaft chain guide (**Figure 52**). Make sure it seats correctly in the notch in the right-hand crankcase (**Figure 56**).

c. Install the clutch as described in Chapter Six.

3. Apply a small amount of liquid sealant to the mating surfaces of the crankcase halves in the area where the cylinder base gasket fits. This will help prevent an oil leak.

4. Install a new cylinder base gasket. Make sure all holes align.

5. Install the dowel pins into the receptacles in the crankcase.

6. Install a piston holding fixture under the piston.

7. Make sure the end gaps of the piston rings are *not* lined up with each other—they must be staggered. Lightly oil the piston rings and the inside of the cylinder bore with assembly oil.

8. Carefully feed the camshaft chain and wire up through the opening in the cylinder and tie it to the engine.

9. Start the cylinder down over the piston. Compress each piston ring with your fingers as it enters the cylinder.

10. Slide the cylinder down until it bottoms on the piston holding fixture.

11. Remove the piston holding fixture and slide the cylinder down into place on the crankcase.

12. Install the cylinder bolts and washers. Tighten in a crisscross pattern in 2-3 steps to the torque specification listed in **Table 2**.

13. Install the bolts securing the cylinder to the crankcase on the right-hand side and tighten to the torque specification listed in **Table 2**.

14. Install the cylinder head, camshaft and cylinder head cover as described in this chapter.

15. Adjust the valves and the camshaft chain tensioner as described in Chapter Three.

16. Follow the *Break-in Procedure* in this chapter if the cylinder was rebored or honed or a new piston or piston rings were installed.

PISTON, PISTON PIN AND PISTON RINGS

The piston is made of an aluminum alloy. The piston pin is made of steel and is a precision fit. The piston pin is held in place by a clip at each end.

Piston Removal

1. Remove the cylinder head cover, cylinder head and cylinder as described in this chapter.

> *WARNING*
> *The edges of all piston rings are very sharp. Be careful when handling them to avoid cutting fingers.*

2. Remove the top ring with a ring expander tool or by spreading the ends with your thumbs just enough to slide the ring up over the piston (**Figure 57**). Repeat for the remaining rings.

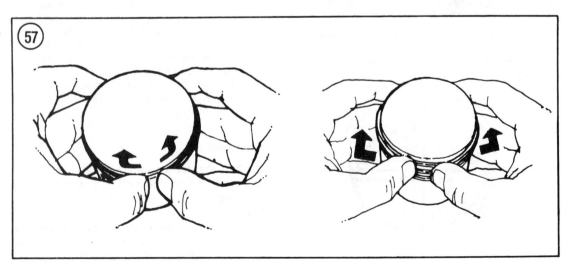

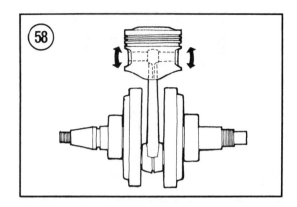

3. Before removing the piston, hold the rod tightly and rock the piston as shown in **Figure 58**. Any rocking motion (do not confuse with the normal sliding motion) indicates wear on the piston pin, piston pin bore, connecting rod small-end bore or, more likely, a combination of these.

NOTE
Wrap a clean shop cloth under the piston so that the piston pin clip will not fall into the crankcase.

4. Remove the clips from each side of the piston pin bore (**Figure 59**) with a small screwdriver or scribe. Hold your thumb over one edge of the clip when removing it to prevent the clip from springing out.

5. Use a proper size wooden dowel or socket extension and push out the piston pin.

CAUTION
Be careful when removing the pin to avoid damaging the connecting rod. If it is necessary to gently tap the pin to remove it, be sure that the piston is properly supported so that lateral shock is not transmitted to the lower connecting rod bearing.

6. If the piston pin is difficult to remove, heat the piston and pin with a hair dryer. The pin will probably push right out. Heat the piston to only about 140° F (60° C), i.e., until it is too warm to touch, but not excessively hot. If the pin is still difficult to push out, use a homemade tool as shown in **Figure 60**.

7. Lift the piston off the connecting rod.

8. If the piston is going to be left off for some time, place a piece of foam insulation tube over the end of the rod to protect it.

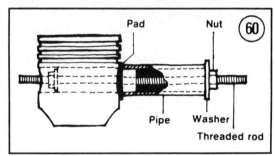

Inspection

1. Carefully clean the carbon from the piston crown with a chemical remover or with a soft scraper (**Figure 61**). Do not remove or damage the carbon ridge around the circumference of the piston above the top ring. If the piston, rings and cylinder are found to be dimensionally correct and can be reused, removal of the carbon ring from the top of the piston or the carbon ridge from the top of the cylinder will promote excessive oil consumption.

CAUTION
Do not wire brush the piston skirts.

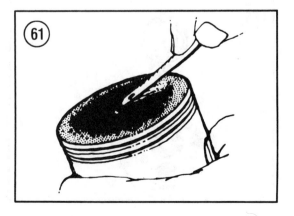

2. Examine each ring groove for burrs, dented edges and wide wear. Pay particular attention to the top compression ring groove as it usually wears more than the others.

3. If damage or wear indicates piston replacement, select a new piston as described under *Piston Clearance* in this chapter.

4. Oil the piston pin and install it in the connecting rod. Slowly rotate the piston pin and check for radial play (**Figure 62**). If any play exists, the piston pin should be replaced, providing the rod bore is in good condition.

5. Measure the inside diameter of the piston pin bore with a snap gauge (**Figure 63**) and measure the outside diameter of the piston pin with a micrometer (**Figure 64**). Compare with dimensions given in **Table 1**. Replace the piston and piston pin as a set if either or both are worn.

6. Check the piston skirt for galling and abrasion which may have been caused by piston seizure. If light galling is present, smooth the affected area with No. 400 emery paper and oil or a fine oilstone. However, if galling is severe or if the piston is deeply scored, replace it.

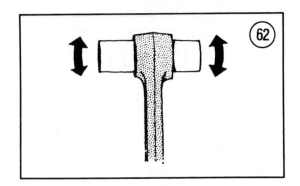

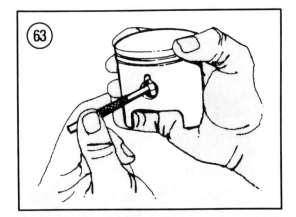

Piston Clearance

1. Make sure the piston and cylinder walls are clean and dry.

2. Measure the inside diameter of the cylinder bore at a point 13 mm (1/2 in.) from the upper edge with a bore gauge (**Figure 65**).

3. Measure the outside diameter of the piston across the skirt (**Figure 66**) at right angles to the piston pin. Measure at a distance 10 mm (0.40 in.) up from the bottom of the piston skirt.

4. Piston clearance is the difference between the maximum piston diameter and the minimum cylinder diameter. Subtract the dimension of the piston from the cylinder dimension and compare to the dimension listed in **Table 1**. If the clearance exceeds that specified, the cylinder should be rebored to the next oversize and a new piston installed.

5. To establish a final overbore dimension with a new piston, add the piston skirt measurement to the specified clearance. This will determine the dimension for the cylinder overbore size. Remember, do not exceed the cylinder maximum service limit inside diameter indicated in **Table 1**.

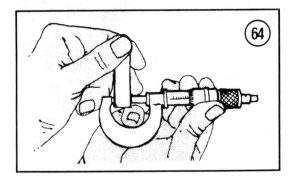

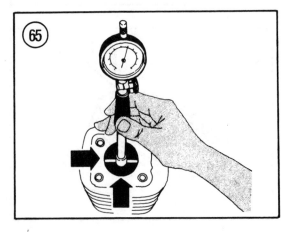

Piston Installation

1. Apply molybdenum disulfide grease to the inside surface of the connecting rod.

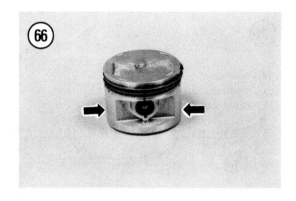

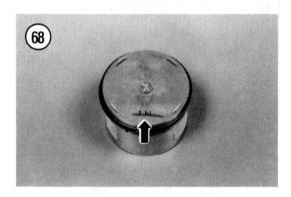

2. Oil the piston pin with assembly oil and install it in the piston until its end extends slightly beyond the inside of the boss (**Figure 67**).

3. Place the piston over the connecting rod with the IN mark (**Figure 68**) on the piston crown directed toward the rear of the engine.

4. Line up the piston pin with the hole in the connecting rod. Push the piston pin through the connecting rod and into the other side of the piston until it is even with the piston pin clip grooves.

CAUTION
If it is necessary to tap the piston pin into the connecting rod, do so gently with a block of wood or a soft-faced hammer. Make sure you support the piston to prevent the lateral shock from being transmitted to the connecting rod bearing.

NOTE
*In the next step, install the clips with the gap away from the cutout in the piston (**Figure 69**).*

5. Install new piston pin clips in both ends of the pin boss. Make sure they are seated in the grooves in the piston.

6. Check the installation by rocking the piston back and forth around the pin axis and from side to side along the axis. It should rotate freely back and forth but not from side to side.

7. Install the piston rings as described in this chapter.

8. Install the cylinder, cylinder head and cylinder head cover as described in this chapter.

Piston Ring
Removal/Inspection/Installation

WARNING
The edges of all piston rings are very sharp. Be careful when handling them to avoid cutting fingers.

1. Remove the top ring by spreading the ends with your thumbs just enough to slide the ring up over the piston (**Figure 57**). Repeat for the remaining rings.

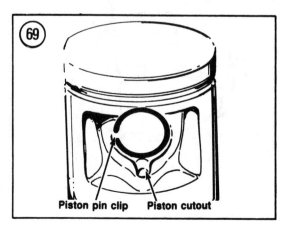

Piston pin clip   Piston cutout

2. Carefully remove all carbon build-up from the ring grooves with a broken piston ring (**Figure 70**). Inspect the grooves carefully for burrs, nicks or broken and cracked lands. Recondition or replace the piston if necessary.

3. Roll each ring around its piston groove as shown in **Figure 71** to check for binding. Minor binding may be cleaned up with a fine-cut file.

4. Measure the side clearance of each ring in its groove with a flat feeler gauge (**Figure 72**) and compare to dimensions given in **Table 1**. If the clearance is greater than specified, the rings must be replaced. If the clearance is still excessive with the new rings, the piston must also be replaced.

5. Measure each ring for wear. Place each ring, one at a time, into the cylinder and push it in about 20 mm (3/4 in.) with the crown of the piston to ensure that the ring is square in the cylinder bore. Measure the gap with a flat feeler gauge (**Figure 73**) and compare to dimensions in **Table 1**. If the gap is greater than specified, the rings should be replaced. When installing new rings, measure their end gap in the same manner as for old ones. If the gap is less than specified, carefully file the ends (**Figure 74**) with a fine-cut file until the gap is correct.

6. Install the piston rings in the order shown in **Figure 75**.

7. Install the oil ring spacer first, then the side rails. New oil ring side rails do not have top and bottom designations. If reassembling used parts, install the side rails as they were removed.

8. Install second compression ring, then the top, by carefully spreading the ends of the ring with your thumbs and slipping the ring over the top of the piston. Remember that the marks on the piston rings are toward the top of the piston.

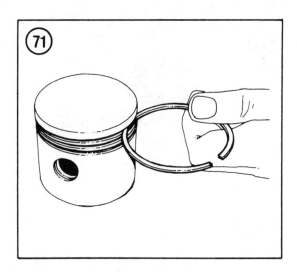

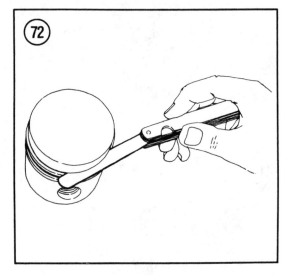

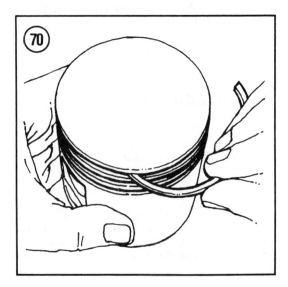

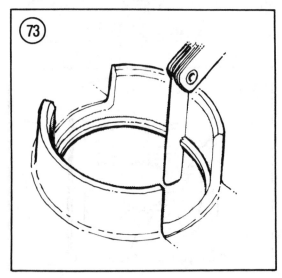

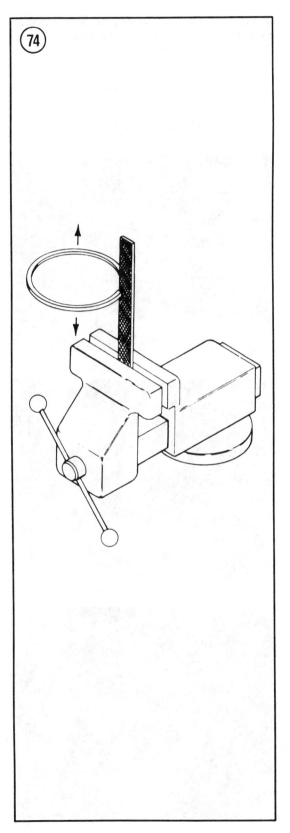

9. Make sure the rings are seated completely in their grooves all the way around the piston and that the ends are distributed around the piston as shown in **Figure 76**. The important thing is that the ring gaps are not aligned with each other when installed.

10. If new rings were installed, measure the side clearance of each ring in its groove with a flat feeler gauge (**Figure 72**) and compare to dimensions given in **Table 1**.

11. Follow the *Break-in Procedure* in this chapter if a new piston or piston rings have been installed or the cylinder was rebored or honed.

PRIMARY DRIVE GEAR

Removal/Installation

1. Place a copper washer (or penny) between the clutch outer housing gear and the primary drive gear.

2. Loosen the primary drive gear locknut and remove the copper washer (or penny).

3. Remove the clutch assembly as described in Chapter Six.

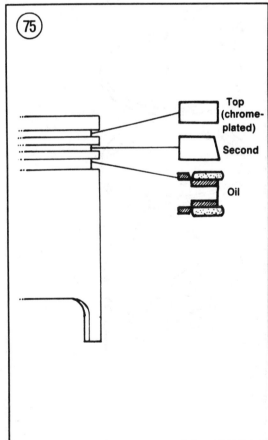

4. Remove the oil pump drive gear (**Figure 77**).

5. Remove the primary drive gear locknut (**Figure 78**) and lockwasher.

6. Remove the oil pump drive gear and pulse generator rotor.

7. Install the primary drive gear.

8. Inspect the primary drive gear, pulse generator rotor and oil pump drive gear for wear or damage. Replace any worn part.

NOTE
The primary drive gear, pulse generator rotor and oil pump drive gear can be installed onto the crankshaft in only one position. During installation match

*up the wide spline groove on the gear
and rotor with the 2 matching splines
on the crankshaft.*

9. Align the splines of the primary drive gear and slide it onto the crankshaft (**Figure 79**).

10. Position the pulse generator with the OUTSIDE mark facing toward the outside.

11. Align the splines of the pulse generator rotor and slide it onto the crankshaft.

12. Install the lockwasher with the OUTSIDE mark facing toward the outside (**Figure 80**).

13. Install the locknut (**Figure 78**) and tighten only finger-tight at this time.

14. Install the clutch as described in Chapter Six. Place a copper washer (or penny) between the clutch outer housing gear and the primary drive gear.

15. Tighten the primary drive gear locknut to the torque specification listed in **Table 2**. Remove the copper washer (or penny).

OIL PUMP

The oil pump is located on the right-hand side of the engine next to the clutch. The oil pump can be removed with the engine in the frame.

Removal/Installation

1. Remove the clutch as described in Chapter Six.

2. Remove the oil pump drive gear (**Figure 77**).

3. Remove the bolts (A, **Figure 81**) securing the oil pipe and remove the oil pipe.

4. Remove the bolts (B, **Figure 81**) securing the oil pump to the crankcase and remove the oil pump assembly.

5. Make sure the oil control orifice and O-ring (**Figure 82**) are installed in the inlet on the crankcase.

6. Install the locating dowels in either the oil pump (A, **Figure 83**) or in the crankcase.

7. Pour engine oil into the pump inlet hole. At the same time rotate the pump shaft counterclockwise until oil flows out the pump outlet hole.

8. Install the oil pump and tighten the screws securely.

9. Make sure the O-ring seals are in place on each end of the oil pipe.

10. Install the oil pipe and bolts. Tighten the bolts securely.

11. After installing the oil pump, start the engine and let it idle for about one minute. Loosen the oil pipe bolt and make sure oil flows from the connection. Retighten the oil pipe bolt.

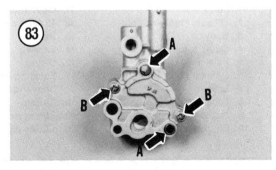

Disassembly/Assembly

Refer to **Figure 84** for this procedure.

The oil pump has dual cavities with main and sub-rotor assemblies. In the inspection steps, the clearance measurements are the same for both the main and sub-rotor assemblies. The main set of rotors (A) is the thicker of the two sets and is assembled into the oil pump body.

On 1989-on models, oil seals have been added to the oil pump body and spacer. These oil seals can be replaced if necessary.

1. Remove the Phillips head screws (B, **Figure 83**) securing the oil pump body to the base and spacer.
2. Remove the pump body and the outer rotor "A" and inner rotor "A."
3. Turn the assembly over and remove the base and the outer rotor "B," inner rotor "B" and the pump shaft from the spacer. Don't lose the dowel pins and the washer on the pump shaft.
4. Inspect the oil pump components as described in this chapter.
5. Into the oil pump base, install the pump drive shaft and dowel pin (**Figure 85**).
6. Into the oil pump base, install the inner rotor "B" (**Figure 86**) and the outer rotor "B."

7. Install the spacer onto the body.
8. Install the washer onto the drive shaft.
9. Install the dowel pin into the pump shaft (**Figure 87**).
10. Remove the inner and outer rotors "A" from the oil pump body.
11. Install the inner and outer rotors "A" (A, **Figure 88**) onto the oil pump spacer and pump shaft.
12. Install the locating dowels (B, **Figure 88**).
13. Install the oil pump body (**Figure 89**) and turn the assembly over.
14. Install the Phillips head screws and tighten securely.

Check Valve
Disassembly/Assembly

1. To disassemble the check valve, perform the following:
   a. Remove the cotter pin at the end of the check valve housing (**Figure 90**). Discard the cotter pin.
   b. Remove the spring seat, spring, check valve and oil seal (**Figure 91**).

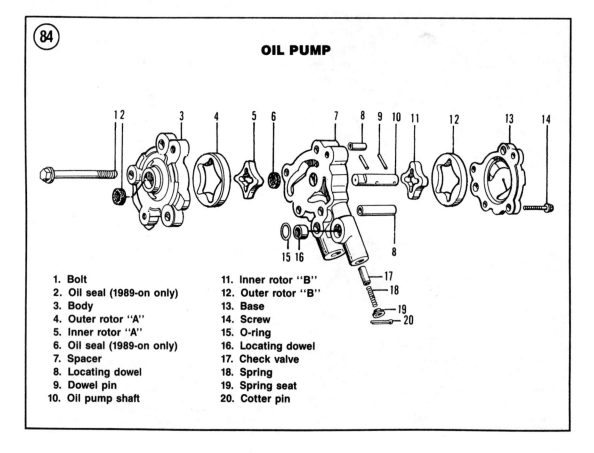

OIL PUMP

1. Bolt
2. Oil seal (1989-on only)
3. Body
4. Outer rotor "A"
5. Inner rotor "A"
6. Oil seal (1989-on only)
7. Spacer
8. Locating dowel
9. Dowel pin
10. Oil pump shaft
11. Inner rotor "B"
12. Outer rotor "B"
13. Base
14. Screw
15. O-ring
16. Locating dowel
17. Check valve
18. Spring
19. Spring seat
20. Cotter pin

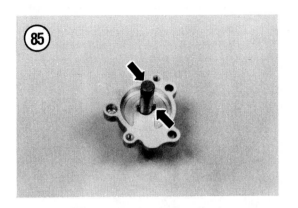

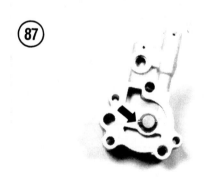

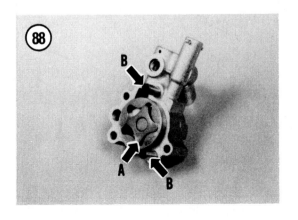

2. Clean all check valve parts in solvent and thoroughly dry. Coat all parts with fresh engine oil before installation.

3. To assemble the check valve, perform the following:

   a. Install the oil seal (large end in first), check valve (small end in first), spring and spring seat.

   b. Install a new cotter pin and bend the ends over completely.

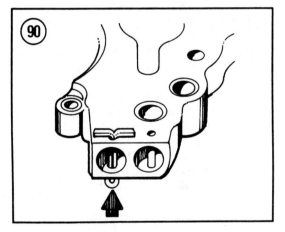

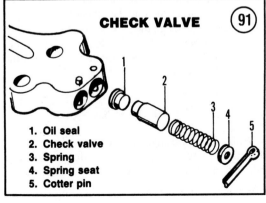

CHECK VALVE

1. Oil seal
2. Check valve
3. Spring
4. Spring seat
5. Cotter pin

Inspection

1. Inspect both sets of inner and outer rotors for scratches and abrasions. Replace parts of each set if evidence of these are found.

2. Clean all parts in solvent and dry thoroughly. Coat all parts with fresh engine oil before installation.

3. Inspect the teeth on the driven gear. Replace the driven gear if the teeth are damaged or any are missing.

4. Install the correct outer rotor into either the oil pump body or base.

5. Measure the clearance between the outer rotor and the oil pump body with a flat feeler gauge (**Figure 92**). If the clearance is 2.25 mm (0.010 in.) or greater, replace the worn part.

6. Install the correct inner rotor into the outer rotor that was installed in Step 5.

7. Measure the clearance between the tip of the inner rotor and the outer rotor with a flat feeler gauge (**Figure 93**). If the clearance is 0.20 mm (0.008 in.) or greater, replace the worn part.

8. Measure the end clearance between both rotors and the oil pump body or base with a straightedge and a flat feeler gauge (**Figure 94**). If the clearance is 0.12 mm (0.005 in.) or greater, replace the worn part.

9. On 1989-1990 XR600R models, inspect the oil seals in the oil pump body and the oil pump spacer. If worn or damaged, replace the oil seals as follows:

   a. Note the position of the oil seal in the body and spacer and note which side of the seal faces out. The new oil seal must face in the same direction.

   b. Measure the distance down the top surface of the body or spacer to the top of the oil seal. This dimension should be 0.5-1.1 mm (0.020-0.043 in.).

   c. Carefully pry the oil seal out of the body or spacer.

   d. Position the new oil seal with the same side facing out as the one that was removed.

   e. Carefully install the new oil seal into the body or spacer until it is down 0.5-1.1 mm (0.020-0.043 in.) from the top surface of the body or spacer.

OIL LINES

With a dry sump engine, the engine oil is stored in the bike's fame. Engine oil is transferred from the bike's frame to the engine via flexible and metal oil lines.

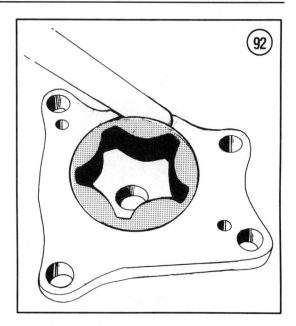

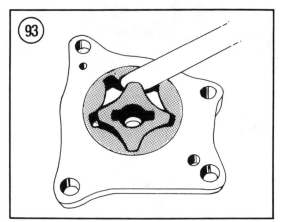

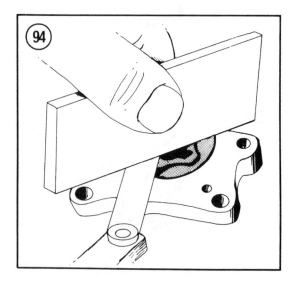

Removal/Inspection/Installation

1. Drain the engine oil as described in Chapter Three.

2. Hold onto the fitting, either on the frame or on the metal oil line, with a wrench and unscrew the flexible oil lines from these fittings (**Figure 95**).

3. Remove the bolts (**Figure 96**) securing the plate that secures the oil lines to the crankcase.

4. Remove the plate and the oil lines.

5. Inspect the oil lines for damage or leakage. If damaged, replace both lines.

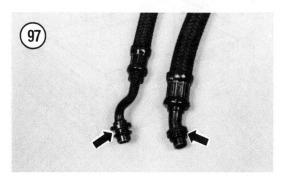

6. Inspect the O-ring seals (**Figure 97**) on the engine end of the oil lines. If damaged or starting to deteriorate, replace the O-ring on each oil line.

7. To remove the metal oil line, perform the following:
   a. Remove the clamping band on the frame.
   b. Disconnect the fitting on the metal oil line from the bike's frame.

8. Install by reversing these removal steps, noting the following.

9. When installing the flexible oil lines, hold onto the fitting, either on the frame or the metal oil line with a wrench and screw the flexible oil lines onto these fittings. Let the flexible oil lines flow in a natural curve; make sure they are not kinked. Tighten the fittings securely.

CAMSHAFT CHAIN

Removal/Installation

1. Remove the cylinder head cover and camshaft as described in this chapter.

2. Remove the clutch assembly as described in Chapter Six.

3. Remove the primary drive gear as described in this chapter.

4. Let the camshaft chain drop down through the passageway in the cylinder head and cylinder and into the outer portion of the right-hand crankcase.

5. Remove the camshaft chain from the camshaft chain sprocket on the crankshaft.

6. Remove the camshaft chain sprocket from the crankshaft.

7. Inspect the camshaft chain for wear and damage. If the chain needs replacing, also check the drive sprocket and the camshaft sprocket. They may require replacement also.

8. Install by reversing these removal steps.

9. The camshaft chain drive gear can be installed onto the crankshaft in only one position. Align the wide spline groove on the camshaft drive gear (A, **Figure 98**) with the 2 matching splines on the crankshaft (B, **Figure 98**) and slide it onto the crankshaft.

10. Attach a piece of wire to the camshaft chain and pull the chain up through the passageway in the cylinder and cylinder head.

CRANKCASE AND CRANKSHAFT

Disassembly of the crankcase (splitting the cases) and removal of the crankshaft assembly require that the engine be removed from the frame.

The thin-walled crankcase is made in 2 halves of precision diecast aluminum alloy. To avoid damage, do not hammer or pry on any of the interior or exterior projected walls. These areas are easily damaged. The cases are split vertically down the centerline of the connecting rod. The cases are assembled with a gasket between the 2 halves. Dowel pins align the halves when they are bolted together.

The crankshaft assembly is made up of 2 full-circle flywheels pressed together on a hollow crankpin. The connecting rod big end bearing on the crankpin is a needle bearing assembly. The crankshaft assembly is supported in 2 ball bearings in the crankcase. Service to the crankshaft assembly is limited to removal and replacement.

The procedure which follows is presented as a complete, step-by-step, major lower end rebuild that should be followed if an engine is to be completely reconditioned. However, if you're replacing a part that you know is defective, the disassembly should be carried out only until the failed part is accessible; there is no need to disassemble the engine beyond that point so long as you know the remaining components are in good condition and that they were not affected by the failed part.

Crankcase Disassembly

1. Remove all exterior engine assemblies as described in this chapter and other related chapters.
   a. Cylinder head cover, camshaft and cylinder head.
   b. Cylinder and piston.
   c. Camshaft chain and tensioner.
   d. Clutch assembly.
   e. Kickstarter.
   f. Alternator.
   g. External shift mechanism.
   h. Oil pump.
2. Remove the engine as described in this chapter.
3. Before removing the crankcase screws, cut a cardboard template approximately the size of the crankcase and punch holes in the template for each screw location. Place each screw in the template hole as it is removed. This will speed up the assembly time by eliminating the search for the correct length screw.
4. Remove the bolts from the left-hand crankcase side that secure the crankcase halves together (**Figure 99**). To prevent warpage, loosen them in a crisscross pattern.

> *NOTE*
> *Set the engine on wood blocks or fabricate a holding fixture of 2×4 inch wood as shown in **Figure 100**.*

5. Remove the bolts from the right-hand crankcase side (**Figure 101**).

> *CAUTION*
> *Perform the next step directly over and close to the workbench as the crankcase halves may separate easily. Do **not** hammer on the crankcase halves or they will be damaged.*

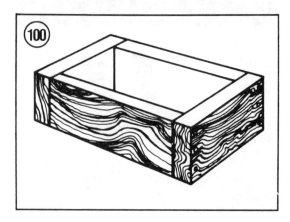

6. Set the crankcase down on the left-hand side. Hold onto the right-hand crankcase and tap on the right-hand end of the crankshaft and transmission shafts with a plastic or soft faced mallet until the crankshaft and crankcase separate.

7. If the crankcase and crankshaft will not separate using this method, check to make sure that all screws are removed. If you still have a problem, it may be necessary to use a puller to remove the right-hand crankcase half. If the proper tools are not available, take the crankcase assembly to a dealer and have it separated. Do not risk expensive crankcase damage with improper tools or techniques.

CAUTION
Never pry between case halves. Doing so may result in oil leaks, requiring replacement of the case halves.

8. Remove the crankcase gasket. Don't lose the locating dowels if they came out of the case. They do not have to be removed from the case if they are secure.

9. Remove the balancer weight assembly.

10. Lift up and carefully remove the transmission, shift drum and shift fork shaft assemblies.

CAUTION
The crankshaft is pressed into the left-hand crankcase half. Do not try to remove it or the crankcase will be damaged. If removal is necessary, take the crankcase and crankshaft to a dealer and have them press it out.

CAUTION
Do not try to drive the crankshaft out of the main bearing with a hammer or crankshaft alignment may be disturbed.

11. If the crankshaft left-hand ball bearing comes out of the crankcase with the crankshaft it must be replaced. Have it removed and a new one installed by a dealer.

12. Inspect the crankcase halves and crankshaft as described in this chapter.

Crankcase Assembly

1. Apply assembly oil to the inner race of all bearings in both crankcase halves and to the crankshaft ball bearings.

2. If the crankshaft was removed, have it installed by a Honda dealer as special tools are required to pull the crankshaft into the left-hand crankcase half.

CAUTION
Do not attempt to drive the crankshaft into the left-hand main bearing with a hammer or mallet or the crankshaft alignment will be disturbed.

NOTE
Set the crankcase half assembly on wood blocks or the wood holding fixture shown in the disassembly procedure.

3. Align the index marks on the balancer weight assembly and the crankshaft (**Figure 102**).

4. Install the balancer weight assembly completely into the left-hand crankcase half.

5. Rotate the crankshaft and balancer several times. Make sure there is no interference between the balancer weight and the crankshaft.

6. Install the transmission assemblies, shift shafts and shift drum in the left-hand crankcase half and lightly oil all shaft ends. Refer to Chapter Six for the correct procedure.

NOTE
Make sure the mating surfaces are clean and free of all old sealant material. Make sure you get a leak-free seal.

7. Install the locating dowels if they were removed and install a new crankcase gasket.
8. Set the right-hand crankcase half over the left-hand crankcase half on the blocks. Push it down squarely into place until it reaches the crankshaft bearing. There is usually about 1/2 inch left to go.
9. Lightly tap the case halves together with a plastic or rubber mallet until they seat.

CAUTION
Crankcase halves should fit together without force. If the crankcase halves do not fit together completely, do not attempt to pull them together with the crankcase screws. Separate the crankcase halves and investigate the cause of the interference. If the transmission shafts were disassembled, recheck to make sure that a gear is not installed backwards. Do not risk damage by trying to force the cases together.

10. After the crankcase halves are completely assembled, rotate the crankshaft and transmission shafts to make sure there is no binding. If any is present, disassemble the crankcase and correct the problem.

NOTE
Set the engine on wood blocks or fabricate a holding fixture of 2×4 inch wood as shown in Figure 100.

11. Install the bolts on the left-hand crankcase side that secure the crankcase halves together (**Figure 99**). Tighten only finger-tight.
12. Securely tighten the bolts in 2 stages in a crisscross pattern to the torque specification listed in **Table 2**.
13. Install the bolts on the right-hand crankcase side (**Figure 101**) and tighten to the torque specification listed in **Table 2**.
14. After the crankcase halves are completely assembled, again rotate the crankshaft and transmission shafts to make sure there is no

binding. If any is present, disassemble the crankcase and correct the problem.
15. After a new crankcase gasket has been installed it must be trimmed. Carefully trim off all excess gasket material where the cylinder base gasket comes in contact with the crankcase. If it is not trimmed the cylinder base gasket will not seal properly.

16. Feed the camshaft chain down through the top of the chain opening in the crankcase and install the chain onto the crankshaft sprocket (**Figure 103**). Make sure it is correctly engaged with the sprocket.

17. Install all exterior engine assemblies as described in this chapter and other related chapters.

    a. Cylinder head, camshaft and cylinder head cover.

    b. Cylinder and piston.

    c. Camshaft chain and tensioner assembly.

    d. Clutch assembly.

    e. Kickstarter.

    f. Alternator.

    g. External shift mechanism.

    h. Oil pump.

Crankcase and Crankshaft Inspection

1. Clean both crankcase halves inside and out with cleaning solvent. Thoroughly dry with compressed air and wipe off with a clean shop cloth. Be sure to remove all traces of old gasket material from all mating surfaces.

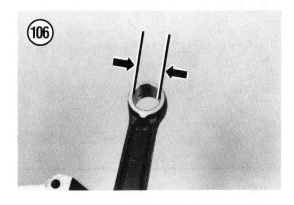

2. Check the transmission bearings (A, **Figure 104**) for roughness, pitting, galling and play by rotating them slowly by hand. If any roughness or play can be felt in the bearing it must be replaced.

3. Carefully inspect the cases for cracks and fractures, especially in the lower areas; they are vulnerable to rock damage. Also check the areas around the stiffening ribs, around bearing bosses and threaded holes. If damage is found, have them repaired by a shop specializing in the repair of precision aluminum castings or replace them.

4. Check the crankshaft main bearings (B, **Figure 104**) for roughness, pitting, galling and play by rotating them slowly by hand. If any roughness or play can be felt in the bearing it must be replaced. This must be entrusted to a dealer as special tools are required. The cam chain sprocket and oil pump drive gear must also be removed and realigned properly upon installation.

5. Check the balancer bearing (C, **Figure 104**) for roughness, pitting, galling and play by rotating it slowly by hand. If any roughness or play can be felt in the bearing it must be replaced.

6. Inspect the balancer gear (A, **Figure 105**) for wear or missing teeth. If either is found, replacement must be performed by a dealer.

7. Inspect the cam chain sprocket for wear or missing teeth. If the sprocket is damaged, the left-hand portion of the crankshaft or the entire crankshaft must be replaced.

8. Measure the inside diameter of the connecting rod small end with a snap gauge and an inside micrometer (**Figure 106**). Compare to dimensions given in **Table 1**. If worn to the service limit the crankshaft assembly must be replaced.

9. Check the connecting rod big end bearing by grasping the rod in one hand and lifting up on it. With the heel of your other hand, rap sharply on the top of the rod. A sharp metallic sound, such as a click, is an indication that the bearing or crankpin or both are worn and the crankshaft assembly should be replaced.

10. Check the connecting rod-to-crankshaft side clearance with a flat feeler gauge (**Figure 107**). Compare to dimensions given in **Table 1**. If the clearance is greater than specified the crankshaft assembly must be replaced.

11. Other inspections of the crankshaft assembly involve accurate measuring equipment and should be entrusted to a dealer or competent machine shop. The crankshaft assembly operates under severe stress and dimensional tolerances are

5

critical. These dimensions are given in **Table 1**. If any are off by the slightest amount it may cause a considerable amount of damage or destruction of the engine. The crankshaft assembly must be replaced as a unit as it cannot be serviced without the aid of a 10-12 ton (9,000-11,000 kilogram) capacity press, holding fixtures and crankshaft jig.

12. Inspect the oil seals. They should be replaced every time the crankcase is disassembled. Refer to *Bearing and Oil Seal Replacement* in this chapter.

Bearing and Oil Seal Replacement

1. Pry out the oil seals with a small screwdriver, taking care not to damage the crankcase bore. If the seals are old and difficult to remove, heat the cases as described in Step 2 and use an awl to punch a small hole in the steel backing of the seal. Install a small sheet metal screw part way into the seal and pull the seal out with a pair of pliers.

> *CAUTION*
> *Do not install the screw too deep or it may contact and damage the bearing behind it.*

2. On bearings so equipped, remove the screws securing the bearing retainer plate (**Figure 108**) and remove the retainer plate.

3. The bearings are installed with a slight interference fit. The crankcase must be heated in an oven to a temperature of about 212° F (100° C). An easy way to check the proper temperature is to drop tiny drops of water on the case; if they sizzle and evaporate immediately, the temperature is correct. Heat only one case at a time.

> *CAUTION*
> *Do **not** heat the cases with a torch (propane or acetylene); never bring a flame into contact with the bearing or case. The direct heat will destroy the case hardening of the bearing and will likely cause warpage of the case.*

4. Remove the case from the oven and hold onto the 2 crankcase studs with a kitchen pot holder, heavy gloves or heavy shop cloths—it is *hot*.

5. Remove the oil seals if not already removed (see Step 1).

6. Hold the crankcase with the bearing side down and tap it squarely on a piece of soft wood. Continue to tap until the bearing(s) fall out. Repeat for the other half.

> *CAUTION*
> *Be sure to tap the crankcase squarely on the piece of wood. Avoid damaging the sealing surface of the crankcase.*

7. If the bearings are difficult to remove, they can be gently tapped out with a socket or piece of pipe the same size as the bearing outer race.

> *NOTE*
> *If the bearings or seals are difficult to remove or install, don't take a chance on expensive damage. Have the work performed by a dealer or competent machine shop.*

8. While heating up the crankcase halves, place the new bearings in a freezer if possible. Chilling them will slightly reduce their overall diameter while the hot crankcase is slightly larger due to heat expansion. This will make bearing installation much easier.

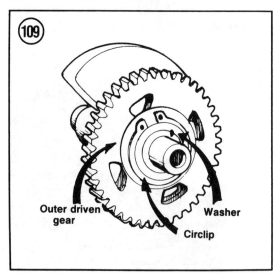

Outer driven gear   Washer   Circlip

9. While the crankcase is still hot, press each new bearing into place in the crankcase by hand until it seats completely. Do not hammer it in. If the bearing will not seat, remove it and cool it again. Reheat the crankcase and install the bearing again.

10. Oil seals are best installed with a special tool available at a dealer or motorcycle supply store. However, a proper size socket or piece of pipe can be substituted. Make sure that the bearings and seals are not cocked in the crankcase hole and that they are seated properly.

BALANCER SYSTEM

The balancer system eliminates the vibration normally associated with a large displacement single cylinder engine. The engine and the frame are designed to be compatible with the balancer system. If the balancer is eliminated it will result in

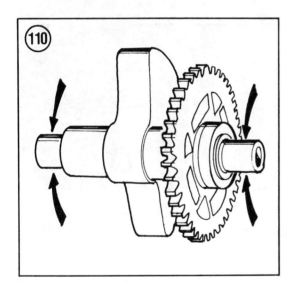

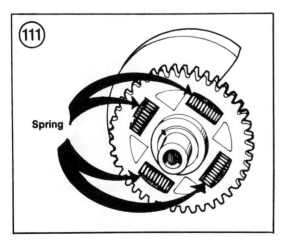

Spring

an excessive amount of vibration. This vibration will result in major fatigue to engine and frame components. Do *not* eliminate this feature.

CAUTION
Any applicable manufacturer's warranty will be voided if the balancer system is modified, disconnected or removed.

The balancer system consists of a balancer weight that is gear-driven by the crankshaft assembly. The balancer construction varies with the different models.

Removal/Installation

Remove and install the balancer assembly as described under *Crankcase and Crankshaft* in this chapter.

Disassembly/Inspection/Assembly (500 cc Models)

The balancer in the 500 cc engine is a one piece unit and cannot be disassembled.

1. Check for broken, chipped or missing teeth on the balancer shaft assembly (A, **Figure 105**). Replace the balancer shaft assembly if the teeth are damaged.

2. Inspect the balancer shaft at each end (B, **Figure 105**) for wear or damage. Replace the balancer shaft assembly if wear is evident.

Disassembly/Inspection/Assembly (600 cc Models)

1. Remove the circlip and washer (**Figure 109**).

2. Remove the outer driven gear and damper springs from the balancer shaft assembly.

3. Check for broken, chipped or missing teeth on the outer driven gear and the gear on the balancer shaft assembly.

4. Check the damper springs. Make sure they are not broken or have sagged. Replace as a set even if only one requires replacement.

5. Measure the outside diameter of the balancer shaft at each end (**Figure 110**) with a micrometer. Replace if worn to the service limit dimension listed in **Table 1** or less.

6. Install the damper springs into the balancer shaft assembly (**Figure 111**).

7. Align the index marks on both gears and install the outer drive gear (**Figure 112**).

8. Install the washer onto the shaft.

9. Install the circlip with the sharp side facing out. Make sure it is completely seated in the groove in the shaft assembly.

KICKSTARTER

Removal

1. Remove the clutch as described in Chapter Six.
2. Remove the kickstarter idle gear and bushing (**Figure 113**).
3. Using Vise Grips, carefully unhook the return spring from the boss on the crankcase.
4. Withdraw the kickstarter assembly from the crankcase.

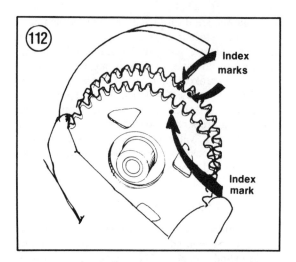

Disassembly/Assembly

Refer to **Figure 114** for this procedure.

The starter decompression components located on the outer end of the kickstarter shaft are not used on 1988-1990 XR600R models.

1. Clean the assembled shaft in solvent and dry thoroughly with compressed air.
2A. On 1988-1990 XR600R models, slide off the thrust washer.
2B. On all other models, slide off the thrust washer, kickstand cam, cam spring, spring seat and circlip.
3. From the other end of the shaft, remove the spring collar, return spring and spring seat.
4. Remove the ratchet spring and the kickstarter ratchet.
5. Remove the circlip and slide off the thrust washer.
6A. On 1987-1990 models, slide off the kickstarter gear and bushing and the other thrust washer.

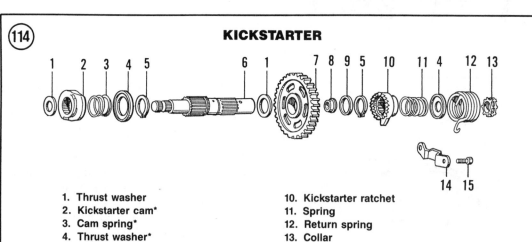

KICKSTARTER

1. Thrust washer
2. Kickstarter cam*
3. Cam spring*
4. Thrust washer*
5. Circlip*
6. Kickstarter shaft
7. Kickstarter gear
8. Kickstarter gear bushing (1987-on)
9. Collar (1983-1986)
10. Kickstarter ratchet
11. Spring
12. Return spring
13. Collar
14. Ratchet guide plate
15. Bolt
* Items not used on 1988-on XR600R models.

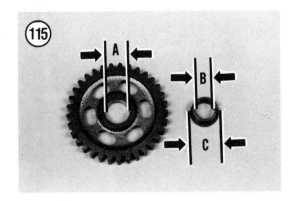

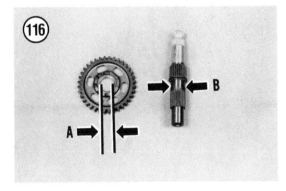

6B. On all other models, slide off the kickstarter gear and the other thrust washer.

7. Measure the inside diameter of the kickstarter gear idle gear (A, **Figure 115**). Replace if worn to the service limit dimension listed in **Table 1** or greater.

8. Measure the inside diameter (B, **Figure 115**) and outside diameter (C) of the kickstarter idle gear bushing. Replace if worn to the service limit listed in **Table 1**.

9. Measure the inside diameter of the kickstarter gear (A, **Figure 116**). Replace if worn to the service limit dimension listed in **Table 1** or greater.

10. Measure the outside diameter of the kickstarter shaft where the kickstarter gear rides (B, **Figure 116**). Replace if worn to the service limit dimension listed in **Table 1** or less.

11. Inspect the gears for chipped or missing teeth. Replace any gears as necessary.

12. Inspect the splines on the kickstarter shaft for wear or damage. Replace as necessary.

13. Make sure the ratchet gear operates properly and smoothly on its shaft.

14. Check all parts for uneven wear; replace any that are questionable.

Assembly

1. Apply assembly oil or fresh engine oil to all sliding surfaces of all parts.

2. Slide on the thrust washer.

3A. On 1987-1990 models, slide the kickstarter gear bushing and the kickstarter gear onto the shaft (**Figure 117**).

3B. On all other models, slide the kickstarter gear onto the shaft.

4. Install the thrust washer and circlip (**Figure 118**). Make sure the circlip is correctly seated in the groove in the shaft.

5. Align the punch marks on the kickstarter shaft and the drive ratchet (**Figure 119**). Slide on the ratchet.

6. Install the ratchet spring and spring seat (**Figure 120**).

7. Install the return spring. Place the hook into the hole in the shaft (**Figure 121**).

8. Slide on the collar and push the collar into place within the return spring (**Figure 122**).

9A. On the 1988-1990 XR600R models, slide on the thrust washer.

9B. On all other models, perform the following:
   a. Install the circlip
   b. Slide on the spring seat and cam spring (**Figure 123**).
   c. Align the punch mark on the kickstarter cam and the punch mark on the shaft (**Figure 124**) and slide on the cam.
   d. Install the thrust washer (**Figure 125**).
   e. Before installing the assembled shaft into the crankcase, check **Figure 126** for correct placement of all components.

Installation

1. Install the assembled shaft into the crankcase.

2. Insert the drive ratchet pawl against the ratchet guide plate on the crankcase.

3. Temporarily install the kickstarter pedal onto the shaft.

4. Hook the return spring onto the crankcase.

5. Rotate the assembly *clockwise* until the ratchet pawl clears the stopper plate. Then push the kickstarter shaft all the way in.

6. Remove the kickstarter pedal.

7. Install the kickstarter idle gear bushing with the shoulder side on first (**Figure 127**).

8. Install the kickstarter idle gear onto the bushing (**Figure 113**).

9. Install the clutch assembly as described in Chapter Six.

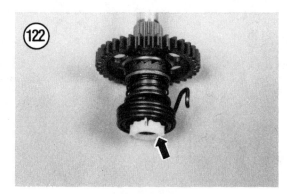

BREAK-IN PROCEDURE

If the rings were replaced, a new piston installed, the cylinder rebored or honed or major lower end work performed, the engine should be broken in just as though it were new. The performance and service life of the engine depends greatly on a careful and sensible break-in.

For the first 5-10 hours of operation, no more than one-third throttle should be used and speed should be varied as much as possible within the one-third throttle limit. Prolonged steady running at one speed, no matter how moderate, is to be avoided as well as hard acceleration.

Following the first 5-10 hours of operation more throttle should not be used until the bike has run for 100 hours and then it should be limited to short bursts of speed until 150 hours have been logged.

During this period, oil consumption may be higher than normal. It is therefore important to frequently check and correct oil level. At no time, during the break-in or later, should the oil level be allowed to drop below the bottom line on the dipstick; if the oil level is low, the oil will become overheated resulting in insufficient lubrication and increased wear.

After 10 Hours Of Operation Service

It is essential that the oil be changed and the oil filter rotor and filter screen be cleaned after the first 10 hours of operation. In addition, it is a good idea to change the oil and clean the oil filter rotor and filter screen at the completion of the 100 hours of operation to ensure that all of the particles produced during break-in are removed from the lubrication system. The small added expense may be considered a smart investment that will pay off in increased engine life.

Table 1 500 AND 600 CC ENGINE SPECIFICATIONS*

Item	Specifications	Wear limit
General		
Type	4-stroke, air-cooled, SOHC	
Number of cylinders	1	
Bore and stroke		
500 cc	92. 0 × 75.0 mm (3.62 × 2.95 in.)	
XL600	100.0 × 75.0 mm (3.93 × 2.95 in.)	
XR600R	97.0 × 80.0 mm (3.82 × 3.15 in.)	
Displacement		
500 cc	498 cc (30.37 cu. In.)	
XL600R	589 cc (35.91 cu. In.)	
XR600R	591 cc (36.1 cu. In.)	
	(continued)	

Table 1 500 AND 600 CC ENGINE SPECIFICATIONS* (continued)

Item	Specifications	Wear limit
Compression ratio		
500 cc	9.2 to 1	
XL600R	8.6 to 1	
XR600R	9.0 to 1	
Compression pressure		
XR600R		
1985-1987	125.2-130.8 psi (8.8-9.2 kg/cm^2)	
1988-1990	185.8-214.2 psi (13-15 kg/cm^2)	
All other models	175 psi (12.5 kg/cm^2)	
Cylinder head warpage	–	0.10 mm (0.004 in.)
Cylinder		
Bore		
500 cc	91.00-91.01 mm (3.5827-3.5831 in.)	91.12 mm (3.587 in.)
XL600R	100.00-100.01 mm (3.3937-39.9375 in.)	100.12 mm (3.942 in.)
1985-1990 XR600R	97.00-97.01 mm (3.8189-3.8193 in.)	97.12 mm (3.824 in.)
Out of round	–	0.05 mm (0.002 in.)
Piston/cylinder clearance	0.01-0.04 mm (0.0004-0.0016 in.)	0.1 mm (0.004 in.)
Warpage across top	–	0.1 mm (0.004 in.)
Piston–500 cc		
Diameter	90.95-90.98 mm (3.5807-3.5819 in.)	90.85 mm (3.577 in.)
Clearance in bore	0.01-0.04 mm (0.0004-0.0016 in.)	0.10 mm (0.004 in.)
Piston pin bore	22.002-22.008 mm (0.8662-0.8665 in.)	22.08 mm (0.869 in.)
Piston pin outer diameter	21.989-21.995 mm (0.8657-0.8659 in.)	21.95 mm (0.864 in.)
Piston–XL600R		
Diameter	99.95-99.98 mm (3.935-3.936 in.)	99.85 mm (3.93 in.)
Clearance in bore	0.01-0.04 mm (0.0004-0.0016 in.)	0.10 mm (0.004 in.)
Piston pin bore	24.002-24.008 mm (0.9450-0.9452 in.)	24.03 mm (0.946 in.)
Piston pin diameter	NA	
Piston–XR600R		
Diameter	96.95-96.98 mm (3.8169-3.8181 in.)	96.85 mm (3.81 in.)
Clearance in bore	0.01-0.04 mm (0.0004-0.0016 in.)	0.10 mm (0.004 in.)
Piston pin bore	24.002-24.008 mm (0.9450-0.9452 in.)	24.03 mm (0.946 in.)
Piston pin diameter	23.989-23.995 mm (0.9444-0.9447 in.)	23.96 mm (0.943 in.)
Piston rings		
Number of rings		
Compression	2	
Oil control	1	
Ring end gap		
Top	0.02-0.04 mm (0.008-0.016 in.)	0.50 mm (0.020 in.)
Second		
1988-1990 XR600R	0.35-0.55 mm (0.014-0.022 in.)	0.65 mm (0.026 in.)

(continued)

Table 1 500 AND 600 CC ENGINE SPECIFICATIONS* (continued)

Item	Specifications	Wear limit
Piston rings		
Ring end gap		
Second (continued)		
All other models	0.02-0.04 mm (0.008-0.016 in.)	0.50 mm (0.020 in.)
Oil (side rail)	0.2-0.9 mm (0.007-0.035 in.)	NA
Ring side clearance		
Top		
1988-1990 XR600R	0.015-0.045 mm (0.0006-0.0018 in.)	0.12 mm (0.006 in.)
All other models	0.030-0.065 mm (0.0012-0.0026 in.)	0.12 mm (0.006 in.)
Second ring	0.015-0.045 mm (0.006-0.018 in.)	0.12 mm (0.006 in.)
Oil control	NA	
Crankshaft/connecting rod		
Small end inner diameter		
500 cc	22.020-22.041 mm (0.8669-0.8678 in.)	22.07 mm (0.869 in.)
600 cc	24.020-24.041 mm (0.9457-0.9465 in.)	24.07 mm (0.948 in.)
Connecting rod big end side clearance	0.05-0.65 mm (0.002-0.0256 in.)	0.80 mm (0.031 in.)
Connecting rod big end radial clearance	0.006-0.018 mm (0.0002-0.0007 in.)	0.05 mm (0.002 in.)
Camshaft lobe height		
500 cc		
Intake	34.023 mm (1.3394 in.)	33.85 mm (1.334 in.)
Exhaust	33.976 mm (1.3376 in.)	33.81 mm (1.331 in.)
600 cc		
Intake	31.023 mm (1.2214 in.)	30.85 mm (1.215 in.)
Exhaust	30.976 mm (1.2195 in.)	30.81 mm (1.213 in.)
1988-1990 XR600R		
Intake	31.155-31.315 mm (1.2266-1.2329 in.)	31.05 mm (1.222 in.)
Exhaust	31.091-31.251 mm (1.2241-1.2304 in.)	31.00 mm (1.220 in.)
Valves		
Valves stem diameter		
Intake	6.575-6.950 mm (0.2589-0.2594 in.)	6.565 mm (0.258 in.)
Exhaust	6.565-6.575 mm (0.2585-0.2589 in.)	6.55 mm (0.2579 in.)
Sub-chamber–600 cc	4.97-4.985 mm (0.1957-0.1963 in.)	4.96 mm (0.195 in.)
Valve guide inner diameter		
Intake and exhaust	6.600-6.615 mm (0.2598-0.2604 in.)	6.63 mm (0.261 in.)
Sub-chamber–600 cc	5.010-5.028 mm (0.1972-0.1980 in.)	5.06 mm (0.199 in.)

(continued)

5

Table 1 500 AND 600 CC ENGINE SPECIFICATIONS* (continued)

Item	Specifications	Wear limit
Stem to guide clearance		
Intake	0.010-0.040 mm	0.065 mm (0.0026 in.)
	(0.0004-0.0016 in.)	
Exhaust	0.025-0.050 mm	0.080 mm (0.0031 in.)
	(0.0010-0.0020 in.)	
Sub-chamber–600 cc	NA	
Valve face width		
Intake	1.20-1.85 mm	2.6 mm (0.10 in.)
	(0.047-0.071 in.)	
Exhaust	0.90-1.70 mm	2.4 mm (0.09 in.)
	(0.040-0.067 in.)	
Sub-chamber–600 cc	1.00-1.40 mm	2.0 mm (0.08 in.)
	(0.039-0.551 in.)	
Valve spring free length		
Intake and exhaust		
Inner	35.1 mm (1.382 in.)	34.1 mm (1.34 in.)
Outer	36.0 mm (1.417 in.)	35.0 mm (1.38 in.)
Sub-chamber–600 cc	40.5 mm (1.5944 in.)	39.3 mm (1.55 in.)
Main rocker arm assembly		
Rocker arm bore ID	11.50-11.518 mm	11.55 mm (0.455 in.)
	(0.4528-0.4535 in.)	
Rocker arm shaft OD	11.466-11.484 mm	11.41 mm (0.449 in.)
	(0.4514-0.4521 in.)	
Sub-rocker arm asssembly		
Rocker arm bore ID		
Intake	8.00-8.015 mm	8.05 mm (0.317 in.)
	(0.3150-0.3155 in.)	
Exhaust	7.00-7.015 mm	7.05 mm (0.277 in.)
	(0.2756-0.2761 in.)	
Rocker arm shaft OD		
Intake	7.969-7.972 mm	7.92 mm (0.312 in.)
	(0.3137-0.3139 in.)	
Exhaust	6.972-6.969 mm	6.92 mm (0.272 in.)
	(0.2744-0.2745 in.)	
Main rocker arm to shaft	0.016-0.052 mm	0.14 mm (0.006 in.)
clearance	(0.0006-0.0020 in.)	
Sub-rocker arm to shaft	0.033-0.043 mm	0.08 mm (0.003 in.)
clearance	(0.0013-0.0017 in.)	
Oil pump (A and B rotors)		
Inner to outer	0.15 mm	0.20 mm (0.008 in.)
rotor tip clearance	(0.006 in.)	
Outer rotor to	0.15-0.21 mm	0.25 mm (0.0010 in.)
body clearance	(0.006-0.008 in.)	
Rotor to body	0.02-0.08 mm	0.12 mm (0.005 in.)
clearance	(0.0008-0.003 in.)	
Counter balance system		
Shaft OD each end		
600 cc	16.977-16.995 mm	16.95 mm (0.667 in.)
	(0.6684-0.6691 in.)	
500 cc	NA	
Kickstarter		
Idle gear ID	20.00-20.021 mm	20.11 mm (0.792 in.)
	(0.7874-0.7882 in.)	
Idle gear bushing		
ID	16.00-16.018 mm	16.03 mm (0.631 in.)
	(0.6299-0.6306 in.)	
OD	19.959-19.98 mm	19.90 mm (0.783 in.)
	(0.7858-0.7866 in.)	
	(continued)	

Table 1 500 AND 600 CC ENGINE SPECIFICATIONS* (continued)

Item	Specifications	Wear limit
Kickstarter		
Gear ID		
1988-1990 XR600R	25.500-25.521 mm (1.0039-1.0048 in.)	25.58 mm (1.007 in.)
All other models	22.000-22.033 mm (0.8661-0.8674 in.)	22.12 mm (0.871 in.)
Shaft OD (where gear rides)	21.959-21.980 mm (0.8645-0.8653 in.)	21.91 mm (0.863 in.)
NA–Not available.		

Table 2 ENGINE TORQUE SPECIFICATIONS

Item	N•m	ft.-lb.
Engine mounting bolts and nuts		
8 mm		
1988-1990 XR600R	27	20
All other models	30-37	22-27
Engine mounting bolts		
10 mm		
1988-1990 XR500R	40	29
All other models		
Upper rear through bolt	35-45	25-33
Lower front through bolt	55-65	40-48
Valve adjuster locknut		
1979-1982 models	15-18	11-13
1983-1984 XR500R	18-22	13-16
XL600R	15-18	11-13
XR600R	23-27	17-19
Cylinder head cover bolts		
6 mm	8-12	6-9
8 mm		
1985-1987	20-26	15-19
1988-1990	23	17
All other models	26-30	19-22
Cylinder head bolts		
XR600R		
1985-1987	28-32	20-23
1988-1990	36	26
All other models	28-32	20-23
Cylinder bolts	47-53	34-38
Cam sprocket bolts	17-23	12-17
Main rocker arm shafts	25-30	18-22
Sub-rocker arm shafts		
Intake	25-30	18-22
Exhaust	20-25	15-18
Drive gear locknut		
1988-1990 XR600R	110	80
All other models	50-60	36-43
Crankcase bolts	8-12	6-9
Right- and left-hand crankcase cover bolts	8-12	6-9
Alternator cover bolts	8-12	6-9
Alternator rotor bolt		
XR600R		
1985-1987	100-120	73-88
1988-1990	125	92
All other models	80-100	59-73

5

CLUTCH AND TRANSMISSION

CLUTCH

The clutch is a wet multi-plate type which operates immersed in the engine oil. It is mounted on the right-hand end of the transmission mainshaft. The inner clutch hub is splined to the mainshaft and the outer housing can rotate freely on the mainshaft. The outer housing is geared to the crankshaft.

The clutch release mechanism is mounted within the right-hand crankcase cover and is operated by the clutch cable and hand lever.

Clutch specifications are listed in **Table 1** at the end of this chapter. **Tables 1-5** are located at the end of this chapter.

CLUTCH (1979-1982 500 CC MODELS)

The clutch assembly used on these models is basically the same but minor differences exist among the models. Where differences occur they are identified.

Refer to **Figure 1** for this procedure.

Removal/Disassembly

The clutch can be removed with the engine in the frame.

1. Remove the seat and side covers.

NOTE
*On XL500S models, reinstall the seat strap bolts as they also hold the upper portion of the shock absorbers to the frame (**Figure 2**). Remove and install one bolt at a time.*

2. Remove the bolts securing the skid plate and remove the skid plate.
3. Drain the engine oil as described in Chapter Three.
4. Place wood blocks under the engine to support it securely.
5. On XL series models, disconnect the battery negative lead or disconnect the main fuse (**Figure 3**).
6. Remove the fuel tank as described in Chapter Seven.
7. Remove the bolt securing the kickstarter pedal and remove the kickstarter pedal.
8. Disconnect the rear brake switch return spring and cable, the front right-hand footpeg and the rear brake pedal.
9. Slacken the clutch cable at the hand lever (**Figure 4**).
10. Disconnect the clutch cable from the clutch release arm (A, **Figure 5**).
11. Disconnect the starter decompressor cable at the crankcase cover (B, **Figure 5**).

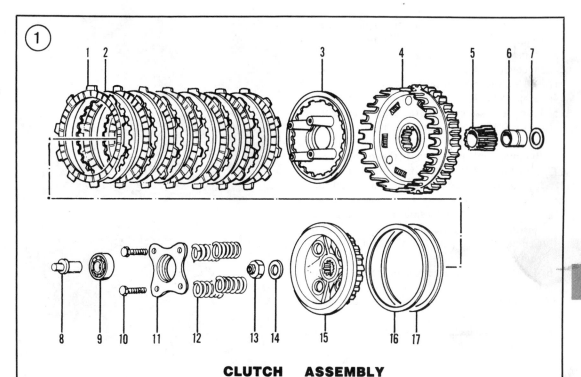

CLUTCH ASSEMBLY
(1979-1982 500CC)

1. Friction disc
2. Clutch plate
3. Pressure plate
4. Clutch outer housing
5. Kickstarter drive gear
6. Outer guide
7. Thrust washer
8. Lifter rod
9. Bearing
10. Bolts
11. Lifter plate
12. Clutch springs
13. Clutch locknut
14. Lockwasher
15. Clutch center
16. Judder seat—Model XL500S only
17. Judder spring—Model XL500S only

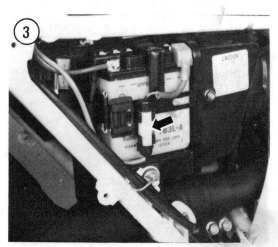

12. Disconnect the pulse generator 2-pin electrical connector. Refer to **Figure 6** or **Figure** 7.

13. Remove the bolts (**Figure 8**) securing the clutch cover and remove the clutch cover and gasket. Don't lose the locating dowels.

14. Remove the lifter rod and bearing (**Figure 9**).

15. Using a crisscross pattern remove the clutch bolts (**Figure 10**) securing the clutch lifter plate and remove the lifter plate.

16. Remove the clutch springs (**Figure 11**).

17. Straighten the locking tab on the clutch nut.

18A. To loosen the clutch nut with a special tool, perform the following:

    a. Hold onto the clutch center to prevent it from turning. Use Honda special tool (Clutch Center Holder—part No. 07923-4280000) or equivalent.

    b. Loosen the clutch nut. Remove the nut and lockwasher.

18B. To remove the clutch nut without the special tool, perform the following:

    a. Hold onto the clutch center to prevent it from turning.

    b. Use an impact driver and loosen the clutch nut. Remove the nut and lockwasher.

19. Slide the entire clutch assembly (clutch center, clutch plates, friction discs, pressure plate and clutch outer housing) off of the transmission mainshaft.

20. On models so equipped, remove the clutch outer housing guide and thrust washer.

21. Separate the components removed in Step 18.

22. Inspect all components as described in this chapter.

Assembly/Installation

NOTE
If new friction discs and clutch plates are being installed, apply new engine oil to all surfaces to avoid having the clutch lock up when used for the first time.

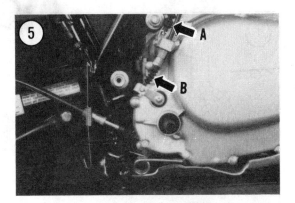

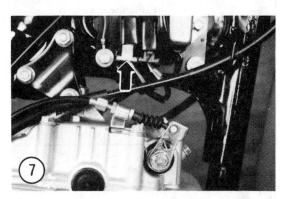

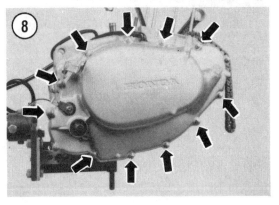

NOTE
The number of friction plates and clutch discs varies among the different models.

1A. On models equipped with a judder spring, perform the following:

   a. Place the clutch center on your workbench with the splines facing up and perform the following.

   b. Install the flat judder seat (**Figure 12**) onto the clutch center.

   c. Install the judder spring on the clutch center with the dished side facing up as shown in **Figure 13**.

   d. Install the only *narrow* friction disc (**Figure 14**) onto the clutch center with the judder seat and spring inboard of it. Refer to **Figure 13**.

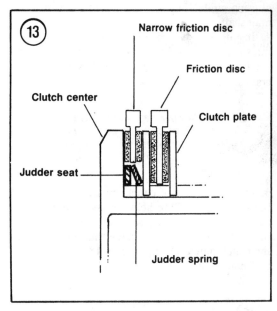

e. Onto the narrow friction disc, install a clutch plate and then a friction disc.

f. Continue to install a clutch plate and then a friction disc, alternating them until all are installed. The last item installed is a friction disc (**Figure 15**).

1B. On all other models, perform the following:

a. Place the clutch center on your workbench with the splines facing up and perform the following.

b. Onto the clutch center, install first a friction disc, then a clutch plate.

c. Continue to install the friction discs and clutch plates, alternating them until all are installed. The last item installed is a friction disc (**Figure 15**).

2. Onto this assembly, install the pressure plate.

3. Install the thrust washer and clutch outer housing guide (**Figure 16**) onto the transmission mainshaft.

4. Install the clutch outer housing onto the transmission shaft (**Figure 17**). Make sure the gears mesh properly with the drive gear on the crankshaft.

NOTE
In the following step, do not tighten the bolts too tight as some play is needed for final alignment when the friction plate tabs slide into the clutch outer housing.

5. Install a couple of clutch springs, washers and bolts (A, **Figure 18**) to hold the assembly made up in Step 1 and Step 2 together. This will aid in installation of these parts. Slide this assembly into the clutch outer housing (**Figure 18**).

6. Remove the bolts, washers and springs.

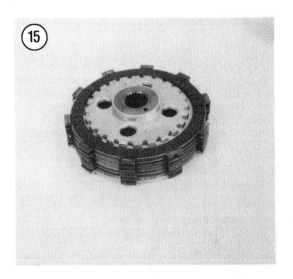

7. Install the lockwasher with the OUTSIDE mark facing toward the outside (**Figure 19**).

> *NOTE*
> *To prevent the clutch outer housing from turning, wedge a soft aluminum or brass bar between the housing gear and the drive gear (**Figure 20**).*

8. Use the same tool set-up used in *Removal/Disassembly* Step 18. Install the clutch nut and tighten to the torque specification listed in **Table 2**.

9. Lock the nut in place by staking the rim of the locknut into the groove in the mainshaft (**Figure 21**). Use a punch and hammer.

9. Install the clutch springs and the lifter plate.

10. Install the clutch bolts. Tighten the bolts securely in a crisscross pattern in 2-3 stages.

11. Install the ball bearing and lifter rod (A, **Figure 22**).

> *NOTE*
> *Make sure the oil screen (B, **Figure 22**) is still in place. This is a good time to remove and clean the screen as described in Chapter Three.*

12. Install a new clutch cover gasket and locating dowels onto the crankcase.

13. Hold the decompressor cam follower in the down position and install the clutch cover. Tighten the bolts to the torque specification listed in **Table 2**.

> *CAUTION*
> *After the clutch cover is installed, check the operation of the clutch and starter decompressor levers. They should operate without binding; if they bind, remove the cover and correct the problem.*

14. Connect the clutch and starter decompressor cables (**Figure 5**).

15. Install the rear brake lever, front footpegs and kickstarter lever.

16. Install the skid plate and tighten the bolt securely.

17. Install the side cover and the seat.

18. Refill the engine with the recommended type and quantity of engine oil as described in Chapter Three.

19. Adjust the clutch, starter decompressor and rear brake as described in Chapter Three.

CLUTCH (1983-1984 XR500R, 1983-1990 XL600R AND XR600R)

Removal/Installation

Refer to **Figure 23** for this procedure.

The clutch assembly can be removed with the engine in the frame.

1. Remove the seat and side covers.

2. Remove the exhaust pipe as described in Chapter Seven.

3. Drain the engine oil as described in Chapter Three.

4A. On XR600R models, remove the bolts (**Figure 24**) securing the engine protector to the frame and remove the protector.

4B. On all other models, remove the bolts securing the skid plate (**Figure 25**) and remove the skid plate.

5. Remove the bolt securing the kickstarter pedal and remove the kickstarter pedal.

6. Disconnect the clutch cable from the clutch release arm and the boss on the engine (**Figure 26**).

7. Remove the bolts securing the right-hand footpeg assembly and remove the assembly.

8. Loosen the brake adjust nut on the end of the brake rod (**Figure 27**).

9. Disconnect the brake pedal return spring from the brake pedal.

10. Disconnect the brake light switch spring from the brake pedal (A, **Figure 28**).

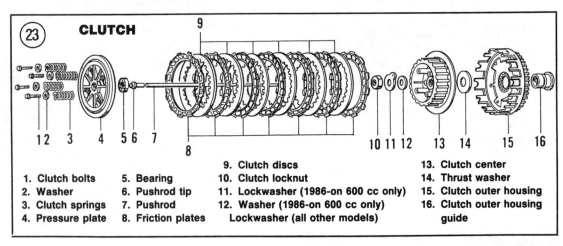

(23) CLUTCH

1. Clutch bolts
2. Washer
3. Clutch springs
4. Pressure plate
5. Bearing
6. Pushrod tip
7. Pushrod
8. Friction plates
9. Clutch discs
10. Clutch locknut
11. Lockwasher (1986-on 600 cc only)
12. Washer (1986-on 600 cc only)
    Lockwasher (all other models)
13. Clutch center
14. Thrust washer
15. Clutch outer housing
16. Clutch outer housing guide

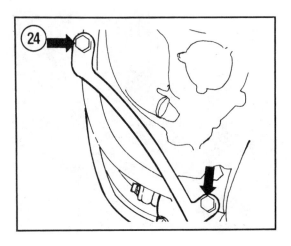

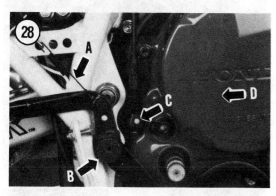

11. Remove the rear brake pedal pinch bolt (B, **Figure 28**) on the pivot shaft.

12. Remove the brake pedal pivot shaft. Move the brake pedal assembly back and out of the way. It is not necessary to remove the assembly from the frame.

13. Remove the oil pipe union bolt from the top of the clutch cover. Don't lose the sealing washers on each side of the oil pipe fitting.

14. On models so equipped, disconnect the starter decompression cable (C, **Figure 28**) from the lever on the crankcase cover.

15. Remove the bolts and nuts (models so equipped) and washers securing the clutch cover (D, **Figure 28**). Remove the clutch cover and gasket. Don't lose the locating dowels.

16. Using a crisscross pattern, remove the clutch bolts (**Figure 29**) securing the clutch pressure plate and remove the pressure plate along with the thrust bearing.

17. Remove the clutch springs and the pressure plate.

18. Remove the friction discs and clutch plates.

19. Remove the clutch lifter (**Figure 30**) and the pushrod (**Figure 31**) from the transmission shaft.

6

20. To keep the clutch center from turning in the next step, attach a clutch holder (**Figure 32**) to it.

CAUTION
Do not clamp the tool on too tightly as it may damage the groove in the clutch center.

21A. On 1986-1990 600 cc models, perform the following:
   a. Straighten the locking tab on the lockwasher
   b. Loosen and then remove the clutch locknut
   c. Remove the clutch holder from the clutch center.
   d. Remove the lockwasher and plain washer. Discard the lockwasher as a new one must be installed.
21B. On all other models, perform the following:
   a. Loosen then remove the clutch locknut.
   b. Remove the clutch holder from the clutch center.
   c. Remove the lockwasher.
22. Remove the clutch center, thrust washer and the clutch outer housing.
23. Slide off the clutch outer housing guide.
24. Inspect all components as described in this chapter.

Assembly/Installation

Refer to **Figure 23** for this procedure.

NOTE
If new friction discs and clutch plates are being installed, apply new engine oil to all surfaces to avoid having the clutch lock up when used for the first time.

1. Position the clutch outer housing guide with the flange side on first and slide it onto the transmission shaft (**Figure 33**).
2. Install the clutch outer housing (A, **Figure 34**) onto the clutch outer housing guide.
3. Slide on the thrust washer (B, **Figure 34**).
4. Install the clutch center (**Figure 35**).
5A. On 1986-1990 600 cc models, perform the following:
   a. Install the plain washer.
   b. Install a new lockwasher and align the hole in the tab with the raised boss in the clutch center.
   c. Install the clutch locknut.

   d. Use the same tool set-up used in Step 20 of *Removal/Disassembly* and tighten the clutch locknut to the torque specification listed in **Table 2**.
   e. Bend a portion of the lock up against one side of the locknut.

5B. On all other models, perform the following:
  a. Install the lockwasher (**Figure 36**) with the OUTSIDE mark facing toward the outside.
  b. Install the clutch locknut.
  c. Use the same tool set-up used in Step 20 of *Removal/Disassembly* and tighten the clutch locknut to the torque specification listed in **Table 2**.
6. Install the clutch pushrod (**Figure 31**).

7. Install the clutch lifter (**Figure 30**).
8. Onto the clutch center install first a friction disc then a clutch plate.
9. Continue to install the friction discs and clutch plates, alternating them until all are installed. The last item installed is a friction disc.
10. Install the pressure plate (A, **Figure 37**) and the clutch springs (B, **Figure 37**).
11. Install the clutch bolts. Tighten the bolts in a crisscross pattern in 2-3 stages to the torque specification listed in **Table 2**.
12. Install a new clutch cover gasket and locating dowels onto the crankcase.
13. Clean off all thread sealant residue from the crankcase cover bolts.
14. On models so equipped, hold the starter decompression cam follower in the down position and install the clutch cover.
15. Position the washers with the cupped side facing toward the crankcase cover and install the bolts, nuts (models so equipped) and washers. Tighten all bolts and nuts to the torque specification listed in **Table 2**.

NOTE
On models equipped with a decompression lever, after the crankcase cover is installed, check the operation of the decompression lever. It should operate without binding. If there is any binding, remove the crankcase cover and correct the problem.

16. Install the kickstarter lever and bolt. Tighten the bolt securely.
17. On models so equipped, connect the starter decompression cable onto the lever on the crankcase cover.
18. Install a new sealing washer on each side of the oil pipe fitting and install the union bolt to the top of the clutch cover. Tighten the union bolt securely.
19. Move the brake pedal assembly back into position and install the brake pedal pivot shaft.
20. Install the rear brake pedal pinch bolt onto the pivot shaft and tighten securely.
21. Connect the brake light switch spring and the brake pedal return spring onto the brake pedal.
22. Install the right-hand footpeg assembly and tighten the bolts to the torque specification listed in **Table 2**.
23. Connect the clutch cable onto the clutch release arm.

24. Refill the engine with the recommended type and quantity of engine oil as described in Chapter Three.

25. Install the exhaust pipe as described in Chapter Seven.

26. Install the skid plate or engine protector.

27. Install the seat and side covers.

28. Adjust the clutch and rear brake as described in Chapter Three.

Inspection (All Models)

Refer to **Table 1** for clutch specifications.

1. Clean all clutch parts in petroleum-based solvent such as kerosene and dry thoroughly with compressed air.

2. Measure the free length of each clutch spring as shown in **Figure 38**. Compare to the specifications listed in **Table 1**. Replace any springs that have sagged to the service limit or less.

3. Measure the thickness of each friction disc at several places around the disc as shown in **Figure 39**. Compare to the specifications listed in **Table 1**. Replace any disc that is worn to the service limit or less.

4. Check the clutch plates for warpage on a surface plate such as a piece of plate glass (**Figure 40**). Compare to the specifications listed in **Table 1**. Replace any plate that is warped to the service limit or more.

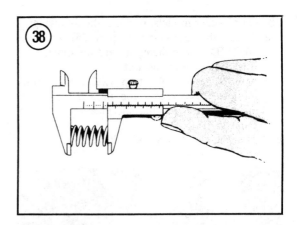

> *NOTE*
> *If any of the friction discs, clutch plates or clutch springs require replacement, you should consider replacing all of them as a set to retain maximum clutch performance.*

5. Inspect the slots in the clutch outer housing (**Figure 41**) for cracks, nicks or galling where they come in contact with the friction disc tabs. If severe damage is evident, the housing must be replaced.

6. Inspect the gear teeth on the outer housing for damage. Remove any small nicks with an oilstone. If damage is severe, the housing must be replaced. Also check the teeth on the driven gear of the crankshaft; if damaged the driven gear may also need replacing.

7. Inspect the damper springs (**Figure 42**). If they are sagged or broken, the housing must be replaced.

8. Inspect the inner splines of the clutch outer housing; replace if damaged.

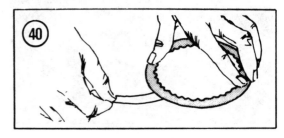

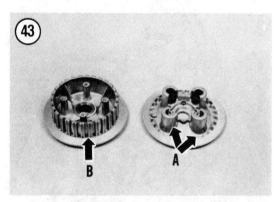

B   A

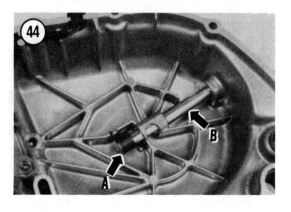

B

A

9. Measure the inside diameter of the clutch outer housing. Compare to the service limit dimensions listed in **Table 1**; replace if worn.

10. Measure the inside diameter and the outside diameter of the outer guide. Compare to the service limit dimensions listed in **Table 1**; replace if worn.

11. Inspect the grooves and studs in the pressure plate (A, **Figure 43**). If either show signs of wear or galling the pressure plate should be replaced.

12. Inspect the inner splines and outer grooves in the clutch center (B, **Figure 43**). If damaged the clutch center should be replaced.

13. Inspect the clutch lifter rod for bending. Roll it on a surface plate or piece of plate glass. Honda does not provide service information for this component, but if the rod is bent or deformed in any way it must be replaced. Otherwise it may hang up in the channel within the transmission shaft, causing erratic clutch operation.

14. Check the movement of the clutch lifter arm assembly in the crankcase cover. If the arm binds or the return spring is weak or broken, it must be replaced. To remove the mechanism perform the following:

    a. Remove the clutch lifter from the lifter arm.

    b. Remove the spring (A, **Figure 44**) and withdraw the lifter arm (B, **Figure 44**) from the cover.

    c. Remove the spring.

    d. Inspect the O-ring seal on the clutch lifter mechanism; replace if necessary.

    e. Check that the return spring is not bent or broken; replace if necessary.

    f. Apply multipurpose grease to the clutch lifter mechanism and install it into the crankcase cover. Secure the mechanism with the spring pin.

CLUTCH CABLE REPLACEMENT

In time the clutch cable will stretch to the point where it is no longer useful and will have to be replaced.

1. Remove the right- and left-hand side covers and seat.

NOTE
On XL500S models, reinstall the seat strap bolts as they also hold the upper portion of the shock to the frame. Remove and reinstall one bolt at a time.

2. Remove the fuel tank as described in Chapter Six.

3. On XL series models, disconnect the battery negative lead or disconnect the main fuse (**Figure 45**).

4. Remove the fuel tank as described in Chapter Seven.

5. Loosen the locknut (A, **Figure 46**) and adjusting barrel (B, **Figure 46**) at the clutch hand lever and remove the cable from the lever.

6A. On RFVC engine models, perform the following:

  a. Remove the clutch cable from the retainer on top of the crankcase.
  b. Slip the cable end out of the clutch activating arm and the boss on the crankcase cover (A, **Figure 47**).
  c. Pull the clutch cable from the retaining clips on the frame down tube (B, **Figure 47**).
  d. Pull the cable out from behind the headlight/steering head area (C, **Figure 47**).

6B. On all other models, perform the following:

  a. Loosen the locknut and adjusting nut (A, **Figure 48**) at the frame lower bracket.
  b. Slip the cable end out of the clutch activating arm (B, **Figure 48**).
  c. Pull the clutch cable from the retaining clip (A, **Figure 49**) on the cylinder head cover.
  d. Pull the cable out from behind the headlight/steering head area and out of the retaining loop on the frame (B, **Figure 49**).

> *NOTE*
> *Before removing the cable, make a drawing of the cable routing through the frame. It is very easy to forget how it was, once it has been removed. Replace the cable exactly as it was, avoiding any sharp turns.*

7. Remove the cable and replace it with a new cable.

8. Install by reversing these removal steps, noting the following.

9. Adjust the clutch as described in Chapter Three.

EXTERNAL SHIFT MECHANISM
(1983-1984 XR500R,
XL600R AND XR600R)

The shifting mechanism is located on the same side of the crankcase as the clutch assembly. To remove the internal shift mechanism (shift levers, shift drum and shift forks), it is necessary to remove the engine and split the crankcase. This procedure is covered in this chapter.

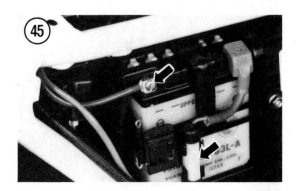

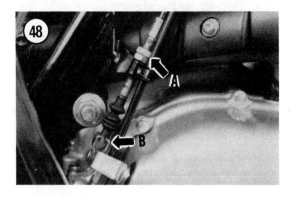

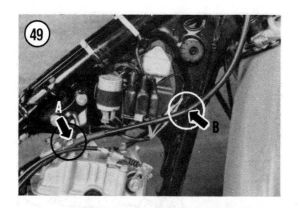

Removal

1. Remove the clutch assembly as described in this chapter.

2. Remove the kickstarter assembly as described in Chapter Five.

3. Remove the bolts securing the oil line to the oil pump and the crankcase.

4. Remove the bolt (**Figure 50**) securing the shift drum stopper plate and remove the stopper plate.

5. Remove the bolt (**Figure 51**) securing the neutral stopper arm and remove the arm.

Inspection

1. Inspect the ramps of the shift drum stopper plate (A, **Figure 52**). They must be smooth and free from burrs or wear; replace as necessary.

2. Inspect the roller on the neutral stopper arm (B, **Figure 52**). It must rotate smoothly with no signs of wear or binding; replace as necessary.

Installation

1. Install the neutral stopper arm and spring (**Figure 51**) onto the crankcase. Tighten the bolt securely.

2. Hold the neutral stopper arm back and out of the way with a screwdriver (A, **Figure 53**).

3. Align the bolt hole in the backside of the shift drum stopper plate with the dowel pin on the shift drum (**Figure 54**). Install the shift drum stopper plate and bolt (B, **Figure 53**). Tighten the bolt securely.

4. Remove the screwdriver and index the stopper arm onto the shift drum stopper plate.

5. Install the oil line from the oil pump to the crankcase. Install and tighten the bolts securely.

6. Install the kickstarter as described in Chapter Five.

7. Install the clutch assembly as described in this chapter.

8. Refill the engine with the recommended type and quantity of engine oil as described in Chapter Three.

9. Adjust the clutch as described in Chapter Three.

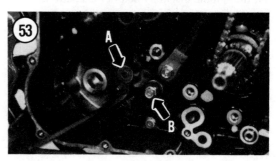

6

EXTERNAL SHIFT MECHANISM (ALL OTHER MODELS)

The shifting mechanism is located under the left-hand crankcase cover. Removal and installation can be accomplished with the engine in the frame. This procedure is shown with the engine removed for clarity.

To remove the internal shift mechanism (shift levers, shift drum and shift forks), it is necessary to remove the engine and split the crankcase. This procedure is covered in this chapter.

Removal/Installation

1. Remove the alternator as described in this chapter.

> *CAUTION*
> *On XL models, shift the transmission into **1st gear**. This will align the neutral indicator rotor with the open area of the shift plate. Do **not** damage this rotor during removal and installation or it will have to be replaced.*

2. Remove the thrust washer (A, **Figure 55**) and carefully remove the gearshift spindle assembly (B, **Figure 55**) and inner thrust washer.
3. Unhook the shift pawl spring (A, **Figure 56**) and remove the bolt (B, **Figure 56**) securing the shift pawl. Remove the shift pawl.
4. If necessary, remove the stopper plate bolt (C, **Figure 56**) and remove the neutral indicator rotor.
5. Remove the bolt (**Figure 51**) securing the neutral stopper arm and remove the arm.
6. If spindle disassembly is necessary, remove the circlips (**Figure 57**) at each end and remove all components. Assemble in the same order as shown in **Figure 57**.
7. Install by reversing these removal steps, noting the following.
8. Make sure the transmission is in 1st gear when installing the gearshift spindle.
9. Make sure the inner thrust washer is installed on the spindle assembly before installation.

TRANSMISSIONS

The transmissions and internal shift mechanisms used among the various models vary considerably.

The transmission used in the RFVC (radial four valve combustion) engines is removed after the internal shift mechanism.

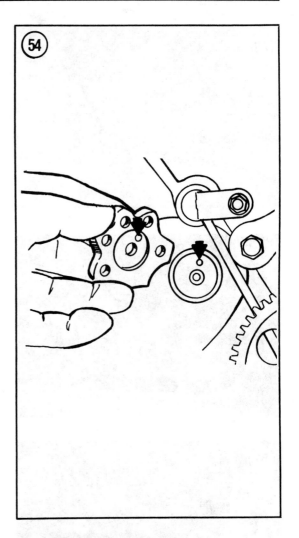

The transmissions used on all other models can be removed and installed without having to remove the internal shift mechanism since the crankcase is split horizontally. Once the crankcase is split, removal and installation of the transmission assemblies is a simple task of pulling the assemblies up and out of the lower crankcase.

There are many different transmissions used among the various models. Some have only small variations and all variations are noted in each procedure. Be sure to use the correct procedure for your specific bike—including model year.

Refer to the various tables at the end of the chapter for transmission and internal shift mechanism specifications.

To gain access to the transmission and internal shift mechanism it is necessary to remove the engine and split the crankcase as described either in Chapter Four or Chapter Five.

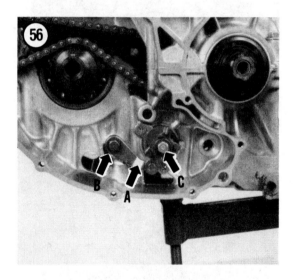

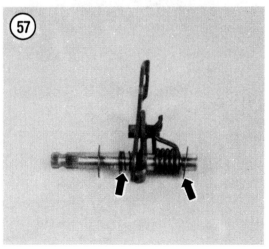

Preliminary Inspection (All Models)

After the transmission shaft assemblies have been removed from the crankcase, clean and inspect the assemblies before disassembling them. Place the assembled shaft into a large can or plastic bucket and thoroughly clean with a petroleum based solvent such as kerosene and a stiff brush. Dry with compressed air or let it sit on rags to drip dry. Repeat for the other shaft assembly.

1. After they have been cleaned, visually inspect the components of the assemblies for excessive wear. Any burrs, pitting or roughness on the teeth of a gear will cause wear on the mating gear. Minor roughness can be cleaned up with an oilstone but there's little point in attempting to remove deep scars.

NOTE
Defective gears should be replaced. It's a good idea to replace the mating gear on the other shaft even though it may not show as much wear or damage.

2. Carefully check the engagement dogs. If any are chipped, worn, rounded or missing the affected gear must be replaced.

3A. On RFVC engines, rotate the transmission bearings in both crankcase halves by hand. Check for roughness, noise and radial play. Any bearing that is suspect should be replaced as described in Chapter Four.

3B. On all other engines, rotate the transmission bearings on the transmission shafts by hand. Check for roughness, noise and radial play. Any bearing that is suspect should be replaced as described in this chapter.

4. If the transmission shafts are satisfactory and are not going to be disassembled, apply assembly oil or engine oil to all components and reinstall them in the crankcase as described in this chapter.

NOTE
If disassembling a used, well run-in (high mileage) transmission for the first time by yourself, pay particular attention to any additional shims that may have been added by a previous owner. These may have been added to take up the tolerance of worn components and must be reinstalled in the same position since the shims have developed a wear pattern. If new parts are going to be installed these shims may be eliminated. This is something you will have to determine upon reassembly.

6

5-SPEED TRANSMISSION
(1979-1982 500 CC ENGINES)

Removal/Installation

1. Remove the engine and split the crankcase as described in Chapter Four.
2. Remove the mainshaft assembly (A, **Figure 58**) and countershaft assembly (B, **Figure 58**).
3. Install by reversing these removal steps, noting the following.

NOTE
Before installation, coat all bearing surfaces with assembly oil.

4. Position the shift forks as shown in A, **Figure 59**.
5. Install the 2 bearing set rings (B, **Figure 59**) and bearing locating dowel (C, **Figure 59**).
6. Engage the balance chain onto the sprocket on the left-hand end of the mainshaft assembly and install it (**Figure 60**).

NOTE
Make sure the shift fork engages properly. Also make sure the bearings are properly indexed into the set ring and oil control orifice on the left-hand side.

7. Install the countershaft assembly (**Figure 61**).

NOTE
*Make sure the shift fork engages properly. Also make sure the bearings are properly indexed into the set ring and locating dowel. The sealing ring on the oil seal must be correctly seated into the groove (A, **Figure 61**) or the crankcase halves will not join properly.*

NOTE
When a new oil seal is installed, apply a light coat of multipurpose grease to the lips before installation.

8. After both transmission assemblies are installed, rotate them by hand. Make sure there is no binding. Also shift through all 5 gears using the shift drum. Make sure the shift forks are operating properly and that you can shift through all gears. This is the time to find that something may be installed incorrectly—not after the crankcase is completely assembled.
9. Reassemble the crankcase and install the engine as described in Chapter Four.

Mainshaft
Disassembly/Inspection/Assembly

Refer to **Figure 62** for this procedure.

NOTE
A helpful "tool" that should be used for transmission disassembly is a large egg flat (the type that restaurants get their eggs in). As you remove a part from the shaft set it in one of the depressions in

the same position from which it was removed. This is an easy way to remember the correct relationship of all parts.

1. If not cleaned in the *Preliminary Inspection* sequence, place the assembled shaft into a large can or plastic bucket and thoroughly clean with solvent and a stiff brush. Dry with compressed air or let it sit on rags to dry.

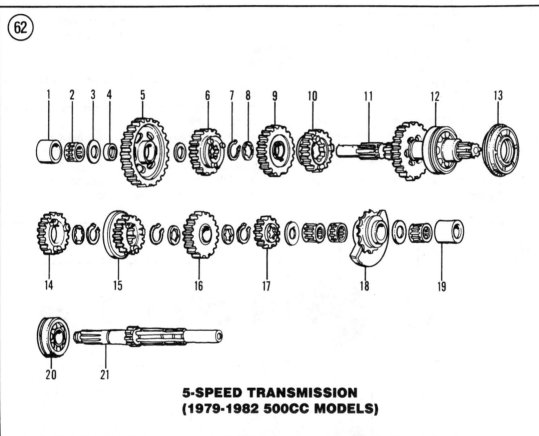

5-SPEED TRANSMISSION
(1979-1982 500CC MODELS)

1. Outer bearing race
2. Needle bearing
3. Thrust washer
4. Countershaft 1st gear spacer
5. Countershaft 1st gear
6. Countershaft 4th gear
7. Circlip
8. Splined washer
9. Countershaft 3rd gear
10. Countershaft 5th gear
11. Countershaft
12. Ball bearing
13. Oil seal
14. Main shaft 4th gear
15. Main shaft 3rd gear
16. Main shaft 5th gear
17. Main shaft 2nd gear
18. Rear balancer
19. Outer bearing race
20. Ball bearing
21. Mainshaft

2. Remove the outer bearing race, needle bearing(s) and thrust washer (1, **Figure 63**).

3. Remove the rear balancer weight (2, **Figure 63**).

4. Remove the needle bearings.

5. Slide off the thrust washer (3, **Figure 63**).

6. Slide off the 2nd gear (4, **Figure 63**).

7. Remove the circlip, splined washer and slide off the 5th gear (5, **Figure 63**).

8. Slide off the splined washer and remove the circlip. Then slide off the 3rd gear (6, **Figure 63**).

9. Remove the circlip and splined washer. Then slide off the 4th gear (7, **Figure 63**).

10. If necessary, remove the ball bearing from the shaft (**Figure 64**).

11. Check each gear for excessive wear, burrs, pitting, or chipped or missing teeth. Make sure the lugs on the gears are in good condition.

NOTE
Defective gears should be replaced. It is a good idea to replace the mating gear on the countershaft even though it may not show as much wear or damage.

12. Make sure that all gears slide smoothly on the mainshaft splines.

NOTE
It is recommended that all circlips be replaced every time the transmission is disassembled to ensure proper gear alignment. Do not expand a circlip more than necessary to slide it over the shaft.

13. Measure the outside diameter of the mainshaft at points "A" and "B". Refer to **Figure 65**. If the shaft is worn to the service limit listed in **Table 3** or less at either location, the shaft must be replaced. The clearance between any gear and shaft is 0.15 mm (0.006 in.).

14. Check the bearings. Make sure they rotate smoothly with no signs of wear or damage; replace as necessary.

15. Assemble by reversing these removal steps, noting the following.

16. Refer to **Figure 66** for correct placement of all gears. Make sure all circlips are seated correctly in the mainshaft grooves.

17. Make sure each gear engages properly to the adjoining gear where applicable.

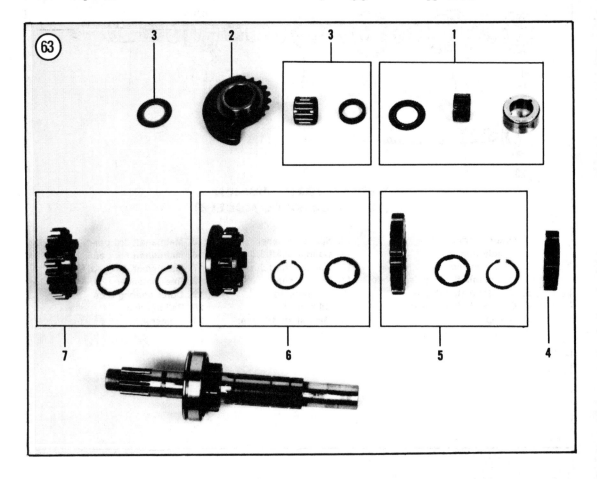

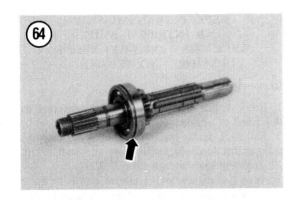

18. Be sure to install the 2nd gear with the recess (**Figure 67**) facing in toward the 5th gear. This recess is necessary to clear the splined washer and circlip securing the 5th gear.

Countershaft
Disassembly/Inspection/Assembly

Refer to **Figure 62** for this procedure.

NOTE
Use the same large egg flat used on the mainshaft disassembly during the countershaft disassembly. This is an easy way to remember the correct relationship of all parts.

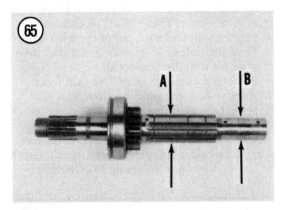

1. If not cleaned in the *Preliminary Inspection* sequence, place the assembled shaft into a large can or plastic bucket and clean thoroughly with solvent and a stiff brush. Dry with compressed air or let it sit on rags to dry.

2. Remove the outer bearing race, needle bearing and thrust washer (1, **Figure 68**).

3. Slide off the 1st gear, 1st gear spacer and the thrust washer (2).

4. Slide off the 4th gear (3).

5. Remove the circlip and splined washer. Then slide off the 3rd gear (4).

6. Slide off the 5th gear (5).

7. Remove the 2nd gear and/or the ball bearing if necessary (**Figure 69**).

NOTE
These 2 components are pressed into place on the countershaft and removal should be entrusted to a Honda dealer or machine shop.

8. Carefully slide off the oil seal (6).

9. Check each gear for excessive wear, burrs, pitting, or chipped or missing teeth. Make sure the lugs on the gears are in good condition.

NOTE
Defective gears should be replaced. It is a good idea to replace the mating gear on the mainshaft even though it may not show as much wear or damage.

10. Make sure that all gears slide smoothly on the mainshaft splines.

NOTE
It is recommended that all circlips be replaced every time the transmission is disassembled to ensure proper gear alignment. Do not expand a circlip more than necessary to slide it over the shaft.

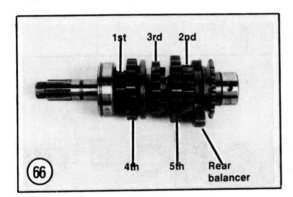

1st   3rd   2nd

4th   5th   Rear balancer

11. Measure the outside diameter of the countershaft at points "A," "B" and "C". Refer to **Figure 70**. If the shaft is worn to the service limit listed in **Table 3** or less at either location, the shaft must be replaced. The clearance between any gear and shaft is 0.15 mm (0.006 in.).

12. Measure the inside diameter (ID) and outside (OD) of the 1st gear spacer. Replace if worn to the service limit dimensions listed in **Table 3**. If either dimension is to the service limit the spacer must be replaced.

13. Check the bearings. Make sure they rotate smoothly with no signs of wear or damage; replace as necessary.

14. Assemble by reversing these removal steps, noting the following.

15. Refer to **Figure 71** for correct placement of all gears. Make sure all circlips are seated correctly in the countershaft grooves.

16. Make sure each gear engages properly to the adjoining gear where applicable.

5-SPEED TRANSMISSION AND INTERNAL SHIFT MECHANISM (1983-1984 XR500R, XL600R AND XR600R)

Removal/Installation

1. Remove the engine and split the crankcase as described in Chapter Five.
2. Pull back on the gear shift plate of the gearshift mechanism to disengage it from the shift drum. Remove the gearshift assembly.
3. Bend down the locking tab on the lockwasher and remove the bolt and lockwasher securing the center shift fork to the shift fork shaft. Discard the lockwasher—never re-use an old lockwasher.
4. Pull the shift fork shaft out of the crankcase.
5. Pivot the shift forks away from the shift drum to allow for shift drum removal.
6. Remove the shift drum and the shift forks.
7. Remove both transmission assemblies.
8. Inspect the shift fork assembly as described in this chapter.
9. Install the transmission assemblies as follows:
   a. Mesh both transmission assemblies together in their proper relationship to each other.

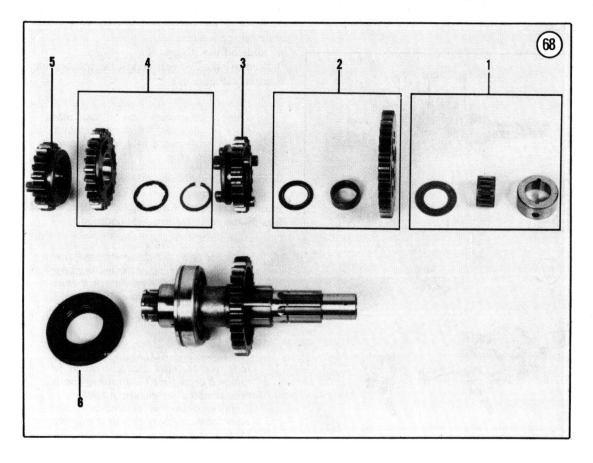

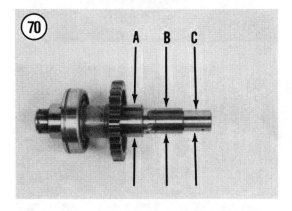

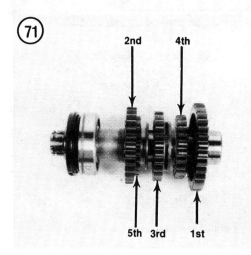

b. Hold the thrust washers in place with your fingers on the both shaft assemblies (**Figure 72**).

c. Install the assembled shafts into the left-hand crankcase.

d. Make sure the thrust washer on both shaft assemblies is still positioned correctly after the assemblies are completely installed.

e. After both assemblies are installed, tap on the end of both shafts with a plastic or soft-faced mallet to make sure they are completely seated.

NOTE
If the thrust washer on the end of the shaft assembly is not seated correctly it will hold the transmission shaft up a little and prevent the crankcase halves from seating completely.

10. Coat all bearing and sliding surfaces of the shift drum with assembly oil and install the shift drum (**Figure 73**).

11. Install the left-hand shift fork (**Figure 74**), center shift fork (**Figure 75**) and the right-hand

6

shift fork (**Figure 76**). Make sure each shift fork is engaged in its respective gear and that all 3 cam pin followers are in mesh with the shift drum grooves.

12. Align the bolt hole in the shift fork shaft and the hole in the center shift fork and install the shift fork shaft (A, **Figure 77**).

13. Install the shift fork shaft bolt and lockwasher (B, **Figure 77**) and tighten to the torque specification listed in **Table 2**.

14. Bend up one of the tabs on the new lockwasher onto the side of the bolt.

15. Install the gearshift mechanism as follows:

 a. Partially install the gearshift assembly with the splined end (for the gearshift pedal) into the left-hand crankcase half.

 b. Pull back on the shift plate and push the shift mechanism all the way down into position.

 c. Release the shift plate and engage it correctly into the shift drum (**Figure 78**).

16. Spin both transmission shafts. Make sure there is no binding.

17. Tilt the left-hand crankcase half and transmission assemblies up to about a 45° angle from horizontal. This is to relieve some of the weight of the gears onto each other. If the next step is done with the crankcase half horizontal you may not be able to shift the transmission through the gears even though all the gears are assembled correctly and the transmission and internal shift mechanism assemblies are installed correctly.

NOTE
The following step is best done with the aid of a helper as the assemblies are loose and won't spin very easily. Have the helper spin the transmission shafts while you turn the shift drum through all the gears.

18. Spin the transmission shafts and shift through all 5 gears using the shift drum. Make sure the shift forks are operating properly and that you can shift through all gears. This is the time to find that something may be installed incorrectly, not after the crankcase is completely assembled.

19. Make sure the thrust washer is installed on the end of the countershaft.

20. Reassemble the crankcase and install the engine as described in Chapter Five.

Mainshaft
Disassembly/Inspection/Assembly

Refer to **Figure 79** for this procedure.

NOTE
A helpful "tool" that should be used for transmission disassembly is a large egg flat (the type that restaurants get their eggs in). As you remove a part from the shaft set it in one of the depressions in the same position from which it was removed (Figure 80). This is an easy way to remember the correct relationship of all parts.

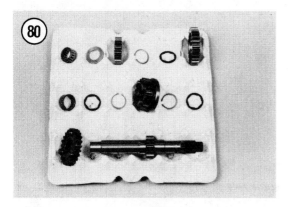

1. If not cleaned in the *Preliminary Inspection* sequence, place the assembled shaft into a large can or plastic bucket and clean thoroughly with solvent and a stiff brush. Dry with compressed air or let it sit on rags to dry.
2. Slide off the needle bearing and thrust washer.
3. Slide off the 2nd gear.
4. Remove the circlip and slide off the splined washer.
5. Slide off the 5th gear and 5th gear bushing.
6. Slide off the splined washer and remove the circlip.
7. Slide off the 3rd gear.
8. Remove the circlip and splined washer.

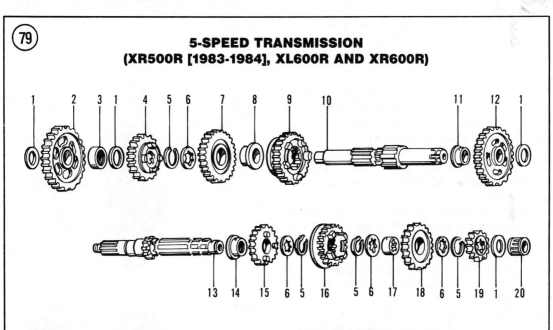

**5-SPEED TRANSMISSION
(XR500R [1983-1984], XL600R AND XR600R)**

1. Washer
2. Countershaft 1st gear
3. Countershaft 1st gear bushing
4. Countershaft 4th gear
5. Circlip
6. Splined washer
7. Countershaft 3rd gear
8. Countershaft 3rd gear bushing (1988-on XR600R)
9. Countershaft 5th gear
10. Countershaft
11. Countershaft 2nd gear bushing
12. Countershaft 2nd gear
13. Mainshaft/1st gear
14. Mainshaft 4th gear bushing (1988-on XR600R)
15. Mainshaft 4th gear
16. Mainshaft 3rd gear
17. Mainshaft 5th gear bushing
18. Mainshaft 5th gear
19. Mainshaft 2nd gear
20. Needle bearing

9A. On 1988-1990 XR600R models, slide off the 4th gear and 4th gear bushing.
9B. On all other models, slide off the 4th gear.
10. Check each gear for excessive wear, burrs, pitting, or chipped or missing teeth. Make sure the lugs on the gears are in good condition.

NOTE
Defective gears should be replaced. It is a good idea to replace the mating gear on the countershaft even though it may not show as much wear or damage.

NOTE
The 1st gear is part of the mainshaft. If the gear is defective the shaft must be replaced.

11. Make sure that all gears slide smoothly on the mainshaft splines.

NOTE
It is recommended that all circlips be replaced every time the transmission is disassembled to ensure proper gear alignment. Do not expand a circlip more than necessary to slide it over the shaft.

12. Measure the outside diameter of the mainshaft by measuring first gear (A, **Figure 81**). If the shaft is worn to the service limit listed in **Table 4** or less at either location, the shaft must be replaced.
13. Measure the inside diameter of the mainshaft 4th and 5th gears. If either gear is worn to the service limit listed in **Table 4** or greater, the gear must be replaced.
14. Measure the outside diameter of the mainshaft 5th gear bushing (**Figure 82**). If the bushing is worn to the service limit dimensions listed in **Table 4** or less, the bushing must be replaced.
15. On 1988-1990 XR600R models, measure the inside and outside diameter of the 4th gear bushing. Replace the bushing if it is worn to or beyond the service limit dimensions listed in **Table 4**.
16A. On 1988-1990 XR600R, perform the following:
   a. Position the 4th gear bushing with the shoulder side going on first and slide on the 4th gear bushing.
   b. Slide on the 4th gear.
   c. Install the splined washer and the circlip.
16B. On all other models, slide on the 4th gear and install the splined washer and circlip (**Figure 83**).
17. Slide on the 3rd gear (A, **Figure 84**) and install the circlip and splined washer (B, **Figure 84**).

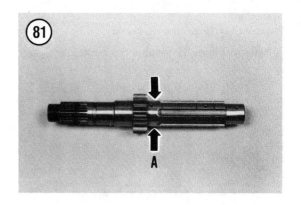
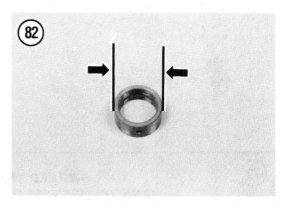
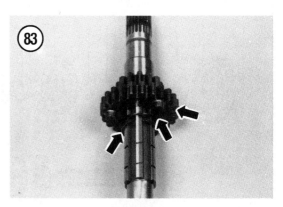
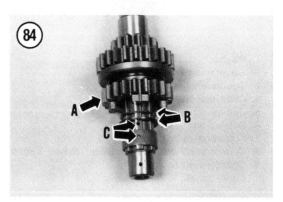

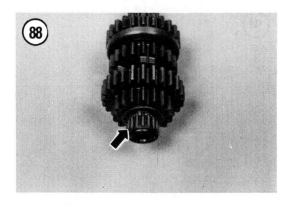

18. Align the oil hole in the 5th gear bushing (C, **Figure 84**) with the oil hole in the mainshaft and slide on the bushing.

19. Slide on the 5th gear and the splined washer (**Figure 85**).

20. Install the circlip (**Figure 86**).

21. Slide on the thrust washer (**Figure 87**) and the needle bearing (**Figure 88**).

22. Before installation, double-check the placement of all gears (**Figure 89**). Make sure all circlips are seated correctly in the mainshaft grooves.

23. Make sure each gear engages properly to the adjoining gear where applicable.

Countershaft
Disassembly/Inspection/Assembly

Refer to **Figure 79** for this procedure.

NOTE
Use the same large egg flat used on the mainshaft disassembly during the countershaft disassembly. This is an easy way to remember the correct relationship of all parts.

1. If not cleaned in the *Preliminary Inspection* sequence, place the assembled shaft into a large can or plastic bucket and thoroughly clean with solvent and a stiff brush. Dry with compressed air or let it sit on rags to dry.

2. Slide off the thrust washer, the 2nd gear and the 2nd gear bushing.

3. Slide off the 5th gear.

4. From the other end of the shaft, slide off the thrust washer, the 1st gear and the 1st gear bushing.

5. Slide off the thrust washer and the 4th gear.

6A. On 1988-1990 XR600R models, remove the circlip and slide off splined washer, 3rd gear and 3rd gear bushing.

6B. On all other models, remove the circlip and slide off the splined washer and the 3rd gear.

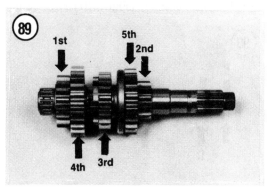

7. Check each gear for excessive wear, burrs, pitting, or chipped or missing teeth. Make sure the lugs on the gears are in good condition.

> *NOTE*
> *Defective gears should be replaced. It is a good idea to replace the mating gear on the mainshaft even though it may not show as much wear or damage.*

8. Make sure that all gears slide smoothly on the countershaft splines.

> *NOTE*
> *It is recommended that all circlips be replaced every time the transmission is disassembled to ensure proper gear alignment. Do not expand a circlip more than necessary to slide it over the shaft.*

9. Measure the outside diameter of the countershaft at points "B", "C", "D" and "E." Refer to **Figure 90**. If the shaft is worn to the service limit in **Table 4** or less at either location, the shaft must be replaced.

> *NOTE*
> *Honda does not provide specifications for the inside or outside diameter of the 3rd gear bushing on 1988-1990 XR600R models. The inside diameter of the bushing is similar to the inside diameter of the 3rd gear on other models, since the transmission shaft at the 3rd gear location is the same on all models.*

10. Measure the inside diameter of the 1st, 2nd and 3rd gears. Replace any gear that is worn to or greater than the service limit dimensions listed in **Table 4.**

11. Measure the inside and outside diameter of the 1st and 2nd gear bushings (**Figure 91**). Replace any

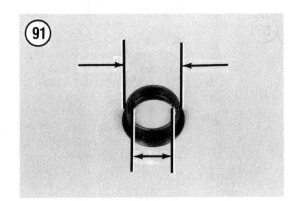

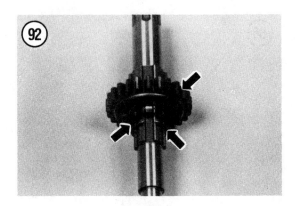

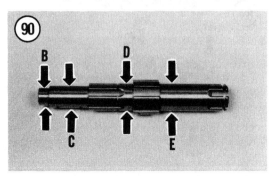

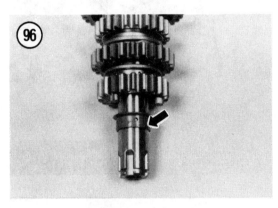

bushing that is worn to or beyond the service limit dimensions listed in **Table 4**.

12A. On 1988-1990 XR600R models, perform the following:

    a. Position the 3rd gear bushing with the shoulder side going on first and slide on the 3rd gear bushing.

    b. Slide on the 3rd gear (flush side on first) and splined washer.

    c. Install the circlip

12B. On all other models, slide on the 3rd gear (flush side on first), splined washer and circlip.

13. Slide on the 4th gear, thrust washer and the 1st gear bushing (**Figure 93**).

14. Slide on the 1st gear (with the higher boss side on first) and the thrust washer (**Figure 94**).

15. Onto the other end of the shaft, slide on the 5th gear (**Figure 95**).

16. Slide on the 2nd gear bushing (**Figure 96**).

17. Slide on the 2nd gear (with the higher boss side on first) and the thrust washer (**Figure 97**).

18. Before installation, double-check the placement of all gears (**Figure 98**). Make sure all circlips are seated correctly in the mainshaft grooves.

19. Make sure each gear engages properly to the adjoining gear where applicable.

20. After both transmission assemblies have been assembled, mesh the 2 assemblies together in the correct position (**Figure 99**). Check that all gears meet correctly. This is your last check before installing the assemblies in the crankcase; make sure they are correctly assembled.

INTERNAL SHIFT MECHANISM (1979-1982 500 CC MODELS)

Removal/Installation

1. Remove the transmission assemblies as described in this chapter.

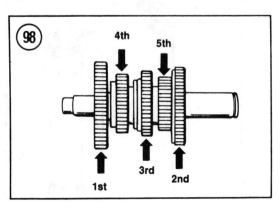

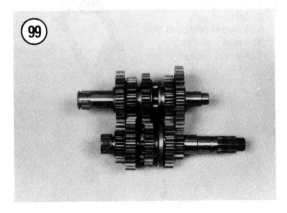

2. Hold onto the shift fork(s) and withdraw one shift fork at a time. Remove both shift fork shafts and the shift fork(s).

3. Remove the bolt (A, **Figure 100**) securing the neutral indicator rotor, collar and stopper plate. Remove all parts.

4. Remove the screws (B, **Figure 100**) securing the bearing set plate and remove the plate.

5. Carefully withdraw the shift drum from the left-hand side.

6. Thoroughly clean all parts in solvent and dry with compressed air.

Inspection

Refer to **Figure 101** and **Figure 102** for this procedure.

1. Inspect each shift fork for signs of wear or cracking. Check for bending and make sure each fork slides smoothly on the shaft. Replace any worn or damaged forks.

2. Check for any arc-shaped wear or burned marks on the shift forks. This indicates that the shift fork has come in contact with the gear. The fork fingers have become excessively worn and the fork must be replaced.

3. Check the grooves in the shift drum (A, **Figure 103**) for wear or roughness. If any of the groove profiles have excessive wear or damage, replace the shift drum.

4. Check the shift drum bearing (B, **Figure 103**). Make sure it operates smoothly with no signs of wear or damage.

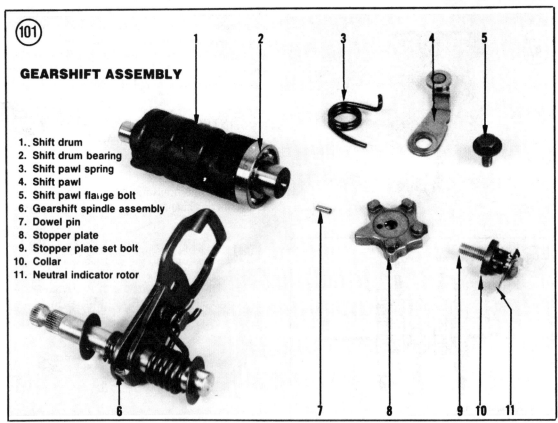

GEARSHIFT ASSEMBLY

1. Shift drum
2. Shift drum bearing
3. Shift pawl spring
4. Shift pawl
5. Shift pawl flange bolt
6. Gearshift spindle assembly
7. Dowel pin
8. Stopper plate
9. Stopper plate set bolt
10. Collar
11. Neutral indicator rotor

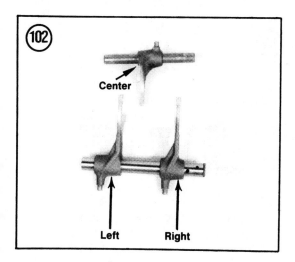

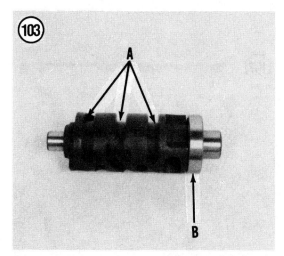

5. Check the cam pin followers on each shift fork. It should fit snugly but not too tight. Check the end that rides in the shift drum for wear or damage; replace as necessary.

6. Measure the outside diameter of the gearshift fork shafts with a micrometer. Replace the ones worn to the service limit listed in **Table 5** or less.

7. Roll each shift fork shaft on a flat surface such as a piece of plate glass and check for any bends. If the shaft is bent, it must be replaced.

8. Measure the width of the gearshift fork fingers with a micrometer (**Figure 104**). Replace the ones worn to the service limit listed in **Table 5** or less.

> *CAUTION*
> *It is recommended that marginal shift forks be replaced. Worn forks can cause the transmission to slip out of gear, leading to more serious and expensive damage.*

9. Measure the inside diameter of the gearshift forks with a micrometer (**Figure 105**). Replace the ones worn to the service limit listed in **Table 5** or greater.

10. Check the stopper plate for wear; replace as necessary.

Assembly/Installation

1. Apply a light coat of oil to the shift fork shafts and the inside bores of the shift forks before installation.

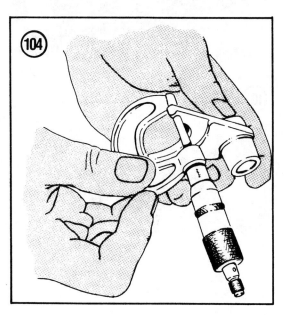

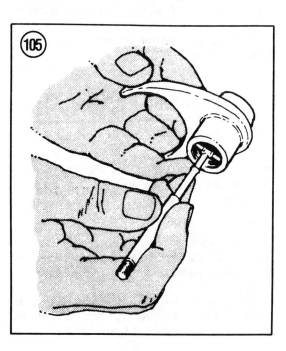

2. Install the shift drum in from the left-hand side.
3. Install the bearing set plate and screws (B, **Figure 100**). Tighten the screws to the torque specification listed in **Table 2**.

NOTE
After installing the shift drum, make sure it rotates smoothly with no binding.

4. Align the dowel pin in the stopper plate with the notch on the end of the shift drum and install the stopper plate.
5. Install the collar, neutral indicator rotor and stopper plate set bolt (A, **Figure 100**). Tighten the bolt securely.

NOTE
*The shift forks have a cast identification mark: "L" left-hand side, "C" center and "R" right-hand side. Refer to **Figure 106**.*

6. Install the right- and left-hand shift forks and shaft (A, **Figure 107**).
7. Install the center shift fork and shaft (B, **Figure 107**).

NOTE
***Figure 102** is shown with the shift forks and shafts removed for clarity. They should be installed at this point in the procedure.*

8. Make sure the shift fork guide pins are properly meshed with the grooves in the shift drum and are correctly positioned on their respective shafts as shown in **Figure 102**.
9. Install the transmission assemblies as described in this chapter.

INTERNAL SHIFT MECHANISM (1983-1984 XR500R, XL600R, XR600R)

The internal shift mechanism on these models is removed and installed during the transmission removal and installation procedures described in this chapter.

Inspection

1. Inspect each shift fork for signs of wear or cracking. Check for bending and make sure each fork slides smoothly on the shaft; replace any worn or damaged forks.
2. Check for any arc-shaped wear or burned marks on the shift forks. This indicates that the shift fork has come in contact with the gear. The fork fingers

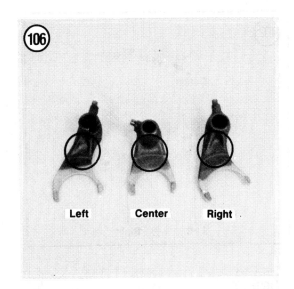
Left   Center   Right

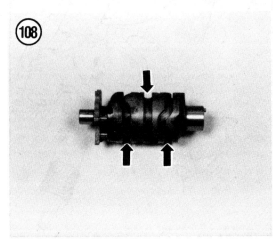

have become excessively worn and the fork must be replaced.

3. Check the grooves in the shift drum (**Figure 108**) for wear or roughness. If any of the groove profiles have excessive wear or damage, replace the shift drum.

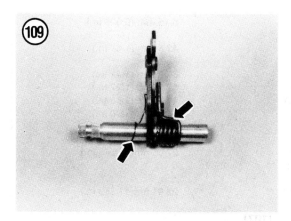

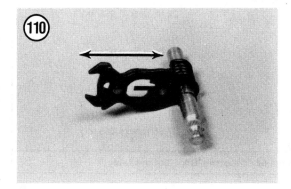

4. Check the cam pin followers on each shift fork. It should fit snugly but not too tight. Check the end that rides in the shift drum for wear or damage; replace as necessary.

5. Measure the outside diameter of the gearshift fork shafts with a micrometer. Replace the ones worn to the service limit listed in **Table 5** or less.

6. Roll each shift fork shaft on a flat surface such as a piece of plate glass and check for any bends. If the shaft is bent, it must be replaced.

7. Measure the width of the gearshift fork fingers with a micrometer (**Figure 104**). Replace ones that are worn to the service limit listed in **Table 5** or less.

> *CAUTION*
> *It is recommended that marginal shift forks be replaced. Worn forks can cause the transmission to slip out of gear, leading to more serious and expensive damage.*

8. Measure the inside diameter of the gearshift forks with a micrometer (**Figure 105**). Replace ones that are worn to the service limit listed in **Table 5** or greater.

9. Apply a light coat of oil to the shift fork shafts and the inside bores of the shift forks before installation.

10. Inspect the shift mechanism for wear or damage. Make sure the return springs (**Figure 109**) have not sagged and are not broken; replace as necessary.

11. Move the shift plate back and forth (**Figure 110**). It must move freely with no binding. Replace the shift mechanism if necessary.

Tables are on the following pages.

Table 1 CLUTCH SPECIFICATIONS*

Item	Standard	Wear limit
Friction disc thickness		
500 cc	2.62-2.78 mm (0.102-0.109 in.)	2.3 mm (0.091 in.)
600 cc	2.92-3.08 mm (0.115-0.121 in.)	2.6 mm (0.10 in.)
Clutch plate warpage	–	0.15 mm (0.006 in.)
Clutch springs free length		
XL500R	44.1 mm (1.74 in.)	42.5 mm (1.67 in.)
XL500S, XR500,		
1979-1982 XR500R	37.3 mm (1.46 in.)	35.8 mm (1.41 in.)
1983-1984 XR500R	33.7 mm (1.32 in.)	32.2 mm (1.27 in.)
XL600R	44.3 mm (1.744 in.)	42.7 mm (1.68 in.)
XR600R	44.7 mm (1.76 in.)	43.1 mm (1.70 in.)
Clutch out housing inner diameter		
(1983-1990 models)	27.000-27.021 mm (1.0630-1.0638 in.)	27.05 mm (1.065 in.)
Clutch outer guide		
Outer diameter	26.959-26.980 mm	26.91 mm (1.059 in.)
(all models)	(1.0614-1.0622 in.)	
Inner diameter		
500 cc		
(1979-1982)	22.000-22.035 mm (0.8661-0.8675 in.)	22.05 mm (0.868 in.)
1983-1984 XR500R	NA	NA
XL600R, XR600R	21.900-22.035 mm (0.8657-0.8675 in.)	22.05 mm (0.868 in.)
Length 500 cc		
(1979-1982)	33.20-33.30 mm (1.307-1.311 in.)	33.10 mm (1.303 in.)
Kickstarter driver gear		
500 cc (1979-1982)	27.000-27.021 mm (1.0630-1.0638 in.)	27.05 mm (1.065 in.)
*Honda does not provide service information for all items or all models. NA = Not available.		

Table 2 CLUTCH TORQUE SPECIFICATIONS

Item	N•m	ft.-lb.
Clutch nut		
XR600R		
1985-1987	70-80	50-58
1988-1990	110	80
All other models	50-60	36-43
Clutch bolts	8-12	6-9
Clutch cover bolts and nuts	8-12	6-9
Footpeg bolt	38-48	27-35
Shift fork shaft bolt	13-17	9-12
Shift drum bearing seat plate screw (500 cc 1979-1982)	9-13	7-10

Table 3 5-SPEED TRANSMISSION–XL500S, XR500, XR500R (1981-1982)

Item	Standard	Service limit
Transmission gears ID		
Mainshaft		
4th, 5th gear	25.020-25.041 mm (0.9850-0.9859 in.)	25.10 mm (0.988 in.)
Countershaft		
3rd, 5th gear	25.020-25.041 mm (0.9850-0.9859 in.)	25.10 mm (0.988 in.)
Gear bushing		
Countershaft 1st gear		
ID	20.020-20.041 mm (0.7866-0.7890 in.)	20.10 mm (0.791 in.)
OD	25.005-25.016 mm (0.9844-0.9849 in.)	24.95 mm (0.982 in.)
Shaft to bushing clearance	0.020-0.54 mm (0.0008-0.0021 in.)	0.10 mm (0.004 in.)
Mainshaft OD @ locations:		
A	24.959-24.980 mm (0.9826-0.9835 in.)	24.91mm (0.981 in.)
B	19.987-20.000 mm (0.7869-0.7874 in.)	19.95 mm (0.785 in.)
Countershaft OD @ locations:		
A	26.959-26.980 mm (1.0614-1.0622 in.)	26.91 mm (1.059 in.)
B	24.959-24.980 mm (0.9826-0.9835 in.)	24.91 mm (0.981 in.)
C	19.987-20.000 mm (0.7869-0.7874 in.)	19.95 mm (0.785 in.)

6

Table 4 5-SPEED TRANSMISSION–XR500R (1983-1984), XL600R AND XR600R

Item	Standard	Service limit
Transmission gears ID		
Mainshaft		
4th gear		
XL600R,		
XR500R (1983-1984)	25.020-25.041 mm (0.9850-0.9859 in.)	25.10 mm (0.988 in.)
XR600R	28.000-28.021 mm (1.1024-1.1032 in.)	28.08 mm (1.106 in.)
5th gear	28.000-28.021 mm (1.1024-1.1032 in.)	28.08 mm (1.106 in.)
Countershaft		
1st gear	25.021-25.041 mm (0.9850-0.9859 in.)	25.10 mm (0.988 in.)
2nd, 3rd gear	28.020-28.041 mm (1.31031-1.1040 in.)	28.10 mm (1.106 in.)
Gear bushing		
Mainshaft		
4th gear OD*	27.979-28.000 mm (1.1015-1.1024 in.)	27.93 mm (1.1000 in.)
4th gear ID*	25.020-25.041 mm (0.9850-0.9859 in.)	25.10 mm (0.9880 in.)
5th gear OD	27.949-27.980 mm (1.1004-1.1016 in.)	27.90 mm (1.1098 in.)

(continued)

Table 4 5-SPEED TRANSMISSION–XR500R (1983-1984), XL600R AND XR600R (continued)

Item	Standard	Service limit
Gear bushing (continued)		
Countershaft		
1st gear ID	20.024-20.041 mm	20.10 mm (0.791 in.)
	(0.7880-0.7890 in.)	
1st gear OD	24.984-25.005 mm	24.93 mm (0.981 in.)
	(0.9836-0.9844 in.)	
2nd gear ID	25.020-25.041 mm	25.10 mm (0.988 in.)
	(0.9850-0.9859 in.)	
2nd gear OD	27.979-28.000 mm	27.93 mm (1.100 in.)
	(1.1015-1.1024 in.)	
Gear-to-bushing clearance		
Mainshaft		
5th gear	0.020-0.072 mm	0.10 mm (0.004 in.)
	(0.0008-0.0028 in.)	
Countershaft		
1st gear	0.015-0.057 mm	0.10 mm (0.004 in.)
	(0.0006-0.0022 in.)	
2nd gear	0.020-0.062 mm	0.10 mm (0.004 in.)
	(0.0008-0.0024 in.)	
Mainshaft OD at location:		
A	24.972-24.993 mm	24.92 mm (0.981 in.)
	(0.9831-0.9840 in.)	
Countershaft OD at location:		
B	15.966-15.984 mm	15.93 mm (0.627 in.)
	(0.6286-0.6293 in.)	
C	19.980-19.993 mm	19.94 mm (0.782 in.)
	(0.7866-0.7871 in.)	
D	24.972-24.993 mm	24.92 mm (0.981 in.)
	(0.9831-0.9840 in.)	
E	24.959-24.980 mm	24.92 mm (0.981 in.)
	(0.9826-0.9835 in.)	

*1988-1990 XR600R models only. Honda does not provide specifications for the 1988-1990 XR600R countershaft 3rd gear bushing.

Table 5 SHIFT FORK AND SHAFT SPECIFICATIONS

1979-1982 500 CC		
Item	**Specifications**	**Wear limit**
Shift fork ID		
Center fork	12.000-12.021 mm	12.05 mm (0.474 in.)
	(0.4724-0.4733 in.)	
Right-hand,	15.000-15.021 mm	15.05 mm (0.592 in.)
left-hand	(0.5906-0.5914 in.)	
Shift fork finger thickness	4.93-5.00 mm	4.50 mm (0.18 in.)
	(0.194-0.197 in.)	
Shift fork shaft OD		
Center fork	11.966-11.984 mm	11.91 mm (0.469 in.)
	(0.4711-0.4718 in.)	
Right-hand,	14.966-14.984 mm	14.91 m (0.587 in.)
left-hand	(0.5892-0.5899 in.)	
Gear shift drum OD	11.966-11.984 mm	11.91 mm (0.469 in.)
	(0.4711-0.4718 in.)	
	(continued)	

Table 5 SHIFT FORK AND SHAFT SPECIFICATIONS (continued)

1983-1990 500 AND 600 CC		
Item	Specifications	Wear limit
Shift fork ID		
All	14.000-14.018 mm (0.5512-0.5519 in.)	14.05 mm (0.553 in.)
Shift fork finger thickness	4.93-5.00 mm (0.194-0.197 in.)	4.50 mm (0.18 in.)
Shift fork shaft OD	13.966-13.984 mm (0.5498-0.5506 in.)	13.90 mm (0.547 in.)

6

FUEL AND EXHAUST SYSTEM

The fuel system consists of the fuel tank, the shutoff valve, a single or dual carburetor (depending on model) and an air filter.

The exhaust system consists of a dual exhaust pipe and a muffler.

This chapter includes service procedures for all parts of the fuel system and exhaust system. Air filter service is covered in Chapter Three.

Carburetor specifications are covered in **Table 1** located at the end of this chapter.

CARBURETOR

Operation

For proper operation, a gasoline engine must be supplied with fuel and air mixed in proper proportions by weight. A mixture in which there is an excess of fuel is said to be rich. A lean mixture is one which contains insufficient fuel. A properly adjusted carburetor supplies the proper mixture to the engine under all operating conditions.

The carburetor consists of several major systems. A float and float valve mechanism maintain a constant fuel level in the float bowl(s). The pilot system supplies fuel at low speeds. The main fuel system supplies fuel at medium and high speeds. A starter (choke) system supplies the very rich mixture needed to start a cold engine.

Some models are equipped with dual-carburetors. The primary carburetor operates alone at low- to mid-range for smooth, precise throttle control. The secondary carburetor opens (along with the primary carburetor) at high-range to provide a large volume of fuel/air mixture for maximum power.

The progressive linkage connecting the 2 carburetors is mechanical and linkage adjustment is covered in this chapter.

Carburetor Service

Major carburetor service (removal and cleaning) should be performed at the intervals indicated in **Table 2** in Chapter Three or when poor engine performance, hesitation and little or no response to mixture adjustment is observed. Alterations in jet size, throttle slide cutaway, and changes in jet needle position, etc., should be attempted only if you're experienced in this type of "tuning" work. A bad guess could result in costly engine damage or, at least, poor performance. If, after servicing the carburetor and making the adjustments described in this chapter, the bike does not perform correctly (and assuming that other factors affecting performance are correct, such as ignition timing and condition, etc.), the bike should be checked by a dealer or a qualified performance tuning specialist.

Dual Carburetors
Removal/Installation

1. Remove both side covers and the seat.
2. On XL series models, disconnect the battery negative lead or disconnect the main fuse (**Figure 1**).
3. Remove the fuel tank as described in this chapter.
4. Loosen the screw on the clamping bands (A, **Figure 2**) on each end of both carburetors. Slide the clamping bands away from the carburetors.
5. Remove the bolts (B, **Figure 2**) securing the intake tube and insulator to the cylinder head. Remove the intake tube and insulator from the engine and carburetor assembly.

NOTE
There is one bolt on the bottom in the center of the intake tubes. It is very difficult to remove.

6. Pull the carburetor assembly forward and out of the air filter intake tube (**Figure 3**).
7. Loosen the throttle cable locknuts (**Figure 4**) at the carburetor assembly.
8. On XL600R models, perform the following:
   a. Loosen the screw (A, **Figure 5**) on the choke cable clamp.
   b. Disconnect the choke cable (B, **Figure 5**) from the carburetor.
9. Partially pull the carburetor assembly out through the left-hand side.
10. Disconnect the "pull" cable (A, **Figure 6**) and the "push" cable (B, **Figure 6**) from the throttle wheel.
11. Note the routing of the carburetor drain tube through the frame. Carefully pull the tube free from the frame and leave it attached to the carburetor.

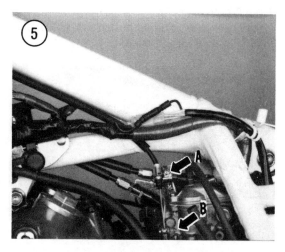

12. Carefully remove the carburetor from the engine and frame and take it to a workbench for disassembly and cleaning.

13. Install by reversing these removal steps, noting the following:

14. Inspect the O-ring seals in the intake tube (A, **Figure 7**) and the insulator (B). Replace if necessary.

15. When installing the throttle cables be sure to install the "pull" cable (A, **Figure 6**) to the bottom receptacle on the throttle wheel and the "push" cable (B) to the upper receptacle on the throttle wheel.

16. Make sure the screws on the clamping bands are tight to avoid a vacuum loss and possible valve damage.

17. Adjust the throttle cables. On models so equipped, also adjust the choke cable as described in Chapter Three.

Single Carburetor (1988-1990 XR600R) Removal/Installation

1. Remove both side covers.

2. Remove the fuel tank as described in this chapter.

3. Loosen the screws on both the front intake tube and rear rubber boot.

4. Disconnect the push and pull throttle cables from the carburetor's throttle wheel.

5. Note the routing of the drain tube through the frame. Carefully pull the tube free from the frame and leave it attached to the carburetor.

6. Carefully pull the carburetor free of the intake tube and the rubber boot and remove it out through the right-hand side. Take it to a workbench for disassembly and cleaning.

7. Install by reversing these removal steps. Note the following during installation.

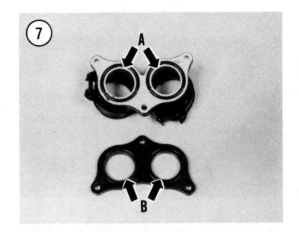

8. Install the carburetor so that the boss on the carburetor aligns with the notch in the rubber intake tube.

9. When installing the throttle cables, be sure to install the "pull" cable to the bottom receptacle on the carburetor's throttle wheel and the "push" cable to the top receptacle on the throttle wheel.

10. Make sure the screws on the clamping bands are tight to avoid a vacuum leak and possible valve damage.

11. Adjust the throttle cable as described in Chapter Three.

Single Carburetor (All Other Models) Removal/Installation

1. Remove both side covers and the seat.

NOTE
On XL500S models, reinstall the seat strap bolts (Figure 8) as they also hold the upper portion of the shocks to the frame. Remove and install one bolt at a time.

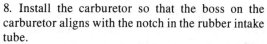

2. On XL series models, disconnect the battery negative lead or disconnect the main fuse (**Figure 1**).

3. Remove the fuel tank as described in this chapter.

NOTE
Although not necessary, removing the air box makes carburetor removal and installation much easier.

4. Disconnect the breather hose (A, **Figure 9**) from the air box.

5. Loosen the screw on the clamping bands on the rear rubber boot (**Figure 10**) and slide the clamping band away from the carburetor.

6. Remove the bolts securing the air box to the frame (B, **Figure 9** and **Figure 11**) and remove the air box.

7. Disconnect the "pull" cable and the "push" cables from the throttle wheel (**Figure 12**).

8. Loosen the screw (**Figure 13**) on the cable clamp and disconnect the choke cable end from the link plate on the carburetor (A, **Figure 14**).

9. Loosen the screw on the clamping bands on the rubber intake tube (B, **Figure 14**) and slide the clamping band away from the carburetor.

10. Note the routing of carburetor drain tube through the frame. Carefully pull the tube free from the frame and leave it attached to the carburetor.

11. Carefully pull the carburetor assembly to the rear and remove it from the engine and frame and take it to a workbench for disassembly and cleaning.

12. Install by reversing these removal steps, noting the following.

13. Install the carburetor so that the boss on the carburetor aligns with the notch in the rubber intake tube.

14. When installing the throttle cables be sure to install the "pull" cable to the bottom receptacle on the throttle wheel and the "push" cable to the upper receptacle on the throttle wheel.

15. Make sure the screws on the clamping bands are tight to avoid a vacuum loss and possible valve damage.

16. Adjust the throttle and choke cables as described in Chapter Three.

Carburetor Disassembly/Assembly (All Models)

The carburetor on all models is basically the same unit. Slight variations exist on the dual-carburetor design. The XL models are equipped with an accelerator pump system.

On models with dual carburetors it is recommended that only one carburetor be disassembled at a time. This will prevent a mixup of parts. The primary carburetor is located on the left-hand side and the secondary carburetor is on the right-hand side.

Refer to **Figure 15** for dual-carburetor models or **Figure 16** for single carburetor models.

1. On dual-carburetor models, separate the carburetors as described in this chapter.

> *NOTE*
> *Carburetor separation is necessary to gain access to the air cutoff valve on the left-hand carburetor.*

2. Remove the vent and overflow tubes (**Figure 17**).

3. Remove the screws (**Figure 18**) securing the top cover and remove cover and the gasket.

4. Remove the screws (**Figure 19**) securing the link arm assembly to the throttle valve and pivot the link arm assembly out of the way.

5. Remove the throttle valve and needle valve from the carburetor. Note the position of the needle valve clip for reassembly.

6. On models equipped with an air cutoff valve, perform the following:

   a. Remove the screws (**Figure 20**) securing the air cutoff valve cover and remove the cover.

   b. Remove the spring and diaphragm (**Figure 21**).

   c. Remove the small O-ring seal (**Figure 22**).

7. On models equipped with an accelerator pump, perform the following:

   a. Remove the screw (**Figure 23**) securing the accelerator pump cover and remove the cover.

   b. Remove the spring (**Figure 24**).

   c. Carefully withdraw the accelerator pump rod assembly (A, **Figure 25**) and remove the rubber boot (B, **Figure 25**).

8. Remove the screws securing the float bowl and remove the float bowl. Refer to **Figure 26** for models with an accelerator pump or A, **Figure 27** for all other models.

9. On models so equipped, unscrew the main jet cover (B, **Figure 27**) from the float bowl.

10. Remove the plastic ferrule (**Figure 28**) from the main jet stanchion.

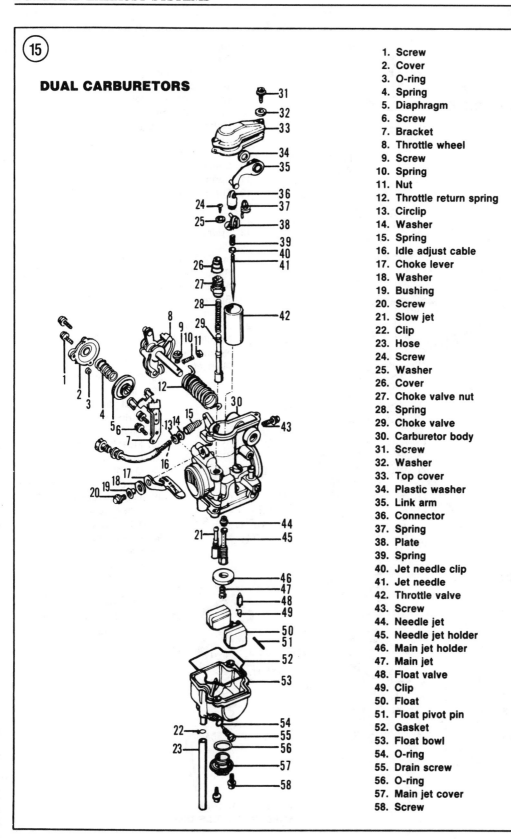

DUAL CARBURETORS

1. Screw
2. Cover
3. O-ring
4. Spring
5. Diaphragm
6. Screw
7. Bracket
8. Throttle wheel
9. Screw
10. Spring
11. Nut
12. Throttle return spring
13. Circlip
14. Washer
15. Spring
16. Idle adjust cable
17. Choke lever
18. Washer
19. Bushing
20. Screw
21. Slow jet
22. Clip
23. Hose
24. Screw
25. Washer
26. Cover
27. Choke valve nut
28. Spring
29. Choke valve
30. Carburetor body
31. Screw
32. Washer
33. Top cover
34. Plastic washer
35. Link arm
36. Connector
37. Spring
38. Plate
39. Spring
40. Jet needle clip
41. Jet needle
42. Throttle valve
43. Screw
44. Needle jet
45. Needle jet holder
46. Main jet holder
47. Main jet
48. Float valve
49. Clip
50. Float
51. Float pivot pin
52. Gasket
53. Float bowl
54. O-ring
55. Drain screw
56. O-ring
57. Main jet cover
58. Screw

7

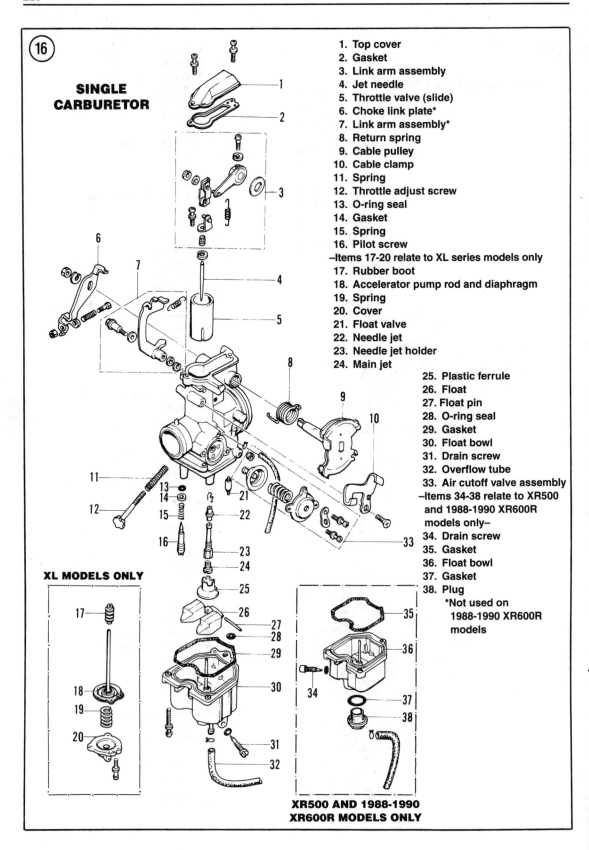

SINGLE CARBURETOR

XL MODELS ONLY

XR500 AND 1988-1990 XR600R MODELS ONLY

1. Top cover
2. Gasket
3. Link arm assembly
4. Jet needle
5. Throttle valve (slide)
6. Choke link plate*
7. Link arm assembly*
8. Return spring
9. Cable pulley
10. Cable clamp
11. Spring
12. Throttle adjust screw
13. O-ring seal
14. Gasket
15. Spring
16. Pilot screw
—Items 17-20 relate to XL series models only
17. Rubber boot
18. Accelerator pump rod and diaphragm
19. Spring
20. Cover
21. Float valve
22. Needle jet
23. Needle jet holder
24. Main jet
25. Plastic ferrule
26. Float
27. Float pin
28. O-ring seal
29. Gasket
30. Float bowl
31. Drain screw
32. Overflow tube
33. Air cutoff valve assembly
—Items 34-38 relate to XR500 and 1988-1990 XR600R models only—
34. Drain screw
35. Gasket
36. Float bowl
37. Gasket
38. Plug
*Not used on 1988-1990 XR600R models

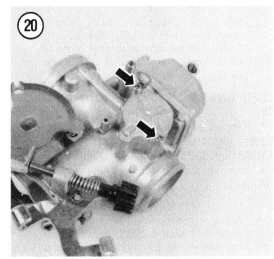

NOTE
Before removing the pilot screw,
*carefully screw it in until it **lightly** seats.*
Count and record the number of turns
so it can be installed in the same
position.

11. Unscrew the pilot screw and spring (**Figure 29**).

12. Remove the small O-ring seal (**Figure 30**) located within the pilot screw receptacle.

13. Remove the float pivot pin (**Figure 31**).

14. Remove the float and float valve needle (**Figure 32**).

NOTE
Before removing the air screw, carefully
*screw it in until it **lightly** seats. Count*
and record the number of turns so it
can be installed in the same position.

15. Remove the air screw on dual-carburetor models; the secondary carburetor is not equipped with an air screw.

16. Remove the main jet (A, **Figure 33**), needle jet holder (**Figure 34**) and the needle jet.

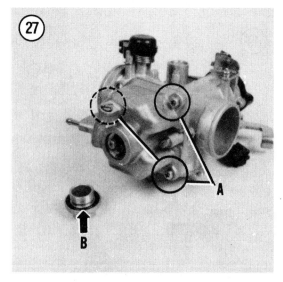

17. Turn the carburetor over and gently tap the side of the body. Catch the needle jet as it falls out into your hand. If the needle jet does not fall out, use a plastic or fiber tool and gently push the needle jet out. Do not use any metal tools for this purpose.

18. On models equipped with a removable slow jet, remove the slow jet (B, **Figure 33**).

19A. On dual-carburetor models, on the primary carburetor only, remove the screw securing the starter choke and remove the choke assembly.

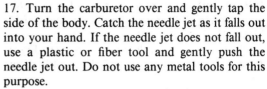

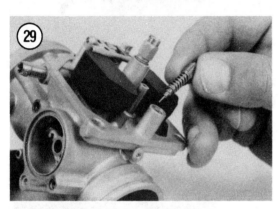

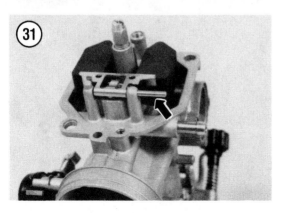

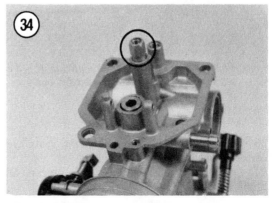

19B. On all other models, unhook the choke return spring and remove the plastic link arm (A, **Figure 35**).

20. Unscrew the throttle adjust screw (B, **Figure 35**) and remove the spring and the throttle adjust screw.

21. Remove the float bowl seal from the float bowl.

22. Remove the main jet cover and O-ring seal.

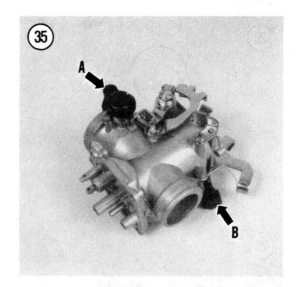

> *NOTE*
> *Further disassembly is neither necessary nor recommended. If throttle or choke shafts or butterflies are damaged, take the carburetor body to a dealer for replacement.*

23. Clean and inspect all parts as described in this chapter.

24. Assembly is the reverse of these disassembly steps, noting the following.

25. Install the needle jet (**Figure 36**) with the chamfered end facing *up* toward the needle jet holder.

26. If removed, install the needle jet clip in its original position; refer to **Table 1** at the end of this chapter.

27. Install the plastic ferrule (**Figure 28**) with the cutout notch facing toward the float pin. This notch is for the overflow tube in the float bowl.

28. Check the float height and adjust, if necessary, as described in this chapter.

29. On models equipped with an accelerator pump, perform the following:
   a. Make sure the tabs on the accelerator pump diaphragm are positioned correctly in the float bowl (**Figure 37**).
   b. Make sure that the rubber boot is completely seated in the carburetor body flange (**Figure 38**).

> *CAUTION*
> *This boot must be correctly seated as it seals off the pump shaft to keep dirt out of the diaphragm area.*

30. Make sure that all small O-ring seals are correctly installed and not forgotten.

31. On dual-carburetor models, repeat all applicable steps for the other carburetor.

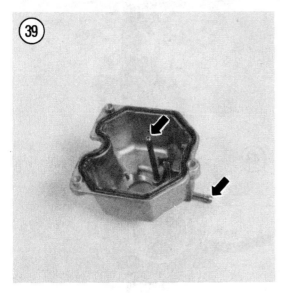

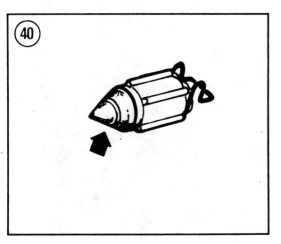

32. After the carburetor has been disassembled the pilot screw, the air screw and the idle speed should be adjusted.

Carburetor Cleaning/Inspection

1. Clean all parts, except rubber or plastic parts, in a good grade of carburetor cleaner. This solution is available at most automotive or motorcycle supply stores in a small, resealable tank with a dip basket for just a few dollars. If it is tightly sealed when not in use, the solution will last for several cleanings. Follow the manufacturer's instructions for correct soak time (usually about 1/2 hour).

2. Remove all parts from the cleaner and blow dry with compressed air. Blow out the jets and needle jet holder with compressed air.

CAUTION
*If compressed air is not available, allow the parts to air dry or use a clean lint-free cloth. Do **not** use a paper towel to dry carburetor parts, as small paper particles may plug openings in the carburetor body or jets.*

CAUTION
*Do **not** use a piece of wire to clean them as minor gouges in the jet can alter flow rate and upset the fuel/air mixture.*

3. Be sure to clean out the overflow tube in the float bowl from both ends (**Figure 39**).

4. Inspect the end of the float valve needle (**Figure 40**) for wear or damage. Also check the inside of the needle valve body. If either part is damaged, replace as a set. A damaged needle valve or a particle of dirt or grit in the needle valve assembly will cause the carburetor to flood and overflow fuel.

5. Inspect all O-ring seals. O-ring seals tend to become hardened with prolonged use and heat and

6. Examine the end of the pilot screw and the throttle adjust screw. If any grooves or roughness are present on either screw, replace it. A damaged end will prevent smooth low-speed engine operation.

Dual-Carburetor Separation

1. Remove the carburetor assembly as described in this chapter.

2. Remove the screws (**Figure 41**) securing the throttle adjust screw bracket and remove the bracket assembly.

3. Remove the screws (A, **Figure 42**) securing the 2 carburetor bodies together.

4. Carefully separate the ball stud from the ball-joint (**Figure 43**) on the throttle drum of the secondary carburetor.

5. Carefully pull the 2 carburetor bodies apart. Do not damage the air joint (**Figure 44**) or the fuel joint (B, **Figure 42**) joining the 2 carburetors.

6. Install new O-ring seals on both the air and fuel joints.

7. Apply a light coat of multipurpose grease to the O-ring seals on the air and fuel joints.

8. Insert the air and fuel joints into their receptacles on the primary carburetor.

9. Place the secondary carburetor onto the primary carburetor, carefully aligning the air joint (**Figure 44**) and fuel joint (B, **Figure 42**). Make sure that the O-ring seals are in place on both joints.

10. Push the 2 carburetor bodies together until they are completely seated.

11. Push the ball stud onto the ball-joint (**Figure 43**).

12. Install the screws (A, **Figure 42**) securing the 2 carburetor bodies together.

13. Align the groove in the throttle adjust screw bracket with the tab on the air vent tube. Install the screws and tighten securely.

14. Check the operation of the throttle as follows:
   a. Move the throttle plate and open and close the throttle a couple of times. It should move freely from open to closed with no binding.
   b. If movement is not free, make sure the ball stud is correctly seated on the throttle drum.
   c. Loosen the carburetor attachment screws a little and slightly move each carburetor body.
   d. Retighten the screws and recheck the movement.

CARBURETOR ADJUSTMENTS

Float Adjustment

The carburetor assembly has to be removed and partially disassembled for this adjustment.

1. Remove the carburetor assembly as described in this chapter.

2A. On dual-carburetor models, remove the screws securing both float bowls and remove them.

2B. On single carburetor models, remove the screws securing the float bowl and remove the float bowl (**Figure 45**).

3. Hold the carburetor assembly with the carburetor inclined 15-45° from vertical so that the

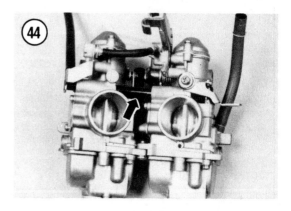

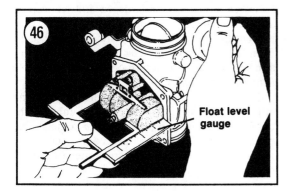

Float level gauge

float arm is just touching the float needle—not pushing it down. Use a float gauge (**Figure 46**), vernier caliper or small ruler and measure the distance from the carburetor body to the bottom surface of the float body (**Figure 47**). The correct height is listed in **Table 1**.

4. Adjust by carefully bending the tang on the float arm. If the float level is too high, the result will be a rich fuel/air mixture. If it is too low, the mixture will be too lean.

> *NOTE*
> *On dual-carburetor models, the floats on both carburetors must be adjusted at the same height to maintain the same fuel/air mixture.*

5. Reassemble and install the carburetors.

Needle Jet Adjustment
(XR Models)

> *NOTE*
> *On XL series models, the needle has only one groove for the clip so it is non-adjustable.*

Needle position can be adjusted to affect the fuel/air mixture for medium throttle openings.

The carburetor assembly has to be removed and partially disassembled for this adjustment.

1. Remove the carburetor assembly as described in this chapter.

2. Remove the screws (**Figure 48**) securing the top cover and remove the cover and gasket.

3. Remove the screws (**Figure 49**) securing the link arm assembly to the throttle valve. Then pivot the link arm assembly back out of the way.

7

4. Remove the throttle valve and needle jet.

5. Remove the needle valve and note the original position of the needle clip. The standard setting is listed in **Table 1**.

6. Raising the needle (lowering the clip) will enrich the mixture during mid-throttle openings, while lowering the needle (raising the clip) will lean out the mixture.

7. Reassemble and install the carburetor by reversing these steps.

Pilot Screw Adjustment (1978-1979)

The air filter element must be cleaned before starting this procedure or the results will be inaccurate. Refer to Chapter Three.

> *NOTE*
> *This pilot jet is pre-set at the factory and adjustment is not necessary unless the carburetor has been overhauled or someone has misadjusted it.*

1. For the preliminary adjustment, carefully turn the pilot screw (**Figure 50**) in until it seats *lightly* and then back it out the number of turns listed in **Table 1**.

> *CAUTION*
> *The pilot screw seat can be damaged if the pilot screw is tightened toohard against the seat.*

2. Start the engine and let it reach normal opeating temperature. Approximately 5-10 minutes of stop and go riding is sufficient. Shut the engine off.

3. Connect a portable tachometer following the manufacturer's instructions.

4. Turn the idle adjust screw (**Figure 51**) in or out ot obtain the idle speed listed in Table 1.

5A. On XL series models, turn the pilot screw *clockwise* until the engine stops running, Back the pilot screw out 2 full turns. Restart the engine and proceed to Step 6.

5B. On XR series models, turn the pilot screw in either direction until the highest idle speed is obtained.

6 Reset the idle speed; refer to Step 4. Open and close the throttle a couple of times; check fo variation in idle speed. Readjust if necessary.

> *WARNING*
> *With the engine idling, move the handlebar from side to side if idle*

speed increases during this movement, the throttle cable needs adjustment or it may be incorrectly routed through the frame. Correct this problem immediately. Do not ride the bike in this unsafe condition.

7. If necessary, repeat Step 5 and Step 6 until the engine runs smoothly at the correct idle speed.

8. Disconnect the portable tachometer.

Pilot Screw Adjustment and New Limiter Cap Installation (1980-1981 XL500S)

In order to comply with U.S. and Canadian emission control standards, a limiter cap is attached to the end of the pilot screw. This is to prevent the owner from readjusting the pilot screw from the factory setting. The limiter cap will allow a maximum of 7/8 of a turn of the pilot screw *to a leaner mixture only.*

The pilot jet is pre-set at the factory and adjustment is not necessary unless the carburetor(s) has been overhauled or someone has misadjusted it. This procedure describes installation of a new pilot screw after carburetor overhaul.

The air filter element must be cleaned before starting this procedure or the results will be inaccurate. Refer to Chapter Three.

> *CAUTION*
> *Do not try to remove the limiter cap from the pilot screw, as it is bonded in place. It will break off and damage the pilot screw if removal is attempted.*

1. For the preliminary adjustment, carefully turn the pilot screw in until it seats lightly and then back it out the number of turns listed in **Table 1**.

> *CAUTION*
> *The pilot screw seat can be damaged if the pilot screw is tightened too hard against the seat.*

2. Start the engine and let it reach normal operating temperature. Approximately 5-10 minutes of stop

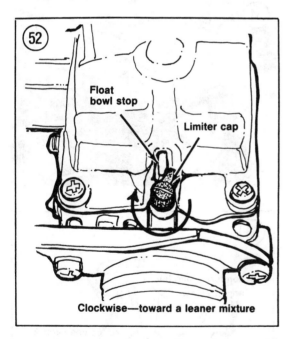

Float bowl stop

Limiter cap

Clockwise—toward a leaner mixture

and go riding is usually sufficient. Shut the engine off

3. Connect a portable tachometer following the manufacturer's instructions.

4. Turn the idle adjust screw in or out to obtain the idle speed listed in **Table 1**.

5. Turn the pilot screw *in* slowly until the engine stops.

6. Turn the pilot screw *out* the number of turns listed in **Table 1**.

7. Start the engine and turn the idle adjust screw in or out to achieve the idle speed listed in **Table 1**.

> *WARNING*
> *With the engine idling, move the handlebar from side to side. If idle speed increases during this movement, the throttle cable needs adjustment or it may be incorrectly routed through the frame. Correct this problem immediately. Do not ride the bike in this unsafe condition.*

8. Disconnect the portable tachometer.

9. Perform this step only if a new limiter cap is to be installed. Install the limiter caps as follows:

  a. Apply Loctite No. 601, or equivalent, to the new limiter cap.

  b. Position the limiter cap against the stop on the float bowl (**Figure 52**) so that the pilot screw can only turn *clockwise*, not counterclockwise.

  c. Install the limiter cap on the pilot screw. Make sure the pilot screw does not move while installing the limiter cap.

10. After this adjustment is completed, test ride the bike. Throttle response from idle should be rapid and without any hesitation.

Air Screw Adjustment (XR500R)

The air filter element must be cleaned before starting this procedure or the results will be inaccurate. Refer to Chapter Three.

1. For the preliminary adjustment, carefully turn the air screw (**Figure 53**) in until it seats *lightly* and then back it out the number of turns listed in **Table 1**.

> *CAUTION*
> *The air screw seat can be damaged if the air screw is tightened too hard against the seat.*

2. Start the engine and let it reach normal operating temperature. Approximately 5-10 minutes of stop and go riding is usually sufficient. Shut the engine off:

3. Connect a portable tachometer following the manufacturer's instructions.

7

4. Turn the idle adjust screw (**Figure 54**) in or out to obtain the idle speed listed in **Table 1**.

5. Open and close the throttle a couple of times. Engine speed should increase smoothly with no hesitation.

6. Turn the air screw in or out to obtain the highest idle speed.

7. Turn the idle adjust screw in or out to obtain the idle speed listed in **Table 1**.

WARNING
With the engine idling, move the handlebar from side to side. If idle speed increases during this movement, the throttle cable needs adjustment or it may be incorrectly routed through the frame. Correct this problem immediately. Do not ride the bike in this unsafe condition.

8. Turn the engine off and disconnect the portable tachometer.

9. After this adjustment is completed, test ride the bike. Throttle response from idle should be rapid and without any hesitation.

Air Screw or Pilot Screw Adjustment and New Limiter Cap Installation (XL600R)

In order to comply with U.S. and Canadian emission control standards, a limiter cap is attached to the end of the air screw (1983 models) or the pilot screw (1984-on models). This is to prevent the owner from readjusting the air or pilot screw from the factory setting. The limiter cap will allow a maximum of 7/8 of a turn of the air or pilot screw *to a leaner mixture only.*

The pilot jet is pre-set at the factory and adjustment is not necessary unless the carburetor(s) has been overhauled or someone has misadjusted it.

The air filter element must be cleaned before starting this procedure or the results will be inaccurate. Refer to Chapter Three.

CAUTION
Do not try to remove the limiter cap from the pilot screw, as it is bonded in place. It will break off and damage the pilot screw if removal is attempted.

1A. On 1983 models, for the preliminary adjustment, carefully turn the air screw (**Figure 53**) in until it seats *lightly* and then back it out the number of turns listed in **Table 2**.

1B. On 1984-on models, for the preliminary adjustment, carefully turn the pilot screw in until it seats *lightly* and then back it out the number of turns listed in **Table 1**.

CAUTION
The pilot screw seat can be damaged if the pilot screw is tightened too hard against the seat.

2. Start the engine and let it reach normal operating temperature. Approximately 5-10 minutes of stop and go riding is usually sufficient. Shut the engine off.

3. Connect a portable tachometer following the manufacturer's instructions.

4. Turn the idle adjust screw in or out to obtain the idle speed listed in **Table 1**.

5. Turn the air or pilot screw in slowly until the engine stops.

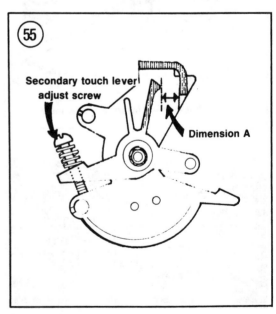

Secondary touch lever
adjust screw

Dimension A

6. Turn the air or pilot screw *out* the number of turns listed in **Table 1**.

7. Start the engine and turn the idle adjust screw in or out to achieve the idle speed listed in **Table 1**.

WARNING
With the engine idling, move the handlebar from side to side. If idle speed increases during this movement, the throttle cable needs adjustment or it may be incorrectly routed through the frame. Correct this problem immediately. Do not ride the bike in this unsafe condition.

8. Disconnect the portable tachometer.

9. Perform this step only if a new limiter cap is to be installed. Install the limiter caps as follows:

   a. Apply Loctite No. 601, or equivalent, to the new limiter cap.

   b. Position the limiter cap against the stop on the float bowl (**Figure 52**) so that the pilot screw can only turn *clockwise*, not counterclockwise.

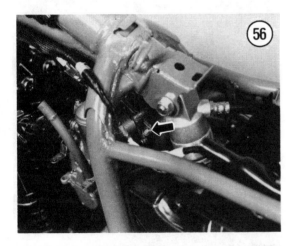

   c. Install the limiter cap on the air or pilot screw. Make sure the air or pilot screw does not move while installing the limiter cap.

10. After this adjustment is completed, test ride the bike. Throttle response from idle should be rapid and without any hesitation.

Secondary Carburetor Touch Lever Adjustment (XL600R)

Refer to **Figure 55** for this procedure.

1. Turn the throttle adjust screw (**Figure 54**) *counterclockwise* until it stops. Record the number of turns.

2. Turn the secondary touch lever adjust screw *out* until the stopper on the secondary touch lever lightly bottoms out on the lug on the throttle lever.

3. Turn the secondary touch lever adjust screw *in* until the clearance (dimension A) between the stopper and the lug is 4.5-5.0 mm (0.177-0.207 in.).

4. Turn the throttle adjust screw (**Figure 54**) *clockwise* to the position recorded in Step 1.

5. Adjust idle speed as described in this chapter.

Carburetor Synchronization (1983 XR500R)

The 1983 XR500R is the only model with dual carburetors that can be synchronized.

1. Remove the seat and side cover.

2. Loosen the adjusting screw (**Figure 56**) on the secondary throttle drum.

3. Make sure both throttle valves are in the closed position.

4. Measure the distance between the primary and secondary throttle drums (A, **Figure 57**). The correct clearance is 7.8-8.0 mm (0.30-0.32 in.).

5. If adjustment is necessary, carefully bend (open or close) the fork end (B, **Figure 57**) of the secondary throttle drum.

6. Screw in the adjusting screw until it just comes in contact with the primary throttle drum.

Fast Idle Adjustment (XL500S)

1. Start the engine and let it reach normal operating temperature. Approximately 5-10 minutes of stop and go riding is usually sufficient. Shut the engine off.

2. Connect a portable tachometer following the manufacturer's instructions.

7

3. Start the engine and pull the choke knob out (**Figure 58**) to its detent position. The correct high speed idle is 2000-2500 rpm.

> *NOTE*
> **Figure 59** *is shown with the fuel tank and side covers removed for clarity only; do not remove them for this adjustment.*

> *NOTE*
> *The locknut and adjusting screw are covered with locking paint at the factory so they will be difficult to adjust the first time.*

4. Adjust by loosening the locknut and turning the adjust screw (**Figure 59**) until the fast idle speed is correct.
5. Open and close the throttle a couple of times and check for variations. Readjust if necessary.
6. Turn the engine off and disconnect the portable tachometer.

Choke Adjustment
(1984-1987 XL Series)

First make sure the choke operates smoothly with no binding. If the cable binds, lubricate it as described under *Control Cables* in Chapter Three. If the cable still does not operate smoothly it must be replaced as described in this chapter.
1. Remove the seat and both side covers.
2. Remove the fuel tank as described in this chapter.
3. Operate the choke lever and check for smooth operation of the cable and choke mechanism.

> *NOTE*
> *The choke circuit is a "bystarter" system in which the choke lever opens a valve rather than closing a butterfly in the venturi area as on many carburetors. In the open position, the slow jet discharges a stream of fuel into the carburetor venturi to richen the mixture when the engine is cold.*

4. Pull the choke lever (**Figure 60**) all the way back to the fully open position and then to the fully closed position.
5. Measure the choke valve stroke (**Figure 61**). The correct stroke 5-7 mm (3/16-1/4 in.).
6. To adjust, loosen the cable clamping screw (A, **Figure 5**) and move the cable sheath either up or down to achieve the correct amount of stroke.
7. Repeat Steps 4 through 6 until the correct stroke can be achieved.

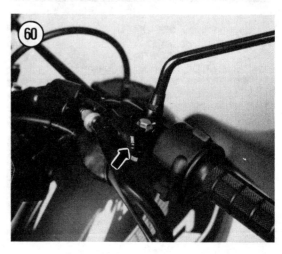

8. If proper adjustment cannot be achieved using this procedure the cable has stretched and must be replaced as described in this chapter.
9. Reinstall the fuel tank, seat and the side covers.

High Altitude Adjustment (XR500)

If the bike is going to be ridden for any sustained period of time at high elevations (2,000 m/6,500 ft.) the carburetor must be readjusted to improve performance and decrease exhaust emissions.

CAUTION
When the bike is returned to lower elevations (near sea level), the main jet must be changed back to the original size and the idle speed readjusted to idle speed listed in **Table 1.**

1. Remove the carburetor assembly as described in this chapter.
2. Remove the screws securing the float bowl and remove the bowl.
3. Remove the standard main jet (**Figure 62**) and install the new smaller one. The sizes are listed in **Table 1.**

4. Reassemble and install the carburetor.
5. Adjust idle speed as described in Chapter Three. The idle speed is the same as with the standard main jet.
6. If the engine idle is rough or the engine misses or stalls, adjust the pilot screw as described in this chapter except for the following. The pilot screw must be backed out 1 3/4 turns (not 2 1/2 turns as with the standard main jet).

High Altitude Adjustment (XL600R)

If the bike is going to be ridden for any sustained period of time at high elevations (2,000 m/6,500 ft.) the carburetor must be readjusted to improve performance and decrease exhaust emissions.

CAUTION
When the bike is returned to lower elevations (near sea level), the main jet must be changed back to the original size and the idle speed readjusted to idle speed listed in **Table 1.**

1. Remove the carburetor assembly as described in this chapter.
2. Remove the screws securing the float bowls and remove both bowls.
3. Remove the standard main jet and install a new smaller jet in each carburetor. The sizes are listed in **Table 1.**
4. Turn the air screw *clockwise* 1/2 turn.
5. Reassemble and install the carburetor.
6. Adjust idle speed as described in Chapter Three. The idle speed is the same as with the standard main jet.

High-altitude and Temperature Adjustment (XR500R and XR600R)

High-altitude and temperature adjustments consist of 3 different changes to the carburetor: main jet size change, a different location of the clip on the jet needle and a different pilot screw setting. Refer to **Figure 63**.

If the bike is going to be ridden for any sustained period of time at high elevations (above 2,000 m/6,500 ft.), the main jet should be changed to a 1-step smaller jet. Never change a jet by more than one size at a time without test riding the bike and running a spark plug test as described in Chapter Three.

CAUTION
If the carburetor has been adjusted for higher elevations, it must be changed

7

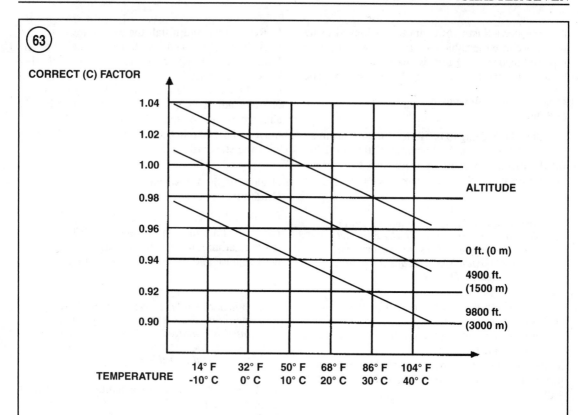

The chart is divided in three directions:

Ambient temperature—vertical lines at bottom.

Altitude—Angled lines on right.

Correction (C) factor—horizontal lines on left.

Determine the approximate altitude and air temperature and note where these two factors intersect (vertical and angled lines). Determine the C factor by moving horizontally to the left from the altitude and temperature intersection.

For example, at 4900 ft. and 68° F the correction factor is approximately 0.96.

To Determine Main Jet Size

Multiply the standard main jet number by the C factor. Use the main jet number closest to the result.

For example, (152 × 0.96 = 145.92)—use main jet number 146.

To Determine the Pilot Screw Setting and Jet Needle Clip Position

If the C factor is above 0.95 no adjustment is necessary to the pilot screw or clip position on the jet needle for proper engine operation.

If the C factor is 0.95 or below, turn the pilot screw out by 1/2 additional turn and raise the clip on the jet needle by one groove.

back to the standard settings when the bike is returned to lower elevations (near sea level). Engine overheating and piston seizure will occur if the engine runs too lean.

Rejetting the Carburetors

Do not try to solve a poor running engine problem by rejetting the carburetors if all of the following conditions hold true.

   a. The engine has held a good tune in the past with the standard jetting.

   b. The engine has not been modified.

   c. The motorcycle is being operating in the same geographical region under the same general climatic conditions as in the past.

   d. The motorcycle was and is being ridden at average highway speeds.

If those conditions all hold true, the chances are that the problem is due to a malfunction in the carburetor or in another component that needs to be adjusted or repaired. Changing carburetor jet size probably will not solve the problem. Rejetting the carburetors may be necessary if any of the following conditions hold true.

   a. A non-standard type of air filter element is being used.

   b. A non-standard exhaust system is installed on the motorcycle.

   c. Any of the top end components in the engine (pistons, cams, valves, compression ratio, etc.) have been modified.

   d. The motorcycle is in use at considerably higher or lower altitudes or in a considerably hotter or colder climate than in the past.

   e. The motorcycle is being operated at considerably higher speeds than before and changing to colder spark plugs does not solve the problem.

   f. Someone has previously changed the carburetor jetting.

   g. The motorcycle has never held a satisfactory engine tune.

If it necessary to rejet the carburetors, check with a dealer or motorcycle performance tuner for recommendations as to the size of jet to install for your specific situation.

If you do change the jets do so only one size at a time. After rejetting, test ride the bike and perform a spark plug test; refer to *Reading Spark Plugs* in Chapter Three.

THROTTLE CABLE REPLACEMENT

1988-1990 XR600R Models

1. Remove both sides covers and the seat.

2. Remove the fuel tank as described in this chapter.

3. Remove the screws securing the throttle body together and separate the parts.

4. Remove the screw and throttle cover (A, **Figure 64**).

5. Remove the cover gasket (B, **Figure 64**).

6. Remove the throttle cable roller (C, **Figure 64**).

7. Disengage the throttle cables from the throttle grip and withdraw them from the upper half of the throttle body.

8. Loosen the throttle cable locknuts at the carburetor assembly.

9. Disconnect the throttle "pull" and "push" cables from the throttle wheel on the carburetor.

NOTE
The piece of string attached in the next step will be used to pull the new throttle cables back through the frame so they will be routed in exactly the same position as the old ones were.

10. Tie a piece of heavy string or cord (approximately 7 ft./2 m long) to the carburetor end of both throttle cables. Wrap this end with masking tape or duct tape. Do not use an excessive amount of tape as it must be pulled through the frame during removal. Tie the other end of the string to the frame or air box.

11. At the throttle grip end of the cables, carefully pull the cables (and attached string) out through the frame. Make sure the attached string follows the same path as the cables through the frame.

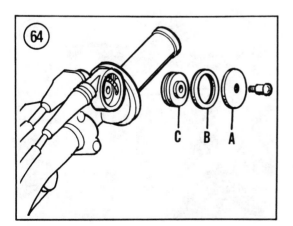

(64)

C   B   A

7

12. Remove the tape and untie the string from the old cables.

13. Lubricate the new cables as described in Chapter Three.

14. Tie the string to the carburetor end of the new throttle cables and wrap them with tape.

15. Carefully pull the string back through the frame routing the new cables through the same path as the old cables.

16. Untie the string from the cables and remove it from the frame.

CAUTION
*The throttle cables are the push/pull type and must be installed as described in Step 17 and Step 18. Do **not** interchange the 2 cables.*

17. Attach the "pull" cable to the bottom receptacle in the throttle wheel on the carburetor.

18. Attach the "push" cable to the top receptacle in the throttle wheel on the carburetor.

19. Apply grease to the upper ends of the throttle cables and to the throttle cable roller.

20. Install the throttle cables through the upper half of the throttle body housing.

21. Attach the throttle cables onto the throttle grip.

22. Install the throttle cable roller (C, **Figure 64**).

23. Install the cover gasket (B, **Figure 64**).

24. Install the throttle cover and screw (A, **Figure 64**). Tighten the screw securely.

25. Install the lower half of the throttle body and install the screws securing the throttle body halves together. Tighten the screws securely.

26. Operate the throttle grip several times and make sure the throttle linkage operates correctly, with no binding. If operation is incorrect or there is binding, carefully check that the cables are attached correctly and there are no tight bends in the cables.

27. Adjust the throttle operation as described in Chapter Three.

28. Install the fuel tank as described in this chapter.

29. Install both side covers and the seat.

30. Test ride the bike slowly at first and make sure the throttle is operating correctly.

All Other Models

1. Remove both side covers and the seat.

2. Remove the fuel tank as described in this chapter.

3. Remove the screws securing the throttle housing together and disengage the throttle cables from the throttle grip.

4. In order to gain access to the throttle wheel on the carburetor, partially remove the carburetor assembly as described in this chapter.

5. Loosen both throttle cable locknuts (**Figure 65**) at the carburetor assembly.

6. Disconnect the "pull" cable (A, **Figure 66**) and the "push" cable (B, **Figure 66**) from the throttle wheel.

NOTE
The piece of string attached in the next step will be used to pull the new throttle cables back through the frame so they will be routed in exactly the same position as the old ones were.

7. Tie a piece of heavy string or cord (approximately 7 ft./2 m long) to the carburetor

end of both throttle cables. Wrap this end with masking or duct tape. Do not use an excessive amount of tape as it must be pulled through the frame loop during removal. Tie the other end of the string to the frame or air box.

8. At the throttle grip end of the cables, carefully pull the cables (and attached string) out through the frame. Make sure the attached string follows the same path as the cables through the frame.

9. Remove the tape and untie the string from old cables.

10. Lubricate the new cables as described in Chapter Three.

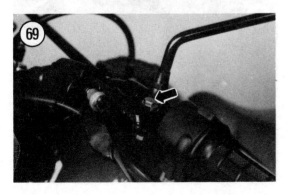

11. Tie the string to the new throttle cables and wrap it with tape.

12. Carefully pull the string back through the frame routing the new cables through the same path as the old cables.

13. Remove the tape and untie the string from the cables and the frame.

CAUTION
*The throttle cables are the push/pull type and must be installed as described and shown in Step 14 and Step 15. Do **not** interchange the 2 cables.*

14. Attach the throttle "pull" cable to the bottom receptacle in the throttle wheel (A, **Figure 66**).

15. Attach the throttle "push" cable to the top receptacle in the throttle wheel (B, **Figure 66**).

16. Install the throttle/switch housing and tighten the screws securely.

17. Operate the throttle grip and make sure the carburetor throttle linkage is operating correctly, with no binding. If operation is incorrect or there is binding, carefully check that the cables are attached correctly and there are no tight bends in the cables.

18. Install the carburetor assembly, fuel tank and seat.

19. Adjust the throttle cables as described in Chapter Three.

20. Test ride the bike slowly at first and make sure the throttle is operating correctly.

7

CHOKE CABLE REPLACEMENT (MODELS SO EQUIPPED)

1. Remove the side covers and the seat.

2. Remove the fuel tank as described in this chapter.

3A. On single-carburetor models, loosen the cable clamp screw (**Figure 67**) and disconnect the cable from the link plate on the carburetor.

3B. On dual-carburetor models, loosen the cable clamp screw (A, **Figure 68**) and disconnect the cable from the carburetor (B, **Figure 68**).

4A. On 1978-1983 models, loosen the locknut and remove the choke cable from the bracket on the upper fork bridge.

4B. On 1984-1990 models, remove the screw (**Figure 69**) securing the cable lever and cable to the housing and remove the cable end from the lever.

NOTE
The piece of string attached in the next step will be used to pull the new choke cable back through the frame so it will be routed in the same position as the old cable.

5. Tie a piece of heavy string or cord (approximately 7 ft./2 m long) to the carburetor end of the choke cable. Wrap this end with masking or duct tape. Do not use an excessive amount of tape as it must be pulled through the frame loop during removal.

6. At the choke lever end of the cable, carefully pull the cable (and attached string) out through the frame. Make sure the attached string follows the same path that the cable does through the frame.

7. Remove the tape and untied the string from the old cable.

8. Lubricate the new cable as described in Chapter Three.

9. Tie the string to the new choke cable and wrap it with tape.

10. Carefully pull the string back through the frame, routing the new cable through the same path as the old cable.

11. Remove the tape and untie the string from the cable and the frame.

12A. On 1978-1983 models, install the cable into the bracket on the upper fork bridge. Tighten the locknut

12B. On 1984-1990 models, attach the cable to the lever and install the lever and screw onto the housing. Tighten the screw securely.

13A. On single-carburetor models, connect the cable onto the link plate on the carburetor. Tighten the cable clamp screw (**Figure 67**).

13B. On dual-carburetor models, connect the cable onto the carburetor. Tighten the cable clamp screw (A, **Figure 68**).

14. Operate the choke lever and make sure the carburetor choke linkage is operating correctly, with no binding. If operation is incorrect or there is binding carefully check that the cable is attached correctly and there are no tight bends in the cable.

15. Adjust the choke cable as described in this chapter.

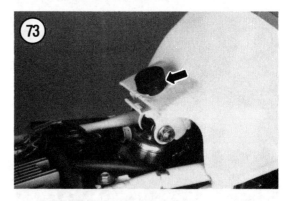

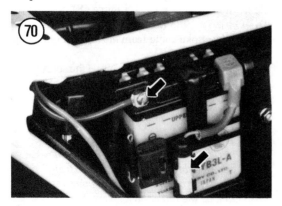

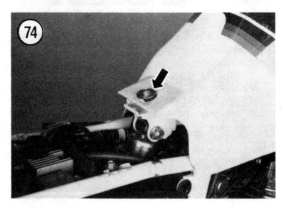

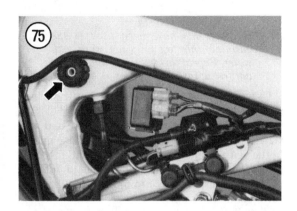

FUEL TANK

Removal/Installation (Metal Tank)

1. Remove both side covers and the seat.

NOTE
On XL500S models, reinstall the seat strap bolts as they also hold the upper portion of the shocks to the frame. Remove and install one bolt at a time.

2. On XL series models, disconnect the battery negative lead or disconnect the main fuse (**Figure 70**).

3. Turn the fuel shutoff valve to the OFF position (A, **Figure 71**).

4. Remove the fuel line to the carburetor assembly (B, **Figure 71**).

5. Pull the fuel filler cap vent tube (**Figure 72**) from the steering head receptacle or fuel filler cap.

6. On models so equipped, remove the rubber cushion (**Figure 73**) from the rear bolt.

7. Remove the bolt and washer (**Figure 74**) securing the rear of the fuel tank. Don't lose the metal spacer in the rubber cushion.

8. Lift up and pull the tank to the rear and remove the fuel tank.

9. Install by reversing these removal steps, noting the following.

10. Inspect the rubber cushions (**Figure 75**) where the front of the fuel tank attaches to the frame. Replace if they are damaged or starting to deteriorate.

11. Turn the fuel shutoff valve ON (**Figure 76**) and check for fuel leaks.

Removal/Installation (Plastic Tank)

1. Remove both side covers and the seat.

2. Turn the fuel shutoff valve to the OFF position.

3. Remove the fuel line to the carburetor assembly.

4. Unhook the rubber strap (A, **Figure 77**) securing the rear of the tank.

5. Remove the bolt and spacer on each side of the front of the fuel tank (B, **Figure 77**).

6. Pull the fuel filler cap vent tube (C, **Figure 77**) from the steering head receptacle.

7. Lift up and pull the tank to the rear and remove the fuel tank.

8. Inspect the rubber protective bands (**Figure 78**) or rubber covers (**Figure 79**) on the nuts of the engine upper hanger plate. Replace as a set if any are damaged or starting to deteriorate.

WARNING
If the protective bands or rubber covers are worn through or not installed, the

7

bolt heads or nuts may wear a hole through the fuel tank. This presents a real fire danger.

9. Install by reversing these removal steps.

FUEL FILTER

The bike is equipped with a small fuel filter screen in the fuel shutoff valve. Considering the dirt and residue that is often found in today's gasoline, it is a good idea to install an inline fuel filter to help keep the carburetor clean. A good quality inline fuel filter (A.C. part No. GF453 or equivalent) is available at most auto and motorcycle supply stores. Just cut the fuel line from the fuel tank to the carburetor and install the filter. Cut out a section of the fuel line the length of the filter body so the fuel line does not kink and restrict fuel flow. Insert the fuel filter and make sure the fuel line is secured to the filter at each end.

GASOLINE/ALCOHOL BLEND TEST

Gasoline blended with alcohol is available in many areas. Most states and most fuel suppliers require labeling of gasoline pumps that dispense gasoline containing a certain percentage of alcohol (methyl or wood). If in doubt, ask the service station operator if their fuel contains any alcohol. A gasoline/alcohol blend, even if it contains co-solvents and corrosion inhibitors for methanol, may be damaging to the fuel system. It may also cause poor performance, hot engine restart or hot-engine running problems.

If you are not sure if the fuel you purchased contains alcohol, run this simple and effective test. A blended fuel doesn't look any different from straight gasoline so it must be tested.

WARNING
Gasoline is very volatile and presents an extreme fire hazard. Be sure to work in a well-ventilated area away from any open flames (including pilot lights on household appliances). Do not allow anyone to smoke in the area and have a fire extinguisher rated for gasoline fires handy.

During this test keep the following facts in mind.
a. Alcohol and gasoline mix together.
b. Alcohol mixes *easier* with water.
c. Gasoline and water do *not* mix.

NOTE
If cosolvents have been used in the gasoline, this test may not work with water. Repeat this test using automotive antifreeze instead of water.

Use an 8 oz. transparent baby bottle with a sealable cap.
1. Set the baby bottle on a level surface and add water up to the 1.5 oz mark. Mark this line on the bottle with a fine-line permanent marking pen. This will be the reference line used later in this test.
2. Add the suspect fuel into the baby bottle up to the 8 oz. mark.
3. Install the sealable cap and shake the bottle vigorously for about 10 seconds.

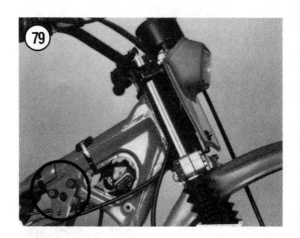

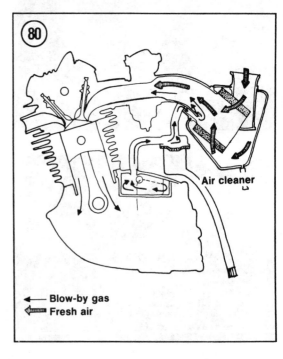

← Blow-by gas
⇐ Fresh air
Air cleaner

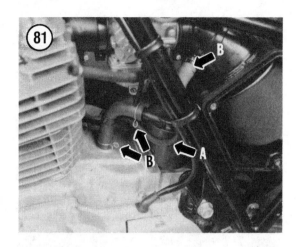

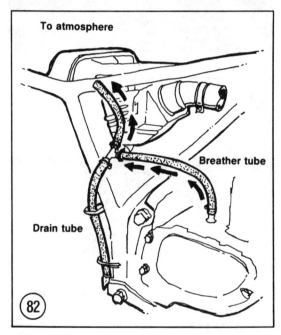

To atmosphere

Breather tube

Drain tube

4. Set the baby bottle upright on the level surface used in Step 1 and wait for a few minutes for the mixture to settle down.

5. If there is *no* alcohol in the fuel the gasoline/water separation line will be exactly on the 1.5 oz. reference line made in Step 1.

6. If there *is* alcohol in the fuel the gasoline/water separation line will be *above* the 1.5 oz. reference line made in Step 1. The alcohol has separated from the gasoline and mixed in with the water (remember it is easier for the alcohol to mix with water than gasoline).

> *WARNING*
> *After the test, discard the baby bottle or place it out of reach of small children. There will always be a gasoline and alcohol residue, and it should **not** be used to drink out of.*

CRANKCASE BREATHER SYSTEM (U.S. ONLY)

To comply with air pollution standards, the XL series models are equipped with a closed crankcase breather system. The system shown in **Figure 80** has a breather separator unit (A, **Figure 81**) and the blowby gases from the crankcase are recirculated into the fuel/air mixture and thus into the engine to be burned. The system used on the XR series models differs in that the gasses are not routed to the air filter air box nor are they burned in the engine. They are routed as shown in **Figure 82** and are vented to the atmosphere.

Inspection/Cleaning

Make sure all hose clamps (B, **Figure 81**) are tight. Check all hoses for deterioration and replace as necessary.

Remove the plug on the XL series (**Figure 83**) or XR series (**Figure 84**) from the drain hose and drain out all residue. This cleaning procedure should be done more frequently if a considerable amount of riding is done at full throttle or in the rain.

> *NOTE*
> *Be sure to install the drain plug and clamp.*

EVAPORATIVE EMISSION CONTROL SYSTEM (1984-1987 CALIFORNIA XL SERIES MODELS ONLY)

Fuel vapor from the fuel tank is routed into a charcoal canister (**Figure 85**). This vapor is stored

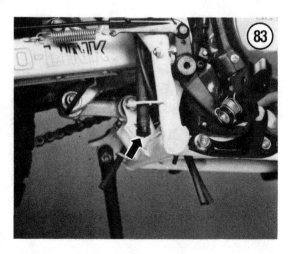

when the engine is not running. When the engine is running these vapors are drawn through a purge control valve and into the carburetors. Make sure all hose clamps are tight. Check all hoses for deterioration and replace as necessary (**Figure 86**).

Refer to **Figure 87** for correct hose routing to the PV valve. When removing the hoses from the PC valve, mark the hose and the fitting with a piece of masking tape and identify where the hose goes. There are so many vacuum hoses on these models that reconnection can be very confusing.

The charcoal canister and the PC valve are located just forward of the rear wheel.

Removal/Installation

1. Remove both side covers and the seat.
2. Remove the fuel tank as described in this chapter.
3. Remove the rear wheel as described in Chapter Nine.

> *NOTE*
> *Before removing the hoses from the PC valve, mark the hose and the fitting with a piece of masking tape and identify where the hose goes.*

4. Disconnect the hoses (**Figure 86**) going to the charcoal canister from the PC valve.
5. Remove the bolt(s) securing the charcoal canister to the canister bracket on the frame and remove the canister assembly.
6. Install by reversing these removal steps.
7. Be sure to install the hoses to their correct fitting on the PC valve.
8. Make sure the hoses are not kinked, twisted or in contact with any sharp surfaces.

AIR FILTER CASE

Removal/Installation

> *NOTE*
> *The air filter case must be removed for rear shock absorber removal and installation. This procedure represents a typical air filter case removal and installation. Minor variations exist among the various models.*

1. Remove the seat and both side covers.
2. On California models, remove the charcoal canister and the PC valve as described in this chapter.
3. Remove the battery as described in Chapter Three.

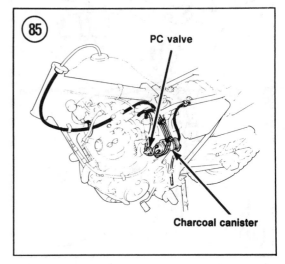

PC valve

Charcoal canister

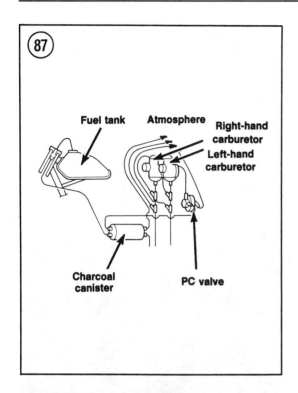

Fuel tank   Atmosphere   Right-hand carburetor

Left-hand carburetor

Charcoal canister   PC valve

4. Loosen the screws on the clamping bands on each carburetor at the back where they attach to the air box inlet tube.

5. On models so equipped, remove the bolt securing the air box on the side.

6. On models so equipped, disconnect the electrical connector to the AC regulator and remove the regulator (A, **Figure 88**).

7. Remove the bolts (B, **Figure 88**) securing the top of the air box to the frame.

8. On some models, remove the muffler as described in this chapter.

9. Unhook the metal band securing the electrical harness to the air box. Move the wiring harness out of the way.

10. Disconnect the crankcase breather hose from the air box.

11. Remove the air filter air box out of the frame.

12. Install by reversing these removal steps.

EXHAUST SYSTEM

The exhaust system is a vital performance component and frequently, because of its design, it is vulnerable to damage. Check the exhaust system for deep dents and fractures and repair or replace them immediately. Check the muffler frame mounting flanges for fractures and loose bolts. Check the cylinder head mounting flanges for tightness. A loose exhaust pipe connection can rob the engine of power.

The exhaust system consists of a dual exhaust pipe, single muffler and a spark arrestor.

Removal/Installation

1. Remove the seat and side covers.

2. Remove the fuel tank as described in this chapter.

3A. On 1988-1990 XR600R models, remove the nuts (**Figure 89**) securing the exhaust pipe flanges to the cylinder head. Remove the two individual exhaust pipe flanges from each exhaust pipe.

3B. On all other models, remove the nuts (**Figure 89**) securing the exhaust pipe flanges to the cylinder head. Slide each exhaust pipe flange down the exhaust pipe.

4. Loosen the clamping bolts (A, **Figure 90**) securing the exhaust pipe to the muffler. Withdraw the exhaust pipe from the muffler and the cylinder head and remove it.

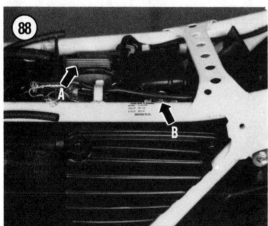

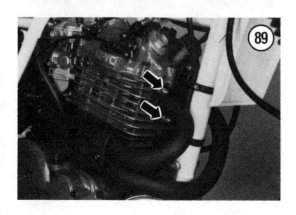

NOTE
Don't lose the 2 collars at each exhaust port when the exhaust pipe is removed from the cylinder head.

NOTE
On some XL series models, the rear directional lights are secured to the frame with the same mounting hardware as the muffler.

5. Remove the bolt(s) and washer(s) (B, **Figure 90**) securing the muffler to the frame. Withdraw the muffler out through the rear and remove it.

6. Inspect the gaskets at all joints; replace as necessary.

7. Be sure to install a new gasket in each exhaust port in the cylinder head.

8. Install the muffler onto the frame.

9. Install the exhaust pipe assembly into position and install one cylinder head nut (at each exhaust port) only finger-tight until the muffler bolts and washers are installed.

10. Install the muffler mounting bolt(s) and washer(s); do not tighten at this time. Make sure the head pipe inlet is correctly seated in the exhaust port.

11. Remove both cylinder head nuts. Install the 4 collars into place (2 collars per exhaust port) and

slide the exhaust flange into position. Make sure the collars are correctly seated into the cylinder head exhaust port.

NOTE
Tightening the cylinder head nuts first will minimize exhaust leaks at the cylinder head.

12. Tighten the muffler bolts securely.

13. Install the fuel tank, seat and side covers.

14. After installation is complete, start the engine and make sure there are no exhaust leaks.

Tables are on the following pages.

Table 1 CARBURETOR SPECIFICATIONS[1]

Item	1979 XL500S	1980-1981 XL500S
Model No.	PD07A	PD07B
Main jet No.	155	155
High altitude jet	NA	NA
Slow jet	55	55
Initial pilot screw opening	2 1/4 turns	2 3/8 turns
Needle jet clip position from top	Fixed	Fixed
Float level	14.5 mm (0.57 in.)	14.5 mm (0.49 in.)
Idle speed	1,200 ± 100 rpm	1,200 ± 100 rpm

Item	1979 XR500	1980 XR500
Model No.	PD06A	PD11A
Main jet No.	158	155
High altitude jet	152	150, 152, 158, 160
Slow jet	55	55
Initial pilot screw opening	2 turns	2 1/4 turns
Needle jet clip position from top	3rd groove	3rd groove
Float level	14.5 mm (0.57 in.)	14.5 mm (0.49 in.)
Idle speed	1,200 ± 100 rpm	1,200 ± 100 rpm

Item	1981-1982 XR500R	XL500R
Model No.	PD11B	PD77A
Main jet No.	152	135
High altitude jet	138, 140, 142, 145, 148, 150, 155, 158	130
Slow jet	55	52
Initial pilot screw opening	2 1/4 turns	2 1/4 turns
Needle jet clip position from top	3rd groove	Fixed
Float level	14.5 mm (0.57 in.)	18.0 mm (0.71 in.)
Idle speed	1,200 ± 100 rpm	1,200 ± 100 rpm

Item	1983-1984 XR500R	1983 XL600R
Model No.		PH60A
1983	PH50A	
1984	PH51A	
Main jet No.		
Primary carb.	135	125
Secondary carb.	108	112
High altitude jet	NA	NA
Slow jet	55	55
Initial pilot screw opening	1 1/8 turns	1 1/8 turns
Needle jet clip position from top		
Primary carb.	4th groove	NA
Secondary carb.	2nd groove (1984: 3rd groove)	NA
Float level	20.0 mm (0.79 in.)	18.0 mm (0.71 in.)
Idle speed	1,300 ± 100 rpm	1,200 ± 100 rpm

(continued)

Table 1 CARBURETOR SPECIFICATIONS[1] (continued)

1984-1990 XL600R		
Item	**49-STATE**	**CALIF**
Models No.		
1984	PH64A	PH66A
1985	PH68A-A	PH68B-B
1986-1990	PH68G	PH68H
Main jet No.		
Primary carb.		
1984	120	118
1985-1990	118	118
Secondary carb.		
1984	120	118
1985-1990	115	115
High altitude main jet		
Primary carb.	112	110
Secondary carb.	112	110
Slow jet		
1984-1985	65	65
1986-1990	62	62
Intital pilot		
screw opening	2 turns	2 turns
Needle jet clip position from top		
Primary carb.	NA	NA
Secondary carb.	NA	NA
Float level		
1984-1985	20.0 mm (0.79 in.)	20.0 mm (0.79 in.)
1986-1990	18.0 mm (0.71 in.)	18.0 mm (0.71 in.)
Idle speed	1,300 ± 100 rpm	1,300 ± 100 rpm

XR600R	
Item	**1985-1990**
Models No.	
1985-1987	PH52A
1988	PD8AA
1989-1990	PD8AD
Main jet No.	
Primary carb.	122
Secondary carb.	122
1988-1990	165
High altitude main jet	NA
Slow jet	
1985-1987	45
1988	60
1989-1990	62
Intial pilot screw opening	
1985-1987	1 3/8 turns
1988	2 5/8 turns
1989-1990	2 turns
Needle jet clip position from top	
Primary carb.	4th groove
Secondary carb.	2nd groove
1988-1990	3rd groove
Float level	
1985-1987	18.0 mm (0.71 in.)
1988-1990	14.5 mm (0.57 in.)
Idle speed	1,300 ± 100 rpm

NOTES

7

CHAPTER EIGHT

ELECTRICAL SYSTEM

This chapter contains operating principles and service and test procedures for all electrical and ignition components. Information regarding the battery and spark plug are covered in Chapter Three.

The electrical systems vary between the XL and XR series models. The XL series is equipped with components approved for a street legal bike. The XR series is equipped only with a headlight and taillight (no battery) and is for off-road use only.

Where differences occur between the XL and XR series they are identified.

The electrical system includes the following systems:

    a. Charging system (XL series models).
    b. Ignition system.
    c. Lighting system.

Tables 1-7 are at the end of this chapter.

CHARGING SYSTEM
(XL SERIES MODELS)

The charging system consists of the battery, alternator and a solid-state voltage regulator/rectifier. See **Figures 1-3** for the various charging systems used among the different models.

Alternating current generated by the alternator is rectified to direct current. The voltage regulator maintains the voltage to the electrical load (lights, ignition, etc.) at a constant voltage regardless of variations in engine speed and load.

Charging System Test
(XL500S, XL500R)

Whenever charging system trouble is suspected, make sure the battery is fully charged and in good condition before going any further. Clean and test the battery as described in Chapter Three. Make sure all electrical connectors are tight and free of corrosion.

1. Start the engine and let it reach normal operating temperature; shut off the engine.
2. Disconnect both battery wires leading to the voltage regulator/rectifier.
3. Connect a 0-15 DC voltmeter and 0-15 DC ammeter as shown in **Figure 4**.
4. Start the engine and let it idle.
5. Increase engine speed and check output at the engine speeds indicated in **Table 1**.
6. If the charging current is considerably lower than specified, check the alternator and/or the voltage regulator/rectifier.
7. If the charging current is too high the voltage regulator/rectifier is probable at fault.
8. Test these components as described in. this chapter. If found faulty they must be replaced as described in this chapter.
9. After the test is completed, disconnect the voltmeter and ammeter. Reconnect the voltage regulator/rectifier wires to the battery.

Charging System Test
(XL600R)

Whenever a charging system trouble is suspected, make sure the battery is fully charged

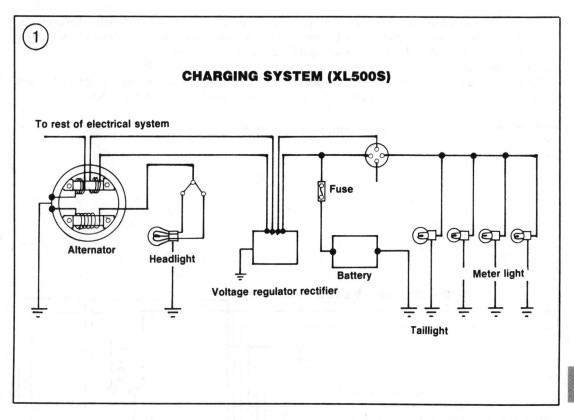

CHARGING SYSTEM (XL500S)

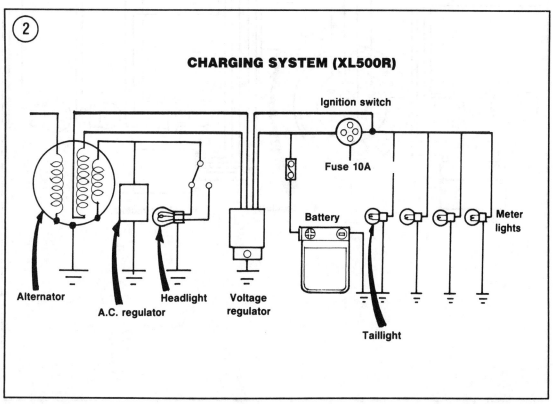

CHARGING SYSTEM (XL500R)

and in good condition before going any further. Clean and test the battery as described in Chapter Three. Make sure all electrical connectors are tight and free of corrosion.

1. Start the engine and let it reach normal operating temperature; shut off the engine.

2. Connect a 0-15 DC voltmeter between the battery terminals. Do not disconnect the battery cables from the battery.

3. Start the engine and let it idle.

4. Gradually increase engine speed and check voltage output at various engine speeds.

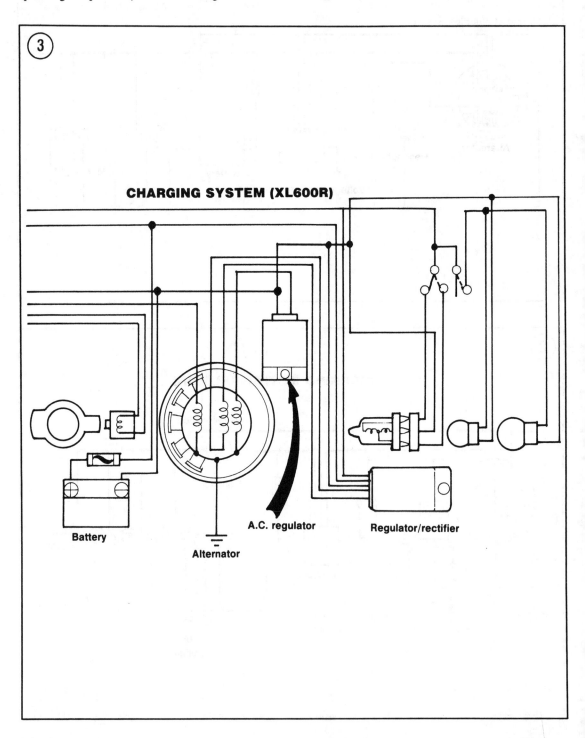

CHARGING SYSTEM (XL600R)

Battery

Alternator

A.C. regulator

Regulator/rectifier

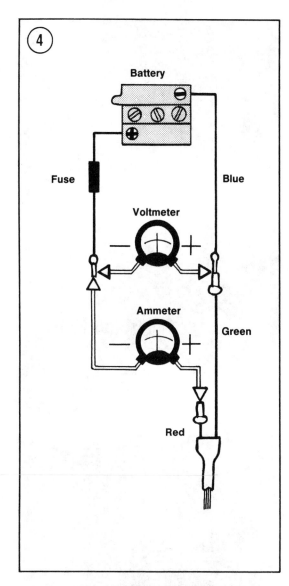

5. The voltage should not exceed 13.5-14.5 volts.

6. Shut the engine off.

7. If the charging voltage is greater than specified, perform the following:

    a. Turn the ignition switch ON.

    b. Use a voltmeter and check the voltage between the black and the green terminals of the voltage regulator/rectifier. There should be battery voltage (12 volts).

    c. If there is no battery voltage, check for an open circuit in the black and green wires in the wiring harness.

    d. If battery voltage is present, replace the voltage regulator/rectifier as described in this chapter.

8. If the charging voltage does not reach that specified even though engine speed increases, perform the following:

    a. Check the voltage regulator/rectifier electrical connector for loose or disconnected terminals.

    b. Use a voltmeter and check the voltage between the red (+) and green (-) terminals of the voltage regulator/rectifier. There should be battery voltage (12 volts).

    c. If there is no battery voltage, check for an open circuit in the red and green wires in the wiring harness.

    d. Use a voltmeter and check the voltage between the black and the green terminals of the voltage regulator/rectifier. There should be battery voltage (12 volts).

    e. If there is no battery voltage, check for an open circuit in the black and green wires in the wiring harness.

    f. If battery voltage is present, inspect the charging coil of the alternator rotor as described in this chapter.

9. Disconnect the voltmeter from the battery.

ALTERNATOR ROTOR

Removal/Installation

1. Remove the bolts securing the skid plate (**Figure 5**) and remove the skid plate.

2. Remove the seat and both side covers.

> *NOTE*
> *On XL500S models, reinstall the seat strap bolts as they also hold the upper portion of the shock to the frame. Remove and reinstall one bolt at a time.*

3. Drain the engine oil as described in Chapter Three.

4. Remove the fuel tank as described in Chapter Seven.

5. On XL series models, disconnect the battery negative lead or the main fuse (**Figure 6**).

6. Disconnect the alternator electrical connector.

7. Shift the transmission into 5th gear.

8. Remove the clamping bolt on the gearshift lever (A, **Figure 7**) and remove the gearshift lever.

9. On 1983-1990 models, perform the following:

   a. Loosen the locknut on the clutch cable at the hand lever. This will allow slack in the clutch cable.

   b. Disconnect the clutch cable from the actuating arm (B, **Figure 7**) on the alternator cover.

10. Remove the bolts securing the drive sprocket cover (**Figure 8**) and remove the cover.

11. Remove the bolts securing the alternator cover and stator assembly (**Figure 9**) and remove the cover and gasket. Do not lose the locating dowels.

12. Have an assistant apply the rear brake. This will keep the rotor from rotating while removing the nut.

13A. On 1988-1990 XR600R models, remove the shoulder bolt and washer (**Figure 10**) securing the alternator rotor.

13B. On all other models, remove the shoulder bolt (**Figure 10**) securing the alternator rotor.

14. Screw in a flywheel puller (**Figure 11**) until it stops. Use the Honda flywheel puller (part No. 07733-0020001), K&N (part No. 81-0170) or equivalent. Refer to **Figure 12** for RFVC engine models or **Figure 13** for all other models.

> *CAUTION*
> *Do not try to remove the rotor without a puller; any attempt to do so will ultimately lead to some form of damage to the engine and/or rotor. Many aftermarket types of pullers are available from most motorcycle dealers or mail order houses. The cost of one of these pullers is very reasonable and it makes an excellent addition to any mechanic's tool box. If you can't buy or*

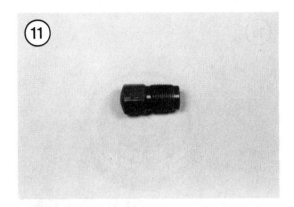

borrow one, have a dealer remove the rotor.

15. Hold the puller with a wrench and gradually tighten the center bolt until the rotor disengages from the crankshaft.

NOTE
If the rotor is difficult to remove, strike the puller center bolt with a hammer a few times. This will usually break it loose.

CAUTION
Never strike the rotor with a hammer as this could destroy the magnetism in the rotor. If destroyed, the rotor must be replaced.

CAUTION
If normal rotor removal attempts fail, do not force the puller as the threads may be stripped out of the rotor causing expensive damage. Take the vehicle to a dealer and have them remove the rotor.

16. Remove the rotor and the puller. Remove the puller from the rotor.

17. Make sure the Woodruff key is still in place in the slot in the crankshaft. Refer to **Figure 14** for RFVC engine models or **Figure 15** for all other models.

CAUTION
*Carefully inspect the inside of the rotor (**Figure 16**) for small bolts, washers or other metal "trash" that may have been picked up by the magnets. These small metal bits can cause severe damage to the alternator stator plate components.*

18. Install by reversing these removal steps, noting the following.

19. Make sure the Woodruff key is in place on the crankshaft and align the keyway in the rotor with the key when installing the rotor.

20. Have an assistant apply the rear brake. This will keep the rotor from rotating while tightening the bolt.

21. Install and tighten the rotor bolt to the torque specification listed in **Table 2**.

22. Install the locating dowels and a new gasket.

23. Adjust the clutch as described in Chapter Three.

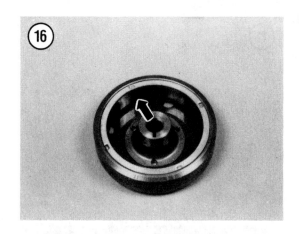

ALTERNATOR STATOR

Removal/Installation

1. Perform Steps 1-11, *Alternator Rotor Removal/Installation* in this chapter.

2A. On RFVC engine models, perform the following:

  a. Remove the bolts (A, **Figure 17**) securing the stator assembly to the alternator cover.

  b. Pull the electrical harness and rubber grommet (B, **Figure 17**) from the notch in the cover.

  c. Remove the stator assembly.

2B. On 1982 XL500R models, perform the following:

  a. Remove the bolts (**Figure 18**) securing the stator assembly to the stator coil base in the alternator cover.

  b. Remove the bolt (**Figure 18**) securing the wire clamp and remove the stator assembly.

  c. Remove the rubber grommets and electrical wire harness from the 2 notches in the alternator cover.

  d. To remove the stator coil base, remove the screws securing the base to the alternator cover. To install the base, position the groove on the base facing upward (**Figure 19**). Tighten the screws securely.

2C. On all other models, perform the following:

  a. Remove the bolts (A, **Figure 20**) securing the stator assembly and set plates to the alternator cover.

  b. Remove the bolt (B, **Figure 20**) securing the wire clamp and remove the wire clamp.

  c. Pull the electrical harness and both rubber grommets from the 2 notches in the cover.

  d. Remove the stator assembly.

3. Install by reversing these removal steps, noting the following.

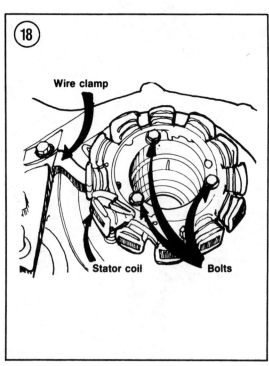

Wire clamp

Stator coil   Bolts

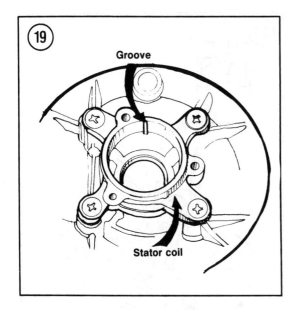

Groove

Stator coil

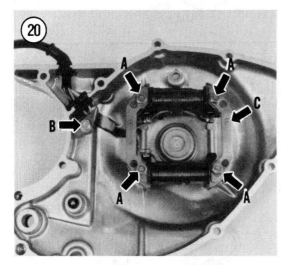

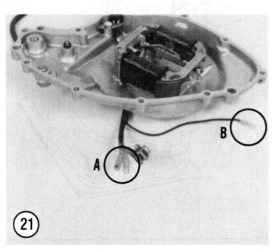

4. On all models except the RFVC engine models, be sure to install the stator assembly with the "F" mark (C, **Figure 20**) toward the front of the alternator cover.

5. Make sure all electrical connectors are free of corrosion and are tight.

Stator Coil Testing

It is not necessary to remove the stator plate to perform the following tests. It is shown removed in the following procedure for clarity.

Accurate results are *not required* in the procedure—just continuity.

1. Remove the seat and side covers.

2. Remove the fuel tank as described in Chapter Seven.

3. On XL series models, disconnect the battery negative lead or disconnect the main fuse (**Figure 6**).

4. Disconnect the alternator electrical connector coming from the alternator stator assembly and make the following tests.

5A. *Lighting coil*—Use an ohmmeter set at R×1 and check for continuity between the following wires (A, **Figure 21**):

    a. XL series: White/yellow wire and ground.

    b. XR series: Blue wire and ground.

If there is continuity (low resistance) the coil is good. If there is no continuity (infinite resistance) the coil is bad and the stator assembly must be replaced. The individual coil cannot be replaced.

5B. *Exciter coil*—On XL series models, use an ohmmeter set at R×1 and check for continuity between the pink/yellow wire and ground (B, **Figure 21**). On XR series models, use an ohmmeter set at R×1 and check for continuity between the black/red wire and ground. If there is continuity (low resistance) the coil is good. If there is no continuity (infinite resistance) the coil is bad and the stator assembly must be replaced. The individual coil cannot be replaced.

6. Connect the electrical connectors. Make sure all connectors are free of corrosion and are tight.

7. Install all items removed.

VOLTAGE REGULATOR/RECTIFIER (XL SERIES MODELS)

Removal/Installation

1. Remove the seat and both side covers.

2. Remove the fuel tank as described in Chapter Seven.

3. Disconnect the battery lead or disconnect the main fuse (**Figure 6**).

8

4. Disconnect the electrical connector (A, **Figure 22**) going to the voltage regulator from the wiring harness.

5. Remove the bolt securing the voltage regulator (B, **Figure 22**) to the frame and remove the voltage regulator.

6. Install by reversing these removal steps, noting the following.

7. Make sure all electrical connectors are free of corrosion and are tight.

Performance Test

1. Remove the right-hand side cover.

2. Connect a voltmeter to the battery negative and positive terminals. Leave the battery cables attached.

3A. On 6-volt systems perform the following:
  a. Start the engine and let it idle.
  b. Increase engine speed until the voltage going to the battery reaches 8.0-8.9 volts (usually at 5,000 rpm).

3B. On 12-volt systems perform the following:
  a. Start the engine and let it idle.
  b. Increase engine speed until the voltage going to the battery reaches 13.5-14.5 volts (usually at 5,000 rpm).

4. At this point the voltage regulator should prevent any further increase in voltage. If this does not happen and the voltage increases above the specified amount, the voltage regulator/rectifier is faulty and must be replaced.

5. Disconnect the voltmeter and shut off the engine.

6. Install the right-hand side cover.

A/C REGULATOR TEST (XL500R, XL600R)

1. Remove the headlight lens assembly from the housing as described in this chapter. Leave the electrical connector attached to the headlight bulb.

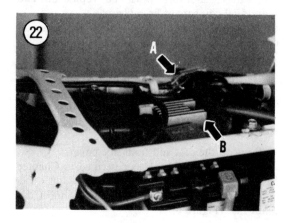

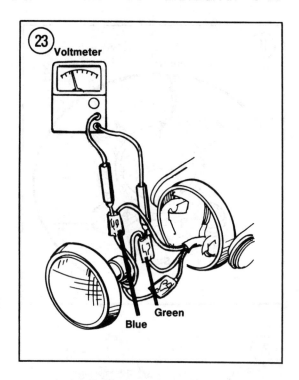

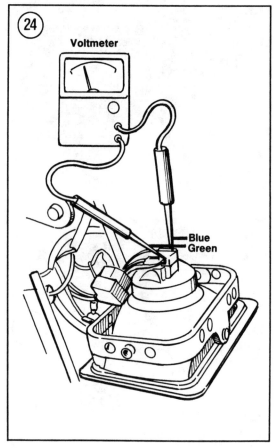

2. Turn the headlight dimmer switch to the HI position.

3. Connect a voltmeter to the headlight green and blue electrical wires. Refer to **Figure 23** for XL500R models or **Figure 24** for XL600R models.

4. Start the engine and let it idle. Increase engine speed slowly until engine speed reaches 5,000 rpm.

5. The voltage should be as follows at this engine speed.

    a. XL500R, 1983-1986 XL600R: 13.5-14.5 volts.

    b. 1987 XL600R: 13.7-14.4 volts.

6. At this point the A/C regulator should prevent any further increase in voltage. If this does not happen and the voltage increases above the specified amount, shut the engine OFF and perform the following:

    a. Test the dimmer switch as described under *Headlight Dimmer Switch Testing* in this chapter.

    b. Check for loose or corroded electrical connectors at the dimmer switch or at the A/C regulator connector. Replace or repair.

    c. Use an ohmmeter and check for an open or short in the A/C regulator circuit portion of the wiring harness.

7. If all of the items tested in Step 6 check out okay, the A/C regulator is faulty and must be replaced.

8. Disconnect the voltmeter.

9. Install the headlight lens assembly.

CAPACITOR DISCHARGE IGNITION

All models are equipped with a capacitor discharge ignition (CDI) system, a solid-state system that uses no breaker points. The ignition circuit is shown in the following illustrations:

    a. **Figure 25**: XL500S.

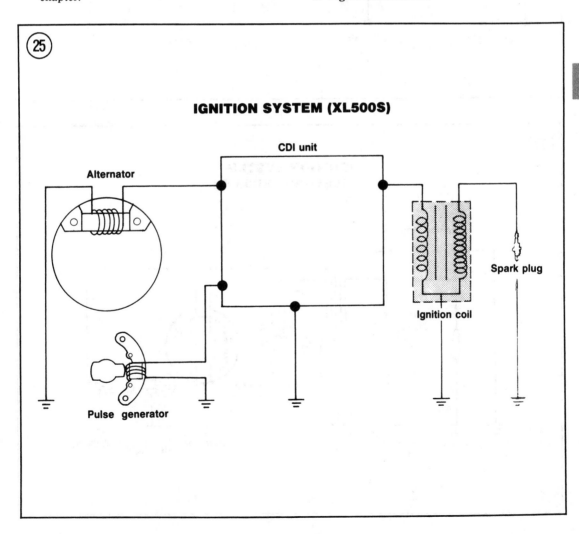

IGNITION SYSTEM (XL500S)

CDI unit

Alternator

Spark plug

Ignition coil

Pulse generator

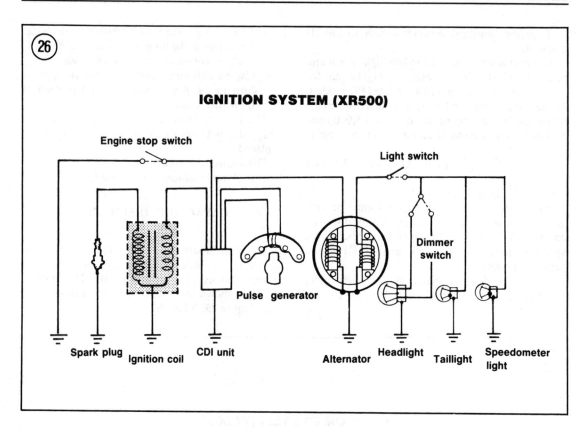

26

IGNITION SYSTEM (XR500)

Engine stop switch

Light switch

Dimmer switch

Pulse generator

Spark plug   Ignition coil   CDI unit   Alternator   Headlight   Taillight   Speedometer light

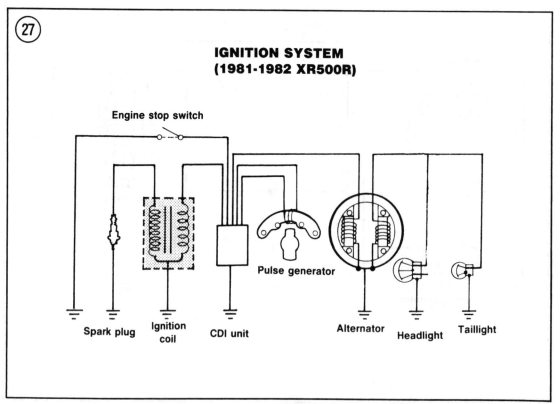

27

IGNITION SYSTEM
(1981-1982 XR500R)

Engine stop switch

Pulse generator

Spark plug   Ignition coil   CDI unit   Alternator   Headlight   Taillight

b. **Figure 26**: XR500.

c. **Figure 27**: 1981-1982 XR500R.

d. **Figure 28**: XL500R.

e. **Figure 29**: 1983-1984 XR500R.

f. **Figure 30**: XR600R.

g. **Figure 31**: XL600R.

As the crankshaft turns the rotor, the permanent magnets within the rotor cause an electronic pulse to develop in the primary coil of the stator assembly. A pulse from the pickup coil in the stator assembly is used to trigger the output of the CDI unit which in turn triggers the output of the ignition coil and fires the spark plug.

CDI Precautions

Certain measures must be taken to protect the capacitor discharge system.

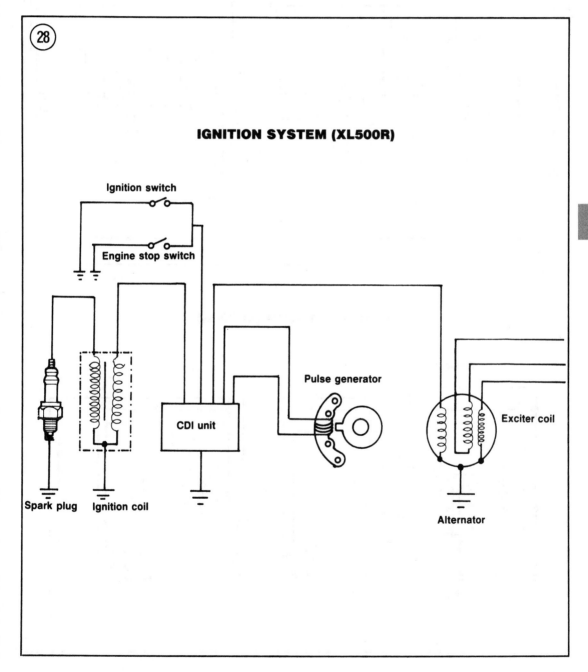

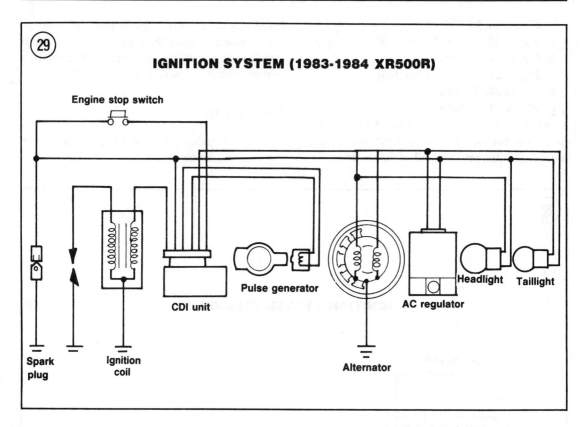

IGNITION SYSTEM (1983-1984 XR500R)

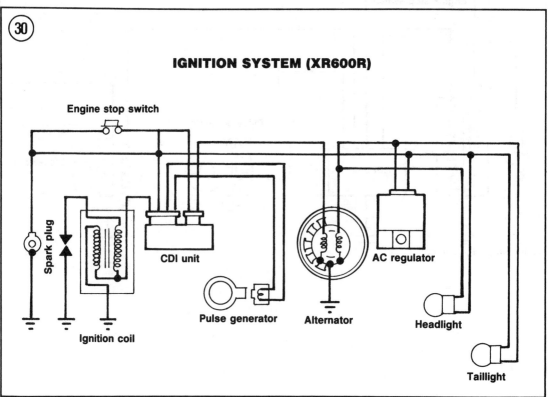

IGNITION SYSTEM (XR600R)

1. Never disconnect any of the electrical connections while the engine is running.

2. Keep all connections between the various units clean and tight. Be sure that the wiring connectors are pushed together firmly to help keep out moisture.

3. Do not substitute another type of ignition coil.

4. The CDI unit is mounted to the frame in a rubber mount. Always be sure that the CDI unit is mounted by this means as it is designed to help isolate vibrations.

CDI Troubleshooting

Problems with the capacitor discharge system fall into one of the following categories. See **Table 3**.

    a. Weak spark.

    b. No spark.

CDI Testing (1982-on Models)

NOTE

*This procedure covers only models from 1982 on. On models not listed, if you suspect a faulty CDI unit, take your bike to a dealer and have them test it. Chances are they will perform a "remove and replace" test to see if the CDI unit is faulty. This type of test is expensive if performed by yourself. Remember if you purchase a new CDI unit and it does **not** solve your particular ignition system problem, you cannot return the CDI unit for refund. Most motorcycle dealers will **not** accept returns on any electrical component since they could be damaged internally even though they look okay externally.*

The manufacturer does not provide test specifications for the CDI unit. The following test proce-

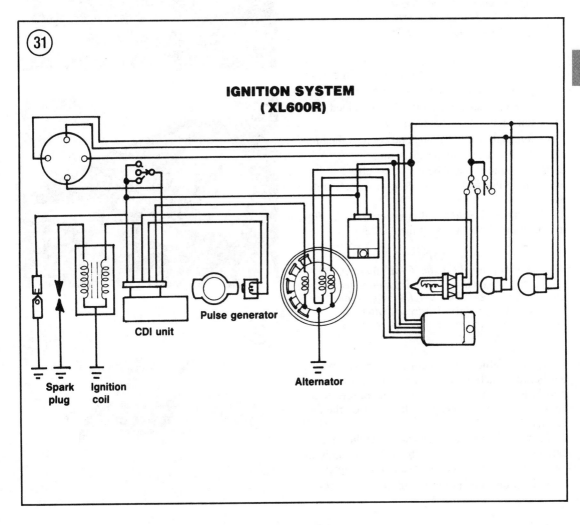

(31)

**IGNITION SYSTEM
(XL600R)**

Pulse generator

CDI unit

Alternator

**Spark
plug**　**Ignition
coil**

8

dures measure the resistance values of the individual components and their associated wiring.

1. Test the CDI units ability to produce a spark. Perform the following:

   a. Disconnect the high voltage lead from the spark plug. Remove the spark plug from the cylinder head.

   b. Connect a new or known good spark plug to the high voltage lead and place the spark plug base on a good ground like the engine cylinder head (**Figure 32**). Position the spark plug so you can see the electrodes.

> *WARNING*
> *If it is necessary to hold the high voltage lead, use an insulated pair of pliers. The high voltage generated by the CD1 could produce serious or fatal shocks.*

> *NOTE*
> *The engine must be kicked over rapidly since the ignition system does not produce a spark at low rpm.*

   c. Kick the engine over rapidly with the kickstarter and check for a spark. If there is a fat blue spark, replace the spark plug.

   d. If a weak spark or no spark is obtained continue with this procedure.

   e. Reinstall the spark plug and connect the high voltage lead onto the spark plug.

2. Remove the seat and both side covers.

3. Remove the fuel tank as described in Chapter Seven.

4. Disconnect the electrical connector(s) (A, **Figure 33**) from the backside of the CDI unit.

> *NOTE*
> *For best results, in the following step, use a quality digital multimeter (Honda part No. KS-AHM-32-003) or equivalent. Install a fresh battery in the multimeter before performing these tests.*

5. Refer to **Table 4** and measure the resistance values between each of the electrical connector(s) terminals on the *wire harness side* of the electrical connector(s). Do not perform these test on the terminals of the CDI unit.

6. If any of the test results do not meet the specifications, then test and inspect the following ignition system components as described in this chapter.

   a. Ignition coil: primary and secondary resistance.

   b. Alternator exciter coil.

   c. Pulse generator.

   d. Engine stop switch.

7. If all of the ignition components are okay, then check the following:

   a. Check for an open or short in the wire harness between each component.

   b. Make sure all connections between the various components are clean and tight. Be sure that the wiring connectors are pushed together firmly to help keep out moisture.

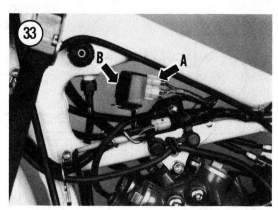

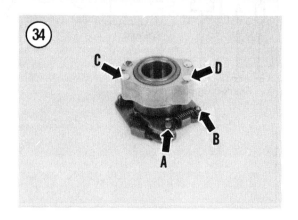

8. If Steps 1-7 meets all specifications, then the CDI unit is faulty and must be replaced as described in this chapter.

Replacement

1. Remove the seat and side covers.
2. Remove the fuel tank as described in Chapter Seven.
3. Disconnect the electrical connectors (A, **Figure 33**) from the backside of the CDI unit.
4. On models so equipped, remove the screws securing the CDI unit to the frame. On all other models, remove the CDI unit from the rubber isolator (B, **Figure 33**) on the frame.

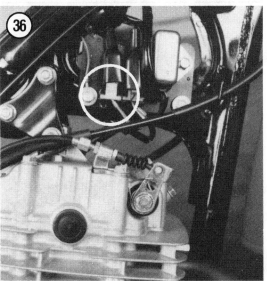

5. Remove the CDI unit.
6. Install a new CDI unit onto the frame and attach the electrical wires to it. Make sure all electrical connectors are free of corrosion and are tight.
7. Install all parts removed.

MECHANICAL IGNITION ADVANCE MECHANISM (XL500S, XL500R, XR500, 1981-1982 XR500R)

NOTE
All models not listed here have an ignition advance circuit built into the CDI unit. This circuit senses speed of the pulse generator rotor as it passes the pulse generator and changes ignition timing accordingly.

The mechanical ignition advance mechanism advances the ignition (fires the spark plug sooner) as engine speed increases. If it does not advance properly and smoothly, the ignition will be incorrect at high engine rpm. It must be inspected periodically to make certain it operates smoothly.

1. Remove the ignition advance mechanism as described in Chapter Four.
2. Inspect the rotor pivot points (A, **Figure 34**) of each weight. The rotor must pivot smoothly to maintain the proper ignition advance. Apply lightweight grease to the pivot pins.
3. Inspect the rotor return springs (B, **Figure 34**). Make sure they are taut and return the rotor to its fully seated position completely.
4. If the rotor is removed from the base, install it, aligning the punch mark (C, **Figure 34**) with the hole in the base.

NOTE
*If the ignition advancer rotor is replaced, the new one must have the same letter designation. Refer to D, **Figure 34**. Failure to do so will result in poor engine performance.*

5. Install by reversing these removal steps.

PULSE GENERATOR

Testing

1A. On RFVC engine models, disconnect the electrical connector going to the pulse generator.
1B. On all other models, disconnect the electrical connector going to the pulse generator. Refer to **Figure 35** for XL series models or **Figure 36** for XR series models.

8

2. On all other models, use an ohmmeter set at R×100 and check the resistance between both wires in the electrical connector. The specified resistance is listed in **Table 5**.

3. If the resistance shown is greater or there is infinite resistance between the 2 terminals, the pulse generator has an open or short and must be replaced as described in this chapter.

Removal/Installation
(RFVC Engine)

1. Remove the right-hand crankcase cover (clutch cover) as described under *Clutch Removal/ Disassembly* in Chapter Six.

2. Remove the bolts (A, **Figure 37**) securing the pulse generator to the crankcase.

3. Carefully remove the electrical harness and rubber grommet (B, **Figure 37**) from the crankcase.

4. Install by reversing these removal steps, noting the following.

5. Make sure all electrical connectors are free of corrosion and are tight.

Removal/Installation
(All Other Models)

1. Remove the right-hand crankcase cover (clutch cover) as described under *Clutch Removal/ Disassembly* in Chapter Six.

2. Remove the Phillips head screws (A, **Figure 38**) securing the pulse generator to the right-hand crankcase cover.

3. Carefully remove the electrical harness and rubber grommet from the right-hand crankcase cover.

4. Install by reversing these removal steps, noting the following.

NOTE
*If the pulse generator is replaced, the new one must have the same letter designation stamped on it (B, **Figure 38**). Failure to do so will result in poor engine performance.*

5. Route the electrical harness through the crankcase cover and out the rubber grommet as shown in **Figure 38**.

6. Make sure all electrical connectors are free of corrosion and are tight.

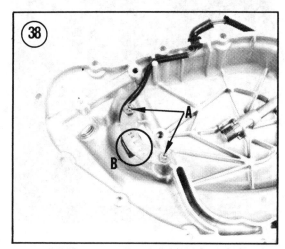

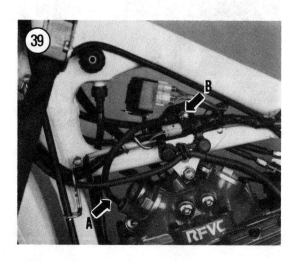

IGNITION COIL

Removal/Installation

1. Remove the seat and side covers.
2. Remove the fuel tank as described in this chapter.
3. On XL series models, disconnect the battery negative lead or the main fuse (**Figure 6**).
4. Disconnect the secondary high voltage lead (A, **Figure 39**) from the spark plug.
5A. On XR600R models, perform the following:
   a. Disconnect the primary electrical wires from the ignition coil.
   b. Remove the bolt securing the ignition coil to the frame.
   c. Remove the ignition coil.
5B. On all other models, perform the following:
   a. Disconnect the primary electrical wires (**Figure 40**) from the ignition coil.

b. On models so equipped, remove the bolts (**Figure 41**) or nuts (B, **Figure 39**) securing the ignition coil to the frame.
c. Withdraw and remove the ignition coil and rubber isolator from the mounting tab on the frame.
6. Install by reversing these removal steps. Note the following during installation.
7. Make sure all electrical connections are free of corrosion and are tight.

Testing (1979-1982 Models)

The ignition coil is a form of transformer which develops the high voltage required to jump the spark plug gap. The only maintenance required is that of keeping the electrical connections clean and tight and occasionally checking to see that the coil is mounted securely.

If the condition of the coil is doubtful, there are several checks which may be made.

First as a quick check of coil condition, disconnect the high voltage lead from the spark plug. Remove the spark plug from the cylinder head. Connect a new or known good spark plug to the high voltage lead and place the spark plug base on a good ground like the engine cylinder head (**Figure 32**). Position the spark plug so you can see the electrode.

> *WARNING*
> *If it is necessary to hold the high voltage lead, do so with an insulated pair of pliers. The high voltage generated by the CDI could produce serious or fatal shocks.*

Turn the engine over with the kickstarter. If a fat blue spark occurs the coil is in good condition; if not proceed as follows. Make sure that you are using a known good spark plug for this test. If the spark plug used is defective the test results will be incorrect.

Reinstall the spark plug in the cylinder head.
Refer to **Figure 42** for this procedure.
Disconnect all ignition coil wires (including the spark plug lead from the spark plug) before testing.

> *NOTE*
> *In order to get accurate resistance measurements the coil must be warm (minimum temperature is 20° C/68° F). If necessary, start the engine and let it warm up to normal operating temperature. If the engine won't run, warm the coil with a hair dryer.*

1. Use an ohmmeter set at R×1 and measure the primary coil resistance between the primary terminal and the mounting flange. Refer to specified resistance values listed in **Table 6**.

2. Use an ohmmeter set at R×1 and measure the secondary lead (spark plug lead with the spark plug cap attached) and the mounting flange. Refer to specified resistance values listed in **Table 6**.

3. If the coil resistance does not meet either of these specifications, the coil must be replaced. If the coil exhibits visible damage, it should be replaced.

4. Reconnect all ignition coil wires to the ignition coil.

Testing (1983-on Models)

The ignition coil is a form of transformer which develops the high voltage required to jump the spark plug gap. The only maintenance required is that of keeping the electrical connections clean and tight and occasionally checking to see that the coil is mounted securely.

If the condition of the coil is doubtful, there are several checks which may be made.

First as a quick check of coil condition, disconnect the high voltage lead from the spark plug. Remove the spark plug from the cylinder head. Connect a new or known good spark plug to

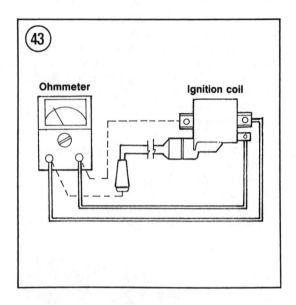

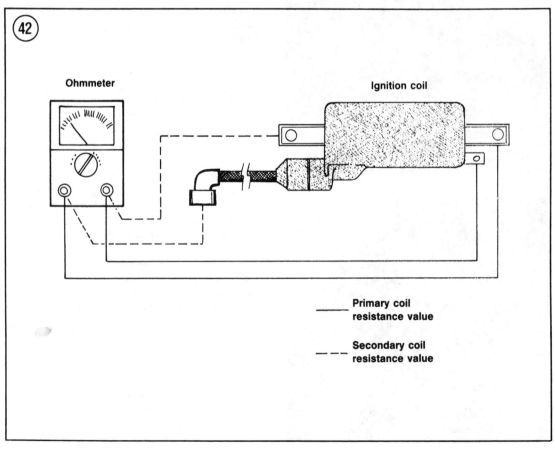

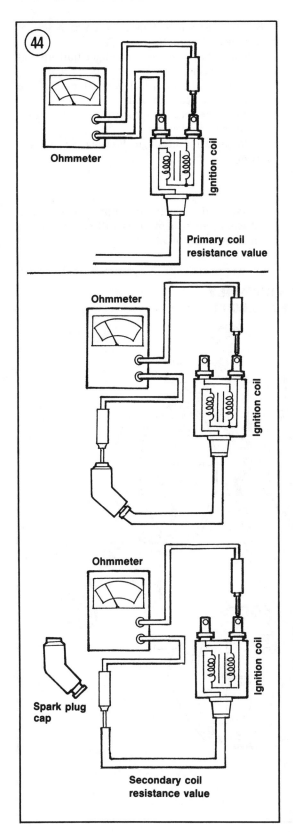

44

Ohmmeter

Ignition coil

Primary coil
resistance value

Ohmmeter

Ignition coil

Ohmmeter

Ignition coil

Spark plug
cap

Secondary coil
resistance value

the high voltage lead and place the spark plug base on a good ground like the engine cylinder head (**Figure 32**). Position the spark plug so you can see the electrode.

> *WARNING*
> *If it is necessary to hold the high voltage lead, use an insulated pair of pliers. The high voltage generated by the CDI could produce serious or fatal shocks.*

Turn the engine over with the kickstarter. If a fat blue spark occurs the coil is in good condition; if not, proceed as follows. Make sure that you are using a known good spark plug for this test. If the spark plug used is defective the test results will be incorrect.

Reinstall the spark plug in the cylinder head.

Refer to **Figure 43** for 1983-1984 XR500R models or **Figure 44** for XL600R and XR600R for this procedure.

Disconnect all ignition coil wires (including the spark plug lead from the spark plug) before testing.

> *NOTE*
> *In order to get accurate resistance measurements the coil must be warm (minimum temperature is 20° C/68° F). If necessary, start the engine and let it warm up to normal operating temperature. If the engine won't run, warm up the coil with a hair dryer.*

1. Use an ohmmeter set at R×1 and measure the primary coil resistance between the positive (+) and the negative (-) terminals on the top of the ignition coil. Refer to specified resistance values listed in **Table 6**.
2. Use an ohmmeter set at R×1,000 to measure the secondary coil resistance between the positive (+) terminal on the top of the ignition coil and spark plug lead with the spark plug cap attached. Refer to specified resistance values listed in **Table 6**.
3. Use an ohmmeter set at R×1,000 to measure the secondary coil resistance between the positive (+) terminal on the top of the ignition coil and spark plug lead with the spark plug cap removed. Refer to specified resistance values listed in **Table 6**. Reconnect the spark plug cap.
4. If the coil resistance does not meet any of these specifications, the coil must be replaced. If the coil exhibits visible damage, it should be replaced.
5. Reconnect all ignition coil wires to the ignition coil.

8

LIGHTING SYSTEM

The lighting system consists of a headlight and taillight. XL series models are also equipped with directional lights, indicator lights and a speedometer illumination light. **Table 7** lists replacement bulbs for these components.

Always use the correct wattage bulb as indicated in this section. The use of a larger wattage bulb will give a dim light and a smaller wattage bulb will burn out prematurely.

Headlight Replacement and Headlight Housing Removal/Installation (XL500S, XL500R)

Refer to **Figure 45** for this procedure.

1. Remove the screw (**Figure 46**) on each side of the headlight housing.
2. Pull the trim bezel and headlight unit up and out of the housing.
3. Disconnect the electrical connector from the backside of the headlight unit.
4. Remove the retainer securing the sealed beam unit and remove the unit.
5. To remove the headlight housing perform the following:

a. Mark all electrical connectors before disconnecting them. This will ensure correct re-connection of all wires.

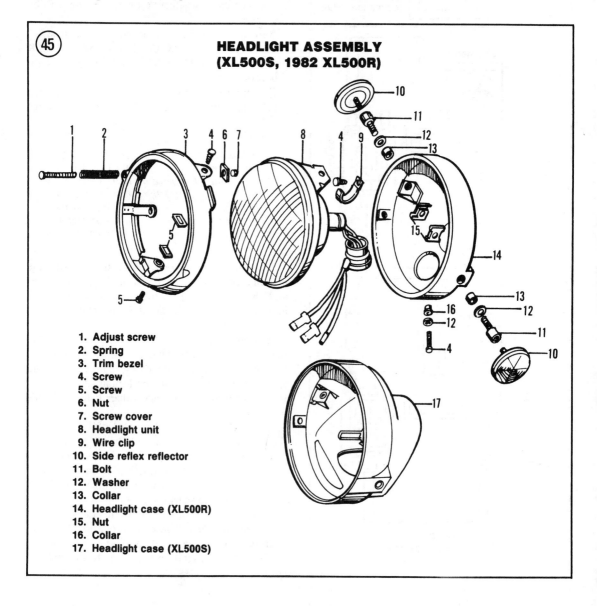

**HEADLIGHT ASSEMBLY
(XL500S, 1982 XL500R)**

1. Adjust screw
2. Spring
3. Trim bezel
4. Screw
5. Screw
6. Nut
7. Screw cover
8. Headlight unit
9. Wire clip
10. Side reflex reflector
11. Bolt
12. Washer
13. Collar
14. Headlight case (XL500R)
15. Nut
16. Collar
17. Headlight case (XL500S)

b. Disconnect all electrical connectors within the headlight housing.

c. Unscrew the reflex reflector on each side.

d. Unscrew the bolt, washer, collar and nut on each side securing the headlight housing to the front fork.

e. Carefully withdraw the electrical wires out through the opening in the backside of the headlight housing.

f. Remove the headlight housing.

6. Install by reversing these removal steps.

7. Adjust the headlight as described in this chapter.

**Headlight Replacement and
Headlight Holder Removal/Installation
(XR500, 1981-1982 XR500R)**

Refer to **Figure 47** for this procedure.

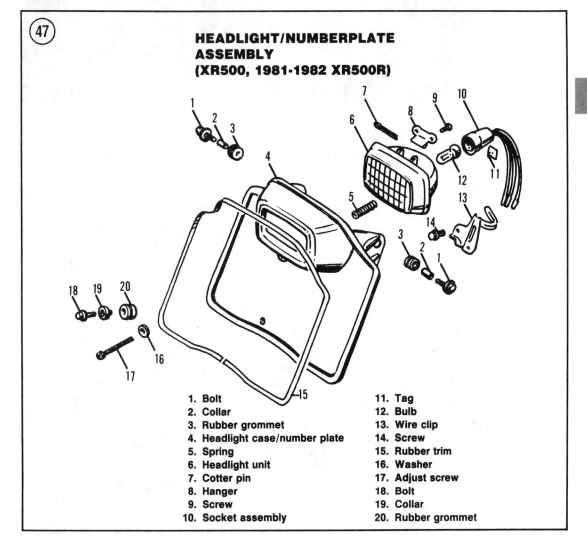

HEADLIGHT/NUMBERPLATE ASSEMBLY (XR500, 1981-1982 XR500R)

1. Bolt	11. Tag
2. Collar	12. Bulb
3. Rubber grommet	13. Wire clip
4. Headlight case/number plate	14. Screw
5. Spring	15. Rubber trim
6. Headlight unit	16. Washer
7. Cotter pin	17. Adjust screw
8. Hanger	18. Bolt
9. Screw	19. Collar
10. Socket assembly	20. Rubber grommet

8

1. Remove the bolts and washers (**Figure 48**) securing the headlight holder.

2. Pivot the holder and headlight assembly down.

3. Rotate the electrical connector/socket (**Figure 49**) and remove it from the backside of the headlight lens unit.

4. Remove the headlight holder.

5. Remove the bulb from the electrical connector/socket and replace with a new bulb.

6. Install by reversing these removal steps.

7. Adjust the headlight as described in this chapter.

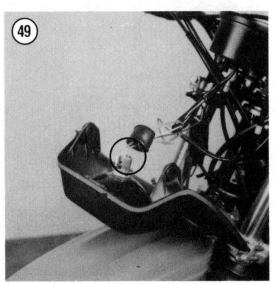

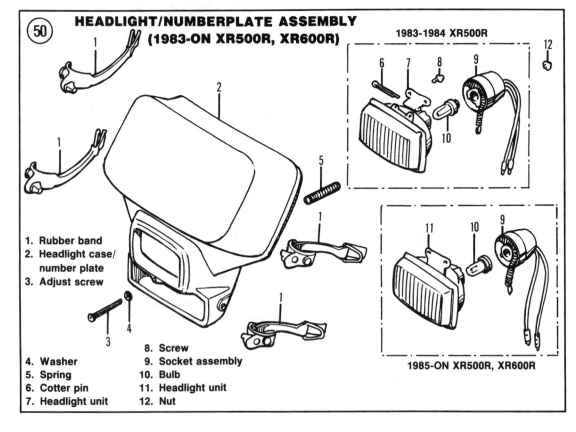

HEADLIGHT/NUMBERPLATE ASSEMBLY (1983-ON XR500R, XR600R)

1983-1984 XR500R

1985-ON XR500R, XR600R

1. Rubber band
2. Headlight case/number plate
3. Adjust screw
4. Washer
5. Spring
6. Cotter pin
7. Headlight unit
8. Screw
9. Socket assembly
10. Bulb
11. Headlight unit
12. Nut

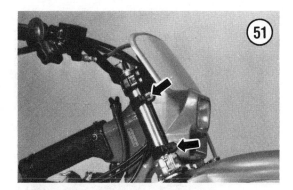

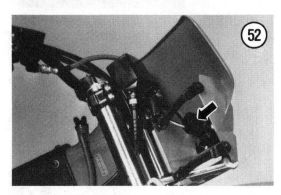

Headlight Replacement and Number Plate Removal/Installation (1983-on XR500R, XR600R)

Refer to **Figure 50** for this procedure.
1. Unhook the rubber mounting bands (**Figure 51**) securing the number plate/headlight assembly to the front forks.
2. Pivot the number plate/headlight assembly out away from the forks and disconnect the electrical connectors going to the bulb socket (**Figure 52**).
3. Remove the number plate.
4. Unhook the spring securing the electrical connector/socket to the backside of the headlight lens unit.
5. Remove the bulb from the electrical connector/socket and replace with a new bulb.
6. Install by reversing these removal steps.
7. Adjust the headlight as described in this chapter.

Headlight Replacement and Number Plate Removal/Installation (XL600R)

Refer to **Figure 53** for this procedure.

8

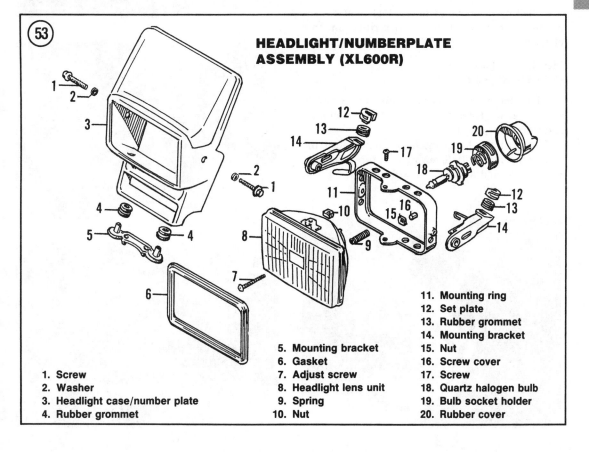

HEADLIGHT/NUMBERPLATE ASSEMBLY (XL600R)

1. Screw
2. Washer
3. Headlight case/number plate
4. Rubber grommet
5. Mounting bracket
6. Gasket
7. Adjust screw
8. Headlight lens unit
9. Spring
10. Nut
11. Mounting ring
12. Set plate
13. Rubber grommet
14. Mounting bracket
15. Nut
16. Screw cover
17. Screw
18. Quartz halogen bulb
19. Bulb socket holder
20. Rubber cover

1. Remove the mounting bolt (**Figure 54**) on each side securing the number plate/headlight assembly to the mounting brackets on the front forks.

2. Pivot the number plate down and unhook it from the locating tabs on the lower fork bridge. Remove the number plate.

3. Pull out on the mounting arms (**Figure 55**) on each side and rest the headlight assembly on the front fork.

4. Disconnect the electrical connector (**Figure 56**) from the backside of the socket assembly.

5. Carefully remove the rubber cover (**Figure 57**) from the bulb holder.

6. Unhook the socket holder (**Figure 58**) and remove the socket holder and bulb (**Figure 59**) from the lens unit.

CAUTION
Carefully read all instructions shipped with the replacement quartz halogen bulb. Do not touch the new bulb glass with your fingers because of oil on your skin. Any traces of oil on the glass will drastically reduce the life of the bulb. Clean any traces of oil from the new bulb with a cloth moistened in alcohol or lacquer thinner.

7. Install by reversing these removal steps.

8. Adjust the headlight as described in this chapter.

Headlight Adjustment
(XL500S, XL500R)

Adjust the headlight horizontally and vertically according to Department of Motor Vehicles regulations in your area.

To adjust the headlight horizontally, turn the screw (A, **Figure 60**). Screwing it in turns the light to the right and loosening it will turn the light to the left.

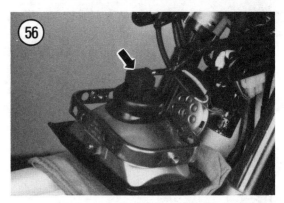

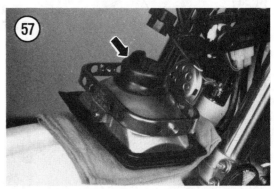

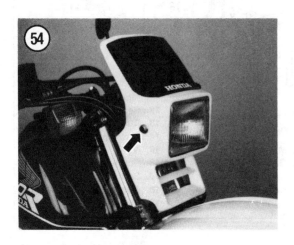

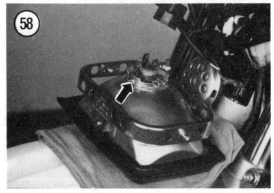

For vertical adjustment, unscrew the front reflex reflectors, then loosen the mounting bolts on each side (B, **Figure 60**). Tilt the headlight housing and tighten the mounting bolts. Install the reflex reflectors.

Headlight Adjustment
(XR500, XR500R, XR600R)

The headlight on these models is limited to vertical adjustment only and adjust to your own personal preference.

For vertical adjustment, turn the adjust screw (**Figure 61**) at the base of the headlight lens.

Headlight Adjustment
(XL600R)

Adjust the headlight horizontally and vertically according to Department of Motor Vehicles regulations in your area.

To adjust the headlight horizontally, turn the screw (A, **Figure 62**). Screwing it in turns the light to the right and loosening it will turn the light to the left.

For vertical adjustment loosen the mounting bolts on each side (B, **Figure 62**). Tilt the headlight housing and tighten the mounting bolts.

Taillight/Brakelight Replacement
(XL500S)

1. Remove the screws (**Figure 63**) securing the lens and remove the lens and gasket.
2. Wash out the inside and outside of the lens with a mild detergent and wipe dry.
3. Inspect the lens gasket and replace it if damaged or deteriorated.
4. Replace the bulb and install the lens; do not overtighten the screws as the lens may crack.

8

Taillight Replacement
(XR500, 1981-1982 XR500R)

1. Remove the screws (**Figure 64**) securing the lens and remove the lens and gasket.
2. Wash out the inside and outside of the lens with a mild detergent and wipe dry.
3. Inspect the lens gasket and replace it if damaged or deteriorated.
4. Replace the bulb and install the lens. Do not overtighten the screws as the lens may crack.

Taillight Replacement
(1983-1984 XR500R, XR600R)

1. From underneath the rear fender, remove the screws, washers and metal collars securing the lens and remove the lens.
2. Wash out the inside and outside of the lens with a mild detergent and wipe dry.
3. Replace the bulb and install the lens; do not overtighten the screws as the lens may crack.

Taillight Replacement
(XL600R)

1. Remove the screws (**Figure 65**) securing the lens and remove the lens and gasket.
2. Wash out the inside and outside of the lens with a mild detergent and wipe dry.
3. Inspect the lens gasket and replace it if damaged or deteriorated.
4. Replace the bulb (**Figure 66**) and install the lens. Do not overtighten the screws as the lens may crack.

Directional Signal Light
Replacement
(XL Series Models)

1. Remove the screws (**Figure 67**) securing the lens and remove the lens.
2. Wash out the inside and outside of the lens with a mild detergent and wipe dry.
3. Replace the bulb and install the lens. Do not overtighten the screws as the lens may crack.

Speedometer Illumination
Light Replacement
(1979-1980 XL500S, XL500R)

1. Remove the headlight housing (A, **Figure 68**) as described in this chapter.
2. Disconnect the speedometer drive cable (B, **Figure 68**).

3. Remove the acorn nuts and washers (C, **Figure 68**) and pull the instrument cluster forward and turn it upside down.
4. Pull the defective lamp holder/electrical wire assembly up and out of the housing.
5. Remove and replace the defective bulb.

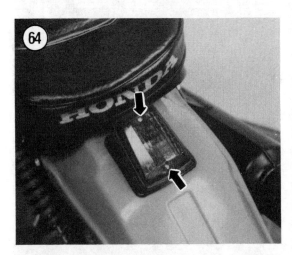

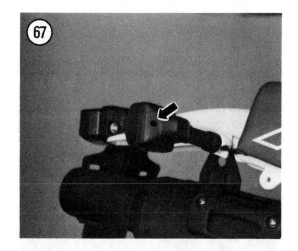

NOTE
If a new bulb will not work, check the wire connections for loose or broken wires. Also check the bulb socket for corrosion. Replace as necessary.

6. Install by reversing these removal steps.

Speedometer Illumination
Light Replacement
(1981 XL500S)

1. Carefully pull the bulb socket/electrical wire assembly from the backside of the speedometer housing.
2. Remove and replace the defective bulb.
3. Push the bulb socket/electrical wire assembly back into the speedometer housing. Make sure it is completely seated to prevent the entry of water and moisture.

NOTE
If a new bulb will not work, check the wire connections for loose or broken wires. Also check the bulb socket for corrosion; replace as necessary.

Speedometer Illumination
Light Replacement
(XR500, XR500R)

1. Remove the headlight housing as described in this chapter.
2. Carefully pull the lamp holder/electrical wire assembly (**Figure 69**) down and out of the housing.
3. Remove and replace the defective bulb.

NOTE
If a new bulb will not work, check the wire connections for loose or broken wires. Also check the bulb socket for corrosion. Replace as necessary.

4. Install by reversing these removal steps.

Speedometer Illumination
Light Replacement
(XR500, XR500R)

1. Remove the headlight housing as described in this chapter.
2. Carefully pull the lamp holder/electrical wire assembly (**Figure 69**) down and out of the housing.
3. Remove and replace the defective bulb.

NOTE
If a new bulb will not work, check the wire connections for loose or broken wires. Also check the bulb socket for corrosion. Replace as necessary.

4. Install by reversing these removal steps.

8

Speedometer Illumination Light Replacement (XL600R)

1. Remove the headlight number plate assembly as described in this chapter.
2. Unscrew the speedometer drive cable collar (A, **Figure 70**) from the base of the speedometer housing. Withdraw the speedometer cable.
3. Remove the nuts and collars (B, **Figure 70**) securing the speedometer housing to the mounting bracket.
4. Carefully pull the speedometer housing away from the mounting bracket.
5. Carefully pull the defective lamp holder/electrical wire assembly from the backside of the housing.
6. Remove and replace the defective bulb.

NOTE
If a new bulb will not work, check the wire connections for loose or broken wires. Also check the bulb socket for corrosion; replace as necessary.

7. Push the lamp socket/electrical wire assembly back into the housing. Make sure it is completely seated to prevent the entry of water and moisture.
8. Install the speedometer housing onto the mounting bracket and install the collars and nuts. Tighten the nuts securely.
9. Screw on the speedometer drive cable collar and tighten securely.
10. Install the headlight/number plate assembly as described in this chapter.

Neutral, High Beam and Directional Signal Indicator Light Replacement (1978-1980 XL500S)

Follow the procedure for replacement of the speedometer illumination light as described in this chapter.

Neutral, High Beam and Turn Signal Indicator Light Replacement (1981-on XL Series Models)

1. Remove the headlight/number plate assembly as described in this chapter.
2. Carefully pull the lamp holder/electrical wire assembly down and out of the backside of the instrument cluster.
3. Remove and replace the defective bulb (**Figure 71**).

NOTE
If a new bulb will not work, check the wire connections for loose or broken wires. Also check the bulb socket for corrosion; replace as necessary.

4. Push the lamp socket/electrical wire assembly back into the housing. Make sure it is completely seated to prevent the entry of water and moisture.
5. Install the headlight/number plate assembly as described in this chapter.

SWITCHES

Ignition Switch Continuity Test (XL Series Models)

1. Remove the headlight/number plate assembly as described in this chapter.
2. In the area in front of the steering stem locate and disconnect the necessary electrical connectors.

NOTE
Some models have a single multi-pin electrical connector while others have a multi-pin electrical connector and a separate connector(s). On all models, there are a total of 4 wires to be tested and wire colors are the same for all models.

3. Locate the electrical connector(s) containing 3 or 4 wires (1 black, 1 red, 1 black/white, 1 green). Disconnect the electrical connector(s).
4. Use an ohmmeter and check for continuity. Connect the test leads to the ignition switch side of the electrical connector as follows:

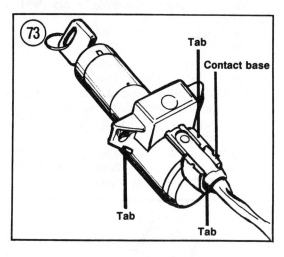

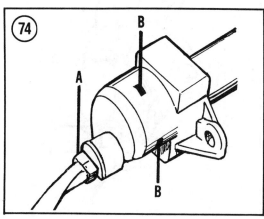

a. Turn the ignition switch ON: there should be continuity (low resistance) between the black and red wires.
b. Turn the ignition switch OFF: there should be continuity (low resistance) between the black/white and green wires.
c. On XL500R models, turn the ignition switch to the LOCK position: there should be continuity (low resistance) between the black/green and green wires.

5. If the ignition switch fails any one of these tests, the electrical contact portion of the switch must be replaced as described in this chapter.
6. Reconnect the 4-pin electrical connector and install all items removed.

Ignition Switch Removal/Installation (XL500S)

1. Disconnect the electrical connector from the ignition switch.
2. Remove the ignition switch from the instrument cluster.
3. Install by reversing these removal steps.

Ignition Switch Removal/Installation (XL500R, XL600R)

1. Remove the headlight/number plate assembly as described in this chapter.
2. Disconnect the electrical connector from the ignition switch.
3. Remove the mounting bolts securing the ignition switch (**Figure 72**) and remove the switch assembly from the upper fork bridge.
4. Install by reversing these removal steps.

Ignition Switch Disassembly/Assembly (XL500R, XL600R)

1. Remove the ignition switch as described in this chapter.
2. Insert the ignition key in the switch and turn the tumbler so it is part way between the ON and OFF position.
3A. On XL500R models, push in on the lugs (**Figure 73**) of the electrical contact switch portion, depressing them enough to clear the slots in the mechanical portion of the switch assembly.
3B. On 1983-1985 XL600R models perform the following:
   a. Open the wire retainer (A, **Figure 74**) securing the electrical harness to the switch.

8

b. Push in on the lugs (B, **Figure 74**) of the electrical contact switch portion, depressing them enough to clear the slots in the mechanical portion of the switch assembly.

3C. On 1986-1987 XL600R models perform the following:

a. Open the wire retainer (A, **Figure 75**) securing the electrical harness to the switch.

b. Remove the screws (B, **Figure 75**) securing the electrical contact portion.

c. Push in on the lug of the electrical contact switch portion, depressing it enough to clear the slot in the mechanical portion of the switch assembly.

4. Withdraw the electrical portion of the switch from the mechanical portion of the ignition switch.

5. Replace the defective component.

6. Assemble by reversing these disassembly steps, noting the following.

7. Make sure the lugs are completely indexed into the slots in the mechanical portion of the switch.

Engine Kill Switch Testing

1. Disconnect the electrical connector from the engine kill switch on the handlebar.

2A. On 1985-1987 XR600R models, use an ohmmeter set at R×1 and connect the 2 leads of the ohmmeter to the black/white and black wires.

2B. On all other models, use an ohmmeter set at R×1 and connect the 2 leads of the ohmmeter to the black/white and green wires.

3. Turn the kill switch button to on the OFF positions and then to the other OFF position. If the switch is good there will be continuity (very low resistance) in both OFF positions.

4. Turn the kill switch button to the RUN position. If the switch is good there will be no continuity (infinite resistance).

5. If the switch fails to pass any of these tests, the switch is faulty and must be replaced.

6. Reconnect the electrical connectors.

7. Install all items removed.

Headlight Dimmer Switch Testing

XL500S

1. Remove the headlight as described in this chapter.

2. Within the headlight housing disconnect the black, black/white and white electrical connectors from the dimmer switch.

3. Turn the dimmer switch to the HI position. Use an ohmmeter set at R×1 and connect the 2 leads of

the ohmmeter to the black and black/white wires. If the switch is good there will be continuity (very low resistance).

4. Turn the dimmer switch to the N position. Use an ohmmeter set at R×1 and connect the 2 leads of the ohmmeter to the following colors.

a. Black/white and white.

b. Black and white.

c. Black and black/white.

If the switch is good there will be continuity (very low resistance) between each of these wires.

5. Turn the dimmer switch to the LO position. Use an ohmmeter set at R×1 and connect the 2 leads of the ohmmeter to the black/white and white wires. if the switch is good there will be continuity (very low resistance).

6. If the switch fails to pass any of these tests, the switch is faulty and must be replaced.

7. Install the headlight assembly as described in this chapter.

XL500R, XL600R

1. Remove the headlight housing as described in this chapter.

2. In the area in front of the steering stem locate and disconnect the white/yellow, blue and white electrical connectors from the dimmer switch.

3. Turn the dimmer switch to the HI position. Use an ohmmeter set at R×1 and connect the 2 leads of the ohmmeter to the white/yellow and blue wires. If the switch is good there will be continuity (very low resistance).

4. Turn the dimmer switch to the N position. Use an ohmmeter set at R×1 and connect the 2 leads of the ohmmeter to the following colors:

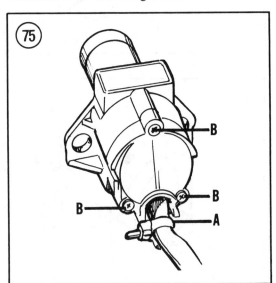

(75)

a. White/yellow and blue.

b. White/yellow and white.

c. Blue and white.

If the switch is good there will be continuity (very low resistance) between each of these wires.

5. Turn the dimmer switch to the LO position. Use an ohmmeter set at R×1 and connect the 2 leads of the ohmmeter to the white/yellow and white wires. If the switch is good there will be continuity (very low resistance).

6. If the switch fails to pass any of these tests, the switch is faulty and must be replaced.

7. Install the headlight assembly as described in this chapter.

Turn Signal Switch Testing
(XL Series Models)

1. Remove the headlight as described in this chapter.

2. Within the headlight housing disconnect the light blue, gray and orange electrical connectors from the turn signal switch.

3. Turn the turn signal switch to the R position. Use an ohmmeter set at R×1 and connect the 2 leads of the ohmmeter to the light blue and gray wires. If the switch is good there will be continuity (very low resistance).

4. Turn the turn signal switch to the L position. Use an ohmmeter set at R×1 and connect the 2 leads of the ohmmeter to the gray and orange wires. If the switch is good there will be continuity (very low resistance) between each of these wires.

5. If the switch fails to pass any of these tests, the switch is faulty and must be replaced.

6. Install the headlight assembly as described in this chapter.

Front Brake Light Switch Testing

1. Remove the headlight as described in this chapter.

2A. On XL500S models, perform the following:

a. Within the headlight housing disconnect the brown and green/yellow electrical connectors from the front brake light switch.

b. Have an assistant apply the front brake. Use an ohmmeter set at R×1 and connect the 2 leads of the ohmmeter to the brown and green/yellow wires. If the switch is good there will be continuity (very low resistance).

2B. On XL600R models perform the following:

a. Within the headlight housing disconnect the black and green/yellow electrical connectors from the front brake light switch.

b. Have an assistant apply the front brake. Use an ohmmeter set at R×1 and connect the 2 leads of the ohmmeter to the black and green/yellow wires. If the switch is good there will be continuity (very low resistance).

3. If the switch fails to pass this test, the switch is faulty and must be replaced.

4. Install the headlight assembly as described in this chapter.

Rear Brake Light Switch Testing
(All XL Series Models)

1. Disconnect the electrical connector wires going to the rear brake pedal switch.

2. Have an assistant apply the rear brake. Use an ohmmeter set at R×1 and connect the 2 leads of the ohmmeter to the electrical wires of the switch connector.

3. If the switch is good there will be continuity (very low resistance).

4. If the switch fails to pass this test, the switch is faulty and must be replaced.

5. To remove the switch, completely unscrew the adjust nut and remove the switch body (**Figure 76**) from the chassis.

6. Install a new switch and adjust as described in this chapter.

7. Connect the electrical connector wires to the rear brake pedal switch.

ELECTRICAL COMPONENTS

Instrument Cluster
Removal/Installation
(XL500S)

1. Disconnect the battery negative lead or the main fuse.

2. Remove the headlight (A, **Figure 77**) as described in this chapter.

3. Disconnect the speedometer drive cable (B, **Figure 77**).

4. Remove the acorn nuts and washers (C, **Figure 77**), pull the instrument cluster forward and turn upside down.

5. Carefully pull the lamp holder/electrical wire assemblies.

6. Disconnect the ignition switch 4-pin electrical connector located within the headlight housing.

7. Pull the ignition switch (D, **Figure 77**) and electrical harness out from the cluster and remove the ignition switch from the cluster.

8. Remove the instrument cluster assembly.

9. Install by reversing these removal steps, noting the following.

10. Be sure the rubber isolators are in place on the mounting studs (C, **Figure 77**).

Speedometer Removal/Installation

XR500, 1981-1982 XR500R

1. Disconnect the speedometer cable from the base of the speedometer.

2. Carefully pull the lamp holder/electrical wire assembly down and out of the backside of the speedometer housing.

3. At the base of the speedometer, remove the acorn nuts and washers (models so equipped) securing the speedometer to the mounting bracket on the upper fork bridge.

4. Remove the speedometer housing assembly.

5. Install by reversing these removal steps.

1983-1984 XR500R

1. Remove the headlight housing as described in this chapter.

2. Disconnect the speedometer cable from the base of the speedometer.

3. Carefully pull the lamp holder/electrical wire assemblies down and out of the backside of the speedometer housing.

4. Remove the mounting bolts securing the speedometer to the mounting bracket on the upper fork bridge.

5. Remove the speedometer housing assembly.

6. Install by reversing these removal steps.

XL600R

1. Remove the headlight/number plate assembly as described in this chapter.

2. Disconnect the speedometer cable (A, **Figure 70**) from the base of the speedometer.

3. Disconnect the electrical connector.

4. Remove the nuts and washer (B, **Figure 70**) securing the speedometer to the mounting bracket on the upper fork bridge.

5. Remove the speedometer housing and electrical wire harness assembly.

6. To remove the speedometer housing from the mounting bracket, remove the nuts and collars securing the housing and remove the housing and the gasket.

7. Install by reversing these removal steps.

Digital Enduro Meter (XR600R)

Meter removal/installation and battery replacement

1. Remove the headlight housing as described in this chapter.

2. Disconnect the electrical wires going to the meter from the sensor on top of the speedometer drive bracket (attached to the upper fork bridge).

3. Remove the bolt on each side of the front hold-down bracket and remove the bracket.

4. Remove the meter assembly from the upper mounting bracket that is attached to the handlebar upper holders.

> *NOTE*
> *Disassembly of the meter is not recommended since replacement parts are not available. If the meter is faulty, the entire meter must be replaced.*

5. To replace the batteries perform the following:
   a. Turn the lockscrew on the bottom of the meter assembly and open the access door.
   b. Replace the three AAA batteries, close the door and turn the lock screw.

6. Install by reversing these removal steps.

Sensor removal/installation

1. Remove the meter assembly as described in this chapter.
2. Disconnect the speedometer cable from the sensor.
3. Remove the bolt securing the sensor and mounting bracket to the upper fork bridge. Remove the assembly.
4. Install by reversing these removal steps.

Sensor inspection

1. Remove the sensor as described in this chapter.
2. Using an ohmmeter, connect the test leads to the electrical wires on the sensor.
3. Have an assistant insert a narrow flat-bladed screwdriver into the base of the sensor where the speedometer cable attaches.
4. Rotate the sensor with the screwdriver and observe the needle on the ohmmeter. The ohmmeter needle should swing back and forth twice for every single complete revolution of the screwdriver and sensor.
5. If the sensor fails this test, the sensor must be replaced.

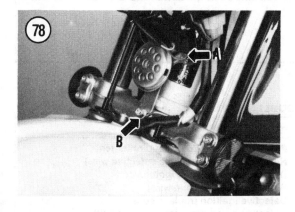

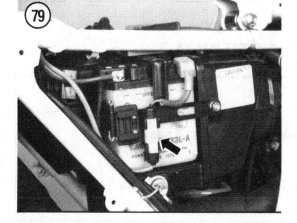

Horn (XL Series Models)

Removal/Installation

1. Remove the headlight housing as described in this chapter.
2. Disconnect the electrical connectors (A, **Figure 78**) from the horn.
3. Remove the bolt (B, **Figure 78**) securing the horn to the bracket.
4. Install by reversing these removal steps.

Testing

1. Disconnect horn wires from harness.

> *WARNING*
> *To prevent a battery explosion, connect the wires exactly as described in Step 2.*

2. Depending on model, connect a 6-volt or 12-volt battery to the horn as follows:
   a. Connect a jumper wire to the battery positive terminal, then to one horn terminal.
   b. Connect another jumper wire to the battery negative terminal, then to the other horn terminal.
3. If the horn is good it will sound. If not, replace it.

FUSE (XL SERIES MODELS)

There is one 10A main fuse in the electrical system on XL series models. The fuse (**Figure 79**) is located next to the battery under the right-hand side cover.

XR series models do not have a fuse.

> *NOTE*
> *Always carry a spare fuse. On some later models, there is a spare fuse next to the main fuse.*

Whenever the fuse blows, find out the reason for the failure before replacing the fuse. Usually, the trouble is a short circuit in the wiring. This may be caused by worn-through insulation or a disconnected wire shorted to ground.

> *CAUTION*
> *Never substitute metal foil or wire for a fuse. Never use a higher amperage fuse than specified. An overload could result in a fire and complete loss of the bike.*

WIRING DIAGRAMS

Wiring diagrams for all models are located at the end of this book.

Table 1 CHARGING CURRENT

XL500S	
Disconnect black wire @ voltage regulator	
Light switch OFF	
5000 rpm	3.2A/8.0V
8000 rpm	5.5A/8.9V
Light switch ON (high beam)	
5000 rpm	1.8A/7.5V
8000 rpm	4.0A/8.0V
XL500R	
Disconnect black wire @ voltage regulator;	
disconnect headlight, taillight, running lights	
2500 rpm	2.7A/16.8V
8000 rpm	5.5A/18.4V
1983-1985 XL600R	
Disconnect black wire @ voltage regulator;	
disconnect headlight, taillight, running lights	
2500 rpm	3.0A/16.8V
8000 rpm	6.5A/18.4V
1986-1987 XL600R	
Information not available from Honda.	

Table 2 ALTERNATOR ROTOR BOLT TORQUE SPECIFICATIONS

Model	N•m	ft.-lb.
XR600R		
1985-1987	100-120	73-88
1988-1990	125	92
All other models	80-100	59-73

Table 3 C.D.I. TROUBLESHOOTING

Symptoms	Probable cause
Weak spark	Poor connections (clean and retighten)
	High voltage leak (replace defective wire)
	Defective coil (replace ignition coil
No spark	Wiring broken (replace wire)
	Defective ignition (replace coil)
	Defective pulse generator (replace coil)

Table 4 IGNITION SYSTEM TEST POINTS

XL500R, XL600R		
Item	Terminal	Standard resistance values
Ignition coil primary circuit	Green and black/yellow wires	0.1-0.3 ohms*
Ignition coil secondary circuit with spark plug cap installed	Green wire and spark plug cap	8.5-11.0K ohms*

(continued)

Table 4 IGNITION SYSTEM TEST POINTS (continued)

XL500R, XL600R		
Item	**Terminal**	**Standard resistance values**
Alternator exciter coil	Black/red and green wires	230-320 ohms *
Pulse generator	Green/white and blue/yellow wires	360-440 ohms *
Engine stop switch (in RUN position)	Black/white and green wires	No continuity (infinity)
Ignition switch (in ON position)	Black/white and green wires	No continuity (infinity)
1983-1984 XR500R, XL600R		
Item	**Terminal**	**Standard resistance values**
Ignition coil primary circuit	Green and black/yellow wires	0.1-0.3 ohms *
Ignition coil secondary circuit with spark plug cap installed	Black yellow wire and spark plug cap	7.4-11.0K ohms *
Alternator exciter coil	Black/red and green wires	230-320 ohms *
Pulse generator	Green/white and blue/yellow wires	360-440 ohms *
Engine stop switch (in RUN position)	Black/white and green wires	No continuity (infinity)

* For accurate readings the components must be @ a minimum temperature of 20° C (68° F).

Table 5 PULSE GENERATOR SPECIFIED RESISTANCE

Model	Standard resistance values
XL500S, XR500	20-60 ohms
XL500R	510-570
XR500R	
1981-1982	90-110
1983-1984	450-550
XL600R, XR600R	360-440

Table 6 IGNITION COIL SPECIFIED RESISTANCE

Models	Primary	Secondary
XL500S, XR500	0.2-0.8 ohms	8-15K ohms
XL500R	0.2-0.8 ohms	3.4-4.2K ohms
XR500R		
1981-1982	0.2-0.8 ohms	2-6k ohms
1983-1984	0.7-0.9 ohms	3.6-4.6K ohms
XR600R	0.1-0.3 ohms	
With spark plug cap installed		7.4-11K ohms
With spark plug cap removed		3.7-4.5K ohms
XL600R		0.1-0.3 ohms
With spark plug cap installed		8.5-11K ohms
		3.7-4.5K ohms

Table 7 REPLACEMENT BULBS

Model	Headlight	Taillight-Brakelight	Turn signal
XL500S	6V 35/36.5W	6V/32W	6V/17W
XL500R	12 V 35/36.5W	12V/32W	12V/23W
XR500	6V 25/25W	6V/3W	–
XR500R			
1981-1982	6V 25/25W	6V/3W	–
1983	12V 25/25W	12V/3W	–
1984	12V 55W	12V 8/27W	–
XL600R	H4JA 12V/60/55W	12V 8/27W	12V/23W
XR600R			
1985-1987	12V 55W	12V 3.4W	–
1988-1990	12V 35W	12V 3.8W	–
All indicator and illuminator bulbs 6V or 12V and 1.7W or 3.4W.			

CHAPTER NINE

FRONT SUSPENSION AND STEERING

This chapter describes repair and maintenance procedures for the front wheel, forks and steering components.

Front suspension torque specifications are covered in **Table 1**. **Tables 1-4** are at the end of this chapter.

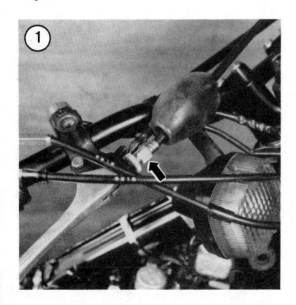

FRONT WHEEL (DRUM BRAKE)

Removal (XL500S, XR500)

1. Place wood blocks under the skid plate to support the bike securely with the front wheel off the ground.
2. Slacken the brake cable at the hand lever (**Figure 1**).
3. Remove the speedometer cable set screw (A, **Figure 2**).
4. Pull the speedometer cable (B, **Figure 2**) free from the speedometer gear box.
5. Loosen the locknut (A, **Figure 3**) at the fork leg bracket.
6. Remove the cable end from the brake arm (B, **Figure 3**).
7. Remove the axle nut (**Figure 4**).
8. Loosen the axle holder nuts (**Figure 5**) and loosen the axle holder. It is not necessary to remove the axle holder, just loosen it enough to clear the front axle.
9. Remove the front axle from the left-hand side.
10. Pull the wheel down and forward. This allows the brake panel to disengage from the boss on the left-hand fork slider.

11. Remove the front wheel.

12. Inspect the wheel as described in this chapter.

Installation (XL500S, XR500)

1. Make sure the axle bearing surfaces of the fork slider and axle are free from burrs and nicks.

2. Clean the axle in solvent and thoroughly dry it. Make sure all surfaces that the axle comes in contact with are clean and free from road dirt and old grease before installation.

3. Position the wheel into place, carefully inserting the groove in the brake panel into the groove in the left-hand fork slider. This is necessary for proper brake operation.

4. Insert the front axle from the right-hand side through the axle holder and the wheel hub and install the axle nut.

5. If removed, install the axle holder with the UP mark facing upward. Install the axle holder nuts and tighten finger-tight at this time.

6. Tighten the front axle nut to the torque specification listed in **Table 1**.

7. Tighten the front axle holder nuts a little tighter, but not to the full torque specification.

8. Install the front brake cable to the brake arm.

9. Slowly rotate the wheel and install the speedometer cable into the speedometer housing. Install the cable set screw.

10. Remove the wood block(s) from under the skid plate.

11. With the front brake applied, push down hard on the handlebars and pump the forks several times to seat the front axle.

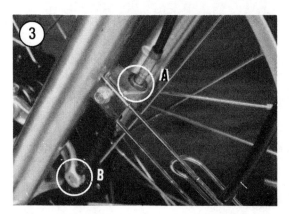

> *WARNING*
> *The axle holder nuts must be tightened in the manner and to the torque value described in Step 12. After installation is complete, there will be a slight gap at the bottom, with no gap at the top. If done incorrectly the studs in the fork slider may fail, resulting in the loss of control of the bike when riding.*

12. Tighten the axle holder upper nuts first and then the lower nuts to the torque specification listed in **Table 1**.

13. After the wheel is completely installed, rotate it several times and apply the brakes a couple of times to make sure that it rotates freely and that the brake is operating correctly.

14. Adjust the front brake as described in Chapter Three.

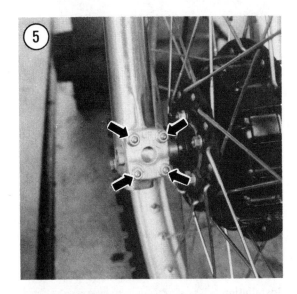

Removal (1981-1982 XR500R, XL500R)

1. Place wood blocks under the skid plate to support the bike securely with the front wheel off the ground.
2. Slacken the brake cable at the hand lever.
3. Remove the speedometer cable set screw (A, **Figure 6**).
4. Pull the speedometer cable free from the speedometer gear box.
5. Loosen the screws on the brake cable clamp on the left-hand fork slider. This is to allow movement of the cable for the next step.
6. At the brake panel perform the following:
    a. Loosen the locknut (A, **Figure 7**).
    b. Remove the cable end from the brake arm (B, **Figure 7**).
    c. Remove the brake cable from the bracket on the brake panel.
7. Loosen the axle holder nuts (B, **Figure 6**) and loosen the axle holder. It is not necessary to remove the axle holder, just loosen it enough to clear the front axle.
8. Unscrew the front axle (C, **Figure 6**) from the left-hand fork leg. Withdraw the front axle.
9. Pull the wheel down and forward. This allows the brake panel to disengage from the boss on the left-hand fork slider.
10. Remove the front wheel.
11. Inspect the wheel as described in this chapter.

Installation (1981-1982 XR500R, XL500R)

1. Make sure the axle bearing surfaces of the fork slider and axle are free from burrs and nicks.
2. Clean the axle in solvent and thoroughly dry it. Make sure all surfaces that the axle comes in contact with are clean and free from road dirt and old grease before installation.
3. Position the wheel into place, carefully inserting the groove in the brake panel into the groove in the left-hand fork slider. This is necessary for proper brake operation.
4. Position the tang on the speedometer gear box under the lip on the fork slider.
5. Insert the front axle from the right-hand side through the axle holder, the speedometer gear box and the wheel hub. Screw the axle into the left-hand fork slider and temporarily tighten the axle.
6. If removed, install the axle holder with the UP mark facing upward. Install the axle holder nuts and tighten finger-tight.
7. Tighten the front axle to the torque specification listed in **Table 1**.

8. Tighten the front axle nuts a little tighter, but not to the full torque specification.

9. Install the front brake cable to the brake arm.

10. Tighten the screws on the brake cable clamp on the left-hand fork slider.

11. Slowly rotate the wheel and install the speedometer cable into the speedometer housing. Install the cable set screw.

12. Remove the wood block(s) from under the skid plate.

13. With the front brake applied, push down hard on the handlebars and pump the forks several times to seat the front axle.

> *WARNING*
> *The axle holder nuts must be tightened in the manner and to the torque value described in Step 14. After installation is complete, there will be a slight gap at the bottom, with no gap at the top. If done incorrectly the studs in the fork slider may fail, resulting in the loss of control of the bike when riding.*

14. Tighten the axle holder upper nuts first and then the lower nuts to the torque specification listed in **Table 1**.

15. After the wheel is completely installed, rotate it several times and apply the brakes a couple of times to make sure that it rotates freely and that the brake is operating correctly.

16. Adjust the front brake as described in Chapter Three.

FRONT WHEEL (DISC BRAKE)

Removal

1. Place wood blocks under the skid plate to support it securely with the front wheel off the ground.

2. Remove the set screw (**Figure 8**) securing the speedometer or tripmeter cable. Pull the cable free from the gear box on the wheel hub.

3. Loosen the axle holder nuts and loosen the axle holder (A, **Figure 9**). It is not necessary to remove the axle holder, just loosen it enough to clear the front axle.

4. Unscrew the front axle (B, **Figure 9**) from the left-hand fork leg. Withdraw the front axle.

5. Pull the wheel down and forward and remove it. This allows the brake disc to slide out of the caliper assembly.

6. Remove the wheel.

> *CAUTION*
> *Do not set the wheel down on the disc surface as it may get scratched or warped. Set the sidewalls on 2 wood blocks.*

> *NOTE*
> *Insert a piece of vinyl tubing or wood in the caliper in place of the brake disc. That way if the brake lever is inadvertently squeezed, the piston will not be forced out of the cylinder. If this does happen, the caliper may have to be disassembled to reseat the piston and the system will have to be bled.*

Installation

1. Make sure the axle bearing surfaces of the fork slider and axle are free from burrs and nicks.

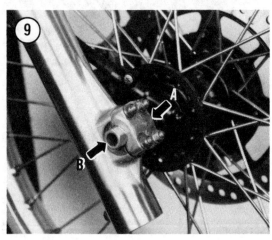

2. Remove the vinyl tubing or pieces of wood from the brake calipers.

3. Position the wheel into place. Carefully insert the brake disc between the brake pads in the caliper assembly.

4. Align the housisng with the tang on the right-hand fork slider (**Figure 10**).

5. Insert the front axle from the right-hand side through the speedometer gear box and the wheel hub. Screw it into the left-hand fork leg.

6. If removed, install the axle holder with the UP mark facing upward. Install the axle holder nuts and tighten finger-tight.

7. Tighten the front axle to the torque specification listed in **Table 1**.

8. Tighten the front axle holder nuts a little tighter, but not to the full torque specification.

9. Slowly rotate the wheel and install the speedometer or tripmeter cable into the gear box. Install the cable set screw.

10. Remove the wood blocks from under the skid plate.

11. With the front brake applied, push down hard on the handlebars and pump the forks several times to seat the front axle.

> *WARNING*
> *The axle holder nuts must be tightened in the manner and to the torque value described in Step 12. After installation is complete, there will be a slight gap at the bottom, with no gap at the top. If done incorrectly the studs in the fork slider may fail, resulting in the loss of control of the bike when riding.*

12. Tighten the axle holder upper nuts first and then the lower nuts to the torque specification listed in **Table 1**.

13. After the wheel is completely installed, rotate it several times and apply the brakes a couple of times to make sure that it rotates freely and that the brake pads are against the disc correctly.

WHEEL INSPECTION
(ALL MODELS)

Measure the axial and radial runout of the wheel with a dial indicator as shown in **Figure 11**. The maximum axial and radial runout is 2.0 mm (0.08 in.). If the runout exceeds this dimension, check the wheel bearing condition.

If the wheel bearings are okay, tighten or replace bent or loose spokes as described in this chapter.

Check the front axle runout as described under *Front Hub* in this chapter.

FRONT HUB

Inspection

Inspect each wheel bearing before removing it from the wheel hub.

> *CAUTION*
> *Do not remove the wheel bearings for inspection purposes as they will be damaged during the removal process. Remove wheel bearings only if they are to be replaced.*

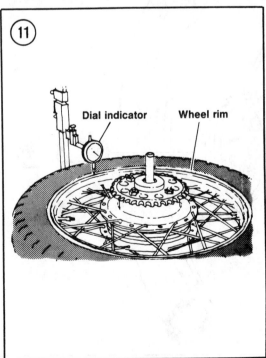

Dial indicator   Wheel rim

1. Perform Steps 1-7 of *Disassembly* in this chapter.

2. Turn each bearing by hand. Make sure bearings turn smoothly.

3. On non-sealed bearings, check the balls for evidence of wear, pitting or excessive heat (bluish tint). Replace the bearings if necessary; always replace as a complete set. When replacing the bearings, be sure to take your old bearings along to ensure a perfect matchup.

> *NOTE*
> *Fully sealed bearings are available from many bearing specialty shops. Fully sealed bearings provide better protection from dirt and moisture that may get into the hub.*

4. Check the axle for wear and straightness. Use V-blocks and a dial indicator as shown in **Figure 12**. If the runout is 0.2 mm (0.01 in.) or greater, the axle should be replaced.

Disassembly

Refer to the following illustrations for this procedure.

a. **Figure 13**: drum brake.
b. **Figure 14**: 1984 XR500R disc brake.
c. **Figure 15**: all other disc brake models.

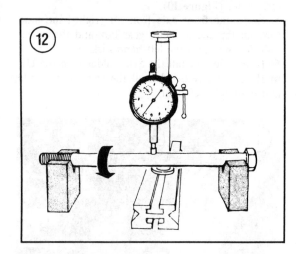

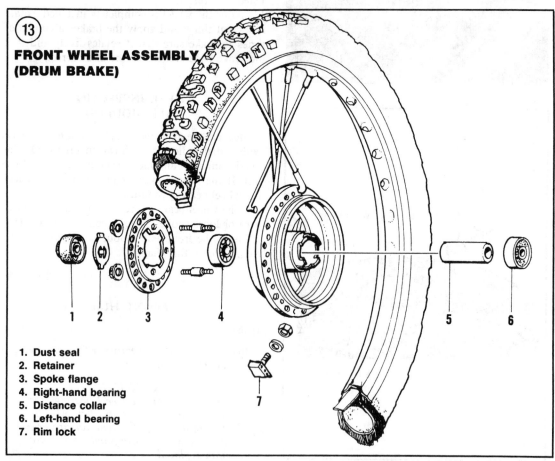

FRONT WHEEL ASSEMBLY (DRUM BRAKE)

1. Dust seal
2. Retainer
3. Spoke flange
4. Right-hand bearing
5. Distance collar
6. Left-hand bearing
7. Rim lock

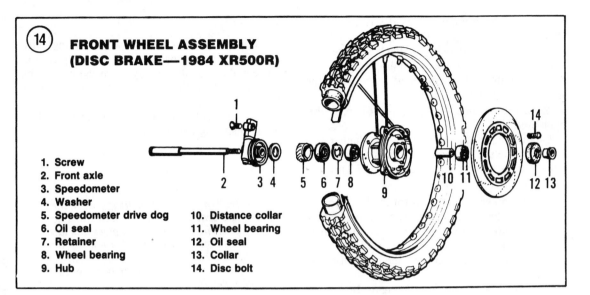

14 FRONT WHEEL ASSEMBLY (DISC BRAKE—1984 XR500R)

1. Screw
2. Front axle
3. Speedometer
4. Washer
5. Speedometer drive dog
6. Oil seal
7. Retainer
8. Wheel bearing
9. Hub
10. Distance collar
11. Wheel bearing
12. Oil seal
13. Collar
14. Disc bolt

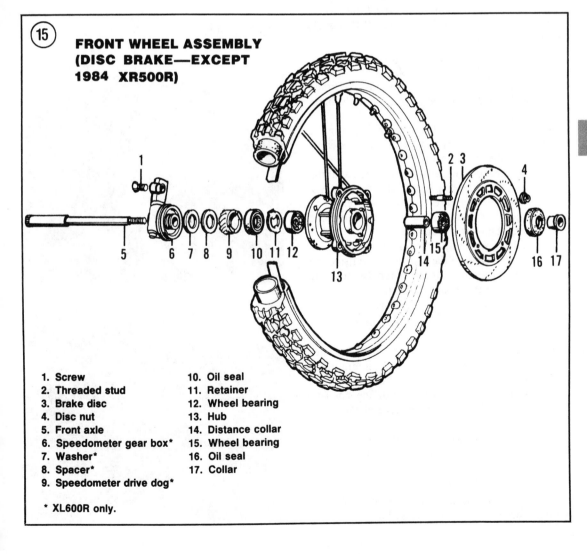

15 FRONT WHEEL ASSEMBLY (DISC BRAKE—EXCEPT 1984 XR500R)

1. Screw
2. Threaded stud
3. Brake disc
4. Disc nut
5. Front axle
6. Speedometer gear box*
7. Washer*
8. Spacer*
9. Speedometer drive dog*
10. Oil seal
11. Retainer
12. Wheel bearing
13. Hub
14. Distance collar
15. Wheel bearing
16. Oil seal
17. Collar

* XL600R only.

9

1. Remove the front wheel as described in this chapter.

2. On drum brake models, pull the brake assembly straight up and out of the brake drum.

3. On models so equipped, remove the speedometer gear box.

4. Remove the dust seal (**Figure 16**) from the right-hand side.

5. On disc brake models, remove the retainer.

6. On models equipped with a speedometer, remove the speedometer drive dog (A, **Figure 17**) and grease seal (B, **Figure 17**).

7. On disc brake models perform the following.

    a. On models so equipped, remove the screws (A, **Figure 18**) securing the plastic dust cover and remove the cover.

    b. Remove the bolts securing the brake disc and remove the disc.

    c. Remove the grease seal (B, **Figure 18**).

8. Before proceeding further, inspect the wheel bearings as described in this chapter. If they must be replaced, proceed as follows.

9A. A special Honda tool set-up can be used to remove the wheel bearings as follows:

    a. Install the 15 mm bearing remover (Honda part No. 07746-0050400) into the right-hand bearing.

    b. Turn the wheel over (left-hand side up) on the workbench so the bearing remover is touching the workbench surface.

    c. From the left-hand side of the hub, install the bearing remover expander (Honda part No. 07746-0050100) into the bearing remover. Using a hammer, tap the expander into the bearing remover with a hammer.

    d. Stand the wheel up to a vertical position.

    e. Tap on the end of the expander and drive the right-hand bearing out of the hub. Remove the bearing and the distance collar.

    f. Repeat for the left-hand bearing.

9B. If special tools are not used perform the following:

    a. To remove the right- and left-hand bearings and distance collar, insert a soft aluminum or brass drift into one side of the hub.

    b. Push the distance collar over to one side and place the drift on the inner race of the lower bearing.

    c. Tap the bearing out of the hub with a hammer, working around the perimeter of the inner race.

    d. Repeat for the other bearing.

10. Clean the inside and the outside of the hub with solvent. Dry with compressed air.

Assembly

1. On non-sealed bearings, pack the bearings with a good quality bearing grease. Work the grease in between the balls thoroughly. Turn the bearing by hand a couple of times to make sure the grease is distributed evenly inside the bearing.

2. Blow any dirt or foreign matter out of the hub before installing the bearings.

> *CAUTION*
> *Install non-sealed bearings with the single sealed side facing outward. Tap the bearings squarely into place and tap on the outer race only. Do not tap on the inner race or the bearing might be damaged. Be sure that the bearings are completely seated.*

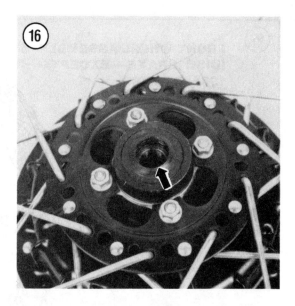

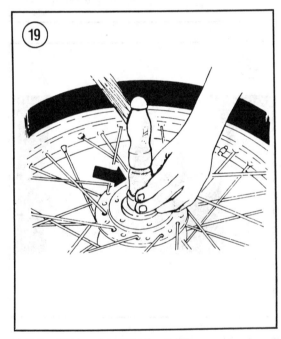

3A. A special Honda tool set-up can be used to install the wheel bearings as follows:

   a. Install the 32×35 mm attachment (Honda part No. 07746-010100) and the 15 mm pilot (Honda part No. 07746-0040300) into the right-hand bearing and drive in the right-hand bearing.

   b. Turn the wheel over (left-hand side up) on the workbench and install the distance collar.

   c. Use the same tool set-up and drive in the left-hand bearing.

3B. If special tools are not used, perform the following:

   a. Tap the right-hand bearing squarely into place and tap on the outer race only. Use a socket (**Figure 19**) that matches the outer race diameter. Do not tap on the inner race or the bearing might be damaged. Be sure that the bearing is completely seated.

   b. Turn the wheel over (left-hand side up) on the workbench and install the distance collar.

   c. Use the same tool set-up and drive in the left-hand bearing.

4. On disc brake models perform the following:

   a. Install the grease seal (B, **Figure 18**).

   b. Install the brake disc and bolts (A, **Figure 18**). Tighten to the torque specifications listed in **Table 1**.

   c. On models so equipped, install the plastic dust seal and screws. Tighten the screws securely.

5. Install the grease seal (B, **Figure 17**) and the speedometer drive dog (A, **Figure 17**).

6. On models so equipped, on the right-hand side, align the tangs of the retainer with the slots in the hub and install the retainer. Push the retainer all the way down onto the surface of the bearing and the hub.

7. Apply grease to the dust seal and install the dust seal (**Figure 16**) next to the retainer.

8. On models equipped with a speedometer, align the tangs (**Figure 20**) of the speedometer drive gear with the notches in the front hub and install the speedometer gear box.

NOTE
Make sure the speedometer gear box seats completely. If the speedometer components do not mesh properly the wheel will be to wide for installation.

9. Install the front wheel as described in this chapter.

9

WHEELS

Wheel Balance

An unbalanced wheel is unsafe. Depending on the degree of unbalance and the speed of the motorcycle, the rider may experience anything from a mild vibration to a violent shimmy which may even result in loss of control.

On spoke wheels, the weights are attached to the spokes on the light side of the wheel.

Before you attempt to balance the wheel, check to be sure that the wheel bearings are in good condition and properly lubricated and that the brakes do not drag. The wheel must rotate freely.

> *NOTE*
> *When balancing the rear wheel do so with the final drive sprocket assembly attached, as it rotates with the rear wheel and affects the balance. The front brake panel does not rotate with the front wheel so it should be removed from the front wheel.*

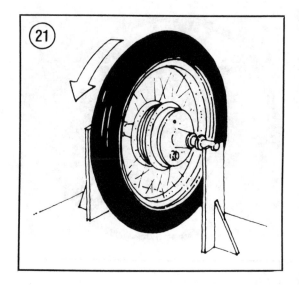

1. Remove the wheel as described in this chapter or Chapter Ten.
2. Mount the wheel on a fixture such as the one shown in **Figure 21** so it can rotate freely.
3. Give the wheel a spin and let it coast to a stop. Mark the tire at the lowest point.
4. Spin the wheel several more times. If the wheel keeps coming to rest at the same point, it is out of balance.
5. Attach a weight to the upper (or light) side of the wheel at the spoke (**Figure 22**). Weights come in 4 sizes: 5, 10, 15 and 20 grams. They are crimped onto the spoke with ordinary gas pliers.
6. Experiment with different weights until the wheel, when spun, comes to a rest at a different position each time.

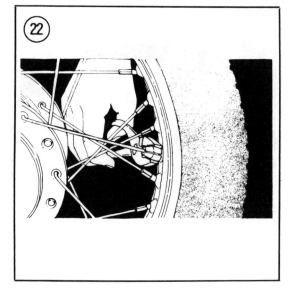

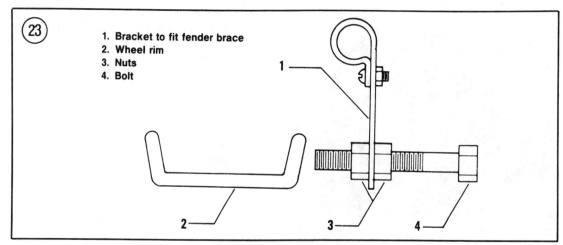

1. Bracket to fit fender brace
2. Wheel rim
3. Nuts
4. Bolt

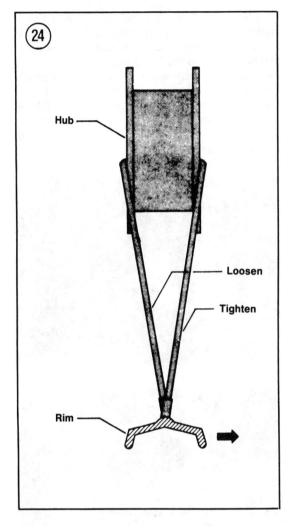

Spoke Adjustment

Spokes loosen with use and should be checked periodically. If all appear to be loose, tighten all spokes on one side of the hub, then tighten all spokes on the other side of the hub. One-half to one turn should be sufficient; do not overtighten.

After tightening the spokes check rim runout to be sure you haven't pulled the rim out of shape.

One way to check rim runout is to mount a dial indicator onto the front fork so that it bears against one side of the rim.

If you don't have a dial indicator, improvise a device like the one shown in **Figure 23**. Adjust the position of the bolt until it just clears the rim. Rotate the wheel and note whether the clearance increases or decreases. Mark the tire with chalk or crayon at areas that produce significantly larger or smaller clearance. Clearance must not change by more than 2.0 mm (0.08 in.).

To pull the rim out, tighten the spokes which terminate on the same side of the hub and loosen spokes which terminate on the opposite side of the hub (**Figure 24**). In most cases, only a slight amount of adjustment is necessary to true a rim. After adjustment is complete, rotate the wheel and make sure another area has not been pulled out of true. Continue adjustment and checking until runout does not exceed 2.0 mm (0.08 in.).

Wheel Alignment

Refer to **Figure 25** for this procedure.
1. Measure the tires at their widest point.
2. Subtract the small dimension from the larger dimension.

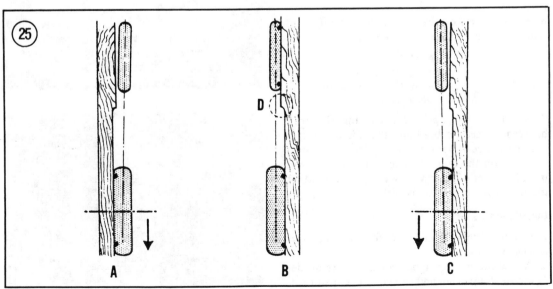

3. Make an alignment tool out of wood, approximately 7 feet long, with an offset equal to one-half of the dimension obtained in Step 2. Refer to (D).

4. If the wheels are not aligned as in (A) and (C), the rear wheel must be shifted to correct the alignment.

5A. On dual-shock models perform the following:
 a. Loosen the rear axle nut.
 b. Loosen the drive chain adjuster locknut and turn the adjuster (**Figure 26**) until the wheels align.

5B. On Pro-Link models perform the following:
 a. Loosen the rear axle nut (A, **Figure 27**).
 b. Turn both snail adjusters (B, **Figure 27**) as required until the wheels align.

6. Adjust the drive chain as described in Chapter Three.

TIRE CHANGING

Removal

1. Remove the valve core to deflate the tire. On models so equipped, loosen the rim locknuts (**Figure 28**) fully, but do not remove them.

2. Press the entire bead on both sides of the tire into the center of the rim.

3. Lubricate the beads with soapy water.

4. Insert the tire iron under the bead next to the valve (**Figure 29**). Force the bead on the opposite side of the tire into the center of the rim and pry the bead over the rim with the tire iron.

5. Insert a second tire iron next to the first to hold the bead over the rim. Then work around the tire with the first tire iron, prying the bead over the rim. Be careful not to pinch the inner tube with the tire irons.

6. Remove the valve from the hole in the rim and remove the inner tube from the tire.

NOTE
Step 7 is required only if it is necessary to completely remove the tire from the rim, as in tire replacement.

7. Stand the tire upright. Insert the tire iron between the second bead and the side of the rim that the first bead was pried over (**Figure 30**). Force the bead on the opposite side from the tire iron into the center of the rim. Pry the second bead off the rim, working around as with the first.

Installation

1. Carefully inspect the tire for any damage, especially inside.

2. A new tire may have balancing rubbers inside. These are not patches and should not be disturbed.

A colored spot near the bead indicates a lighter point on the tire. This spot should be placed next to the valve stem or on models so equipped, midway between the 2 rim locks.

3. Check that the spoke ends do not protrude through the nipples into the center of the rim. If they do they will puncture the inner tube. File off any protruding spoke ends.

4. Make sure the rubber rim tape is in place with the rough side toward the rim.

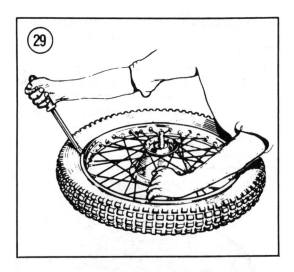

5. Install the tube valve core into the tube valve. Place the tube into the tire and inflate it just enough to round it out. Too much air will make installing the tire difficult and too little will increase the chances of pinching the tube with tire irons.

6. Lubricate both beads of the tire with soapy water. Pull the tube partly out of the tire at the valve. Squeeze the beads together to hold the tube and insert the valve into the hole in the rim (**Figure 31**). The lower bead should go into the center of the rim with the upper bead outside it.

7. Place the lower bead of the tire into the center of the rim on each side of the valve stem. Work around the tire in both directions (**Figure 32**). Use a tire iron for the last few inches of bead (**Figure 33**).

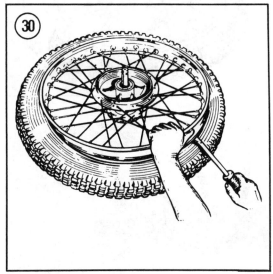

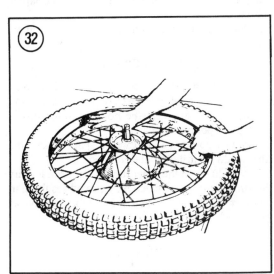

9

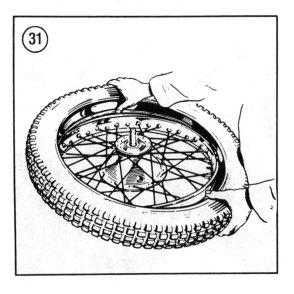

8. Press the upper bead into the rim opposite the valve stem. Pry the bead into the rim on both sides of the initial point with a tire iron, working around the rim to the valve (**Figure 34**).

9. Wiggle the valve stem to be sure the tube is not trapped under the tire bead. Set the valve squarely in the rim hole before screwing on the valve stem nut.

10. Check the bead on both sides of the tire for even fit around the rim.

11. Bounce the wheel several times, rotating it each time. This will force the tire beads against the rim flanges. After the tire beads are in contact with the rim evenly, inflate the tire to seat the beads.

12. Inflate the tire to more than the recommended inflation pressure for the initial seating of the rim flanges. Once the beads are seated correctly, deflate the tire to the correct pressure described in Chapter Three.

13. Balance the wheel as described in this chapter.

TIRE REPAIRS

Patching an inner tube on the road is very difficult. A can of pressurized tire sealant may inflate the tire and seal the hole, although this is only a temporary fix.

Another solution is to carry a spare inner tube that could be installed and inflated.

If you do patch the inner tube, do not run for any length of time as the patch may rub off resulting in another flat. Install a new inner tube as soon as possible.

HANDLEBAR

Removal/Installation
(Drum Brake Models)

1. On XL series models perform the following:
   a. Remove the right-hand rear view mirror (A, **Figure 35**).
   b. Remove the clamping screws on the turn signal bracket and remove the turn signal assembly from the handlebar.

2. Disconnect the brake light switch electrical connector.

3. Remove the screws securing the right-hand handlebar switch assembly (B, **Figure 35**) and remove the electrical wires from the clips (C, **Figure 35**) on the handlebar. Remove the switch assembly from the handlebar.

4. Remove the throttle assembly (D, **Figure 35**) and carefully lay the throttle assembly and cables over the fender or back over the frame. Be careful that the cables do not get crimped or damaged.

5. On XL series models perform the following:
   a. Remove the left-hand rear view mirror (A, **Figure 36**).
   b. Remove the clamping screws on the turn signal bracket (B, **Figure 36**) and remove the turn signal assembly from the handlebar.

6. On models so equipped perform the following:
   a. Disconnect the choke cable from the choke lever (C, **Figure 36**).

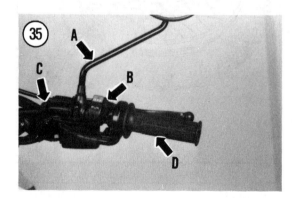

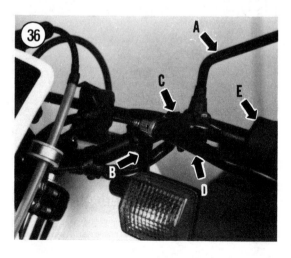

b. Remove the bolt securing the clutch lever assembly (D, **Figure 36**).

7. Lay the clutch and choke (models so equipped) lever assemblies and cable(s) back over the frame or front fender. Be careful that the cables do not get crimped or damaged.

8. Remove the screws securing the left-hand handlebar switch assembly (E, **Figure 36**) and remove the electrical wires from the clips on the handlebar.

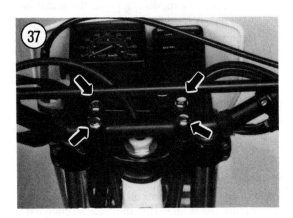

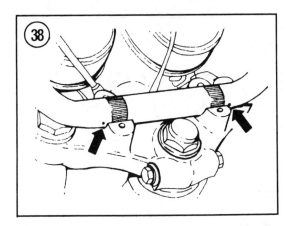

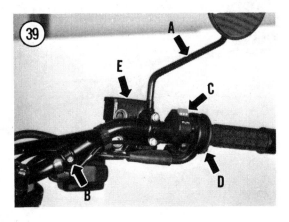

9. Remove the bolts (**Figure 37**) securing the handlebar upper holders in place. Remove the handlebar upper holders then remove the handlebar.

10. To maintain a good grip on the handlebar and to prevent it from slipping down, clean the knurled section of the handlebar with a wire brush. It should be kept rough so it will be held securely by the holders. The holders should also be kept clean and free of any metal that may have been gouged loose by handlebar slippage.

11. Install by reversing these removal steps, noting the following.

12. Position the handlebar on the upper fork bridge so the punch mark on the handlebar is aligned with the top surface of the raised portion of the upper fork bridge (**Figure 38**).

13. Install the handlebar holders and install the bolts. Tighten the forward bolts first and then the rear bolts. Tighten all bolts to the torque specification listed in **Table 1**.

14. Apply a light coat of multipurpose grease to the throttle grip area on the handlebar before installing the throttle grip assembly.

NOTE
When installing all assemblies, align the punch mark on the handlebar with the slit on the mounting bracket.

WARNING
*After installation is complete make sure the brake lever does **not** come in contact with the throttle grip assembly when it is pulled on fully.*

15. Adjust the throttle operation as described in Chapter Three.

**Removal/Installation
(Disc Brake Models)**

1. Remove the headlight housing as described Chapter Eight.
2. Remove the fuel tank as described in Chapter Seven.
3. On XL series models perform the following:
   a. Remove the right-hand rear view mirror (A, **Figure 39**).
   b. Remove the clamping screws on the turn signal bracket (B, **Figure 39**) and remove the turn signal assembly from the handlebar.
4. Disconnect the brake light switch electrical connector.
5. Remove the screws securing the right-hand handlebar switch assembly (C, **Figure 39**) and

remove the electrical wires from the clips on the handlebar.

CAUTION
Cover the frame with a heavy cloth or plastic tarp to protect it from accidental spilling of brake fluid. Wash any spilled brake fluid off any painted or plated surface immediately, as it will destroy the finish. Use soapy water and rinse thoroughly.

6A. On 1988-1990 XR600R models, perform the following:
   a. Remove the screws securing the throttle body together and separate the parts.
   b. Remove the screw and throttle cover (A, **Figure 40**).
   c. Remove the cover gasket (B, **Figure 40**).
   d. Remove the throttle cable roller (C, **Figure 40**).
   e. Disengage the throttle cables from the throttle grip and withdraw them from the upper half of the throttle body.
   f. Lay the throttle cables over the fender or back over the frame. Be careful that the cables do not get kinked.
6B. On all other models, remove the bolts securing the throttle assembly (D, **Figure 39**) and carefully lay the throttle assembly and cables over the fender or back over the frame. Be careful that the cables do not get kinked.
7. Remove the bolts (E, **Figure 39**) securing the brake master cylinder and lay it over the frame. Keep the reservoir in the upright position to minimize loss of brake fluid and to keep air from entering into the brake system. It is not necessary to remove the hydraulic brake line.
8. On XL series models perform the following:
   a. Remove the left-hand rear view mirror (A, **Figure 41**).
   b. Remove the clamping screws on the turn signal bracket (B, **Figure 41**) and remove the turn signal assembly from the handlebar.
9. Remove the bolts securing the clutch lever assembly (C, **Figure 41**).
10. On models so equipped, disconnect the choke cable from the choke lever.
11. Lay the clutch and choke (models so equipped) lever assemblies and cable back over the frame or front fender. Be careful that the cables do not get crimped or damaged.
12. Remove the screws securing the left-hand handlebar switch assembly (D, **Figure 41**) and remove the electrical wires from the clips on the handlebar.

13. On 1985-1986 XR600R models, disconnect the speedometer cable from the Digital Enduro Meter.
14. Remove the bolts (**Figure 42**) securing the handlebar upper holders in place.
15A. On 1985-1986 XR600R models, remove the handlebar upper holders, the Digital Enduro Meter assembly and mounting brackets from upper fork bridge.
15B. On all other models, remove the handlebar upper holders.
16. Remove the handlebar.
17. Install by reversing these removal steps, noting the following.
18. To maintain a good grip on the handlebar and to prevent it from slipping down, clean the knurled section of the handlebar with a wire brush. It should be kept rough so it will be held securely by the holders. The holders should also be kept clean and free of any metal that may have been gouged loose by handlebar slippage.
19. Position the handlebar on the upper fork bridge so the punch mark on the handlebar is aligned with

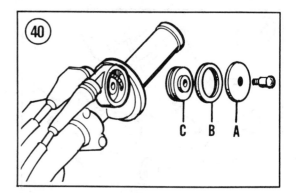

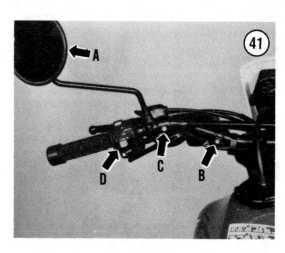

the top surface of the raised portion of the upper fork bridge (**Figure 38**).

20. Install the handlebar holders and install the bolts. Tighten the forward bolts first and then the rear bolts. Tighten all bolts to the torque specification listed in **Table 1**.

21. Apply a light coat of multipurpose grease to the throttle grip area on the handlebar before installing the throttle grip assembly.

> *NOTE*
> *When installing all assemblies, align the punch mark (**Figure 38**) on the handlebar with the slit on the mounting bracket.*

22. Install the brake master cylinder onto the handlebar. Install the clamp with the UP arrow facing up and align the clamp mating surface with the punch mark on the handlebar. Tighten the upper bolt first and then the lower bolt.

> *WARNING*
> *After installation is completed, make sure the brake lever does not come in contact with the throttle grip assembly when it is pulled on fully. If it does, the brake fluid may be low in the reservoir; refill as necessary. Refer to **Front Disc Brakes** in Chapter Eleven.*

23. On 1988-1990 XR600R models, perform the following:
   a. Apply grease to the upper ends of the throttle cables and to the throttle cable roller.
   b. Install the throttle cables through the upper half of the throttle body housing.
   c. Attach the throttle cables onto the throttle grip.
   d. Install the throttle cable roller (C, **Figure 40**).
   e. Install the cover gasket (B, **Figure 40**).

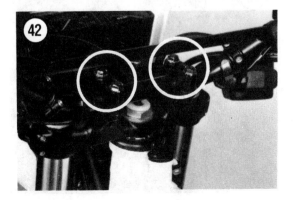

   f. Install the throttle cover and screw (A, **Figure 40**). Tighten the screw securely.
   g. Install the lower half of the throttle body and install the screws securing the throttle body halves together. Tighten the screws securely.

24. Adjust the throttle operation as described in Chapter Three.

STEERING HEAD AND STEM (LOOSE BALL BEARINGS)

Disassembly

Refer to **Figure 43** for this procedure.

1. Remove the front wheel as described in this chapter.
2. Remove the handlebar as described in this chapter.
3. Remove the headlight and number plate assembly as described in Chapter Seven.
4. Remove the instrument cluster or speedometer as described in Chapter Seven.
5. Remove the horn as described in Chapter Seven.
6. Remove the ignition switch as described in Chapter Seven.
7. Remove the bolts (**Figure 44**) securing the front fender and remove the front fender.
8. Loosen the upper and lower fork bridge bolts (**Figure 45**) and slide out both fork tube assemblies.
9. Remove the steering stem nut and washer (**Figure 46**) and remove the upper fork bridge.
10. Loosen the steering stem adjust nut with the pin spanner provided in the factory tool kit, large drift and hammer or the easily improvised tool shown in **Figure 47**.
11. Have an assistant hold a large pan under the steering stem to catch any loose balls that may fall out while you carefully lower the steering stem.
12. Lower the steering stem assembly down and out of the steering head.
13. Remove the upper race from the steering head.
14. Remove the ball bearings from the upper and lower race. There are 36 ball bearings total (18 in the upper race and 18 in the lower racer).

Inspection

1. Clean the bearing races in the steering head and the bearings with solvent.
2. Check the welds around the steering head for cracks and fractures. If any are found, have them repaired by a competent frame shop or welding service.
3. Check the balls for pitting, scratches or discoloration indicating wear or corrosion. Replace them in sets if any are bad.

9

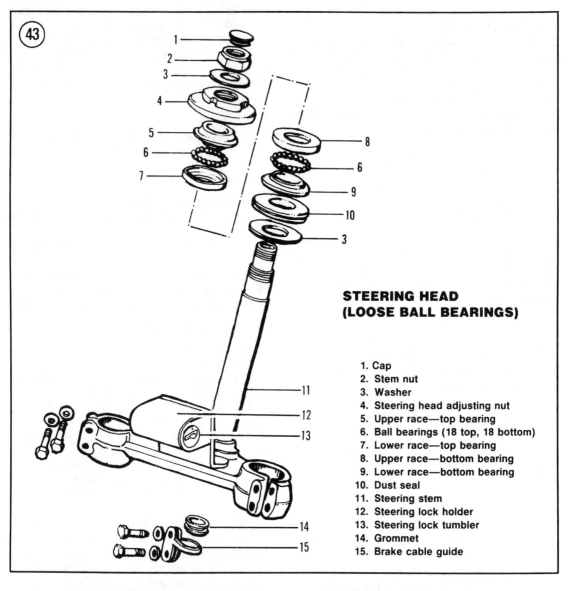

**STEERING HEAD
(LOOSE BALL BEARINGS)**

1. Cap
2. Stem nut
3. Washer
4. Steering head adjusting nut
5. Upper race—top bearing
6. Ball bearings (18 top, 18 bottom)
7. Lower race—top bearing
8. Upper race—bottom bearing
9. Lower race—bottom bearing
10. Dust seal
11. Steering stem
12. Steering lock holder
13. Steering lock tumbler
14. Grommet
15. Brake cable guide

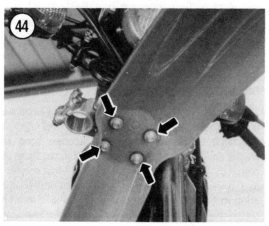

4. Check the races for pitting, galling and corrosion. If any of these conditions exist, replace the races as described in this chapter.

5. Check the steering stem for cracks and check its race for damage or wear. If this race or any race is damaged, the bearings should be replaced as a complete bearing set. Take the old races and bearings to your dealer to ensure accurate replacement.

Steering Stem Assembly

Refer to **Figure 43** for this procedure.

1. Make sure the steering head and stem races are properly seated.

2. Apply a coat of cold grease to the upper bearing race cone and fit 18 ball bearings around it (**Figure 48**).

3. Apply a coat of cold grease to the lower bearing race cone on the steering stem and fit 18 ball bearings around it (**Figure 49**).

4. Install the steering stem into the head tube and hold it firmly in place.

5. Install the upper race of the top bearing.

6. Install the steering stem adjust nut (**Figure 50**) and tighten it until it is snug against the upper race, then back it off 1/8 turn.

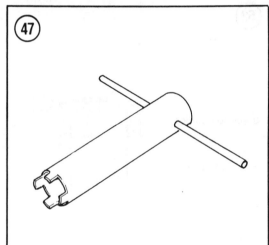

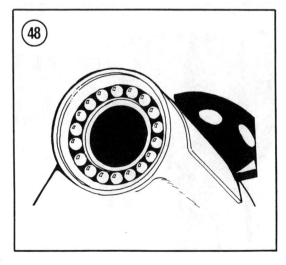

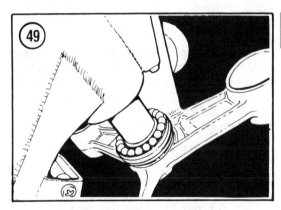

NOTE
*The adjusting nut should be just tight enough to remove both horizontal and vertical play (**Figure 51**), yet loose enough so that the assembly will turn to both lock positions under its own weight after an assist.*

7. Install the upper fork bridge, washer and steering stem nut.

NOTE
Steps 8-10 must be performed in this order to assure proper upper and lower fork bridge to fork alignment.

8. Install the fork tubes so that the top of the fork tube aligns with the top surface of the upper fork bridge (**Figure 52**).
9. Tighten the *lower* fork bridge bolts to the torque specification listed in **Table 1**.
10. Tighten the steering stem nut to the torque specification listed in **Table 1**.
11. Tighten the *upper* fork bridge bolts to the torque specification listed in **Table 1**.
12. Install all items removed.
13. After a few hours of riding, the bearings have had a chance to seat; readjust the free play in the steering stem with the steering stem adjusting nut. Refer to Step 6.

Steering Stem Adjustment

If play develops in the steering system, it may only require adjustment. However, don't take a chance on it. Disassemble the stem and look for possible damage. Then reassemble and adjust as described in Step 6 of the *Steering Head Assembly* procedure.

STEERING HEAD AND STEM (ROLLER BEARINGS)

Disassembly

Refer to **Figure 53** for this procedure.
1. Remove the front wheel as described in this chapter.
2. Remove the headlight and number plate assembly as described in Chapter Seven.
3. Remove the speedometer as described in Chapter Seven.
4. Remove the horn as described in Chapter Seven.
5. Remove the ignition switch as described in Chapter Seven.
6. Remove the bolts securing the front fender and remove it.
7. Remove the handlebar (A, **Figure 54**) as described in this chapter.

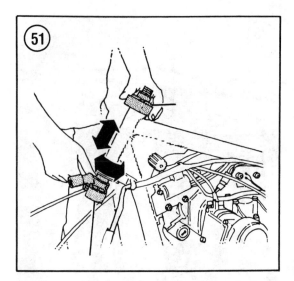

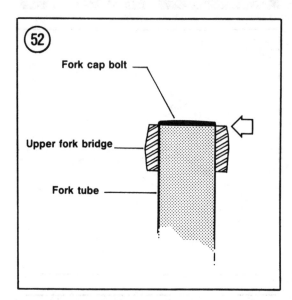

Fork cap bolt

Upper fork bridge

Fork tube

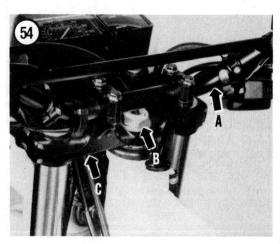

STEERING STEM (ROLLER BEARINGS)

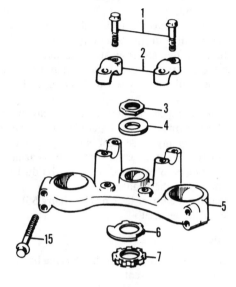

1. Bolt
2. Handlebar upper holder
3. Steering stem nut
4. Washer
5. Upper fork bridge
6. Lockwasher (models so equipped)
7. Steering stem adjust nut
8. Grease seal (models so equipped)
9. Roller bearing set
10. Roller bearing outer race
11. Dust seal
12. Steering stem
13. Grommet
14. Cable holder
15. Bolt

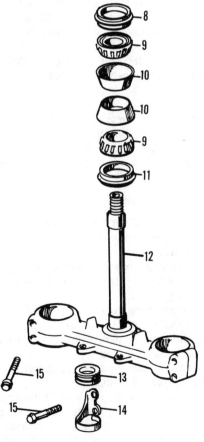

9

8. Remove the steering stem nut and washer (B, **Figure 54**).

9. Loosen the upper fork bridge bolts and remove the upper fork bridge (C, **Figure 54**).

10. On models so equipped, remove the lockwasher. Discard the lockwasher as a new one must be installed during assembly.

11. Remove the steering stem adjust nut. To loosen the adjust nut, use a large drift and hammer or use the easily improvised tool shown in **Figure 47**.

12. Lower the steering stem assembly down and out of the steering head (A, **Figure 55**). Don't worry about catching any loose steel balls as the steering stem is equipped with assembled roller bearings.

13. On models so equipped, remove the dust seal from the top of the headset.

14. Remove the upper bearing (B, **Figure 55**) from the top of the headset.

Inspection

1. Clean the bearing races in the steering head and the bearings with solvent.

2. Check the welds around the steering head for cracks and fractures. If any are found, have them repaired by a competent frame shop or welding service.

3. Check the rollers for pitting, scratches or discoloration indicating wear or corrosion. Replace them in sets if any are bad.

4. Check the races for pitting, galling and corrosion. If any of these conditions exist, replace the races as described in this chapter.

5. Check the steering stem for cracks, damage or wear. If damaged in any way replace the steering stem.

Steering Stem Assembly

Refer to **Figure 53** for this procedure.

1. Make sure the steering head and stem races are properly seated.

2. Install the upper bearing into the steering head.

3. Install the steering stem into the head tube and hold it firmly in place.

4. Install the steering stem adjust nut and tighten it to about 1.0-2.0 N•m (0.7-1.5 ft.-lb.).

5. Turn the steering stem from lock-to-lock 4-5 times to seat the bearings.

6. Retighten the steering stem adjust nut to about 1.0-2.0 N•m (0.7-1.5 ft.-lb.).

7. Repeat Step 5 and Step 6 twice. If during these steps the adjust nut will not tighten, remove the nut and inspect both the nut and the steering stem threads for dirt and/or burrs. Clean both parts and repeat Steps 4-7.

8. On models so equipped, install a *new* lockwasher with the locking tab facing toward the rear of the bike.

9. Install the upper fork bridge, washer and steering stem nut only finger-tight at this time.

NOTE
Steps 10-13 must be performed in this order to assure proper upper and lower fork bridge to fork alignment.

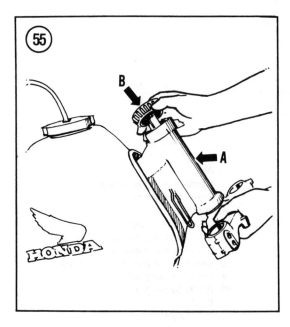

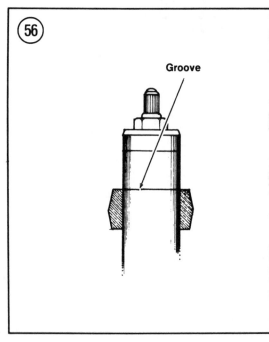

Groove

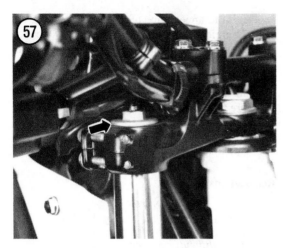

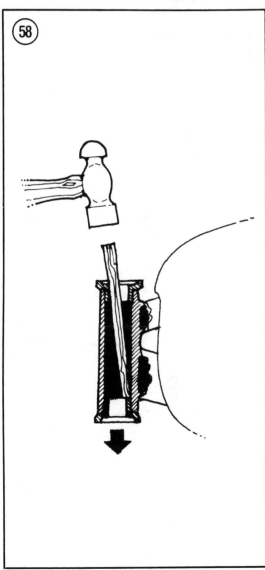

10A. On XL500S, XR500 models, slide the fork tubes into position so the top surface of the fork tube aligns with the top surface of the upper fork bridge (**Figure 52**).

10B. On 1981-1984 XR500R models, slide the fork tubes into position so the *lower* groove on the fork tube aligns with the top surface of the upper fork bridge (**Figure 56**).

10C. On XL500R, XR600R, XL600R models, slide the fork tubes into position so the top surface of the fork tube aligns with the top surface of the upper fork bridge (**Figure 57**).

11. Tighten the *lower* fork bridge bolts to the torque specification listed in **Table 1**.

12. Tighten the steering stem nut to the torque specification listed in **Table 1**.

13. Tighten the upper fork bridge bolts to the torque specification listed in **Table 1**.

14. On models so equipped, bend the lockwasher locking tab up against the back surface of the upper fork bridge.

15. Install all items removed.

Steering Stem Adjustment

If play develops in the steering system, it may only require adjustment. However, don't take a chance on it. Disassemble the stem and look for possible damage, then reassemble and adjust as described in Steps 4-7 of the *Steering Head Assembly* procedure.

STEERING HEAD BEARING RACES

The headset and steering stem bearing races are pressed into place. Because they are easily bent, do not remove them unless they are worn and require replacement.

Headset Bearing Race
Removal/Installation

To remove the headset race, insert a hardwood stick or soft punch into the head tube (**Figure 58**) and carefully tap the race out from the inside. After it is started, tap around the race so that neither the race nor the head tube is damaged.

To install the headset race, tap it in slowly with a block of wood, a suitable size socket or piece of pipe (**Figure 59**). Make sure that the race is squarely seated in the headset race bore before tapping it into place. Tap the race in until it is flush with the steering head surface.

**Steering Stem Bearing Race
and Grease Seal
Removal/Installation**

1. To remove the steering stem race (bottom bearing lower race) try twisting and pulling it up by hand. If it will not come off; carefully pry it up with a screwdriver; work around in a circle, prying a little at a time.

2. On models with loose ball bearings, remove the bottom bearing lower race, dust seal and dust seal washer.

> *CAUTION*
> *On models with roller bearings, do not attempt to remove the lower bearing, inner race and dust seal from the steering stem. Removal of these components requires the use of a hydraulic press and special tools and should be entrusted to a Honda dealer or machine shop.*

3A. On models with loose ball bearings, install the dust seal washer and dust seal. Slide the lower race over the steering stem with the bearing surface facing up.

3B. On models with roller bearings, have the dealer or machine shop install the dust seal, and lower roller bearing and internal race.

4. Tap the lower race down with a piece of hardwood. Work around in a circle so the race will not be bent. Make sure it is seated squarely and is all the way down.

FRONT FORK SERVICE (ALL MODELS)

The front suspension on all models uses spring controlled, hydraulically damped, telescopic fork. Before suspecting major trouble, drain the front fork oil and refill with the proper type and quantity; refer to *Front Fork Oil Change* in Chapter Three. If you still have trouble, such as poor damping, a tendency to bottom or top out or leakage around the rubber seals, follow the service procedures in this section.

To simplify fork service and to prevent the mixing of parts, the legs should be removed, serviced and installed individually.

Some of the fork assemblies used among the various models were originally equipped with a foam seal and a plastic washer. These parts were located between the oil seal and the circlip (**Figure 60**). The Honda factory has determined that the foam seal may work its way down into the oil seal

and give the appearance of a worn or leaking oil seal. Therefore on models so equipped, do *not* reinstall the foam seal and plastic washer under the dust seal during the assembly procedure. If you purchase a new seal kit that still contains these 2 parts in it, discard them; they are not to be used.

Figure 60 shows these 2 parts and indicates that they should be discarded.

FRONT FORK
(XL500S, XR500)

Removal/Installation

> *NOTE*
> *The Allen bolt at the base of the slider is secured with thread sealant and is often very difficult to remove because the damper rod will turn inside the slider. It*

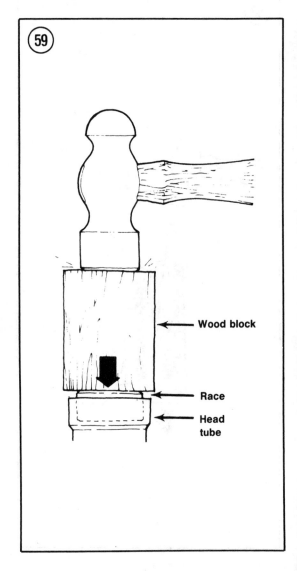

(59)

← **Wood block**

← **Race**

← **Head
tube**

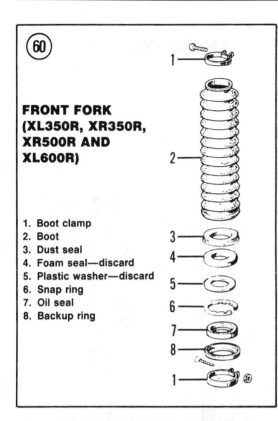

FRONT FORK (XL350R, XR350R, XR500R AND XL600R)

1. Boot clamp
2. Boot
3. Dust seal
4. Foam seal—discard
5. Plastic washer—discard
6. Snap ring
7. Oil seal
8. Backup ring

sometimes can be removed with an air impact driver. If you are unable to remove it, take the fork tubes to a dealer and have the bolts removed.

1. If the fork assembly is going to be disassembled, perform the following:
   a. Have an assistant hold the front brake on, compress the front forks and hold it in this position.
   b. Slightly loosen the Allen bolt at the base of the slider. If the bolt is loosened too much, fork oil may start to drain out of the slider.
2. On XR models, remove the speedometer cable clamp in the left-hand fork slider (**Figure 61**).
3. Loosen the clamp screw (**Figure 62**) on the boot and slide the boot down.
4. Remove the front wheel as described in this chapter.
5. Remove the protective cap from the fork cap bolts.
6. Loosen, but do not remove, the fork cap bolts.
7. Loosen the upper and lower fork bridge bolts (A, **Figure 63**).
8. Remove the fork tubes (B, **Figure 63**). It may be necessary to slightly rotate the fork tube while pulling it down and out.
9. Install by reversing these removal steps, noting the following.
10. Insert the fork tube up through the lower and upper fork bridges.
11. Align the top of the fork tube with the top surface of the upper fork bridge (**Figure 52**).
12. Tighten the upper and lower fork bridge bolts to the torque specifications listed in **Table 1**.

9

64

FRONT FORK ASSEMBLY (XL500S, XR500)

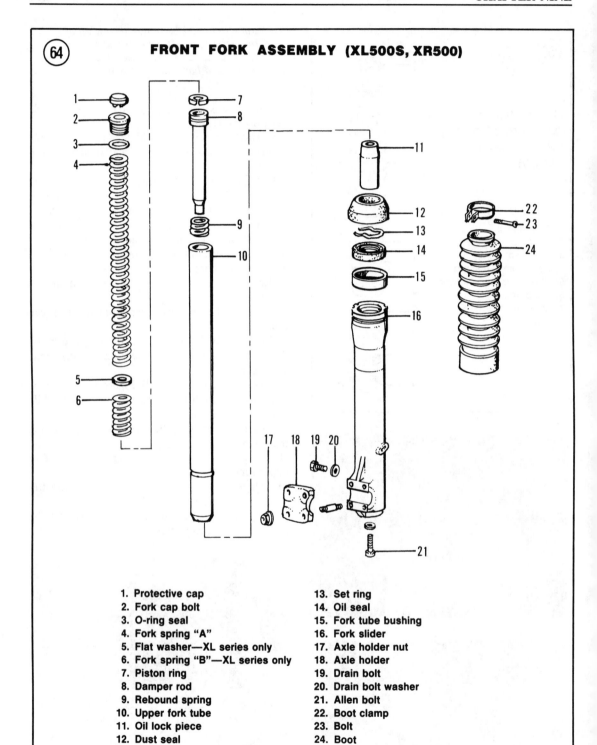

1. Protective cap
2. Fork cap bolt
3. O-ring seal
4. Fork spring "A"
5. Flat washer—XL series only
6. Fork spring "B"—XL series only
7. Piston ring
8. Damper rod
9. Rebound spring
10. Upper fork tube
11. Oil lock piece
12. Dust seal
13. Set ring
14. Oil seal
15. Fork tube bushing
16. Fork slider
17. Axle holder nut
18. Axle holder
19. Drain bolt
20. Drain bolt washer
21. Allen bolt
22. Boot clamp
23. Bolt
24. Boot

Disassembly

Refer to **Figure 64** for this procedure.
1. Clamp the slider in a vise with soft jaws.
2. If not loosened during the fork removal sequence, loosen the Allen bolt on the bottom of the slider.

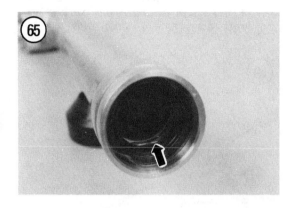

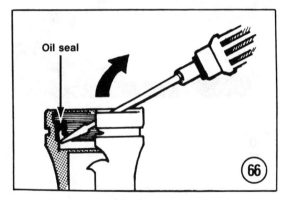

Oil seal

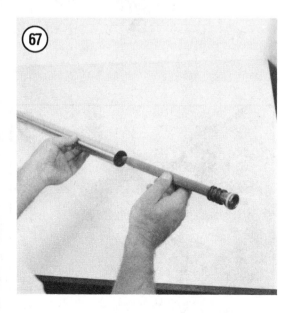

NOTE
This bolt is secured with thread sealant and is often very difficult to remove because the damper rod will turn inside the slider. It sometimes can be removed with an air impact driver. If you are unable to remove it, take the fork tubes to a dealer and have the bolts removed.

3. Remove the 6 mm Allen bolt and gasket from the slider.
4. Hold the upper fork tube in a vise with soft jaws and loosen the fork cap bolt (if it was not loosened during the fork removal sequence).

WARNING
Be careful when removing the fork top cap bolt as the spring(s) is under pressure. Protect your eyes accordingly.

5. Remove the fork top cap bolt from the fork.
6A. On XL series models remove the fork springs and flat washer.
6B. On XR series models remove the fork spring.
7. Remove the fork from the vise, pour the fork oil out and discard it. Pump the fork several times by hand to expel most of the remaining oil.
8. Pull the fork tube out of the slider.
9. Remove the oil lock piece, the damper rod and rebound spring.
10. Remove the dust seal from the slider.
11A. On XL500S models, remove the set ring and oil seal from the slider.
11B. On XR500 models, remove the set ring (**Figure 65**) oil seal and backup ring from the slider.

NOTE
It may be necessary to slightly heat the area on the slider around the oil seal before removal. Use a rag soaked in hot water. Do not apply a flame directly to the fork slider.

CAUTION
*Use a dull screwdriver blade to remove the oil seal (**Figure 66**). Do not damage the outer edge or inner surface of the slider.*

12. Inspect the components as described in this chapter.

Assembly

1. Coat all parts with fresh DEXRON automatic transmission fluid or fork oil before installation.
2. Install the rebound spring onto the damper rod and insert this assembly into the fork tube (**Figure 67**).

9

3A. On XL series models, temporarily install the fork springs. It is not necessary to install the flat washer at this time.

3B. On XR series models, temporarily install the fork spring.

4. Install the fork cap bolt to hold the damper rod in place.

5. Install the oil lock piece onto the damper rod (**Figure 68**).

6. Install the upper fork assembly into the slider (**Figure 69**).

7. Make sure the gasket (**Figure 70**) is on the Allen head screw.

8. Apply Loctite Lock N' Seal to the threads of the Allen bolt before installation. Install it in the fork slider and tighten (**Figure 71**) to the torque specification listed in **Table 1**.

9. To prevent damage to the inside of the new fork seal during installation, wrap the groove in the top of the fork tube with clear tape. Do *not* use duct or masking tape.

10. On XR500 models, position the backup ring with the flange side facing up. Slide the backup ring down the fork tube and into the slider.

11. Install the new oil seal as follows:

  a. Coat the new seal with ATF (automatic transmission fluid).

  b. Position the seal with the marking facing upward and slide it down onto the fork tube.

  c. Drive the seal into the slider with Honda special tool Fork Seal Driver Body (part No. 07947-0010100) and Fork Seal Driver Attachment (part No. 07947-0010600); refer to **Figure 72**.

  d. Drive the oil seal in until the groove in the slider can be seen above the top surface of the oil seal.

  e. Remove the tape from the top of the fork tube.

NOTE
A piece of 2 in. galvanized pipe can also work as a tool. If both ends are

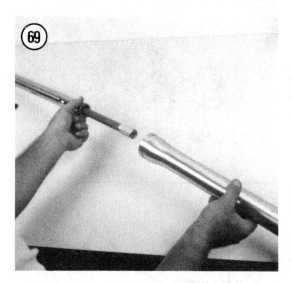

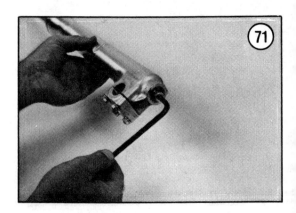

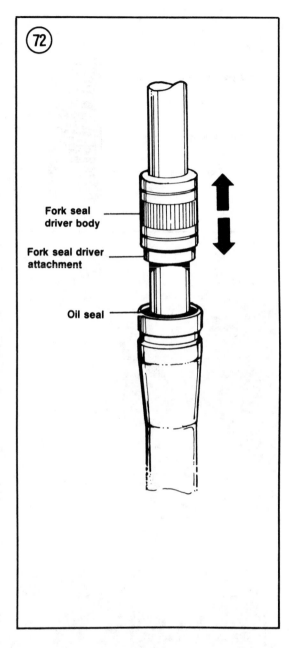

Figure 72 labels: Fork seal driver body, Fork seal driver attachment, Oil seal

threaded (a close nipple pipe fitting), wrap one end with duct tape to prevent the threads from damaging the interior of the slider.

12. Install the set ring. Make sure the set ring is completely seated in the groove in the fork slider.
13. Install the dust seal into the slider (**Figure 73**).
14. Remove the fork cap bolt.
15A. On XL series models remove the fork springs.
15B. On XR series models remove the fork spring.
16. Fill the fork tube with the correct quantity of DEXRON automatic transmission fluid or fork oil. Refer to **Table 2**.
17A. On XL series models perform the following:
  a. Install the short fork spring "B" (**Figure 74**) and the flat washer.
  b. Install the long fork spring "A" (**Figure 75**).

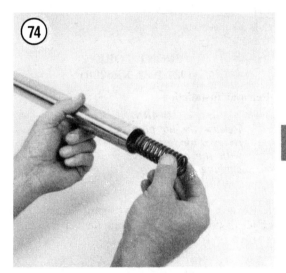

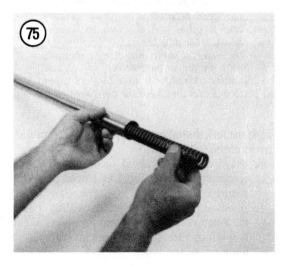

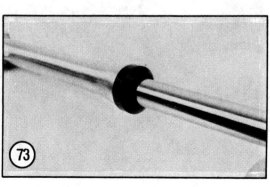

NOTE
Make sure the springs and flat washer are installed as shown in Figure 76.

17B. On XR series models, install the fork spring (**Figure 75**).

18. Inspect the O-ring seal on the fork cap bolt; replace if necessary.

19. Install the fork cap bolt (A, **Figure 77**). Make sure the O-ring seal (B, **Figure 77**) is in place.

20. Push down on the spring(s) and start the bolt slowly; don't cross-thread it.

21. Place the slider in a vise with soft jaws and tighten the fork top cap bolt to the torque specifications listed in **Table 1**.

22. Repeat this procedure for the other fork assembly.

23. Install the fork assemblies as described in this chapter.

FRONT FORK
(1981-1982 XR500R)

Removal/Installation

WARNING
Release the air pressure gradually. If released too fast, fork oil will spurt out with the air. Protect your eyes and clothing accordingly.

1. Remove the air valve cap (**Figure 78**) and bleed off all air pressure by depressing the valve stem.

NOTE
The Allen bolt at the base of the slider has been secured with thread sealant and is often very difficult to remove because the damper rod will turn inside the slider. It sometimes can be removed with an air impact driver. If you are unable to remove it, take the fork tubes to a dealer and have the bolts removed.

2. If the fork assembly is going to be disassembled, perform the following:

  a. Have an assistant hold the front brake on, compress the front forks and hold it in this position.

  b. Using a 6 mm Allen wrench, slightly loosen the Allen bolt at the base of the slider. If the bolt is loosened too much, fork oil may start to drain out of the slider.

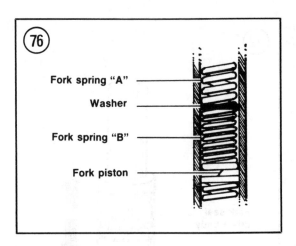

Fork spring "A"
Washer
Fork spring "B"
Fork piston

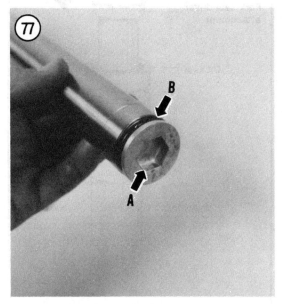

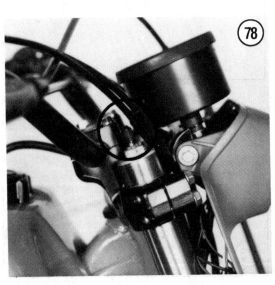

3. Disconnect the brake and speedometer cables from the left-hand fork slider (**Figure 79**).

4. Remove the front wheel as described in this chapter.

5. Remove the bolts securing the front fender (A, **Figure 80**) and remove the fender.

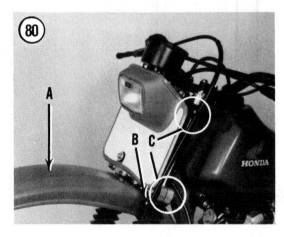

6. Loosen, but do not remove, the fork cap bolt/air valve assembly on each fork assembly.

7. Loosen the upper clamping band and slide the rubber boot (B, **Figure 80**) down and away from the lower fork bridge.

8. Loosen the upper and lower fork bridge bolts (C, **Figure 80**).

9. Remove the fork tube. It may be necessary to slightly rotate the fork tube while pulling it down and out.

10. Install by reversing these removal steps, noting the following.

11. Install the fork tube so the top of the fork tube aligns with the top surface of the upper fork bridge (**Figure 52**).

12. Tighten the upper and lower fork bridge bolts to the torque specifications listed in **Table 1**.

13. Inflate the front forks to the standard air pressure listed in **Table 3**. Do not use compressed air, only use a small hand-operated air pump (**Figure 81**).

WARNING
Never use any type of compressed gas as a lethal explosion may result. Never heat the fork assembly with a torch or place it near an open flame or extreme heat for the same reason.

CAUTION
Never exceed an air pressure of 1.0 kg/cm2 (14 psi) as damage may occur to internal components of the fork assembly.

14. Apply the front brake and pump the forks several times. Recheck the air pressure and readjust if necessary.

Disassembly

Refer to **Figure 82** during the disassembly and assembly procedures.

1. Remove the rubber boot from the slider.

2. Clamp the slider in a vise with soft jaws.

3. If not loosened during the fork removal sequence, loosen the Allen bolt on the bottom of the slider.

NOTE
This bolt has been secured with thread sealant and is often very difficult to remove because the damper rod will turn inside the slider. It sometimes can be removed with an air impact driver. If you are unable to remove it, take the fork tubes to a dealer and have the bolts removed.

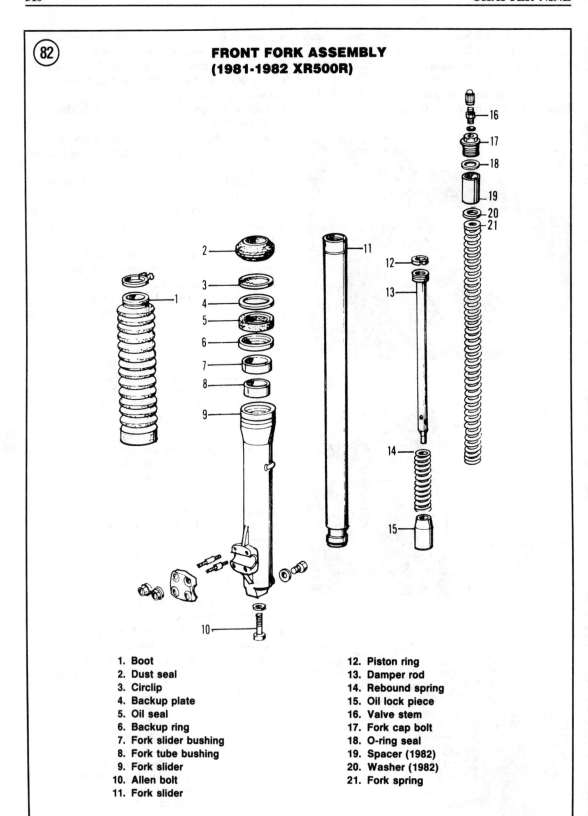

**FRONT FORK ASSEMBLY
(1981-1982 XR500R)**

1. Boot
2. Dust seal
3. Circlip
4. Backup plate
5. Oil seal
6. Backup ring
7. Fork slider bushing
8. Fork tube bushing
9. Fork slider
10. Allen bolt
11. Fork slider
12. Piston ring
13. Damper rod
14. Rebound spring
15. Oil lock piece
16. Valve stem
17. Fork cap bolt
18. O-ring seal
19. Spacer (1982)
20. Washer (1982)
21. Fork spring

4. Remove the Allen bolt and gasket from the slider.

5. Hold the upper fork tube in a vise with soft jaws and loosen the fork cap bolt/air valve assembly if it was not loosened during the fork removal sequence.

WARNING
Be careful when removing the fork cap bolt/air valve assembly as the spring is under pressure. Protect your eyes accordingly.

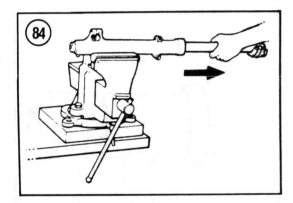

6. Remove the fork cap bolt/air valve assembly from the fork.

7A. On 1981 models remove the fork spring.

7B. On 1982 models remove the collar, spring seat and the fork spring.

8. Remove the fork from the vise, pour the fork oil out and discard it. Pump the fork several times by hand to expel most of the remaining oil.

9. Remove the dust seal from the slider.

10. Remove the circlip (**Figure 83**) and the back up plate from the slider.

NOTE
On this type of fork, force is needed to remove the fork tube from the slider.

11. Install the fork slider in a vise with soft jaws.

12. There is an interference fit between the bushing in the fork slider and the bushing on the fork tube. In order to remove the fork tube from the slider, pull hard on the fork tube using quick in and out strokes (**Figure 84**). Doing this will withdraw the bushing, backup ring and oil seal from the slider.

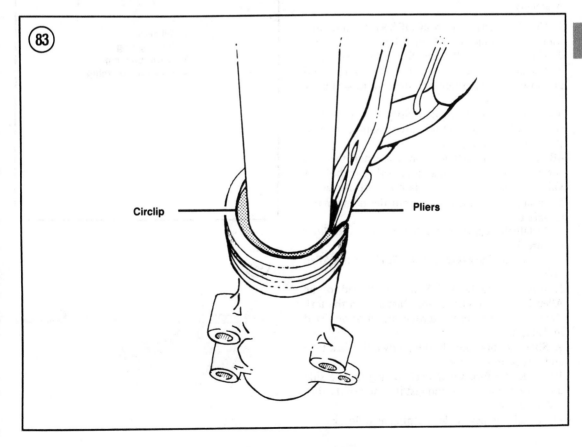

Circlip — — — Pliers

NOTE
It may be necessary to slightly heat the area on the slider around the oil seal before removal. Use a rag soaked in hot water; do not apply a flame directly to the fork slider.

13. Withdraw the fork tube from the slider.

NOTE
Do not remove the fork tube bushing unless it is going to be replaced. Inspect it as described in this chapter.

14. Turn the fork tube upside down and slide off the oil seal, backup ring and slider bushing (**Figure 85**) from the fork tube.
15. Do not discard the slider bushing at this time. It will be used during the installation procedure.
16. Remove the oil lock piece, the damper rod and rebound spring.
17. Inspect the components as described in this chapter.

Assembly

1. Coat all parts with fresh DEXRON automatic transmission fluid or fork oil before installation.
2. If removed, install a new fork tube bushing.
3. Install the rebound spring onto the damper rod and insert this assembly into the fork tube (**Figure 86**).
4A. On 1981 models temporarily install the fork spring and fork cap bolt/air valve assembly to hold the damper rod in place.
4B. On 1982 models temporarily install the fork spring, spring seat, collar and fork cap bolt/air valve assembly to hold the damper rod in place.
5. Install the oil lock piece onto the damper rod (**Figure 87**).
6. Install the upper fork assembly into the slider (**Figure 88**).
7. Make sure the gasket (**Figure 70**) is on the Allen bolt.
8. Apply Loctite Lock N' Seal to the threads of the Allen bolt before installation. Install it in the fork slider and tighten to the torque specification listed in **Table 1**.
9. Slide the fork slider bushing down the fork tube and rest it on the slider.
10. Slide the fork slider backup ring (flange side up) down the fork tube and rest it on top of the fork slider bushing.
11. Install the new slider bushing as follows:

a. Place the old fork slider bushing on top of the backup ring.
b. Drive the bushing into the fork slider with Honda special tool Fork Seal Driver Body (part No. 07947-0010100) and Fork Seal Driver (part No. 07947-3710101).

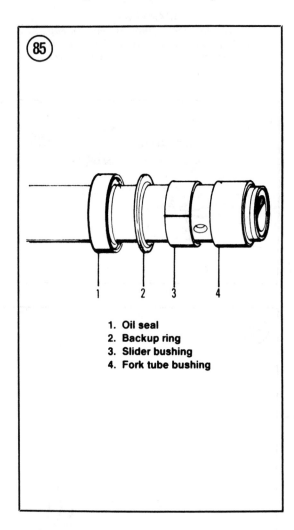

85

1. Oil seal
2. Backup ring
3. Slider bushing
4. Fork tube bushing

86

c. Drive the bushing into place until it seats completely in the recess in the slider.

d. Remove the installation tool and the old fork slider bushing.

> *NOTE*
> *A piece of 2 in. galvanized pipe can also work as a tool. If both ends are threaded (a close nipple pipe fitting), wrap one end with duct tape to prevent the threads from damaging the interior of the slider.*

12. Slide the oil seal backup ring (flange side up) down the fork tube and into the fork slider.

13. To prevent damage to the inside of the new fork seal during installation, wrap the groove in the top of the fork tube with clear tape. Do *not* use duct or masking tape.

14. Install the new fork seal as follows:

a. Coat the new seal with ATF (automatic transmission fluid).

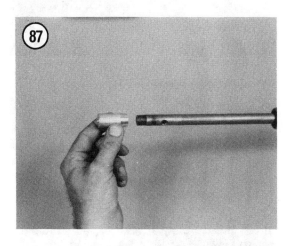

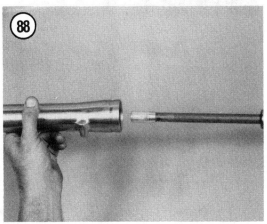

b. Position the seal with the marking facing upward and slide it down onto the fork tube.

c. Drive the seal into the slider with Honda special tool Fork Seal Driver Body (part No. 07947-0010100) and Fork Seal Driver (part No. 07947-0010600); refer to **Figure 72**.

d. Drive the oil seal in until the groove in the slider can be seen above the top surface of the oil seal.

e. Remove the tape from the top of the fork tube.

> *NOTE*
> *A piece of 2 in. galvanized pipe can also work as a tool. If both ends are threaded (a close nipple pipe fitting), wrap one end with duct tape to prevent the threads from damaging the interior of the slider.*

15. Install the circlip with the sharp side facing up. Make sure the circlip is completely seated in the groove in the fork slider.

16. Install the dust seal onto the slider.

17A. On 1981 models remove the fork cap bolt/air valve assembly and the fork spring.

17B. On 1982 models remove the fork cap bolt/air valve assembly, spacer, washer and the fork spring.

18. Fill the fork tube with the correct quantity of DEXRON automatic transmission fluid or fork oil. Refer to **Table 3**.

19. Install the fork spring into the fork tube.

20A. On 1981 models install the fork spring and fork cap bolt/air valve assembly to hold the damper rod in place.

20B. On 1982 models install the fork spring, spring seat, collar and fork cap bolt/air valve assembly to hold the damper rod in place.

21. Inspect the O-ring seal on the fork cap bolt/air valve assembly; replace if necessary.

22. Install the fork cap bolt/air valve assembly while pushing down on the spring. Start the bolt slowly, don't cross-thread it.

23. Place the slider in a vise with soft jaws and tighten the fork cap bolt/air valve assembly to the torque specifications listed in **Table 1**.

24. Slide the rubber boot down the fork tube and snap it into place in the groove in the fork slider. Tighten the clamping band screw securely.

25. Repeat this procedure for the other fork assembly.

26. Install the fork assemblies as described in this chapter.

FRONT FORK
(XL500R, XR500R [1983-1984], XR600R AND XL600R)

Removal/Installation

1. Remove the air valve cap (**Figure 89**) and bleed off all air pressure by depressing the valve stem.

> *WARNING*
> *Release the air pressure gradually. If released too fast, fork oil will spurt out with the air. Protect your eyes and clothing accordingly.*

> *NOTE*
> *On 1988-1990 XR600R models, the bottom bolt at the base of the slider does not screw into the damper rod as the 6 mm Allen bolt does on all other models. On these models, it is not necessary to loosen the bottom bolt at this time.*

> *NOTE*
> *On all models except the 1988-1990 XR600R, the 6 mm Allen bolt at the base of the slider has been secured with a thread sealant and is often difficult to loosen and remove because the damper rod will turn inside the slider. It sometimes can be removed with an air impact driver. If you are unable to remove it, take the fork tubes to a dealer and have the bolts removed.*

2. On all models except the 1988-1990 XR600R, if the fork assembly is going to be disassembled, perform the following:

    a. Have an assistant hold the front brake on, compress the front forks and hold them in this position.

b. Using a 6 mm Allen wrench, slightly loosen the Allen bolt at the base of the slider. If the bolt is loosened too much, fork oil may start to drain out of the slider.

3. On disc brake models, perform the following:

a. Remove the bolts (**Figure 90**) securing the caliper assembly to the left-hand fork slider.

b. Remove the bolts (**Figure 91**) securing the brake hose to the left-hand fork slider.

c. Slide the caliper assembly off the brake disc.

d. Tie the caliper assembly up to the frame with Bungee cord to take the strain off the brake hose.

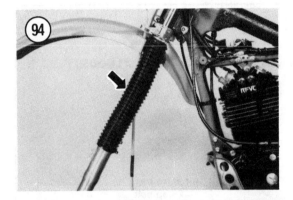

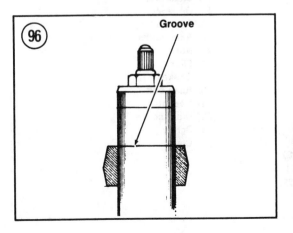

Groove

4. On models so equipped, remove the speedometer cable clamp (**Figure 92**) on the right-hand fork leg.

5. Remove the front wheel as described in this chapter.

6. Loosen, but do not remove, the fork cap bolt/air valve assembly.

7. Loosen the upper and lower fork bridge bolts (**Figure 93**).

8. Loosen the clamping screws on the rubber boot bands. Slide the rubber boots down (**Figure 94**).

9. Remove the fork tube. It may be necessary to slightly rotate the fork tube while pulling it down and out.

10. Install by reversing these removal steps, noting the following.

11A. On XL500R, XR600R and XL600R models, install the fork tubes so that the top of the fork tube aligns with the top surface of the upper fork bridge (**Figure 95**).

11B. On XR500R models, install the fork tubes so that the *lower* groove of the fork tube aligns with the top surface of the upper fork bridge (**Figure 96**).

12. Tighten the upper and lower fork bridge bolts to the torque specifications listed in **Table 1**.

13. Install the rubber fork boots with the greater number of holes toward the rear of the bike.

14. Inflate the forks to the standard air pressure listed in **Table 3**. Do not use compressed air, only use a small hand-operated air pump (**Figure 97**).

9

WARNING
Never use any type of compressed gas as a lethal explosion may result. Never heat the fork assembly with a torch or place it near an open flame or extreme heat for the same reason.

CAUTION
Never exceed an air pressure of 1.0 kg/cm² (14 psi) as damage may occur to internal components of the fork assembly.

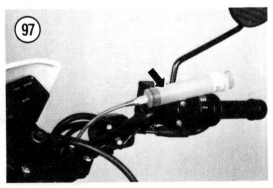

15. Apply the front brake and pump the forks several times. Recheck the air pressure and readjust if necessary.

Disassembly

Refer to **Figure 98** for XL500R, XR500R (1983-1984) an XL600R models or **Figure 99** for XR600R models during the disassembly and assembly procedures.

1. Clamp the slider in a vise with soft jaws.

2A. On all models except 1988-1990 XR600R models, perform the following:

a. If not loosened during the fork removal sequence, loosen the 6 mm Allen bolt at the base of the slider.

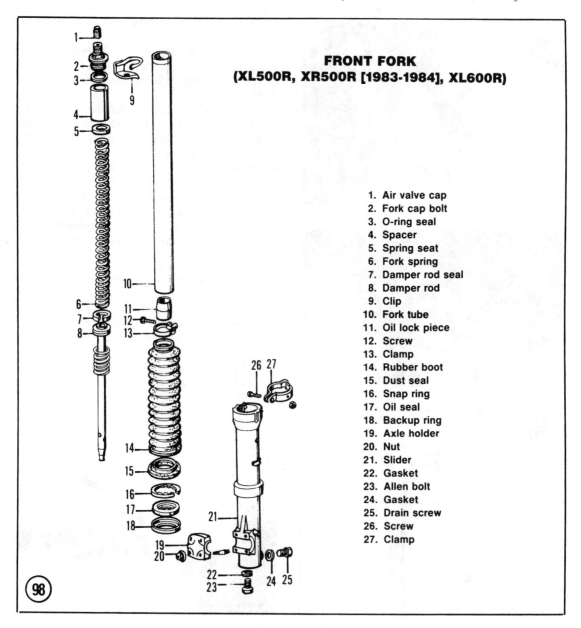

**FRONT FORK
(XL500R, XR500R [1983-1984], XL600R)**

1. Air valve cap
2. Fork cap bolt
3. O-ring seal
4. Spacer
5. Spring seat
6. Fork spring
7. Damper rod seal
8. Damper rod
9. Clip
10. Fork tube
11. Oil lock piece
12. Screw
13. Clamp
14. Rubber boot
15. Dust seal
16. Snap ring
17. Oil seal
18. Backup ring
19. Axle holder
20. Nut
21. Slider
22. Gasket
23. Allen bolt
24. Gasket
25. Drain screw
26. Screw
27. Clamp

98

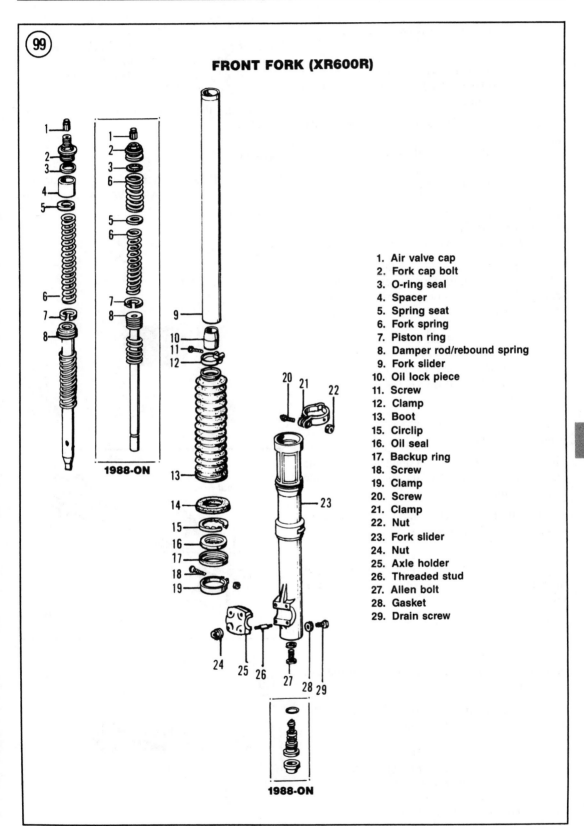

FRONT FORK (XR600R)

1. Air valve cap
2. Fork cap bolt
3. O-ring seal
4. Spacer
5. Spring seat
6. Fork spring
7. Piston ring
8. Damper rod/rebound spring
9. Fork slider
10. Oil lock piece
11. Screw
12. Clamp
13. Boot
15. Circlip
16. Oil seal
17. Backup ring
18. Screw
19. Clamp
20. Screw
21. Clamp
22. Nut
23. Fork slider
24. Nut
25. Axle holder
26. Threaded stud
27. Allen bolt
28. Gasket
29. Drain screw

1988-ON

1988-ON

9

tubes to a dealer and have the bolts removed.

b. Remove the 6 mm Allen bolt and gasket from the base of the slider. Some fork oil may drain out at this time.

2B. On 1988-1990 XR600R models, perform the following:

a. Remove the cap from the base of the slider.
b. Using a suitable size socket, loosen, then remove the bottom bolt and sealing washer from the base of the slider. Some fork oil may drain out at this time.
c. Discard the sealing washer as it cannot be reused since it would allow fork oil leakage.

3. Hold the upper end of the fork tube in a vise with soft jaws and loosen the fork cap bolt/air valve assembly if it was not loosened during the fork removal sequence.

> *WARNING*
> *Be careful when removing the fork cap bolt/air valve assembly as the spring is under pressure. Protect your eyes accordingly.*

4. Remove the fork cap bolt/air valve assembly from the fork tube.

5A. On 1988-1990 XR600R models, remove the upper short fork spring "A," the spring seat and the lower long fork spring "B."

5B. On all other models, remove the spacer, the spring seat and the fork spring.

6. Remove the fork from the vise, pour the remaining fork oil out and discard it. Pump the fork several times by hand to expel most of the remaining fork oil.

7. Remove the dust seal from the slider.

8. Withdraw the fork tube from the slider.

9. Remove the oil lock piece, the damper rod and the rebound spring.

10. Remove the circlip (**Figure 100**), the oil seal and the backup ring from the slider.

> *CAUTION*
> *It may be necessary to slightly heat the area on the slider around the oil seal before removal. Use a rag soaked in hot water. Do not apply a flame directly to the fork slider.*

> *CAUTION*
> *Use a dull screwdriver blade to remove the oil seal (**Figure 101**). Do not damage the outer edge or inner surface of the slider.*

11. Inspect the components as described in this chapter.

Assembly

1. Coat all parts with fresh DEXRON automatic transmission fluid or SAE 10W fork oil before installation.

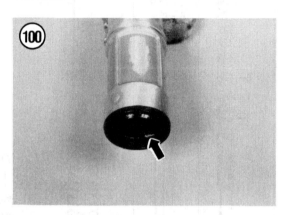

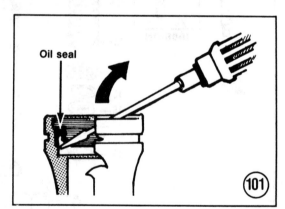

Oil seal

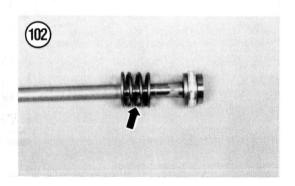

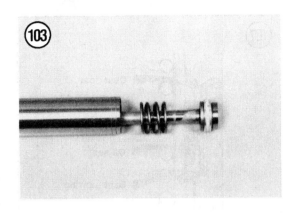

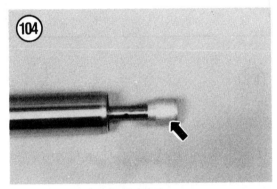

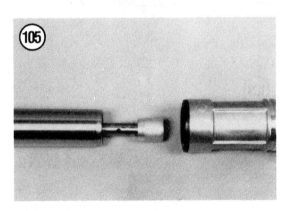

2. Install the rebound spring onto the damper rod (**Figure 102**) and insert this assembly into the fork tube (**Figure 103**).

3A. On 1988-1990 XR600R models, temporarily install the lower long fork spring "B," the spring seat, the upper short fork spring "A" and the fork cap bolt/air valve assembly to hold the damper rod in place.

3B. On all other models, temporarily install the fork spring, the spring seat, spacer and the fork cap bolt/air valve assembly to hold the damper rod in place.

4. Install the oil lock piece onto the damper rod (**Figure 104**).

5. Install the upper fork assembly into the slider (**Figure 105**).

6A. On 1988-1990 XR600R models, perform the following:

    a. Apply Loctite Lock N' Seal to the threads of the bottom bolt prior to installation.

    b. Install a *new* sealing washer onto the bottom bolt. Never reuse an old sealing washer as the fork oil will leak out.

    c. Install the bottom bolt and new sealing washer into the base of the slider.

    d. Using a suitable size socket, tighten the bottom bolt to the torque specification listed in **Table 1**.

6B. On all other models, perform the following:

    a. Apply Loctite Lock N' Seal to the threads of the 6 mm Allen bolt prior to installation.

    b. Make sure the gasket (**Figure 106**) is on the 6 mm Allen bolt.

    c. Install the 6 mm Allen bolt and gasket into the base of the slider.

    d. Tighten the Allen bolt to the torque specification in **Table 1**.

7. Slide the fork slider backup ring (flange side up) down the fork tube and rest it on top of the fork slider bushing.

8. To prevent damage to the inside of the new fork seal during installation, wrap the groove in the top of the fork tube with clear tape. Do not use duct or masking tape.

9. Install the new oil seal as follows:

    a. Coat the new seal with ATF (automatic transmission fluid).

    b. Position the seal with the marking facing upward and slide it down onto the fork tube.

    c. Drive the seal into the slider with Honda special tool Fork Seal Driver Body (part No.

9

07947-KA50100) and Fork Seal Attachment (part No. 07947-KF00100); refer to **Figure 72**.

d. Drive the oil seal in until the groove in the slider can be seen above the top surface of the oil seal.

e. Remove the tape from the top of the fork tube.

NOTE
A piece of 2 in. galvanized pipe can also work as a tool. If both ends are threaded (a close nipple pipe fitting), wrap one end with duct tape to prevent the threads from damaging the interior of the slider.

10. Install the circlip with the sharp side facing up. Make sure the circlip is completely seated in the groove in the fork slider.

11. Install the dust seal into the slider.

12. Refer to **Figure 107** and make sure that all components install in Steps 8-12 are installed in their correct position.

13A. On 1988-1990 XR600R models, remove the upper short fork spring "A," the spring seat and the lower long fork spring "B."

13B. On all other models, remove the spacer, the spring seat and the fork spring.

14. Fill the fork tube with the correct quantity of DEXRON automatic transmission fluid or fork oil. Refer to **Table 3**.

15. Inspect the O-ring seal (**Figure 108**) on the fork cap bolt/air valve assembly; replace if necessary.

16A. On 1988-1990 XR600R models, perform the following:

a. Install the lower long spring "B," the spring seat and the upper short fork spring "A."

b. Install the fork top cap bolt/air valve assembly while pushing down on the spring. Start the bolt slowly, don't cross-thread it.

16B. On all other models, perform the following:

a. Install the fork spring with the tapered end (**Figure 109**) going first.

b. Install the spring seat, the spacer and the fork top cap bolt/air valve assembly (**Figure 110**) while pushing down on the spring. Start the bolt slowly, don't cross-thread it.

17. Install the slider in a vise with soft jaws and tighten the top fork cap bolt/air valve assembly to the torque specification listed in **Table 1**.

18. Repeat for the other fork assemblies.

19. Install the fork assemblies as described in this chapter.

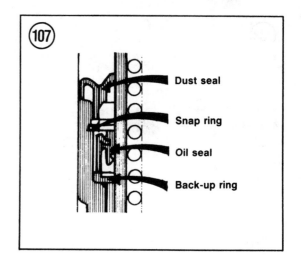

Dust seal

Snap ring

Oil seal

Back-up ring

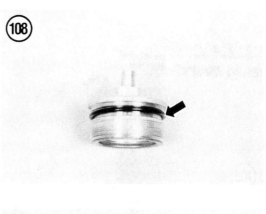

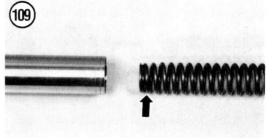

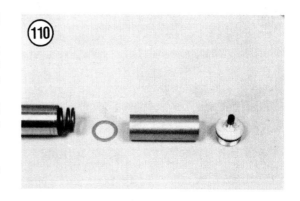

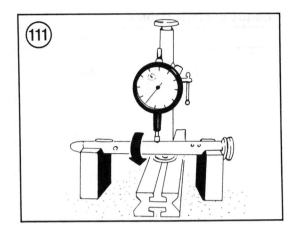

FRONT FORK INSPECTION

1. Thoroughly clean all parts in solvent and dry them. Check the fork tube for signs of wear or scratches.

2. Check the damper rod for straightness. **Figure 111** shows one method. The rod should be replaced if the runout is 0.2 mm (0.008 in.) or greater.

3. Carefully check the damper rod and piston ring(s) for wear or damage. Refer to **Figure 112.**

4. Check the upper fork tube for straightness. If bent or severely scratched, it should be replaced.

5. Check the lower slider for dents or exterior damage that may cause the upper fork tube to hang up during riding. Replace if necessary.

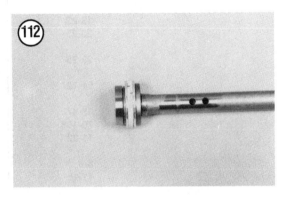

6. Measure the uncompressed length of the fork spring (not rebound spring) as shown in **Figure 113**. If the spring has sagged to the service limit dimensions listed in **Table 4** the spring must be replaced.

7. On models so equipped, inspect the slider and fork tube bushings. If either is scratched or scored they must be replaced. If the Teflon coating is worn off so that the copper base material is showing on approximately 3/4 of the total surface, the bushing must be replaced. Also check for distortion on the check points of the backup ring; replace as necessary. Refer to **Figure 114.**

8. Any parts that are worn or damaged should be replaced. Simply cleaning and reinstalling unserviceable components will not improve performance of the front suspension.

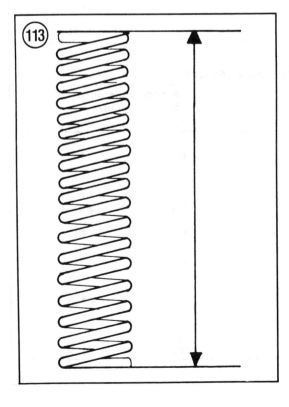

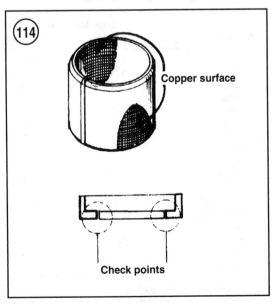

Copper surface

Check points

9

Table 1 FRONT SUSPENSION TORQUE SPECIFICATIONS

Item	N•m	ft.-lb.
Front axle	50-85	36-62
Front axle nut	50-85	36-62
Front axle holder nuts	10-14	7-10
Handlebar holder nuts	18-30	13-22
Upper frok bridge bolts		
XL500S, XR500,		
1981-1982, XR500R	18-25	13-18
XL500R	18-23	13-17
1983-1984 XR500R,		
XL600R	18-30	13-22
XR600R		
1985-1987	25-30	18-22
1988-1990	33	24
Lower fork bridge bolts		
XL500S, XR500,		
1981-1982 XR500R	18-30	13-22
XL500R	30-35	22-25
1983-1984 XR500R,		
XL600R, 1985-1990 XR600R	30-35	22-25
Steering stem nut		
XL500S, XR500	70-100	51-72
XL500R, 1981-1982 XR500R,		
XL500R	80-120	58-87
1983-1984 XR500R, 1985-1990 XR600R	95-140	70-103
Front fork top cap bolt	15-30	11-22
Front fork Allen bolt		
1981-1982 XR500R	8-12	6-9
All other models	15-25	11-18
Front fork bottom bolt		
1988-1990 XR600R	35	25
Brakes disc mounting		
bolts or nuts	14-16	10-12

Table 2 FRONT FORK OIL CAPACITY*

Model	Standard capacity		Standard distance from top of fork	
	cc	fl. oz.	mm	in.
XL500S	190	6.4	–	–
XL500R	379	12.75	163	6.42
XR500	202	6.8	–	–
XR500R				
1981-1982	345	11.7	181	7.1
1983	651	22	141	5.5
1984	651	22		
Maximum	–	–	171	6.73
Minimum	–	–	131	5.16
XL600R	455	15.4	150	5.9
XR600R				
1985-1987	631	21.3		
Maximum	–	–	147	5.8
Minimum	–	–	117	4.6
1988-1990	643	21.8		
Maximum	–	–	130	5.1
Minimum	–	–	100	3.9

*Capacity for each fork leg.

Table 3 FRONT FORK AIR PRESSURE

Model	psi	kg/cm^2
1982 XL500R	0-2.8	0-0.2
XR500R	0-14	0-0.98
All other models	0	0

Table 4 FRONT FORK SPRING FREE LENGTH

Model	Standard		Service length	
	mm	in.	mm	in.
XL500S				
Spring A	481.9	18.97	477.7	18.81
Spring B	NA	NA	68	2.68
XL500R	580.4	22.85	568.8	22.38
XR500	562.4	22.1	552.7	21.8
XL500R				
1981	617.5	24.31	605.1	24
1982	NA	NA	NA	NA
1983-1984	568.9	22.4	563	22.2
XL600R	563.5	22.18	557	21.93
XR600R				
1985-1987	589.8	23.22	583.9	22.99
1988-1990				
Fork spring "A"	63.0	2.480	62.4	2.457
Fork spring "B"	582.8	22.945	577.0	22.717

NA = Information not available from Honda.

9

CHAPTER TEN

REAR SUSPENSION

This chapter includes repair and replacement procedures for the rear wheel and rear suspension components. Tire changing and wheel balancing are covered in Chapter Nine.

Refer to **Table 1** for rear suspension torque specifications. **Tables 1-3** are located at the end of this chapter.

REAR WHEEL (DUAL-SHOCK)

Removal/Installation

1. Place wood blocks under the skid plate to support the bike securely with the rear wheel off the ground.
2. Completely unscrew the rear brake adjusting nut (**Figure 1**) and pull the cable retainer and cable out of the brake arm.
3. Loosen the locknut and axle adjusting bolt (**Figure 2**) on each side.
4. Remove the cotter pin and loosen the rear axle nut (**Figure 3**).
5. Remove the screws (**Figure 4**) securing the drive sprocket cover and remove the cover.
6. Remove the bolts (**Figure 5**) securing the drive sprocket. Remove the sprocket retainer, the sprocket and the drive chain. Let the drive chain rest on the chain slider on the swing arm.

7. Remove the rear axle nut and withdraw the axle from the right-hand side.

8A. On XR500R models, pull the wheel to the rear to disengage the brake panel from the boss on the swing arm.

8B. On XL500S and XR500 models, perform the following:

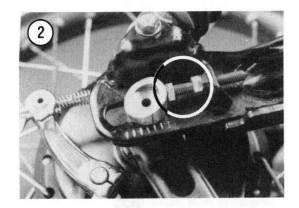

a. Pivot the brake set plate down (**Figure 6**) and slide it off the brake torque link.

b. Remove the brake torque link from the brake panel (**Figure 7**).

c. Let the brake torque link pivot down and rest it on the floor.

9. Remove the drive chain from the wheel sprocket and remove the wheel.

10. Install by reversing these removal steps, noting the following.

11A. On XR500R models, be sure to align the groove in the brake panel onto the boss on the swing arm.

11B. On XL500S and XR500 models, be sure to install the brake set plate onto the brake panel and torque link (**Figure 6**).

10

12. If the drive chain master link was removed, install a new clip on the master link with the closed end facing in the direction of travel (**Figure 8**).

13. Install the rear axle in from the right-hand side.

14. Adjust the drive chain as described in Chapter Three.

15. Tighten the rear axle nut to the torque specification listed in **Table 1**.

16. Install a new cotter pin and bend the ends over completely.

17. After the wheel is installed, completely rotate it and apply the brake several times to make sure it rotates freely and that the brakes work properly.

18. Adjust the rear brake as described in Chapter Three.

REAR WHEEL (PRO-LINK)

Removal/Installation

1. Place wood blocks under the skid plate to support the bike securely with the rear wheel off the ground.

2. Unscrew the brake adjust nut (**Figure 9**) and disconnect it from the brake arm.

3. Remove the rear axle nut (A, **Figure 10**).

4. On models so equipped, loosen the holder nut (**Figure 11**) on the snail adjuster.

5. Rotate the snail adjusters (B, **Figure 10**) toward the front so the wheel can be moved forward for maximum chain slack.

6. Move the wheel forward and position the notch in the snail adjusters onto the stopper pin on the swing arm.

7. Rotate the rear wheel and derail the drive chain from the driven sprocket.

8. On the right-hand side, pull the stopper plate (**Figure 12**) off of the stopper pin on the swing arm.

9. Slide the wheel and axle assembly to the rear and remove it.

10. Install by reversing these removal steps, noting the following.

11. Make sure the groove in the brake panel is properly meshed with the tang on the swing arm. This is necessary for proper brake operation.

12. Adjust the drive chain as described in Chapter Three.

13. Tighten the rear axle nut to the torque specification listed in **Table 1**.

14. After the wheel is installed, completely rotate it and apply the brake several times to make sure it rotates freely and that the brake works properly.

15. Adjust the rear brake as described in Chapter Three.

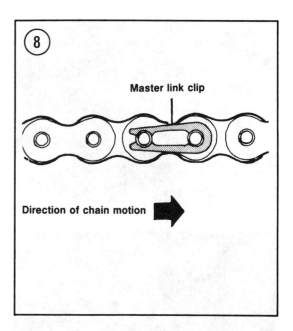

Master link clip

Direction of chain motion

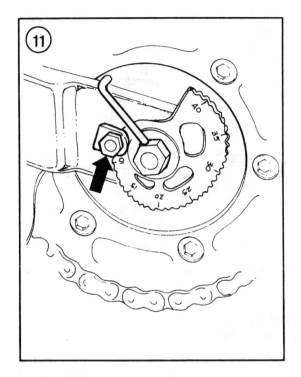

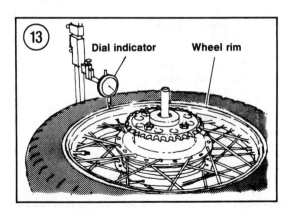

Dial indicator   Wheel rim

REAR WHEEL INSPECTION

Measure the axial and radial runout of the wheel with a dial indicator as shown in **Figure 13**. The maximum axial and radial runout is 2.0 mm (0.08 in.).

Tighten or replace any bent or loose spokes as described under *Spoke Adjustment* in Chapter Nine.

Check axle runout as described in this chapter.

REAR HUB INSPECTION

Inspect each wheel bearing prior to removing it from the wheel hub.

CAUTION
Do not remove the wheel bearings for inspection purposes as they will be damaged during the removal process. Remove wheel bearings only if they are to be replaced.

1A. On XL500S, XL500R, XR500, 1981-1982 XR500R, XL6005R models, perform Steps 1-5 of *Disassembly* in this chapter.

1B. On 1983-1984 XR500R and XR600R models, perform Steps 1-4 of *Disassembly* in this chapter.

2. Turn each bearing by hand. Make sure the bearings turn smoothly.

3. On non-sealed bearings, check the balls for evidence of wear, pitting or excessive heat (bluish tint). Replace the bearings if necessary; always replace as a complete set. When replacing the bearings, be sure to take your old bearings along to ensure a perfect matchup.

NOTE
Fully sealed bearings are available from many bearing speciality shops. Fully sealed bearings provide better protection from dirt and moisture that would otherwise get into the hub.

4. Check the axle for wear and straightness. Use V-blocks and a dial indicator as shown in **Figure 14**. If the runout is 0.2 mm (0.01 in.) or greater, the axle should be replaced.

10

REAR HUB (XL500S, XL500R, XR500, 1981-1982 XR500R, XL600R)

Disassembly

Refer to the following illustrations for this procedure:
  a. **Figure 15**: XL500S and XL500R.
  b. **Figure 16**: XR500 and 1981-1982 XR500R.
  c. **Figure 17**: XL600R.

1. Remove the rear wheel as described in this chapter.
2. Pull the brake assembly straight up and out of the brake drum.
3. Remove the axle spacer (**Figure 18**).
4. To remove the bearing retainer (**Figure 19**), perform the following:

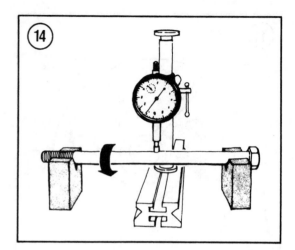

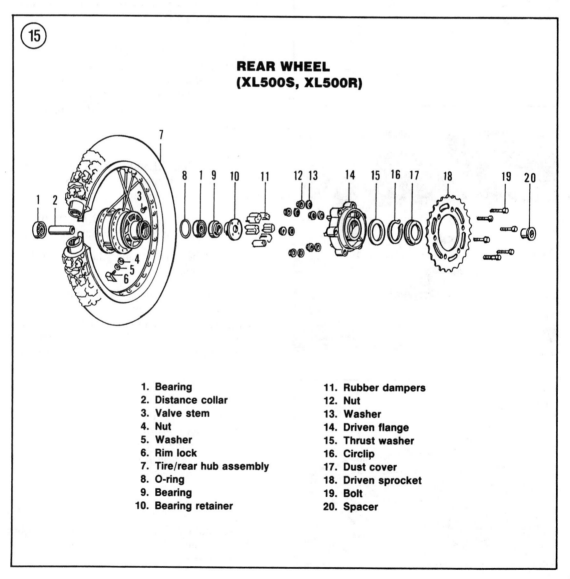

**REAR WHEEL
(XL500S, XL500R)**

1. Bearing
2. Distance collar
3. Valve stem
4. Nut
5. Washer
6. Rim lock
7. Tire/rear hub assembly
8. O-ring
9. Bearing
10. Bearing retainer
11. Rubber dampers
12. Nut
13. Washer
14. Driven flange
15. Thrust washer
16. Circlip
17. Dust cover
18. Driven sprocket
19. Bolt
20. Spacer

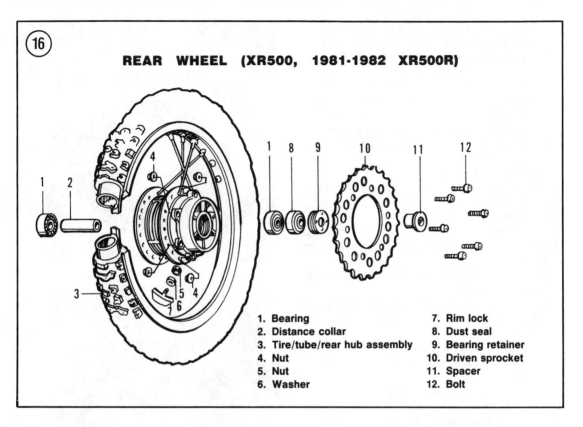

16

REAR WHEEL (XR500, 1981-1982 XR500R)

1. Bearing
2. Distance collar
3. Tire/tube/rear hub assembly
4. Nut
5. Nut
6. Washer
7. Rim lock
8. Dust seal
9. Bearing retainer
10. Driven sprocket
11. Spacer
12. Bolt

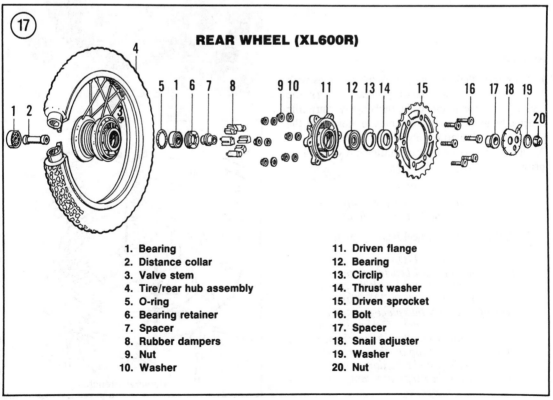

17

REAR WHEEL (XL600R)

1. Bearing
2. Distance collar
3. Valve stem
4. Tire/rear hub assembly
5. O-ring
6. Bearing retainer
7. Spacer
8. Rubber dampers
9. Nut
10. Washer
11. Driven flange
12. Bearing
13. Circlip
14. Thrust washer
15. Driven sprocket
16. Bolt
17. Spacer
18. Snail adjuster
19. Washer
20. Nut

10

a. Install the Honda special tool, Retainer Wrench Body (part No. 07710-0010401) in from the right-hand side (**Figure 20**).

b. Install the Honda special tool, Retainer Wrench A (part No. 07710-0010200) on the left-hand side and onto the bearing retainer.

c. Use a wrench (**Figure 21**) on the Retainer Wrench A and unscrew the bearing retainer.

d. Remove the bearing retainer and the special tools from the rear hub.

5. Remove the dust seal.

6. Before proceeding further, inspect the wheel bearings as described in this chapter. If they must be replaced, proceed as follows.

7. To remove the right- and left-hand bearings (**Figure 22**) and distance collar, perform the following:

a. Insert a soft aluminum or brass drift into one side of the hub.

b. Push the distance collar over to one side and place the drift on the inner race of the lower bearing.

c. Tap the bearing out of the hub with a hammer, working around the perimeter of the inner race.

d. Repeat for the other bearing.

8. Clean the inside and the outside of the hub with solvent. Dry with compressed air.

Assembly

1. On non-sealed bearings, pack the bearings with a good quality wheel bearing grease. Work the grease in between the balls thoroughly; turn the bearing by hand a couple of times to make sure the grease is distributed evenly inside the bearing.

2. Blow any dirt or foreign matter out of the hub prior to installing the bearings.

CAUTION
Install non-sealed bearings with the single sealed side facing outward.

3. Pack the hub with wheel bearing grease.

CAUTION
*Install the standard bearings (they are sealed on one side only) with the sealed side facing out (**Figure 22**). Tap the bearings squarely into place and tap on the outer race only. Use a socket (**Figure 23**) that matches the outer race diameter. Do not tap on the inner race or the bearing might be damaged. Be sure that the bearings are completely seated.*

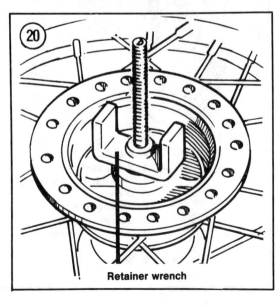

Retainer wrench

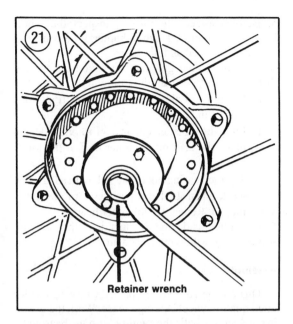

Retainer wrench

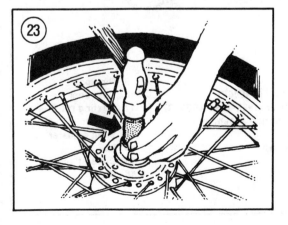

4. Install the right-hand bearing into the hub.

5. Press the distance collar into the hub from the left-hand side.

6. Install the left-hand bearing into the hub.

7. Inspect the bearing retainer threads for damage. Replace if necessary.

8. Apply grease to the lips of the grease seal in the bearing retainer.

9. Screw the bearing retainer into the hub. Use the same tool set-up used in Step 4 of *Disassembly*.

10. After the bearing has been screwed into the hub, lock it in place by staking it with a center punch and hammer (**Figure 24**).

11. Install the rear brake assembly into the hub.

12. Install the rear wheel as described in this chapter.

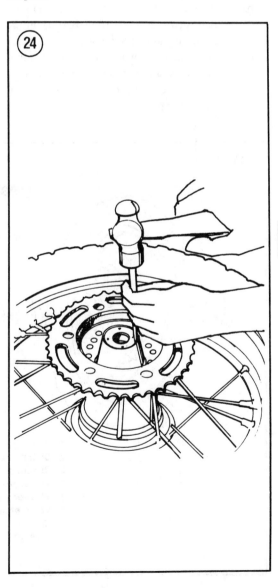

10

REAR HUB
(1983-1984 XR500R, 1985-1990 XR600R)

Disassembly

Refer to **Figure 25** for this procedure.

1. Remove the rear wheel as described in this chapter.
2. Remove the bolts securing the driven sprocket and remove the sprocket.
3. Using 2 wide flat-bladed screwdrivers, carefully pry loose then remove the collar from the left-hand side.
4. To remove the bearing retainer perform the following:
   a. Install the Honda special tool, Retainer Wrench Body (part No. 07910-3000000) in from the right-hand side (**Figure 21**).
   b. Install the Honda special tool, Retainer Wrench A (part No. 07710-0010100) on the left-hand side and onto the bearing retainer.
   c. Use a wrench (**Figure 21**) on the Retainer Wrench A and unscrew the bearing retainer.
   d. Remove the bearing retainer and the special tools from the rear hub.

5. Before proceeding further, inspect the wheel bearings as described in this chapter. If they must be replaced, proceed as follows.
6. To remove the right- and left-hand bearings and distance collar, perform the following:
   a. Insert a soft aluminum or brass drift into one side of the hub.
   b. Push the distance collar over to one side and place the drift on the inner race of the lower bearing.
   c. Tap the bearing out of the hub with a hammer, working around the perimeter of the inner race. d. Repeat for the other bearing.
7. Clean the inside and the outside of the hub with solvent. Dry with compressed air.

Assembly

1. On non-sealed bearings, pack the bearings with a good quality wheel bearing grease. Work the grease in between the balls thoroughly; turn the bearing by hand a couple of times to make sure the grease is distributed evenly inside the bearing.

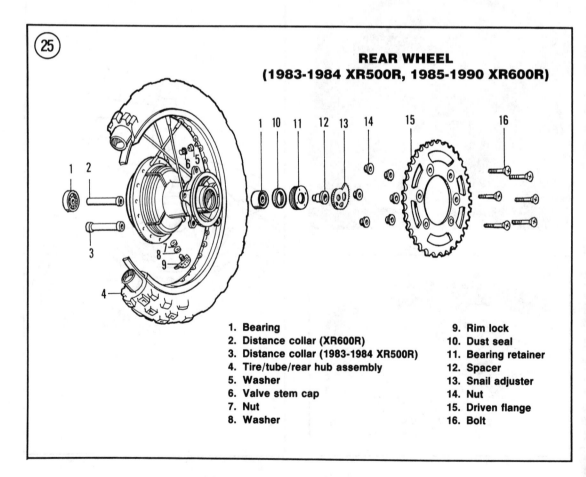

REAR WHEEL
(1983-1984 XR500R, 1985-1990 XR600R)

1. Bearing
2. Distance collar (XR600R)
3. Distance collar (1983-1984 XR500R)
4. Tire/tube/rear hub assembly
5. Washer
6. Valve stem cap
7. Nut
8. Washer
9. Rim lock
10. Dust seal
11. Bearing retainer
12. Spacer
13. Snail adjuster
14. Nut
15. Driven flange
16. Bolt

2. Blow any dirt or foreign matter out of the hub prior to installing the bearings.

CAUTION
Install non-sealed bearings with the single sealed side facing outward.

3. Pack the hub with multipurpose grease.

CAUTION
Install the standard bearings (they are sealed on one side only) with the sealed side facing out (Figure 22). Tap the bearings squarely into place and tap on the outer race only. Use a socket (Figure 23) that matches the outer race diameter. Do not tap on the inner race or the bearing might be damaged. Be sure that the bearings are completely seated.

4. Install the right-hand bearing into the hub.
5A. On XR600R models, position the distance collar with the "LH" mark facing toward the left-hand side. Press the distance collar into the hub from the left-hand side.

5B. On all other models, press the distance collar into the hub from the left-hand side. Either end can go in first as the collar is symmetrical.
6. Install the left-hand bearing into the hub.
7. Inspect the bearing retainer threads for damage. Replace if necessary.
8. Apply grease to the lips of the grease seal in the bearing retainer.
9. Screw the bearing retainer into the hub. Use the same tool set-up used in Step 4 of *Disassembly*.
10. After the bearing has been screwed into the hub, lock it in place by staking it with a center punch and hammer (**Figure 24**).
11. Install the driven sprocket and tighten the bolts to the torque specification listed in **Table 1**.
12. Install the rear wheel as described in this chapter.

FINAL DRIVEN SPROCKET
(XL500S, XL500R, XL600R)

Refer to **Figure 26** for this procedure. Models not listed in this procedure do not have a final driven sprocket assembly with rubber dampers. The sprocket is attached directly to the wheel hub.

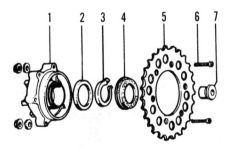

FINAL DRIVEN SPROCKET ASSEMBLY (XL SERIES MODELS)

1. Drive flange
2. Thrust washer
3. Circlip
4. Dust cover
5. Sprocket
6. Bolt
7. Collar

10

Disassembly/Assembly

1. Remove the rear wheel as described in this chapter.

2. Remove the dust cover (A, **Figure 27**).

3. Remove the circlip and thrust washer.

4. Withdraw the final driven sprocket assembly straight up and out of the rear hub.

> *NOTE*
> *If the final driven sprocket assembly is difficult to remove, tap on the backside of the sprocket (from the opposite side of the wheel through the wheel spokes) with a wooden handle of a hammer. Tap evenly around the perimeter of the sprocket until the assembly is free.*

5. If necessary, remove the Allen bolts (B, **Figure 27**) securing the driven sprocket to the driven flange.

6. Install by reversing these removal steps, noting the following.

7. The snap ring and dust cover must be installed as shown in **Figure 28**.

8. If the driven sprocket was removed, tighten the bolts to the torque specification listed in **Table 1**.

Inspection

1. Visually inspect the rubber dampers for signs of damage or deterioration. Replace as a complete set.

2. Inspect the driven flange assembly housing for cracks or damage. Replace if necessary.

3. Inspect the teeth (C, **Figure 27**) of the driven sprocket. If the teeth are visibly worn (**Figure 29**), remove the bolts and replace the sprocket.

4. If the sprocket requires replacement, also inspect the drive chain and the drive sprocket. They also may be worn and need replacing.

SWING ARM (DUAL-SHOCK)

In time, the bushings will wear and have to be replaced. The condition of the bushings can greatly affect handling performance and if worn parts are not replaced they can produce erratic and dangerous handling. Common symptoms are wheel hop, pulling to one side during acceleration and pulling to the other side during braking.

Removal/Installation

1. Remove both side covers.

2. Remove the rear wheel as described in this chapter.

3. Remove the lower mounting bolt securing each shock absorber.

> *NOTE*
> *It is not necessary to remove the shock absorber units, just pivot the units up and out of the way.*

4. Grasp the rear end of the swing arm and try to move it from side to side in a horizontal arc. There should be no noticeable side play. If play is evident, and the pivot bolt is tightened correctly, then the bushings or pivot collar are worn and require replacement.

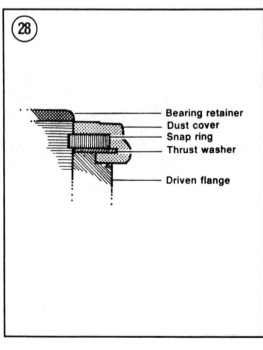

Bearing retainer
Dust cover
Snap ring
Thrust washer

Driven flange

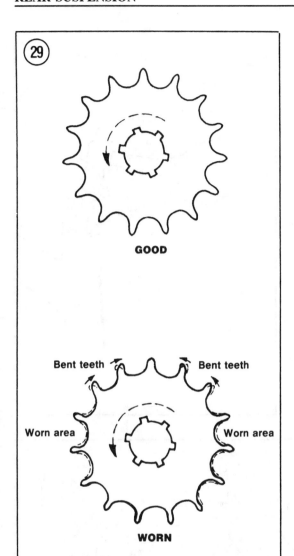

GOOD

Bent teeth   Bent teeth

Worn area   Worn area

WORN

5. Remove the bolts (A, **Figure 30**) securing the drive chain cover and remove the cover.

6. On XL series models, remove the drive chain guide.

7. Remove the self-locking nut (B, **Figure 30**) and withdraw the pivot bolt from the right-hand side.

8. Pull back on the swing arm, free it from the frame and remove it from the frame.

NOTE
Don't lose the dust caps on each side of the pivot points; they may fall off during removal.

9. Install by reversing these removal steps, noting the following.

10. Position the swing arm into the mounting area of the frame. Align the holes in the swing arm with the holes in the frame.

11. Apply a light coat of grease to the pivot bolt prior to installation.

12. Tighten the pivot bolt to the torque specification listed in **Table 1**.

13. Move the swing arm up and down several times to make sure all components are properly seated.

14. Adjust the drive chain and rear brake as described in Chapter Three.

Disassembly/Inspection/Assembly

Refer to **Figure 31** for XL500S models or **Figure 32** for XR500 models for this procedure.

10

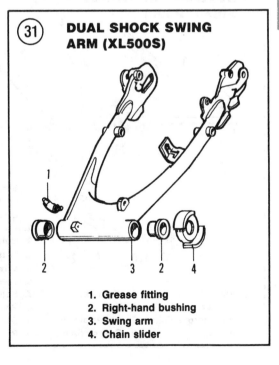

DUAL SHOCK SWING ARM (XL500S)

1. Grease fitting
2. Right-hand bushing
3. Swing arm
4. Chain slider

1. Remove the chain slider from the left-hand side.

2. Remove the dust seal from each side of the swing arm. Discard the dust seals.

3. Withdraw the pivot collar from the swing arm.

4. Secure the swing arm in a vise with soft jaws.

5. Using a suitable size drift or extension and socket tap the bushing out of one end of the swing arm (**Figure 33**).

6. Repeat Step 5 and remove the bushing from the other end.

7. Thoroughly clean out the inside of the swing arm with solvent and dry with compressed air.

8. Measure the outside diameter of the pivot collar at both ends. If the diameter is 21.35 mm (0.841 in.) or less at either end, the collar must be replaced.

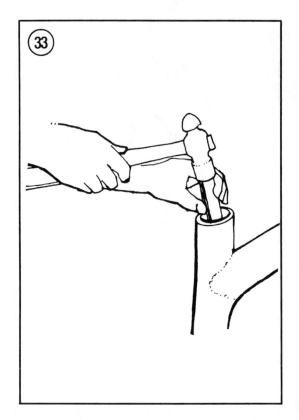

NOTE
Always replace both bushings even though only one may be worn.

9. Measure the inside diameter of each bushing. If the diameter is 21.67 mm (0.853 in.) or greater on either bushing, replace both bushings as a pair.

10. The maximum clearance between the bushings and the collar is 0.32 mm (0.013 in.). Replace one or all parts if this dimension is exceeded.

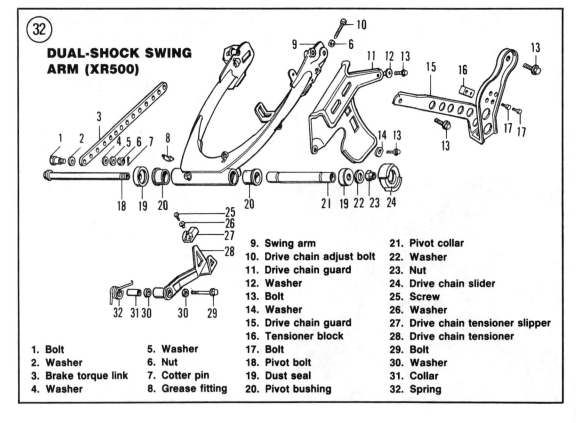

DUAL-SHOCK SWING ARM (XR500)

1. Bolt	17. Bolt
2. Washer	18. Pivot bolt
3. Brake torque link	19. Dust seal
4. Washer	20. Pivot bushing
5. Washer	21. Pivot collar
6. Nut	22. Washer
7. Cotter pin	23. Nut
8. Grease fitting	24. Drive chain slider
9. Swing arm	25. Screw
10. Drive chain adjust bolt	26. Washer
11. Drive chain guard	27. Drive chain tensioner slipper
12. Washer	28. Drive chain tensioner
13. Bolt	29. Bolt
14. Washer	30. Washer
15. Drive chain guard	31. Collar
16. Tensioner block	32. Spring

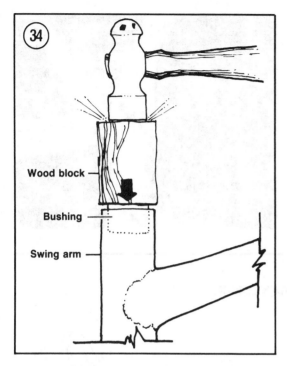

Wood block

Bushing

Swing arm

11. Apply a light coat of oil to the inside and outside surfaces of the new bushing prior to installation.

WARNING
Never reinstall a bushing that has been removed. During the removal procedure it becomes slightly damaged and is no longer true to alignment. If reinstalled, it will damage the pivot collar and create an unsafe riding condition.

12. Tap one bushing into place slowly and squarely into the swing arm with a block of wood (**Figure 34**). Make sure it completely seats and is not cocked in the bore of the swing arm.
13. Repeat Step 12 and install the other bushing.
14. Apply a light coat of molybdenum disulfide grease to the pivot collar and the inside surface of both bushings. Insert the pivot collar into the swing arm.
15. Install new dust seals. Apply a light coat of grease to their lips prior to installation.
16. Inspect the drive chain slider for wear; replace if necessary.

SWING ARM (PRO-LINK)

In time, the needle bearings or pivot collar will wear and will have to be replaced. The condition of the bearings can greatly affect handling performance and if worn parts are not replaced they can produce erratic and dangerous handling. Common symptoms are wheel hop, pulling to one side during acceleration and pulling to the other side during braking.

Removal

1. Place wood blocks under the skid plate to support the bike securely with the rear wheel off the ground.
2. Remove both side covers and the seat.
3. Remove the fuel tank as described in Chapter Seven.
4. Remove the air filter case as described in Chapter Seven.
5. Remove the shock absorber (**Figure 35**) as described in this chapter.
6. Grasp the rear end of the swing arm and try to move it from side to side in a horizontal arc. There should be no noticeable side play. If play is evident and the pivot bolt is tightened correctly, the bearings or pivot collar should be replaced.
7. Remove the bolt and nut (**Figure 36**) securing the shock arm to the shock link.
8. Remove the rear wheel as described in this chapter.

10

9. Remove the self-locking nut (**Figure 37**) and withdraw the pivot bolt from the left-hand side.

10. Pull back on the swing arm, free it from the drive chain and remove the swing arm from the frame.

11. Inspect the swing arm as described in this chapter.

NOTE
Don't lose the dust seals on each side of the pivot points; they will usually fall off when the swing arm is removed.

Installation

1. Position the drive chain over the left-hand side of the swing arm.

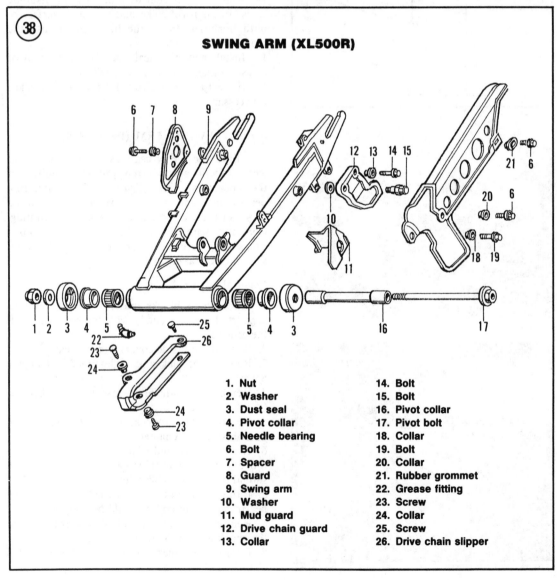

SWING ARM (XL500R)

1. Nut
2. Washer
3. Dust seal
4. Pivot collar
5. Needle bearing
6. Bolt
7. Spacer
8. Guard
9. Swing arm
10. Washer
11. Mud guard
12. Drive chain guard
13. Collar
14. Bolt
15. Bolt
16. Pivot collar
17. Pivot bolt
18. Collar
19. Bolt
20. Collar
21. Rubber grommet
22. Grease fitting
23. Screw
24. Collar
25. Screw
26. Drive chain slipper

2. Position the swing arm into the mounting area of the frame. Align the holes in the swing arm with the holes in the frame. To help align the holes, insert a drift in from the right-hand side.

3. Apply a light coat of molybdenum disulfide grease to the pivot bolt and install the pivot bolt from the left-hand.

4. Install the self-locking nut and tighten to the torque specification listed in **Table 1**.

5. Move the swing arm up and down several times to make sure all components are properly seated.

6. Locate the shock arm into position with the mounting holes in the shock link and install the bolt and nut. Tighten the bolt and nut to the torque specification listed in **Table 1**.

7. Install the rear wheel as described in this chapter.

8. Install the shock absorber as described in this chapter.

9. Install the air filter case as described in Chapter Seven.

10. Install the fuel tank, the seat and side covers.

11. Lubricate the swing arm pivot bolt and shock linkage as described in Chapter Three.

Disassembly/Inspection/Assembly

Refer to the following illustrations for this procedure:

   a. **Figure 38**: XL500R.
   b. **Figure 39**: 1981-1984 XR500R.
   c. **Figure 40**: XR600R.
   d. **Figure 41**: XL600R.

1. Remove the swing arm as described in this chapter.

2. Remove the drive chain guard and mud guard from the swing arm.

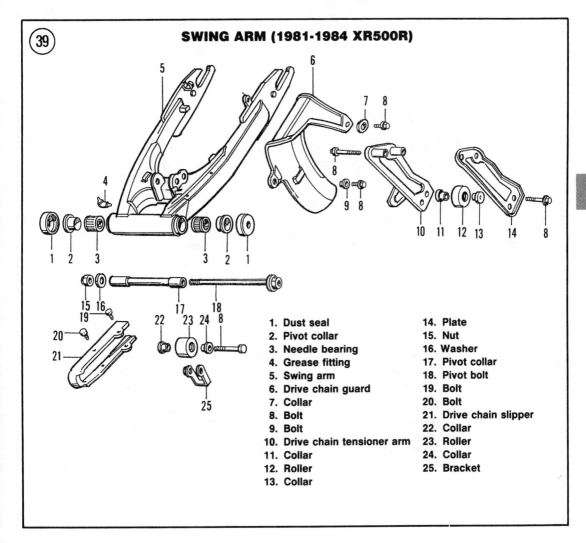

SWING ARM (1981-1984 XR500R)

1. Dust seal	14. Plate
2. Pivot collar	15. Nut
3. Needle bearing	16. Washer
4. Grease fitting	17. Pivot collar
5. Swing arm	18. Pivot bolt
6. Drive chain guard	19. Bolt
7. Collar	20. Bolt
8. Bolt	21. Drive chain slipper
9. Bolt	22. Collar
10. Drive chain tensioner arm	23. Roller
11. Collar	24. Collar
12. Roller	25. Bracket
13. Collar	

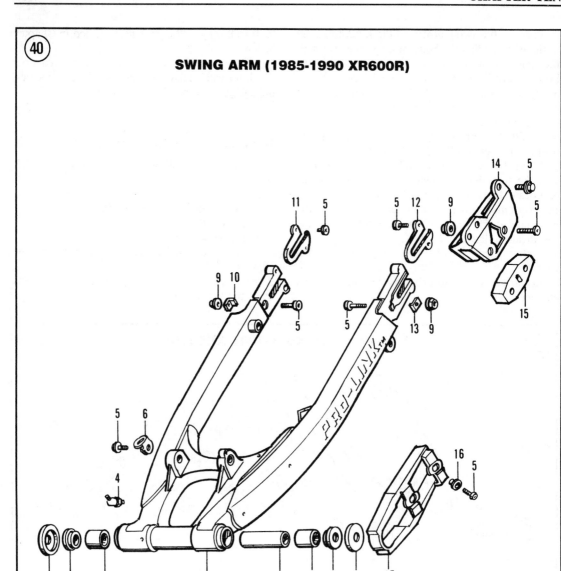

SWING ARM (1985-1990 XR600R)

1. Dust seal
2. Pivot collar
3. Needle bearing
4. Grease fitting
5. Screw
6. Bracket
7. Swing arm
8. Center collar
9. Nut

10. Clip
11. Drive chain adjuster plate
12. Drive chain adjuster plate
13. Clip
14. Drive chain guide
15. Drive chain guide slider
16. Collar
17. Drive chain slider

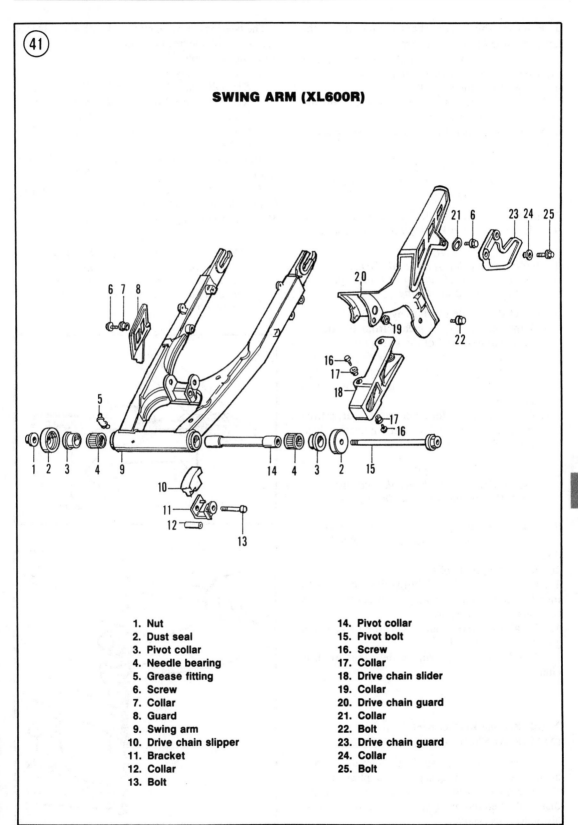

SWING ARM (XL600R)

1. Nut
2. Dust seal
3. Pivot collar
4. Needle bearing
5. Grease fitting
6. Screw
7. Collar
8. Guard
9. Swing arm
10. Drive chain slipper
11. Bracket
12. Collar
13. Bolt
14. Pivot collar
15. Pivot bolt
16. Screw
17. Collar
18. Drive chain slider
19. Collar
20. Drive chain guard
21. Collar
22. Bolt
23. Drive chain guard
24. Collar
25. Bolt

3. Remove the drive chain slider from the left-hand side of the swing arm.

4. If necessary, remove the bolt and nut securing the shock arm to the swing arm. It does not have to be removed for this procedure.

5. Remove both dust seals if they have not already fallen off during the removal sequence.

6. Withdraw the pivot collar, clean in solvent and thoroughly dry.

NOTE
There are no factory specifications for the outside diameter of the pivot collar.

7. Inspect the pivot collar for abnormal wear, scratches or score marks. Replace if necessary.

NOTE
If the pivot collar is replaced, the needle bearing at each end must also be replaced at the same time.

8. Inspect the needle bearings as follows:

a. Wipe off any excess grease from the needle bearing at each end of the swing arm.

b. Turn each bearing with your fingers; make sure they rotate smoothly. The needle bearings wear very slowly and wear is very difficult to measure.

c. Check the rollers for evidence of wear, pitting or color change (bluish tint) indicating heat from lack of lubrication.

NOTE
Always replace both needle bearings even though only one may be worn.

9. Prior to installing the pivot collar, coat the collar and both needle bearings with molybdenum disulfide grease.

10. Insert the pivot collar.

11. Coat the inside of both dust caps with molybdenum disulfide grease and install them onto the ends of the swing arm.

12. Install the drive chain slider, the drive chain guard and mud guard.

13. Install the swing arm as described in this chapter.

Needle Bearing Replacement (XL500R, XL600R)

The swing arm is equipped with a needle bearing at each end. The bearing is pressed in place and has to be removed with force. The bearing will get distorted when removed, so don't remove it unless absolutely necessary.

The bearings must be removed with special tools that are available from a Honda dealer. The special tools are as follows:

a. Bearing remover:
   XL500R—part No. 07936-3710600.
   XL600R—part No. 07936-3710600.

b. Handle: part No. 07936-3710100.

c. Slide hammer weight: part No. 07936-3710200.

1. Remove the swing arm as described in this chapter.

2. Remove the dust seal and bearing assembly from each side of the swing arm.

3. Secure the swing arm in a vise with soft jaws.

NOTE
These special tools grab the inner surface of the bearing and then withdraw it from the swing arm with the use of a tool similar to a body shop slide hammer.

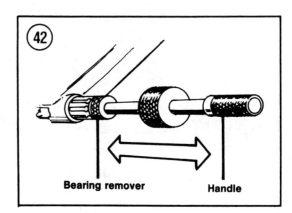

Bearing remover   Handle

4. Either the right- or left-hand bearing race can be removed first.

5. Install the bearing remover through the hole in the bearing and expand the tool behind the bearing.

6. Attach the handle (slide hammer and handle) to the bearing remover.

7. Slide the weight on the hammer back and forth several times until the bearing and bearing collar are withdrawn from the swing arm (**Figure 42**).

8. Remove the bearing and bearing collar from the special tools.

9. Turn the swing arm over in the vise and repeat Steps 5-8 for the other bearing.

10. Thoroughly clean out the inside of the swing arm with solvent and dry with compressed air.

11. Apply a light coat of molybdenum disulfide grease to all parts prior to installation.

NOTE
Either the right- or left-hand bearing race can be installed first.

CAUTION
*For correct alignment, the new needle bearings **should** be pressed into place by a Honda dealer with the use of special tools and a hydraulic press. The following procedure is provided if you choose to perform this operation yourself. If done incorrectly, the needle bearing can be damaged during installation and may not be aligned correctly.*

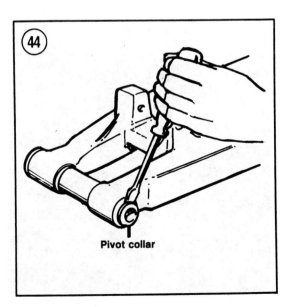

Pivot collar

WARNING
Never reinstall a needle bearing that has been removed. During removal it becomes slightly damaged and is no longer true to alignment. If installed, it will damage the pivot collar and create an unsafe riding condition.

12. Position the new needle bearing with its marks facing up toward the outside.

13. Place the bearing collar onto the needle bearing and place them onto the swing arm.

14. Use the following Honda special tools:
   a. 20 mm Pilot: part No. 07746-0040500.
   b. 32×35 mm Attachment: part No. 07746-0010100.
   c. Driver: part No. 07749-0010000.

15. Place the Honda special tools onto the bearing collar and the needle bearing (**Figure 43**).

16. Using a hammer, slowly and carefully drive the needle bearing and collar into place squarely. Make sure it is properly seated.

17. Remove the special tools.

18. Repeat Steps 13-18 for the other needle bearing.

19. Install a new dust seal on each end of the swing arm.

20. Install the swing arm as described in this chapter.

10

Needle Bearing Replacement (XR600R)

The swing arm is equipped with a needle bearing at each end. The bearing is pressed in place and has to be removed with force. The bearing will get distorted when removed, so don't remove it unless absolutely necessary.

The bearings must be removed and installed with special tools that are available from a Honda dealer.

1. Remove the swing arm as described in this chapter.

2. Remove the dust seal from each side of the swing arm.

3. Secure the swing arm in a vise with soft jaws.

4. Using a wide flat-bladed screwdriver (**Figure 44**) carefully pry the thrust collar from each side of the swing arm.

5. Install the Honda special tool, Needle Bearing Remover (part No. 07946-MA70000) into one end of the swing arm.

6. Using 2 wrenches, turn the bolt heads on the remover and withdraw the needle bearing from the swing arm (**Figure 45**). Discard the needle bearing as it cannot be reused.

7. Turn the swing arm over in the vise and repeat Step 5 and Step 6 for the other side.

8. Thoroughly clean out the inside of the swing arm with solvent and dry with compressed air.

> *NOTE*
> *Either the right- or left-hand bearing race can be installed first.*

9. Apply a light coat of molybdenum disulfide grease to all parts prior to installation.

> *CAUTION*
> *For correct alignment the new needle bearings **should** be pressed into place by a Honda dealer with the use of special tools and a hydraulic press. The following procedure is provided if you choose to perform this operation yourself. If done incorrectly, the needle bearing can be damaged during installation and may not be aligned correctly.*

> *WARNING*
> *Never reinstall a needle bearing that has been removed. During removal it becomes slightly damaged and is no longer true to alignment. If installed, it will damage the pivot collar and create an unsafe riding condition.*

10. Position the new needle bearing with its marks facing up toward the outside.

11. Place the bearing collar onto the needle bearing and place them onto the swing arm.

12. Use the following Honda special tools:
   a. 20 mm Pilot: part No. 07746-0040500.
   b. 32×35 mm Attachment: part No. 07746-0010100.
   c. Driver: part No. 07749-0010000.

13. Place the Honda special tools onto the bearing collar and the needle bearing (**Figure 43**).

14. Using a hammer, slowly and carefully drive the needle bearing and collar into place squarely. Make sure it is properly seated.

15. Remove the special tools.

16. Repeat Steps 10-14 for the other needle bearing.

17. Install a new dust seal on each end of the swing arm.

18. Install the swing arm as described in this chapter.

DUAL SHOCK ABSORBERS

The rear shocks are spring controlled and gas charged. Spring preload can be adjusted on all models. The shock damper unit is sealed and cannot be serviced. Service is limited to removal and replacement of the damper unit and/or spring.

> *WARNING*
> *Do not try to dismantle the gas filled shock damper unit or apply any form of heat to it. If the unit is heated in any way it may result in an extremely dangerous explosion.*

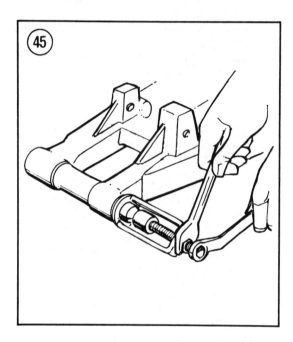

Spring Preload Adjustment

XL500S models

1. Remove the right- and left-hand side covers.

WARNING
The cam ring must be set to the same setting on both sides or it will result in an unsafe riding condition.

2. Use the spanner wrench furnished in the factory tool kit. Rotate the cam ring (**Figure 46**) at the upper end of the shock to one of the 5 positions. *Counterclockwise* to increase spring preload or *clockwise* to decrease spring preload.

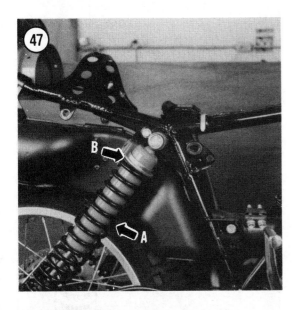

XR500 models

1. Remove the right- and left-hand side covers.
2. Have an assistant pull down on the spring coils (A, **Figure 47**).
3. Make sure the adjust collar (B, **Figure 47**) slides down with the spring.

WARNING
The set ring must be set to the same groove on both sides or it will result in an unsafe riding condition.

4. Remove the set ring and reposition it into a different groove on the damper unit. *Down* to increase spring preload or *up* to decrease spring preload.

NOTE
Make sure the set ring is correctly seated in the groove in the damper unit.

5. After resetting, push down on the rear end of the bike several times to make sure the set rings have been properly seated.

Removal/Installation

Removal and installation of the rear shocks is easier if done separately. The remaining unit will support the rear of the bike and maintain the correct relationship between the top and bottom shock mounts.

1. Place wood blocks under the skid plate to hold the bike securely with the rear wheel off the ground.
2. Remove both side covers and the seat.
3. Adjust both shocks to their softest setting.
4. Remove the upper and lower mounting bolts (**Figure 48**) securing the shock absorber to the frame. Remove the shock.
5. Install by reversing these removal steps, noting the following.
6. Tighten the upper and lower mounting bolts to the torque specifications listed in **Table 1**.
7. Repeat for the other side.

Disassembly/Inspection/Assembly

Refer to **Figure 49** for XL500S or **Figure 50** for XR500 models for this procedure.

WARNING
Without the proper tool, this procedure can be dangerous. The spring can fly loose, causing injury. For a small bench fee, a dealer can do the job for you.

10

REAR SHOCK ABSORBER (XL500S)

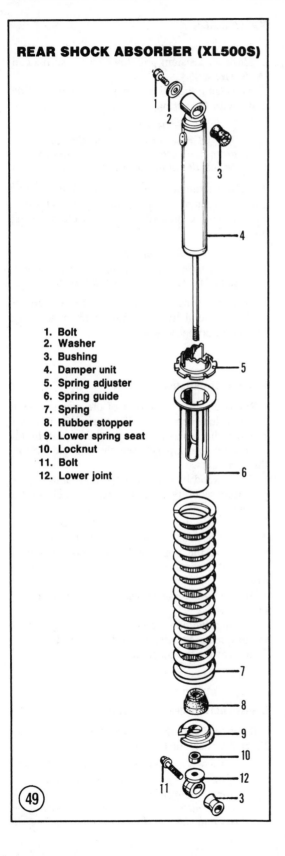

1. Bolt
2. Washer
3. Bushing
4. Damper unit
5. Spring adjuster
6. Spring guide
7. Spring
8. Rubber stopper
9. Lower spring seat
10. Locknut
11. Bolt
12. Lower joint

49

REAR SHOCK ABSORBER (XR500)

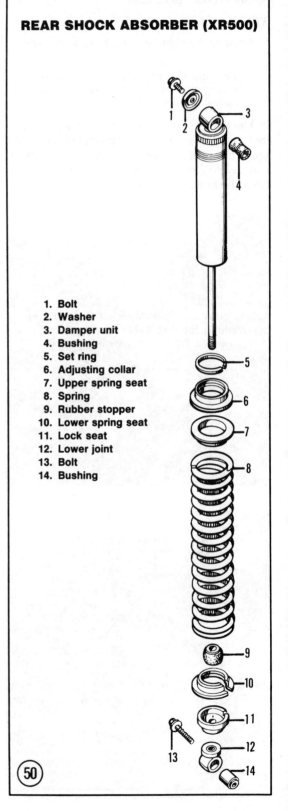

1. Bolt
2. Washer
3. Damper unit
4. Bushing
5. Set ring
6. Adjusting collar
7. Upper spring seat
8. Spring
9. Rubber stopper
10. Lower spring seat
11. Lock seat
12. Lower joint
13. Bolt
14. Bushing

50

1. Install the shock absorber in a compression tool as shown in **Figure 51**. This is a special tool and is available from a Honda dealer. It is the Shock Absorber Compressor Tool (part No. 07959-3290001).

CAUTION
Be sure the compressor tool base is properly adjusted to fit the shock spring seat.

2. Compress the shock spring just enough to gain access to the spring seat. Remove the spring seat.
3. Place the lower joint in a vise with soft jaws and loosen the locknut.
4. Completely unscrew the lower joint. This part may be difficult to break loose as Loctite Lock N' Seal was applied during assembly.
5. Release the spring tension and remove the shock from the compression tool.
6. Remove the spring adjuster, spring and spring guide from the damper unit.
7. Measure the spring free length (**Figure 52**). The spring must be replaced if it has sagged to the service limit listed in **Table 2** or less.

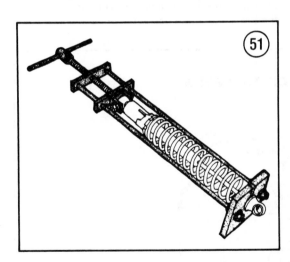

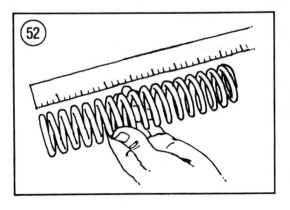

8. Check the damper unit for leakage and make sure the damper rod is straight.

NOTE
The damper unit cannot be rebuilt; it must be replaced as a unit.

9. Inspect the rubber bushings in the upper and lower joints. Replace if necessary.
10. Inspect the rubber stopper. If it is worn or deteriorated, remove the locknut and slide off the rubber stopper. Replace with a new one.
11. Assembly is the reverse of these disassembly steps, noting the following.
12. Apply Loctite Lock 'N Seal to the threads of the damper rod prior to installing the locknut. Temporarily screw the locknut all the way down and tight against the end of the threads.
13. Apply Loctite Lock N' Seal to the threads of the damper rod prior to installing the lower joint. Screw the upper joint on all the way. Secure the lower joint in a vise with soft jaws and tighten the locknut along with the damper rod against the lower joint.

NOTE
After the locknut is tightened completely the locknut must be against the bottom surface of the upper joint and against the end of the threads on the damper rod.

PRO-LINK SUSPENSION SYSTEM

The single shock absorber and linkage of the Pro-Link rear suspension system are attached to the swing arm just aft of the swing arm pivot point and to the lower rear portion of the frame and the shock absorber. All of these items are located forward of the rear wheel.

The shock link and shock arms working together with the matched spring rate and damping rates of the shock absorber combine to achieve a "progressive rising rate" rear suspension. This system provides the rider with the best of two worlds—greater rider comfort and better transfer of power to the ground.

As the rear suspension is moved upward by bumps, the shock absorber is compressed by the movement of the shock arm. As rear suspension travel increases, the portion of the shock link where the shock absorber is attached rises above the swing arm, thus increasing shock absorber travel (compression). This provides a progressive rise rate in which the shock eventually moves at a faster rate than the wheel. At about halfway through the wheel travel the shock begins to move at a faster rate than it did in the beginning.

10

SHOCK ABSORBER (PRO-LINK)

The single shock absorber (**Figure 53**) used in the Pro-Link suspension system has a remote oil/nitrogen reservoir on all models except the XL500R and the XL600R. The remote reservoir allows more rapid oil cooling and helps prevent the oil from frothing. The shock is adjustable for both shock rate and damping action.

Spring Pre-load Adjustment

There must be pre-load on the spring at all times. Never ride the bike without spring pre-load as loss of control may result.

The spring length (pre-load) must be maintained within the dimensions listed in **Table 3**.

1. Place wood block(s) under the skid plate to support the bike securely with the rear wheel off the ground.
2. Remove both side covers.
3. Remove the air filter air box. Cover the exposed carburetor throat(s) with a clean shop cloth to keep out dirt and foreign matter.
4. Measure the existing spring length (**Figure 54**).

NOTE
Special Honda tools are required for the locknut and the adjuster. These are Pin Spanners, part No. 89201-KA4-810 and part No. 89202-KA4810.

5. To adjust, loosen the locknut and turn the adjuster (**Figure 55**) in the desired direction. Tightening the adjuster *increases* spring pre-load and loosening it *decreases* pre-load.
6. One complete turn (360°) of the adjuster moves the spring 1.5 mm (0.006 in.).

NOTE
*Remember the spring length (pre-load) must be maintained within the dimensions listed in **Table 3**.*

7. After the desired spring length is achieved, tighten the locknut securely.
8. Install all items removed.

Rebound Adjustment

Rebound damping can be adjusted to 4 different settings. The adjuster knob is located at the base of the shock absorber (**Figure 56**) between the legs of the lower mounting bracket.

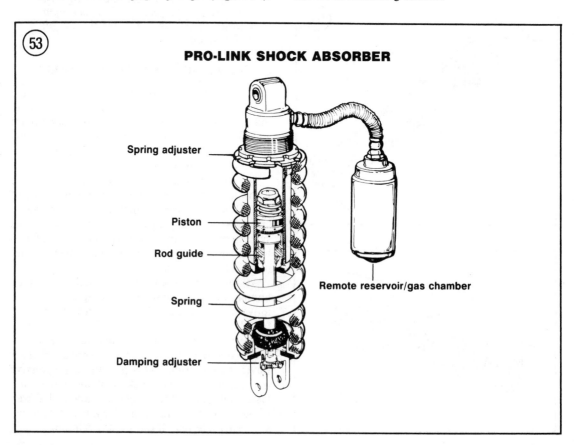

PRO-LINK SHOCK ABSORBER

Spring adjuster

Piston

Rod guide

Spring

Damping adjuster

Remote reservoir/gas chamber

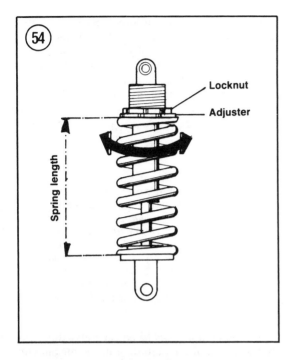

Locknut

Adjuster

Spring length

The rebound setting should be adjusted to personal preference to accommodate rider weight and riding conditions.

Make sure that the adjuster is located into one of the detents and not in between any 2 settings.

Removal

1. Place wood blocks under the engine to support the bike securely with the rear wheel off of the ground.
2. Remove the seat and both side covers.
3. Remove the fuel tank as described in Chapter Seven.
4. Remove the muffler as described in Chapter Seven.
5. On XL500R, remove the bolts securing the drive chain mud guard and remove the mud guard. Cover the exposed carburetor throats with duct tape or a clean shop cloth to keep out dirt and foreign matter.
6. On all models except XL500R models, remove the air filter air box. Cover the exposed carburetor throat(s) with duct tape or a clean shop cloth to keep out dirt and foreign matter.
7. On XL600R models, remove the battery as described in Chapter Three.

> *WARNING*
> *On models so equipped, do not attempt to disconnect the reservoir from the shock absorber body. The compressed nitrogen within the system is pressurized to about 20 kg/cm² (285 psi).*

8. On models so equipped, remove the bolts (A, **Figure 57**) and/or bands securing the remote reservoir to the frame. Don't lose the clamping bands.

10

9. Remove the upper mounting flange bolt (B, **Figure 57**) securing the shock to the frame. Some models have a nut on the bolt, on others the bolt is threaded into the other side of the mounting bracket.

10. Tilt the upper portion of the shock absorber toward the rear.

NOTE
The next step requires the aid of a helper. While raising the rear wheel, make sure the upper portion of the shock absorber clears any mounting brackets on the frame. Do not damage the locknut and adjust nut threads on the upper portion of the shock.

11. Raise the rear wheel as far as possible and have the helper install wood blocks under the rear wheel (**Figure 58**).

12. Remove the shock absorber lower mounting bolt (and nut on models so equipped).

13. On models so equipped, note the location of the remote reservoir hose in relation to the shock absorber and the frame. The shock absorber must be reinstalled in the same direction so the remote reservoir will be on the correct side of the frame.

14. Carefully remove the shock absorber out from the frame.

15. Keep the rear wheel in the raised position for the installation procedure.

Installation

WARNING
*All bolts and nuts used on the Pro-Link suspension must be replaced with parts of the same type. Do **not** use a replacement part of lesser quality or substitute design, as this may affect the performance of the system or result in failure of the part which will lead to loss of control of the bike. Torque values listed must be used during installation to assure proper retention of these parts.*

1. The rear wheel must be in the raised position as shown in **Figure 58**.

2. Apply a light coat of molybdenum disulfide paste grease to the upper mounting bracket on the frame.

3. Position the shock absorber assembly in the frame with the remote reservoir hose on the correct side as noted in Step 13 of *Removal*.

4. Apply a coat of molybdenum disulfide paste grease to the pivot points of the shock link.

5. Position the shock absorber onto the shock link and install the lower mounting bolt (and nut on models so equipped). Do not tighten the bolt at this time.

NOTE
The next step requires the aid of a helper. While lowering the rear wheel, make sure the upper portion of the shock absorber clears any mounting brackets on the frame. Do not damage the locknut and adjust nut threads on the upper portion of the shock. Also on models so equipped, make sure the remote reservoir does not get damaged.

6. Slowly lower the rear wheel and move the upper portion of the shock absorber into alignment with the upper mounting flange on the frame.

7. Install the shock absorber upper mounting bolt.

8. Tighten the upper and lower mounting bolts (and nuts on models equipped) to the torque specification listed in **Table 1**.

9. On models equipped with a remote reservoir, perform the following:

   a. Position the remote reservoir onto the frame.

   b. Attach to the frame with the mounting bands and/or bolts.

   c. Make sure the remote reservoir hose is correctly routed through the frame and is not kinked or touching any moving part of the bike.

10. Remove the wood blocks from under the engine. Push down on the rear of the bike and

make sure the rear suspension is operating properly. Make sure the remote reservoir hose is not rubbing on the shock absorber. Relocate if necessary.

11. On all models except XL500R models, perform the following:

    a. Remove the shop cloth covering the carburetor(s) throat.

    b. Install the air filter air box. Make sure all fittings are tight to avoid an air leak.

12. On XL600R models, install the battery as described in Chapter Three.

13. On XL500R, install the drive chain mud guard and bolts. Tighten the bolts securely.

14. Install the muffler as described in Chapter Seven.
way.

15. Install the fuel tank as described in Chapter Seven.

16. Install the seat and both side covers.

Disassembly/Inspection/Assembly (XR500R, XR600R)

Refer to the following illustrations for this procedure:

    a. **Figure 59**: 1981-1982 XR500R.

    b. **Figure 60**: XR600R.

    c. **Figure 61**: 1983-1984 XR500R.

Service by the home mechanic is limited to removal and installation of the spring. Under no circumstances should you attempt to disconnect the reservoir hose or disassemble the shock absorber unit or reservoir due to the high internal pressure of the nitrogen. If you are satisfied with the existing spring pre-load setting and want to maintain it, measure the spring length (**Figure 62**) prior to disassembly.

1. Hold the shock absorber upside down and secure the upper mounting portion (A, **Figure 63**) of the shock absorber in a vise with soft jaws. Be careful not to kink or damage the remote reservoir hose.

> *NOTE*
> *Special tools are required to loosen the locknut and the adjuster. These are pin spanners, Honda part No. 89201-KA4-810 and 89202-KA4-810.*

2. Use special tools to loosen the locknut and spring adjuster (B, **Figure 63**). Unscrew them to almost the end of the threads. Do not completely unscrew either nut.

3. Remove the shock absorber from the vise.

4. From the lower portion of the shock absorber assembly, compress the spring.

5. On models so equipped, remove the spring seat.

6. Slide out the spring stopper.

7. Slide off the spring.

8. Inspect all components as described in this chapter.

9. Install the spring onto the damper unit.

10. Position the spring seat with the flange side toward the spring and install the spring seat.

11. On models so equipped, install the spring stopper.

12. Hold the shock absorber upside down and secure the upper mounting portion (A, **Figure 63**) of the shock absorber in a vise with soft jaws. Be careful not to kink or damage the remote reservoir hose.

13. Screw the adjuster and locknut on by hand until they contact the spring.

14. Use the special Honda tools used during disassembly and tighten the adjuster to the dimension taken prior to disassembly or to the standard spring length indicated in **Table 2**.

15. Hold onto the adjuster and tighten the locknut to the torque specification listed in **Table 1**.

16. Remove the shock absorber from the vise.

Disassembly/Inspection/Assembly (XL500R, XL600R)

Refer to the following illustrations for this procedure:

    a. **Figure 64**: XL500R.

    b. **Figure 65**: XL600R.

Service by the home mechanic is limited to removal and installation of the spring. Under no circumstances should you attempt to disconnect the reservoir hose or disassemble the shock absorber unit or reservoir due to the high internal pressure of the nitrogen. If you are satisfied with the existing spring pre-load setting and want to maintain it, measure the spring length (**Figure 62**) prior to disassembly.

1. Hold the shock absorber upside down and secure the upper mounting portion of the shock absorber in a vise with soft jaws. Be careful not to kink or damage the remote reservoir hose.

> *NOTE*
> *Special tools are required to loosen the locknut and the adjuster. These are pin spanners, Honda part No. 89201-KA4-810 and 89202-KA4-810.*

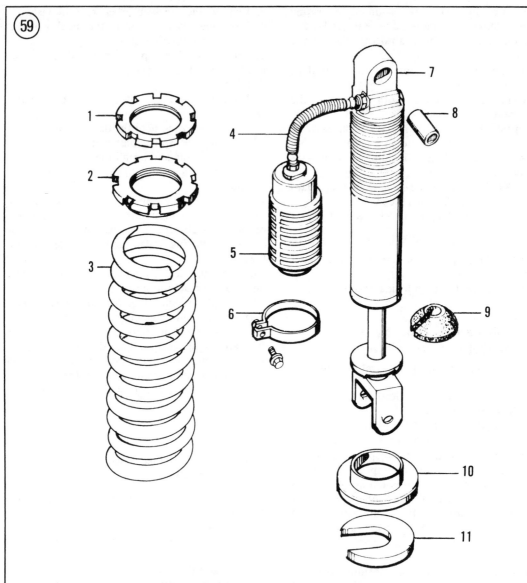

**REAR SHOCK ABSORBER—PRO-LINK
(1981-1982 XR5000R)**

1. Adjuster locknut
2. Spring adjuster
3. Spring
4. Hose
5. Reservoir
6. Reservoir clamp band
7. Damper unit assembly
8. Bushing
9. Rubber stopper
10. Spring seat
11. Spring stopper

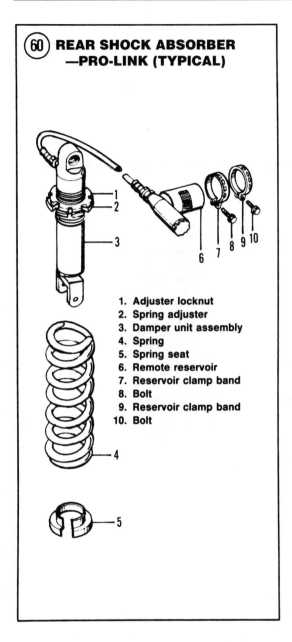

60 REAR SHOCK ABSORBER —PRO-LINK (TYPICAL)

1. Adjuster locknut
2. Spring adjuster
3. Damper unit assembly
4. Spring
5. Spring seat
6. Remote reservoir
7. Reservoir clamp band
8. Bolt
9. Reservoir clamp band
10. Bolt

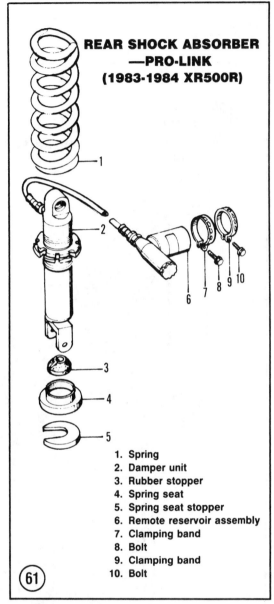

REAR SHOCK ABSORBER —PRO-LINK (1983-1984 XR500R)

1. Spring
2. Damper unit
3. Rubber stopper
4. Spring seat
5. Spring seat stopper
6. Remote reservoir assembly
7. Clamping band
8. Bolt
9. Clamping band
10. Bolt

61

10

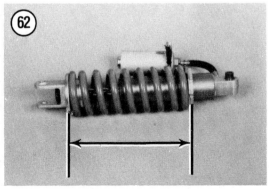

62

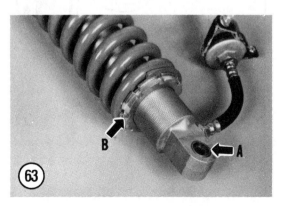

63

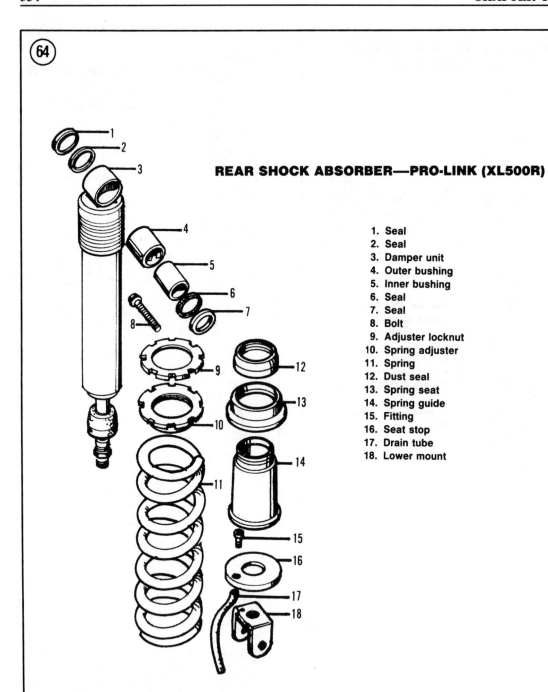

REAR SHOCK ABSORBER—PRO-LINK (XL500R)

1. Seal
2. Seal
3. Damper unit
4. Outer bushing
5. Inner bushing
6. Seal
7. Seal
8. Bolt
9. Adjuster locknut
10. Spring adjuster
11. Spring
12. Dust seal
13. Spring seat
14. Spring guide
15. Fitting
16. Seat stop
17. Drain tube
18. Lower mount

2. Use special tools to loosen the locknut and spring adjuster to almost the end of the threads. Do not completely unscrew either nut at this time.

3. Remove the shock absorber from the vise.

4. Completely unscrew the locknut and adjust nut from the damper unit.

5. Slide the spring off the damper unit.

6A. On XL600R models, no further disassembly is required.

6B. On XL500R models, perform the following:

a. Secure the upper mounting portion of the shock absorber in a vise with soft jaws. Be careful not to kink or damage the remote reservoir hose.

b. Loosen the locknut on the damper rod.

c. Remove the shock absorber from the vise.

d. Completely unscrew the lower mount from the damper rod.

e. Slide off the seat stop, spring guide, spring seat and dust seal.

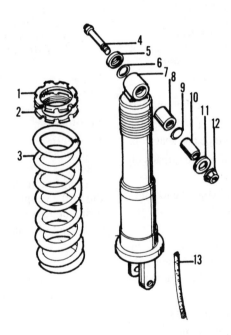

**REAR SHOCK ABSORBER—
PRO-LINK (XL600R)**

1. Adjuster locknut
2. Spring adjuster
3. Spring
4. Bolt
5. Seal
6. O-ring
7. Damper unit
8. Bushing
9. O-ring
10. Bushing
11. Washer
12. Nut
13. Drain tube

10

7. Inspect all components as described in this chapter.

NOTE
The damper unit cannot be rebuilt; it can be recharged with gas, the ATF fluid replaced or the entire unit can be replaced.

WARNING
The shock absorber damper unit and remote reservoir contain nitrogen gas compressed to between 142-284 psi (10-20 kg/cm^2) (pressure varies, depending on year and model). Do not tamper with or attempt to open the damper unit or disconnect the reservoir hose from either unit. Do not place it near an open flame or other extreme heat. Do not dispose of the damper assembly yourself. Take it to a dealer where it can be deactivated and disposed of properly. Never attempt to remove the valve core from the base of the reservoir.

8. On XL500R models, perform the following:

   a. Slide on the dust seal, spring seat (flange side toward the spring), spring guide and seat stop.

   b. Apply Loctite Lock N' Seal to the threads on the damper rod.

   c. Screw on the lower mount. Align the locating pin on the seat stop with the notch on the lower mount.

   d. Secure the upper mounting portion of the shock absorber in a vise with soft jaws. Be careful not to kink or damage the remote reservoir hose.

   e. Tighten the locknut on the damper rod securely.

9. Install the spring onto the damper unit.

10. Screw the adjuster and locknut by hand until they contact the spring.

11. Hold the shock absorber upside down and secure the upper mounting portion of the shock absorber in a vise with soft jaws. Be careful not to kink or damage the remote reservoir hose.

12. Use the special Honda tools used during disassembly and tighten the adjuster to the dimension taken prior to disassembly or to the standard spring length indicated in **Table 3**.

13. Hold onto the adjuster and tighten the locknut securely.

14. Remove the shock absorber from the vise.

Disassembly/Assembly
(1985-1987 XR600R)

Refer to **Figure 66** for this procedure.

Service by the home mechanic is limited to removal and installation of the spring. Under no circumstances should you attempt to disconnect the reservoir hose or disassemble the shock absorber unit or reservoir due to the high internal pressure of the nitrogen. If you are satisfied with the existing spring pre-load setting and want to maintain it, measure the spring length (**Figure 62**) prior to disassembly.

1. Hold the shock absorber upside down and secure the upper mounting portion of the shock absorber in a vise with soft jaws. Be careful not to kink or damage the remote reservoir hose.

NOTE
Special tools are required to loosen the locknut and the adjuster. These are pin spanners, Honda part No. 89201-KA4-BIO and 89202-KA4-810.

2. Use special tools to loosen the locknut and spring adjuster (B, **Figure 63**) to almost the end of the threads. Do not completely unscrew either nut at this time.

3. Remove the shock absorber from the vise.

4. Completely unscrew the locknut and spring adjuster.

5. From the lower portion of the shock absorber, slide off the spring lower seat, the spring and the spring upper seat.

6. Inspect all components as described in this chapter.

NOTE
The damper unit cannot be rebuilt; it can be recharged with gas, the ATF fluid replaced or the entire unit can be replaced.

WARNING
The shock absorber damper unit and remote reservoir contain nitrogen gas compressed to between 142-284 psi (10-20 kg/cm^2) (pressure varies, depending on year and model). Do not tamper with or attempt to open the damper unit or disconnect the reservoir hose from either unit. Do not place it near an open flame or other extreme heat. Do not dispose of the damper assembly yourself. Take it to a dealer where it can be deactivated and disposed of properly. Never attempt to remove the valve core from the base of the reservoir.

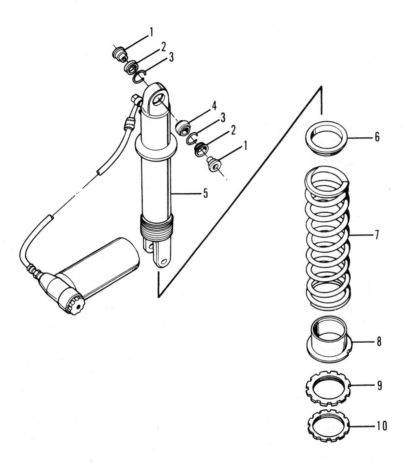

REAR SHOCK ABSORBER—PRO-LINK
(1985-1987 XR600R)

1. Dust seal
2. Collar
3. Clip
4. Bearing
5. Damper/remote
   reservoir assembly
6. Spring upper seat
7. Spring
8. Spring lower seat
9. Spring adjuster
10. Locknut

10

7. Onto the lower end of the damper unit slide on the upper spring seat (flange side toward the spring), the spring and the spring lower seat (flange side toward the spring).

8. Hold the shock absorber upside down and secure the upper mounting portion of the shock absorber in a vise with soft jaws. Be careful not to kink or damage the remote reservoir hose.

9. Screw the adjuster and locknut on by hand until they contact the spring.

10. Use the special Honda tools used during disassembly and tighten the adjuster to the dimension taken prior to disassembly or to the standard spring length indicated in **Table 2**.

11. Hold onto the adjuster and tighten the locknut securely.

12. Remove the shock absorber from the vise.

Disassembly/Assembly
(1988-1990 XR600R)

Refer to **Figure 67** for this procedure.

Service by the home mechanic is limited to removal and installation of the spring. Under no circumstances should you attempt to disconnect the reservoir hose or disassemble the shock absorber unit or reservoir due to the high internal pressure of the nitrogen. If you are satisfied with the existing spring pre-load setting and want to maintain it, measure the spring length (**Figure 62**) prior to disassembly.

1. Hold the shock absorber right side up and secure it in a vise with soft jaws. Be careful not to kink or damage the remote reservoir hose.

NOTE
Special tools are required to loosen the locknut and adjuster. These are pin spanners, Honda part Nos. 89201-K44-810 and 89202-KA4-810.

2. Use the special tools to loosen the locknut and spring adjuster to almost the end of the threads. Do not completely unscrew either nut.

3. Remove the shock absorber from the vise.

4. Turn the shock absorber upside down and remove the spring seat stopper.

5. Slide off the spring seat and the spring.

6. Inspect all components as described in this chapter.

NOTE
The damper unit can be rebuilt; but this should be entrusted to a Honda dealer. It can also be recharged with nitrogen gas and the ATF can also be replaced.

CAUTION
The shock absorber damper unit and remote reservoir contain nitrogen gas compressed to 235 psi (16.5 kg/cm²). Do not tamper with or attempt to open the damper unit or disconnect the reservoir hose from either unit. Do not place it near an open flame or extreme heat. Do not dispose of the damper assembly yourself. Take it to a dealer where it can be deactivated and disposed of properly, Never attempt to remove the valve core from the base of the reservoir.

7. Slide the spring onto the damper unit.

8. Position the spring seat with the flanged side going on last and install the spring seat.

9. Slide the spring seat stopper onto the damper unit and into the spring seat.

10. Screw the adjuster down against the spring until it is hand-tight.

11. Hold the shock absorber right side up and secure it in a vise with soft jaws. Be careful not to kink or damage the remote reservoir hose.

12. Use the special tools used during disassembly and tighten the adjuster to the dimension taken prior to disassembly or to the standard spring length indicated in **Table 2**.

13. Hold onto the adjuster and tighten the locknut securely.

Inspection
(All Models)

1. Measure the free length of the spring (**Figure 67**). Replace the spring if it has sagged to the service limit listed in **Table 2** or less.

2. Check the remote reservoir hose for deterioration or damage. If damaged it replaced by a dealer.

3. Check the damper unit for dents, oil leakage or other damage. Make sure the damper rod is straight.

**REAR SHOCK ABSORBER
(1988-1990 XR600R)**

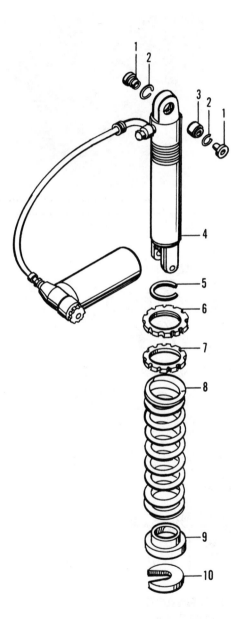

1. Dust seal
2. Washer
3. Bearing
4. Damper/
   remote reservoir assembly
5. Clip
6. Locknut
7. Spring adjuster
8. Spring
9. Spring seat
10. Spring seat stopper

10

NOTE
The damper unit cannot be rebuilt; it can be recharged with gas, the ATF fluid replaced or the entire unit can be replaced.

WARNING
The shock absorber damper unit and remote reservoir contain nitrogen gas compressed to between 142-284 psi (10-17 kg/cm²) (pressure varies, depending on year and model). Do not tamper with or attempt to open the damper unit or disconnect the reservoir hose from either unit. Do not place it near an open flame or other extreme heat. Do not dispose of the damper assembly yourself. Take it to a dealer where it can be deactivated and disposed of properly. Never attempt to remove the valve core from the base of the reservoir.

4A. On XR600R models, the upper bearing must be removed and installed with special tool and hydraulic press. This job should be entrusted to a Honda dealer or machine shop.

4B. On all other models, inspect the upper mounting bushing (**Figure 68**); replace if necessary.

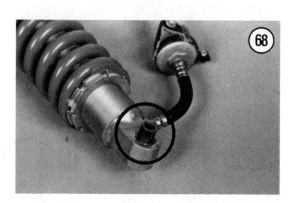

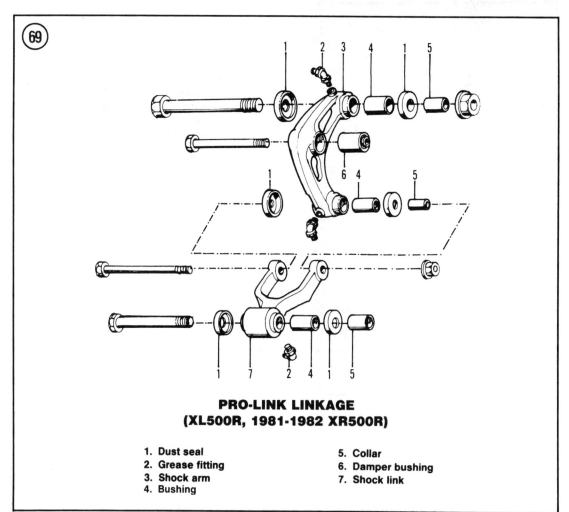

**PRO-LINK LINKAGE
(XL500R, 1981-1982 XR500R)**

1. Dust seal
2. Grease fitting
3. Shock arm
4. Bushing
5. Collar
6. Damper bushing
7. Shock link

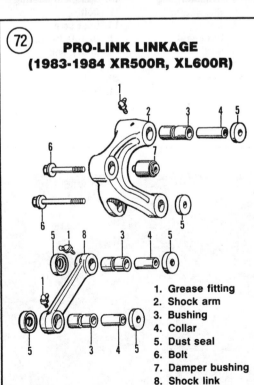

PRO-LINK LINKAGE
(1983-1984 XR500R, XL600R)

1. Grease fitting
2. Shock arm
3. Bushing
4. Collar
5. Dust seal
6. Bolt
7. Damper bushing
8. Shock link

5. Check the remote reservoir hose for deterioration or damage. If damaged have it replaced by a dealer.

6. Check the damper unit for dents, oil leakage or other damage. Make sure the damper rod is straight.

PRO-LINK PIVOT ARM ASSEMBLY
(XL500R, 1981-1982 XR500R)

Removal

Refer to **Figure 69** for this procedure.

1. Remove the shock absorber as described in this chapter.

2. Remove the shock arm pivot bolt (A, **Figure 70**).

3. From the lower portion of the frame, remove the bolt and nut securing the shock link to the frame (B, **Figure 70**).

4. Remove the bolt (**Figure 71**) securing the shock arm to the swing arm.

5. Remove the pivot arm assembly.

6. Inspect all components as described in this chapter.

Installation

1. Apply molybdenum disulfide paste grease to all pivot collars and dust seals prior to installation.

2. Install the shock arm onto the swing arm and install the bolt from the right-hand side (**Figure 71**). Tighten the bolt to the torque specification listed in **Table 1**.

3. Install the shock link onto the frame and install the pivot bolt (B, **Figure 70**) in from the right-hand side. Install the nut and tighten the bolt to the torque specification listed in **Table 1**.

4. Make sure the dust seals are installed on the shock link.

5. Move the shock link up into position with the shock arm and install the shock arm pivot bolt (A, **Figure 70**) from the right-hand side.

6. Install the nut and tighten to the torque specification listed in **Table 1**.

7. Install the shock absorber as described in this chapter.

PRO-LINK PIVOT ARM ASSEMBLY
(1983-1984 XR500R, XL600R, XR600R)

Removal

Refer to the following illustrations for this procedure:

    a. **Figure 72**: 1983-1984 XR500R and XL600R.

    b. **Figure 73**: XR600R.

10

1. Place wood blocks under the skid plate to hold the bike securely with the rear wheel off the ground.

2. Remove the shock absorber as described in this chapter.

3. Remove pivot bolt securing the shock arm to the shock link (A, **Figure 74**).

4. Remove the pivot bolt securing the shock arm to the swing arm (B, **Figure 74**).

5. Remove pivot bolt securing the shock link to the frame (C, **Figure 74**).

NOTE
Don't lose the dust seal on each side of the pivot points; they will usually fall off when the swing arm is removed.

6. Remove the shock link and shock arm from the frame.

7. Inspect all components as described in this chapter.

Installation

1. Apply molybdenum disulfide paste grease to all pivot collars and dust seals prior to installation.

2. Install the shock arm to the swing arm, then install the pivot bolt and nut. Tighten the bolt and nut only finger-tight at this time.

3. Install the shock link onto the frame and install the pivot bolt. Install the nut and tighten to the torque specification listed in **Table 1**.

4. Connect the shock link to the shock arm and install the pivot bolt. Install the nut and tighten to the torque specification listed in **Table 1**.

5. Install the shock absorber as described in this chapter.

6. Move the swing arm up and down several times to make sure all components are properly seated.

Inspection (All Models)

1. Inspect the shock link and shock arm for cracks or damage; replace as necessary.

2. Remove the dust seals at all pivot points and push out the bushings.

3. Clean all parts in solvent and thoroughly dry with compressed air.

4. Inspect the bushings for scratches, abrasion or abnormal wear; replace as necessary.

5. Inspect the dust seals. Replace all of them as a set if any are worn or starting to deteriorate. If the dust seals are in poor condition they will allow dirt to enter into the pivot areas and cause the bushings to wear.

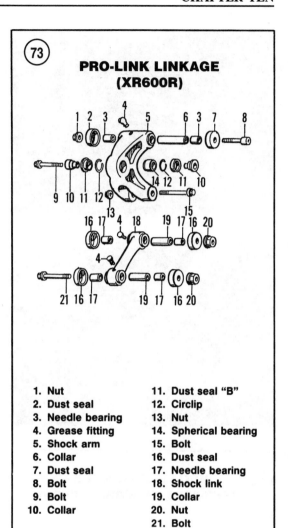

PRO-LINK LINKAGE (XR600R)

1. Nut	11. Dust seal "B"
2. Dust seal	12. Circlip
3. Needle bearing	13. Nut
4. Grease fitting	14. Spherical bearing
5. Shock arm	15. Bolt
6. Collar	16. Dust seal
7. Dust seal	17. Needle bearing
8. Bolt	18. Shock link
9. Bolt	19. Collar
10. Collar	20. Nut
	21. Bolt

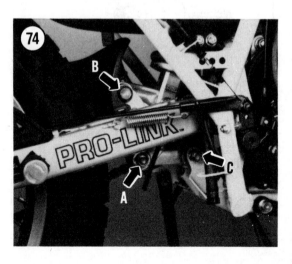

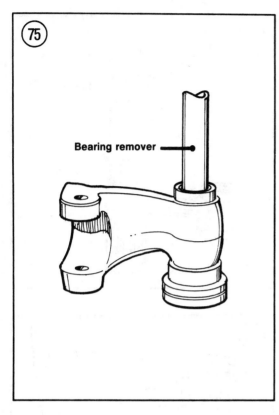

6. Coat all surfaces of the pivot receptacles, the bushings and the inside of the dust seals with molybdenum disulfide paste grease. Insert the bushings into the shock link and the shock arm and install the dust seals.

NOTE
Make sure the dust seal lips seat correctly. If not they will allow dirt and moisture into the bushing areas and cause wear.

PRO-LINK ARM BEARING REPLACEMENT (XR600R)

The bearings in the shock link and shock arm are unique and must be removed and installed with special tools. It is probably less expensive to have this procedure performed by a Honda dealer due to the expense of the special tools. This procedure is present if you choose to perform this task yourself.

Shock Arm Needle Bearing Replacement

1. Support the shock arm so the dust seal sealing surface will not be damaged.

2. Install the Honda special tool (Bearing Remover–part No. 07949-MJ00000) into the shock arm (**Figure 75**) and drive out both needle bearings and distance collar. Discard the needle bearings; never reinstall a needle bearing that has been removed.

3. Thoroughly clean the shock arm in solvent and blow dry with compressed air.

4. Apply a light coat of oil to the inner surface of the shock arm prior to installation of the needle bearings.

5. Support the shock arm so the dust seal sealing surface will not be damaged.

6. Position the needle bearings with their marking facing toward the outside.

7. Correctly position one of the needle bearings onto the shock arm.

8. Install the Honda special tools (Drive–part No. 07749-0010000 and Attachment 32×35 mm–part No. 07746-0010100) into the needle bearing and the shock arm (**Figure 76**).

9. Drive in the needle bearing.

10. Turn the shock arm over and install the distance collar.

11. Repeat Steps 7-9 for the other needle bearing.

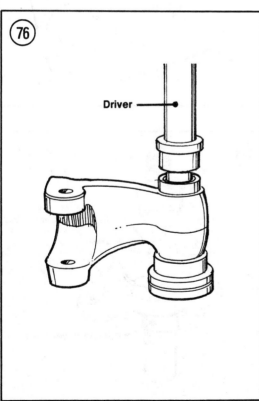

10

Shock Link Needle Bearing Replacement

1. Support the shock link so the dust seal sealing surface will not be damaged.

2. Install the Honda special tool (Bearing Remover—part No. 07946-MJ00000) into the shock link (**Figure 77**) and drive out both needle bearings and distance collar. Discard the needle bearings—never reinstall a needle bearing that has been removed.

3. Repeat Step 2 for the other set of bearings at the other end of the shock link.

4. Thoroughly clean the shock link in solvent and blow dry with compressed air.

5. Apply a light coat of oil to the inner surface of the shock link prior to installation of the needle bearings.

6. Support the shock link so the dust seal sealing surface will not be damaged.

7. Position the needle bearings with their marking facing toward the outside.

8. Correctly position one of the needle bearings onto the shock link.

9. Install the Honda special tools (Driver—part No. 07749-0010000) and (Attachment 32×35 mm—part No. 07746-0010100) into the needle bearing and the shock link (**Figure 78**).

10. Drive in the needle bearing.

11. Turn the shock link over and install the distance collar.

12. Repeat Steps 7-9 for the other needle bearing.

13. Repeat Steps 7-12 for the other set of needle bearings at the other end of the shock link.

Shock Link Spherical Bearing Replacement

This procedure requires a hydraulic press for removal and installation of the spherical bearing.

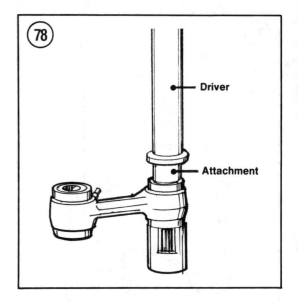

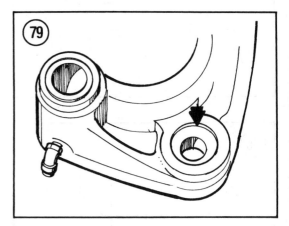

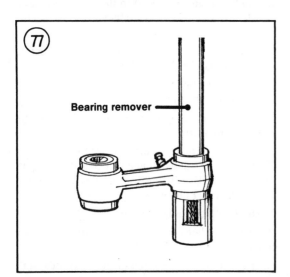

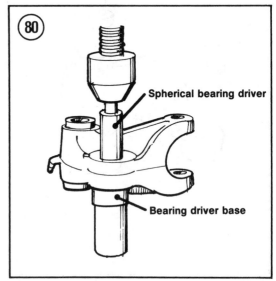

1. Remove the side collars and dust seals.

2. Remove the circlip (**Figure 79**) from each side of the spherical bearing.

3. Support the shock link on the Honda special tool (Bearing Drive Base–part No. 07949-KA30200).

4. Install the Honda special tool (Spherical Bearing Drive–part No. 07946-KA30100) into the shock link (**Figure 80**).

5. Use a hydraulic press and drive the spherical bearing out of the shock link. Discard the spherical bearing; never reinstall a spherical bearing that has been removed.

6. Thoroughly clean the shock link in solvent and blow dry with compressed air.

7. Apply a light coat of oil to the inner surface of the shock link prior to installation of the spherical bearing.

8. Install a circlip into one side of the shock link.

9. Using the same tool set-up used for removal, install the new spherical bearing until it bottoms out against the circlip.

10. Install the other circlip.

11. Apply molybdenum disulfide paste grease to the side collars and dust seals prior to installation.

12. Install the side collars and the dust seals.

Table 1 REAR SUSPENSION TORQUE SPECIFICATIONS

Item	N•m	ft.-lb.
Rear axle nut		
Dual shock models	70-110	51-80
Pro-Link models	80-110	58-80
Final drive sprocket Allen bolts	28-34	20-25
Swing arm pivot bolt and nut		
Dual shock models	70-100	51-72
Pro-Link models		
1981-1982	70-100	51-72
1983-1990	80-100	58-72
Shock absorbers mounting bolts and nuts (Dual-shock models)		
Upper	8-14	6-10
Lower	30-50	22-36
Shock absorber mounting bolts and nuts (Pro-Link models)		
1981-1982 XR500R		
Upper	60-75	43-54
Lower	38-48	27-35
1983-1984 XR500R, XL600R		
Upper and lower	40-50	29-36
XR600R		
Upper	40-50	29-36
Lower	25-35	18-25
Pro-Link Linkage		
1981-1982 XL500R		
Shock arm-to-swing arm pivot bolt	90-120	65-87
Shock link-to-frame pivot bolt	60-75	43-54
Shock arm-to-shock link pivot bolt	60-75	43-54
1983-1984 XR500R, XL600R		
Shock arm-to-swing arm pivot bolt	90-120	65-87
Shock link-to-frame pivot bolt	40-50	29-36
Shock arm-to-shock link pivot bolt	40-50	29-36
XR600R		
Shock arm-to-swing arm pivot bolt	60-80	43-58
Shock link-to-frame pivot bolt		
1985-1987	40-50	29-36
1988-1990	70	51
Shock arm-to-shock link pivot bolt	40-50	29-36

10

Table 2 REAR SHOCK SPRING FREE LENGTH

Model	Service limit	
	mm	in.
XL500S	321.8	12.7
XL500R	248.5	9.78
XR500	332	13.1
XR500R		
1981-1982	219	8.6
1983-1984	264.5	10.41
XL600R	273	10.75
XR600R		
1985-1987	231	9.1
1988-1990	234	9.41

Table 3 PRO-LINK REAR SHOCK SPRING PRE-LOAD STANDARD DIMENSION

Model	mm	in.
XL500R	241	9.49
XR500R		
1981-1982	212.6	8.4
1983-1984	255	10.1
XL600R	265	10.43
XR600R		
1985	225.2	8.87
1986-1990	218.8	8.62

CHAPTER ELEVEN

BRAKES

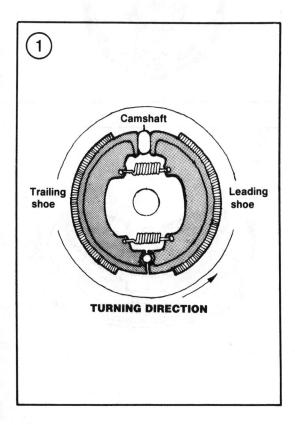

TURNING DIRECTION

Camshaft

Trailing shoe

Leading shoe

The brake system consists of either a drum brake or single disc on the front wheel and a drum brake on the rear.

Table 1 (drum) and **Table 2** (disc) contain brake specifications. **Tables 1-3** are located at the end of this chapter.

DRUM BRAKES

The front brake on the 1981-1982 XR500R is a double leading shoe type. All other models are of the single leading shoe type.

Figure 1 illustrates the major parts of the brake assembly. Activating the brake lever or pedal pulls the lever which in turn rotates the camshaft. This forces the brake shoes out into contact with the brake drum.

Lever and pedal free play must be maintained on both brakes to minimize premature brake wear and maximize braking effectiveness. Refer to Chapter Three for complete adjustment procedures.

Each drum brake is equipped with a wear indicator (**Figure 2**). The indicators should be inspected frequently, especially if riding in competition. When the two arrows align it is time to replace the brake linings.

11

FRONT DRUM BRAKE

Disassembly

1. Remove the front wheel as described in Chapter Nine.

2. Pull the brake assembly straight up and out of the brake drum.

NOTE
Prior to removing the brake shoes from the backing plate, measure them as described under **Inspection** *in this chapter.*

3A. On double leading shoe models, remove the cotter pins and flat washers on both brake camshafts.

3B. On single leading shoe models, remove the cotter pin and flat washer from the brake backing plate (**Figure 3**).

4. Place a clean shop cloth on the brake linings to protect them from oil and grease during removal.

5. Remove the brake shoes from the backing plate. Pull up on the center of each shoe as shown in **Figure 4**.

6. Remove the return springs and separate the brake shoes.

7. Mark the position of the brake arm to the camshaft so it will be installed in the same position.

8. Loosen the clamp bolt on the brake lever.

9. Remove the brake arm, wear indicator, return spring and dust seal.

10. Withdraw the camshaft from the backing plate.

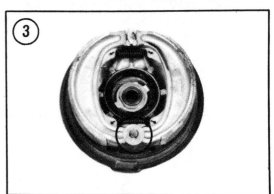

Inspection

1. Thoroughly clean and dry all parts except the brake linings.

2. Check the contact surface of the drum (**Figure 5**) for scoring. If there are grooves deep enough to snag your fingernail, the drum should be turned and new brake shoes fitted. This type of wear can be avoided to a great extent if the brakes are disassembled and thoroughly cleaned after riding in water, mud or deep sand.

3. Clean any oil or grease residue from the brake drum with a clean rag soaked in lacquer thinner. Do not use a solvent that will leave an oil residue.

4. Measure the inside diameter of the brake drum with vernier calipers (**Figure 6**). If the measurement is greater than the service limit listed in **Table 1** the brake drum must be replaced.

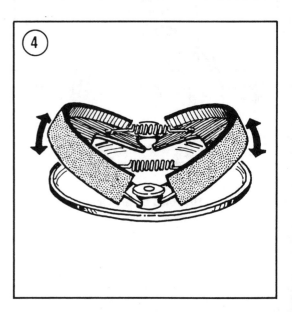

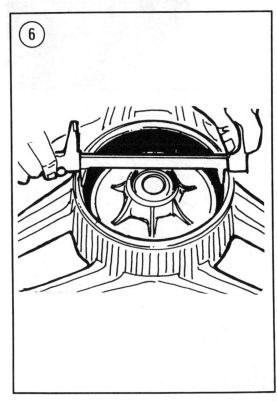

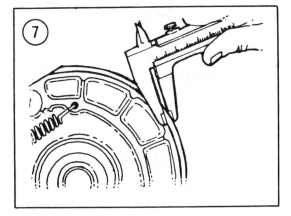

5. If the drum can be turned and still stay within the maximum service limit diameter, the linings will have to be replaced and the new ones arced to conform to the new drum contour.

6. Inspect the linings for embedded foreign material. Dirt can be removed with a stiff wire brush. Check for any traces of oil or grease; if they are contaminated they must be replaced.

7. Measure the brake linings with a vernier caliper (**Figure 7**). They should be replaced if the lining portion is worn to the service limit dimension or less. Refer to specifications listed in **Table 1**.

8. Inspect the cam lobe(s) and pivot pin area of the backing plate for wear or corrosion. Minor roughness can be removed with fine emery cloth.

9. Inspect the bearing surface for the camshaft(s) in the backing plate. If it is worn or damaged the backing plate must be replaced. The camshaft(s) should also be replaced at the same time.

10. Inspect the brake shoe return springs for wear. If they are stretched, they will not fully retract the brake shoes. Replace as necessary.

Assembly

1. Grease the camshaft(s) with a light coat of molybdenum disulfide grease.

2. Install the camshaft(s) into the backing plate from the backside.

3. From the outside of the backing plate install the return spring onto the camshaft.

4. Align the wear indicator to the camshaft as shown in **Figure 8**. Push it onto the camshaft and down all the way to the backing plate.

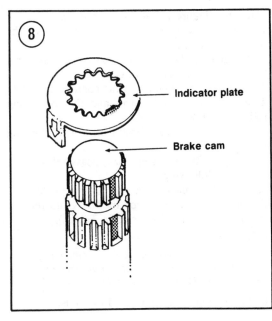

Indicator plate

Brake cam

5. When installing the brake arm(s) onto the camshaft(s), be sure to align the marks on the two parts with the punch marks (**Figure 9**). Tighten the bolt and nut securely.

6. Grease the camshaft(s) and pivot post with a light coat of molybdenum disulfide grease; avoid getting any grease on the brake backing plate where the brake linings may come in contact with it.

> *NOTE*
> *If new linings are being installed, file off the leading edge of each shoe a little so that the brake will not grab when applied (**Figure 10**).*

7. Hold the brake shoes in a "V" formation with the return springs attached and snap them into place on the brake backing plate. Make sure they are firmly seated on it.

8A. On double leading shoe models, install the flat washers and the cotter pins. Bend the ends over completely.

8B. On single leading shoe models, install the flat washer and the cotter pin. Bend the ends over completely.

9. Install the brake panel assembly into the brake drum.

10. Install the front wheel as described in Chapter Nine.

11. Adjust the front brake as described in Chapter Three.

Brake Arm, Brake Cam and Connecting Rod Replacement
(1981-1982 XR500R)

Refer to **Figure 11** for this procedure.

1. Remove the brake assembly and remove the brake shoes as described in this chapter.

2. Remove the bolts and nuts securing brake arm "A" and "B" to each brake camshaft.

3. Loosen both locknuts on the connecting rod.

4. Remove both brake arms and the connecting rod.

5. Unscrew the brake arms from the connecting rod.

6. Assemble by reversing these disassembly steps, noting the following.

7. Align the punch mark on the brake cams and the brake arms and tighten the bolts and nuts to the torque specification listed in **Table 3**.

> *NOTE*
> *After the brake arms and connecting rod have been removed or replaced they have to be adjusted as follows.*

8. Loosen both connecting rod locknuts.

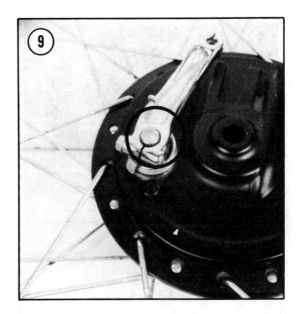

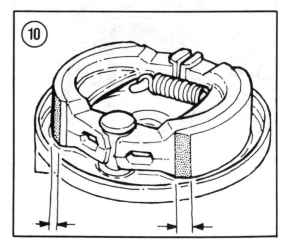

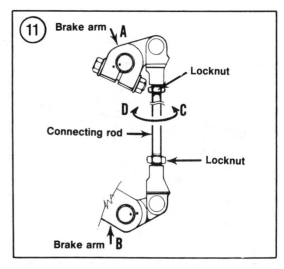

9. Place a clean shop cloth on the brake shoes. With your hands, push both brake shoes together until they are tight against both brake camshafts with no free play.

10. Turn the connecting rod as indicated by direction "C" until there is free play between the connecting rod and the brake arm.

11. Now turn the connecting rod as indicated by direction "D" to just the point where the free play decreases (not any further).

12. Tighten the locknuts securely and recheck the free play. Readjust if necessary.

13. Remove the shop cloth and make sure that both brake cams are parallel to each other. If not, repeat this procedure until correct.

14. Move the brake lever and make sure that both brake arm "A" and "B" start to move at the same time.

FRONT DISC BRAKE

The front disc brake is actuated by hydraulic fluid and is controlled by a hand lever on the master cylinder. As the brake pads wear, the brake fluid level drops in the reservoir and automatically adjusts for wear.

When working on hydraulic brake systems, it is necessary that the work area and all tools be absolutely clean. Any tiny particles of foreign matter and grit in the caliper assembly or the master cylinder can damage the components. Also, sharp tools must not be used inside the caliper or on the piston. If there is any doubt about your ability to correctly and safely carry out major service on the brake components, take the job to a dealer or brake specialist.

FRONT BRAKE PAD REPLACEMENT

There is no recommended mileage interval for changing the friction pads in the disc brake. Pad wear depends greatly on riding habits and conditions. The pads should be checked for wear every 6 months and replaced when the wear indicator reaches the edge of the brake disc. To maintain an even brake pressure on the disc always replace both pads in the caliper at the same time.

CAUTION
Check the pads more frequently when the wear line approaches the disc. On some pads the wear line is very close to the metal backing plate. If pad wear happens to be uneven for some reason

the backing plate may come in contact with the disc and cause damage.

WARNING
When working on the brake system, do not inhale brake dust. It may contain asbestos, which can cause lung injury and cancer. Wear a disposable face mask and wash your hands thoroughly after completing the work.

Replacement –
1988-1990 (XR600R)

Refer to **Figure 12** for this procedure.

1. Remove the pad pin plug at the bottom of the caliper assembly.

2. Remove the pad pin.

3. During the next step the master cylinder brake fluid will rise as the pistons are repositioned in the caliper. Perform the following:

   a. Clean the top of the master cylinder of all dirt and foreign matter.

   b. Remove the screws securing the cover. Remove the cover, plate and diaphragm from the master cylinder.

   c. As the pistons are being repositioned in the caliper, constantly check the reservoir to make sure brake fluid does not overflow. Remove fluid, if necessary, prior to it overflowing.

CAUTION
In Step 4, do not press real hard on the brake disc as the disc may become slightly warped. The brake disc is thin in order to dissipate heat and can be easily damaged by the pressure of a side load.

4. Slowly and carefully push the caliper assembly against the brake disc. This will reposition the pistons in the caliper assembly to allow room for the new thicker brake pads. Constantly check the reservoir to make sure brake fluid does not overflow. Remove fluid, if necessary, prior to it overflowing.

5. Slide the brake pads out from the lower portion of the caliper assembly.

6. Carefully remove any rust or corrosion from the brake disc.

7. Lightly coat the backs of the new pads (not the friction material) with disc brake lubricant.

NOTE
When purchasing new pads, check with the dealer to make sure the friction

11

compound of the new pads is compatible with the disc material. Remove any roughness from the backs of the pads with a fine-cut file; blow them clean with compressed air.

8. Install the new brake pads into the caliper from the lower portion of the caliper.

9. Push the brake pads up and into position and install the pad pin. Tighten the pad pin to the torque specification listed in **Table 3.**

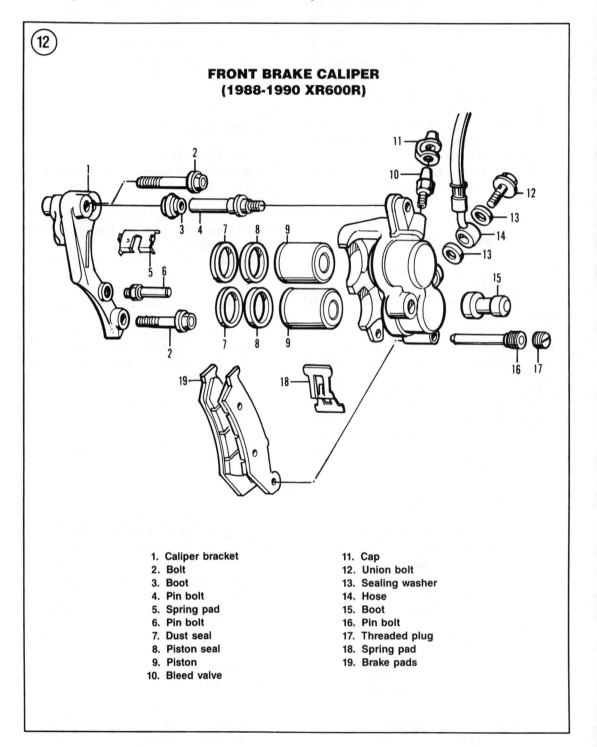

**FRONT BRAKE CALIPER
(1988-1990 XR600R)**

1. Caliper bracket
2. Bolt
3. Boot
4. Pin bolt
5. Spring pad
6. Pin bolt
7. Dust seal
8. Piston seal
9. Piston
10. Bleed valve
11. Cap
12. Union bolt
13. Sealing washer
14. Hose
15. Boot
16. Pin bolt
17. Threaded plug
18. Spring pad
19. Brake pads

10. Install the pad pin plug.

11. Place wood block(s) under the frame so the front wheel is off of the ground. Spin the front wheel and activate the brake lever as many times as it takes to refill the cylinders in the caliper and correctly locate the pads.

> *WARNING*
> *Use brake fluid clearly marked DOT 3 or DOT 4 from a sealed container. Other types may vaporize and cause brake failure. Always use the same brand name; do not intermix as many brands are not compatible. Do not intermix silicone based (DOT 5) brake fluid as it can cause brake component damage leading to brake failure.*

12. Refill the master cylinder reservoir, if necessary, to maintain the correct fluid level as seen through the viewing port on the side. Install the diaphragm, plate and cover. Tighten the screws securely.

> *WARNING*
> *Do not ride the motorcycle until you are sure the brake is operating correctly with full hydraulic advantage. If necessary, bleed the front brake as described in this chapter.*

13. Remove the wood block(s) from under the frame.

14. Bed the brakes in gradually for the first 10 days of riding by using only light pressure as much as possible. Immediate hard application will glaze the friction pads and greatly reduce the effectiveness of the brake.

Replacement—All Other Models

Refer to **Figure 13** for this procedure.

1. Unscrew the threaded plugs covering the pad pins.

2. Loosen both pad pins (A, **Figure 14**) but do not remove them at this time.

3. Remove the bolts (B, **Figure 14**) securing the brake caliper assembly to the front fork.

4. Carefully slide the caliper assembly off the brake disc and remove the caliper assembly.

5. Remove both pad pins.

6. Remove both brake pads and the shim.

7. Clean the pad recess and the end of the pistons with a soft brush. Do not use solvent, a wire brush or any hard tool which would damage the cylinders or pistons.

8. Carefully remove any rust or corrosion from the disc.

9. Lightly coat the end of the pistons and the backs of the new pads (*not* the friction material) with disc brake lubricant.

> *NOTE*
> *When purchasing new pads, check with your dealer to make sure the friction compound of the new pad is compatible with the disc material. Remove any roughness from the backs of the new pads with a fine-cut file; blow them clean with compressed air.*

10. When new pads are installed in the caliper the master cylinder brake fluid level will rise as the caliper pistons are repositioned. Perform the following:

   a. Clean the top of the master cylinder of all dirt and foreign matter.

   b. Remove the screws securing the cover. Remove the cover, plate (models so equipped) and the diaphragm from the master cylinder and slowly push the caliper pistons into the caliper. Constantly check the reservoir to make sure brake fluid does not overflow. Remove fluid, if necessary, prior to it overflowing.

   c. The pistons should move freely. If they don't and there is evidence of them sticking in the cylinder, the caliper should be removed and serviced as described in this chapter.

11. Push the caliper pistons in all the way to allow room for the new pads.

12. Install the anti-rattle spring as shown in A, **Figure 15**.

13. Install the shim into the caliper (B, **Figure 15**).

14. Install the outboard pad (**Figure 16**).

15. Install the inboard pad (**Figure 17**).

16. Push both pads against the anti-rattle spring, then insert one of the pin bolts (**Figure 18**).

17. Install the other pad pin bolt (**Figure 19**).

18. Tighten the pad pin bolts only finger tight at this time.

19. Carefully install the caliper assembly onto the disc being careful not to damage the leading edge of the brake pads.

11

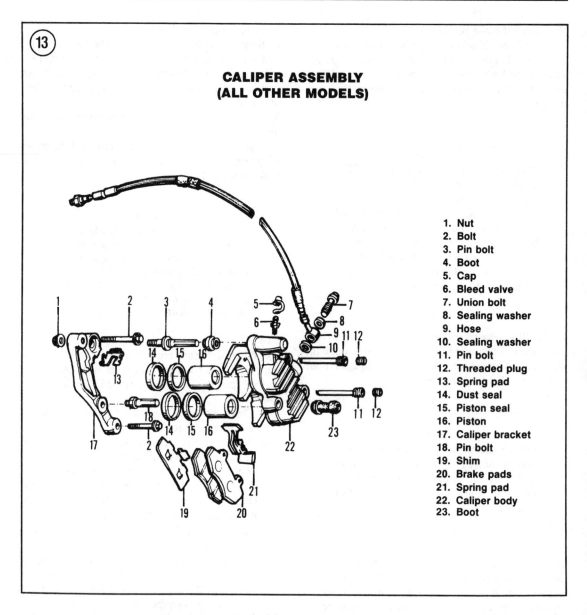

**CALIPER ASSEMBLY
(ALL OTHER MODELS)**

1. Nut
2. Bolt
3. Pin bolt
4. Boot
5. Cap
6. Bleed valve
7. Union bolt
8. Sealing washer
9. Hose
10. Sealing washer
11. Pin bolt
12. Threaded plug
13. Spring pad
14. Dust seal
15. Piston seal
16. Piston
17. Caliper bracket
18. Pin bolt
19. Shim
20. Brake pads
21. Spring pad
22. Caliper body
23. Boot

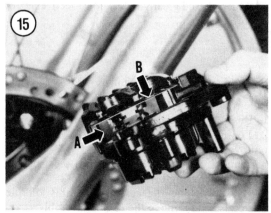

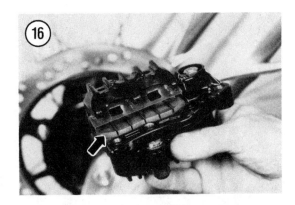

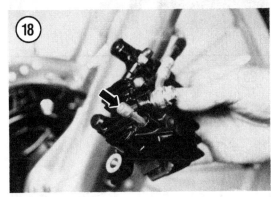

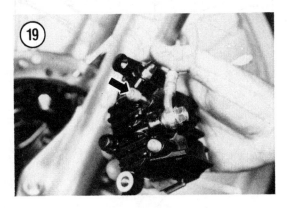

20. Install the bolts securing the brake caliper assembly to the front fork and tighten to the torque specification listed in **Table 3**.

21. Tighten the pad pin bolts to the torque specification listed in **Table 3**.

22. Install the threaded plugs and tighten securely.

23. Place wood block(s) under the skid plate so that the front wheel is off the ground. Spin the front wheel and activate the brake lever as many times as it takes to refill the cylinder in the caliper and correctly locate the pads.

> *WARNING*
> *Use brake fluid clearly marked DOT 3 or DOT 4 from a sealed container. Other types may vaporize and cause brake failure. Always use the same brand name; do not intermix as many brands are not compatible. Do not intermix silicone based (DOT 5) brake fluid as it can cause brake component damage leading to brake system failure.*

24. Refill the master cylinder reservoir, if necessary, to maintain the correct fluid level as seen through the viewing port on the side. Install the diaphragm, plate (models so equipped) and cover. Tighten the screws securely.

> *WARNING*
> *Do not ride the motorcycle until you are sure the brakes are operating correctly with full hydraulic advantage. If necessary, bleed the brake as described in this chapter.*

25. Bed the pads in gradually for the first 10 days of riding by using only light pressure as much as possible. Immediate hard application will glaze the new friction pads and greatly reduce the effectiveness of the brake.

FRONT MASTER CYLINDER

Removal/Installation

1. On XL600R models, remove the rear view mirror from the master cylinder.

> *CAUTION*
> *Cover the fuel tank, front fender and speedometer or instrument cluster with a heavy cloth or plastic tarp to protect them from accidental brake fluid spills. Wash brake fluid off any painted or plated surfaces or plastic parts immediately, as it will destroy the finish. Use soapy water and rinse completely.*

11

2. On XL600R models, pull back the rubber boot on the hand lever.

3A. On XL600R models, remove the bolt (**Figure 20**) and nut securing the hand lever and remove the hand lever.

3B. On all other models, remove the bolt and nut securing the hand lever and remove the knuckle protector and hand lever.

4A. On XR500R models, perform the following:

   a. Unscrew the fitting (A, **Figure 21**) securing the brake hose to the master cylinder.

   b. Remove the brake hose and tie it up, then cover the end to prevent the entry of foreign matter.

4B. On XL600R models, unscrew the fitting securing the brake hose to the metal brake line at the top of the upper fork bridge (A, **Figure 22**).

4C. On XR600R models, unscrew the union bolt securing the brake hose to the master cylinder. Don't lose the sealing washer on each side of the hose fitting.

5. On XL6000R models, disconnect the front brake light switch wires.

6. Remove the clamping bolts (B, **Figure 21**) and clamp securing the master cylinder to the handlebar and remove the master cylinder.

7. Install by reversing these removal steps, noting the following.

8. Install the clamp with the "UP" arrow facing up. Align the face of the clamp with the punch mark on the handlebar. Tighten the upper bolt first, then the lower to the torque specification listed in **Table 3**.

9A. On XR500R models, screw the brake hose fitting (A, **Figure 21**) onto the master cylinder. Tighten the fitting to the torque specifications listed in **Table 3**.

9B. On XL600R models, screw the brake hose onto the metal brake line at the top of the upper fork bridge (A, **Figure 22**). Tighten to the torque specification listed in **Table 3**.

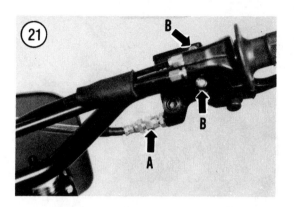

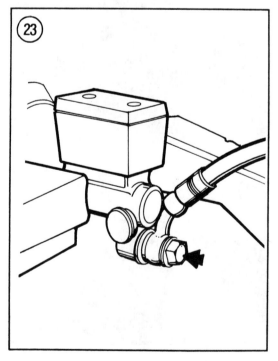

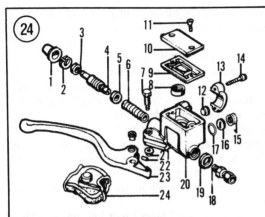

FRONT MASTER CYLINDER (1983-1984 XR500R)

1. Rubber boot	13. Clamp
2. Circlip	14. Bolt
3. Secondary cup	15. Viewing port
4. Piston	16. Window
5. Primary cup	17. O-ring
6. Spring	18. Fitting
7. Bolt	19. Sealing washer
8. Separator	20. Body
9. Diaphagm	21. Nut
10. Cover	22. Pin
11. Screw	23. Hand lever
12. Plug	24. Rubber boot

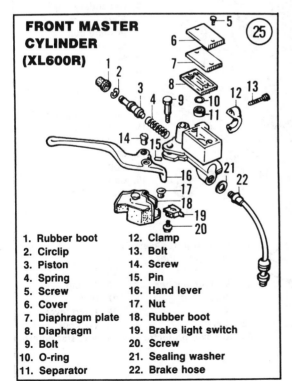

FRONT MASTER CYLINDER (XL600R)

1. Rubber boot	12. Clamp
2. Circlip	13. Bolt
3. Piston	14. Screw
4. Spring	15. Pin
5. Screw	16. Hand lever
6. Cover	17. Nut
7. Diaphragm plate	18. Rubber boot
8. Diaphragm	19. Brake light switch
9. Bolt	20. Screw
10. O-ring	21. Sealing washer
11. Separator	22. Brake hose

9C. On XR600R models, perform the following:
   a. Place a sealing washer on each side of the brake hose fitting and install the union bolt.
   b. Position the brake hose as shown in **Figure 23** and tighten the union bolt to the torque specification listed in **Table 3**.
10. Bleed the brake as described in this chapter.

Disassembly

Refer to the following illustrations for this procedure:
   a. **Figure 24**: 1983-1984: XR500R.
   b. **Figure 25**: XL600R.
   c. **Figure 26**: 1985-1987 XR600R.
   d. **Figure 27**: 1988-1990 XR600R.
1. Remove the master cylinder as described in this chapter.

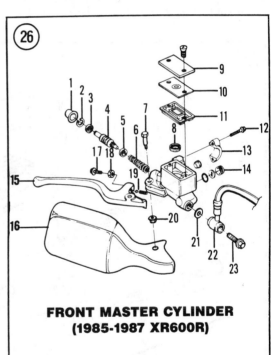

FRONT MASTER CYLINDER (1985-1987 XR600R)

1. Rubber boot	13. Clamp
2. Circlip	14. Viewing port assembly
3. Secondary cup	15. Hand lever
4. Piston	16. Knuckle protector
5. Primary cup	17. Adjuster screw
6. Spring	18. Locknut
7. Bolt	19. Steel ball and spring
8. Separator	20. Nut
9. Cover	21. Sealing washer
10. Plate	22. Brake line
11. Diaphragm	23. Union bolt
12. Screw	

11

2. On XL600R models, unscrew the brake hose and sealing washer from the master cylinder.

3. Remove the screws securing the cover and remove the cover, diaphragm plate (models so equipped) and diaphragm.

4. Pour out the brake fluid and discard it. *Never reuse brake fluid.*

5. Remove the rubber boot from the area where the hand lever actuates the internal piston.

6. Using circlip pliers, remove the internal circlip from the body (**Figure 27**).

7. Remove the piston assembly and the spring (**Figure 28**).

8. On models so equipped, remove the brake light switch if necessary.

Inspection

1. Clean all parts in denatured alcohol or fresh brake fluid. Inspect the cylinder bore and piston contact surfaces for signs of wear and damage. If either part is less than perfect, replace it.

2. Check the end of the piston for wear caused by the hand lever. Replace if worn.

3. Replace the piston assembly if either the primary or secondary cup requires replacement.

4. Inspect the pivot hole in the hand lever. If worn or elongated it must be replaced.

5. Make sure the passages in the bottom of the brake fluid reservoir are clear. Check the reservoir cap and diaphragm for damage and deterioration and replace as necessary.

6. Inspect the threads in the bore for the brake line.

7. Check the hand lever pivot lugs on the master cylinder body for cracks.

8. Measure the cylinder bore (**Figure 29**). Replace the master cylinder if the bore exceeds the specifications given in **Table 2**.

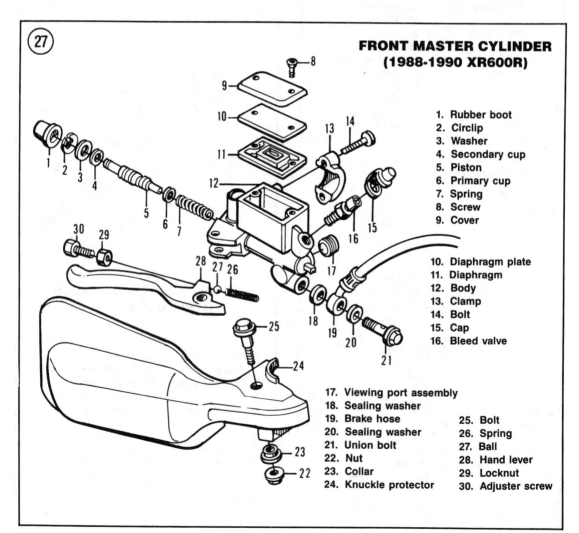

27

FRONT MASTER CYLINDER (1988-1990 XR600R)

1. Rubber boot
2. Circlip
3. Washer
4. Secondary cup
5. Piston
6. Primary cup
7. Spring
8. Screw
9. Cover
10. Diaphragm plate
11. Diaphragm
12. Body
13. Clamp
14. Bolt
15. Cap
16. Bleed valve
17. Viewing port assembly
18. Sealing washer
19. Brake hose
20. Sealing washer
21. Union bolt
22. Nut
23. Collar
24. Knuckle protector
25. Bolt
26. Spring
27. Ball
28. Hand lever
29. Locknut
30. Adjuster screw

9. Measure the outside diameter of the piston as shown in **Figure 30** with a micrometer. Replace the piston assembly if it is less than the specifications given in **Table 2**.

Assembly

1. Soak the new cups in fresh brake fluid for at least 15 minutes to make them pliable. Coat the inside of the cylinder with fresh brake fluid prior to the assembly of parts.

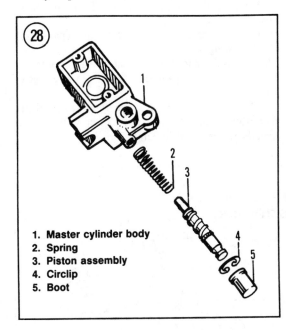

1. **Master cylinder body**
2. **Spring**
3. **Piston assembly**
4. **Circlip**
5. **Boot**

CAUTION
When installing the piston assembly, do not allow the cups to turn inside out as they will be damaged and allow brake fluid leakage within the cylinder bore.

2. Install the spring and piston assembly into the cylinder together. Install the spring with the tapered end facing toward the secondary cup on the piston.
3. Install the circlip and slide in the rubber boot.
4. Install the diaphragm plate (models so equipped) and cover. Do not tighten the cover screws at this time as fluid will have to be added later when the system is bled.
5. On XL600R models, perform the following:
   a. Install a sealing washer onto the brake hose and screw the brake hose onto the master cylinder body.
   b. Tighten the hose to the torque specification listed in **Table 3**.
6. If removed, install the brake light switch.
7. Install the master cylinder as described in this chapter.

FRONT CALIPER

Removal/Installation

Refer to the following illustrations for this procedure:
   a. **Figure 31**: 1988-1990 XR600R.
   b. **Figure 32**: All other models.
It is not necessary to remove the front wheel in order to remove the caliper assembly.

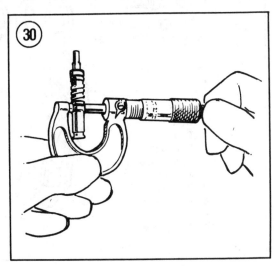

CAUTION
Do not spill any brake fluid on the front fork or front wheel. Wash off any spilled brake fluid immediately, as it will destroy the finish. Use soapy water and rinse completely.

1. On XL600R models, remove the flexible brake line from the clamp on the left-hand fork slider. It is not necessary to disconnect the metal brake line from the flexible brake line at this connection.
2. Clean the top of the master cylinder of all dirt and foreign matter.
3. Loosen the screws securing the master cylinder cover. Pull up and loosen the cover, plate (models so equipped) and the diaphragm. This will allow air to enter the reservoir and allow the brake fluid to drain out more quickly in the next step.
4. Place a container under the brake line at the caliper. Remove the union bolt and sealing washers (A, **Figure 33**) securing the brake hose or metal brake line to the caliper assembly.

5. Remove the brake line and let the brake fluid drain out into the container. Dispose of this brake fluid—never reuse brake fluid. To prevent the entry of moisture and dirt, cap the end of the brake line and tie the loose end up to the forks.
6. Loosen the bolts (B, **Figure 33**) securing the brake caliper assembly to the front fork. Push in on the caliper while loosening the bolts to push the pistons back into the caliper bores.
7. Remove the bolts securing the brake caliper assembly to the front fork.
8. Remove the caliper assembly from the brake disc.
9. Install by reversing these removal steps, noting the following.
10. Carefully install the caliper assembly onto the disc being careful not to damage the leading edge of the brake pads.
11. Install the bolts securing the brake caliper assembly to the front fork and tighten to the torque specifications listed in **Table 3**.

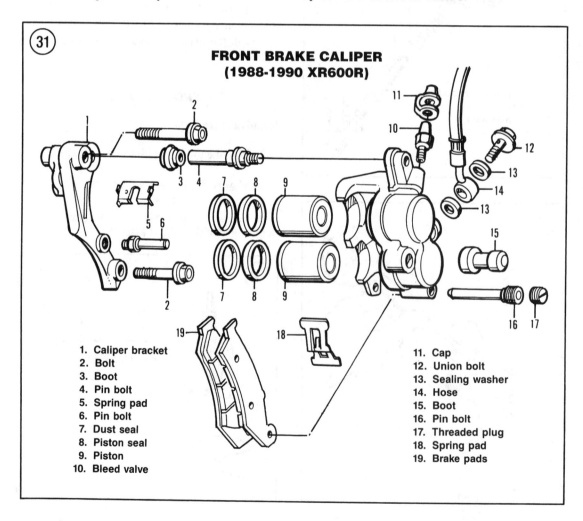

(31)

FRONT BRAKE CALIPER
(1988-1990 XR600R)

1. Caliper bracket
2. Bolt
3. Boot
4. Pin bolt
5. Spring pad
6. Pin bolt
7. Dust seal
8. Piston seal
9. Piston
10. Bleed valve
11. Cap
12. Union bolt
13. Sealing washer
14. Hose
15. Boot
16. Pin bolt
17. Threaded plug
18. Spring pad
19. Brake pads

12. If the caliper bracket was removed from the caliper, lubricate the caliper pin bolts and pin bushing on the caliper bracket with silicone grease.
13. Install the brake hose or brake line with a sealing washer on each side of the fitting, onto the caliper. Install the union bolt and tighten to the torque specifications listed in **Table 3**.

14. Remove the master cylinder top cover, plate (models so equipped) and diaphragm.

WARNING
Use brake fluid clearly marked DOT 3 or DOT 4 from a sealed container. Other types may vaporize and cause brake failure. Always use the same brand name; do not intermix as many brands are not compatible. Do not intermix silicone-based (DOT 5) brake fluid as it can cause brake component damage leading to brake system failure.

15. Place wood blocks under the skid plate to support the bike securely with the front wheel off the ground.
16. Spin the front wheel several times and activate the front brake lever as many times as it takes to refill the cylinders in the caliper and correctly locate the pads.
17. Refill the master cylinder reservoir. Install the diaphragm, plate (models so equipped) and cover. Do not tighten the screws at this time.

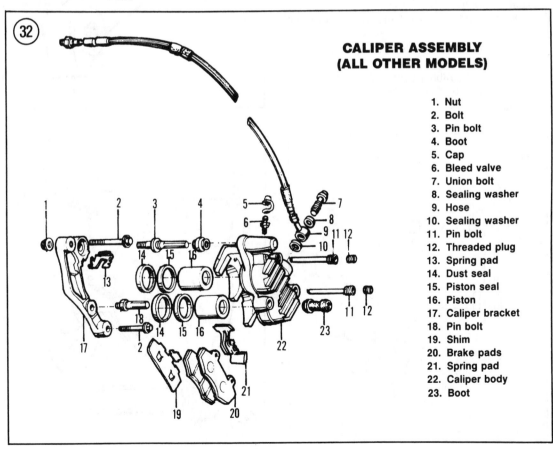

CALIPER ASSEMBLY (ALL OTHER MODELS)

1. Nut
2. Bolt
3. Pin bolt
4. Boot
5. Cap
6. Bleed valve
7. Union bolt
8. Sealing washer
9. Hose
10. Sealing washer
11. Pin bolt
12. Threaded plug
13. Spring pad
14. Dust seal
15. Piston seal
16. Piston
17. Caliper bracket
18. Pin bolt
19. Shim
20. Brake pads
21. Spring pad
22. Caliper body
23. Boot

11

18. Bleed the brake as described in this chapter.

> *WARNING*
> *Do not ride the motorcycle until you*
> *are sure that the brakes are operating*
> *properly.*

Caliper Rebuilding

> *WARNING*
> *When working on the brake system, do*
> ***not*** *inhale brake dust. It may contain*
> *asbestos, which can cause lung injury*
> *and cancer. Wear a disposable face*
> *mask and wash your hands thoroughly*
> *after completing the brake work.*

Refer to the following illustrations for this procedure:

  a. **Figure 31**: 1988-1990 XR600R.
  b. **Figure 32**: All other models.

1. Remove the caliper and brake pads as described in this chapter.

2. Separate the caliper bracket (A, **Figure 34**) from the caliper assembly (B, **Figure 34**).

3A. On 1988-1990 XR600R models, perform the following:

  a. Remove the pad spring (C, **Figure 34**) from the caliper.
  b. Remove the rubber boot (A, **Figure 35**) and pad shim (B, **Figure 35**) from the caliper bracket.

  c. Remove the caliper pivot boot (A, **Figure 36**).

3B. On all other models, perform the following:

  a. Remove the brake pad shim and spring pad (A, **Figure 37**).

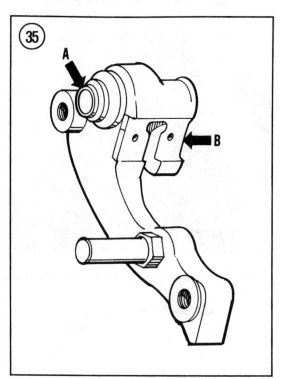

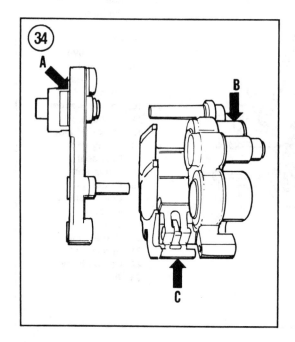

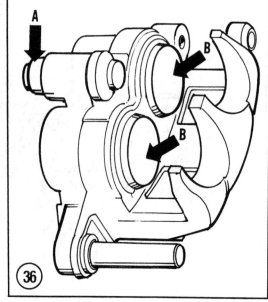

b. Remove the caliper pivot boots (B, **Figure 37**).

4. Place a shop cloth or a piece of soft wood in the area normally occupied by the brake pads.

5. Place the caliper assembly on the workbench with the pistons facing down.

WARNING
In the next step, the pistons may shoot out of the caliper body like bullets. Keep your fingers out of the way.

*Wear shop gloves and apply air pressure gradually. Do **not** use high pressure air or place the air hose nozzle directly against the hydraulic line fitting inlet in the caliper body. Hold the air nozzle away from the inlet allowing some of the air to escape.*

6. Apply air pressure in short spurts to the hydraulic line fitting inlet (**Figure 38**) and force the pistons out. Refer to B, **Figure 36** for 1988-1990 XR600R models or C, **Figure 37** for all other models. If you don't have a compressor, have a dealership or competent service station mechanic perform this for you.

CAUTION
In the following step, do not use a sharp tool to remove the dust and piston seals from the caliper cylinders. Do not damage the cylinder surfaces.

7. Use a piece of plastic or wood and carefully push the dust and piston seals in toward the caliper cylinder and out of their grooves. Refer to **Figure 39** for 1988-1990 XR600R models or **Figure 40** for all other models. Remove the dust and piston seals from both cylinders and discard all seals.

8. Inspect the caliper body and bracket for damage. Replace the caliper body and bracket if necessary.

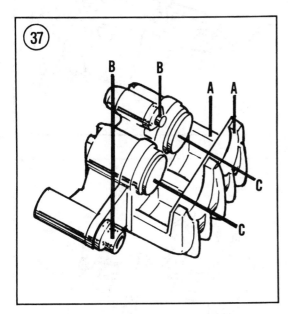

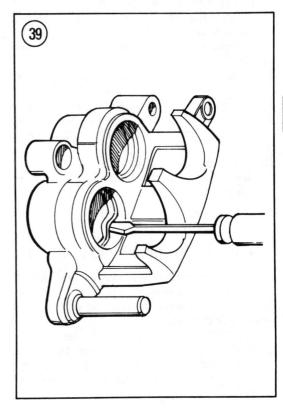

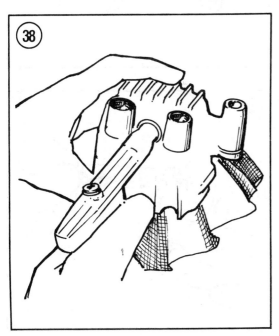

9. Inspect the cylinders and the pistons for scratches, scoring or other damage. Light dirt and rust may be removed with fine emery paper. If rust is severe, replace the caliper body. Replace the caliper body if necessary.

10. If serviceable, clean the caliper body with rubbing alcohol and rinse with clean brake fluid.

11. Measure the inside diameter of both caliper cylinders (**Figure 41**) with an inside micrometer. If worn to the service limit dimension listed in **Table 2**, or greater, replace the caliper assembly.

12. Measure the outside diameter of the pistons (**Figure 42**) with a micrometer. If worn to the service limit dimension listed in **Table 2**, or less, replace the pistons.

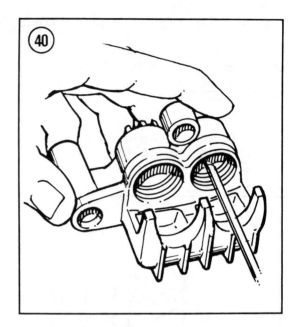

NOTE
Never reuse the old dust seals and piston seals. Very minor damage or age deterioration can make the seals useless.

13. Coat the new dust seals and piston seals with fresh DOT 3 or DOT 4 brake fluid.

14. Carefully install the new dust seals and piston seals in the grooves in each caliper cylinder. Make sure the seals are properly seated in their respective grooves.

15. Coat the pistons and caliper cylinders with fresh DOT 3 or DOT 4 brake fluid.

16. Position the pistons with the insulated ends or dished ends toward the brake pads and install the pistons into the caliper cylinders. Push the pistons in until they bottom out.

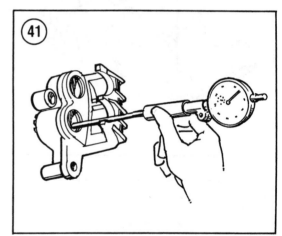

17. Inspect the caliper pin boots. Replace if damaged or starting to deteriorate.

18. Apply silicone grease to the caliper pivot boots and install the boots into the caliper body. Make sure the boots are properly seated in the caliper body grooves.

19. Install the brake pad shim and spring.

20. Install the brake pads and the caliper as described in this chapter.

FRONT BRAKE HOSE REPLACEMENT

There is no factory-recommended replacement interval but it is a good idea to replace all brake hoses every four years or when they show signs of cracking or damage.

The XL600R has a combination of 2 flexible brake hoses and 2 metal brake lines (**Figure 43**).

On all other models there is only one flexible brake hose that runs from the master cylinder to the caliper assembly.

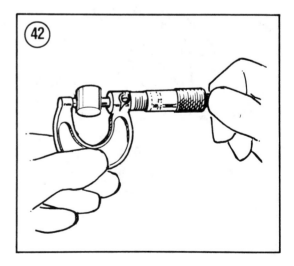

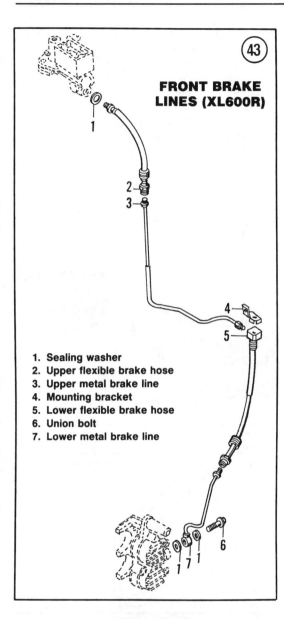

FRONT BRAKE LINES (XL600R)

1. Sealing washer
2. Upper flexible brake hose
3. Upper metal brake line
4. Mounting bracket
5. Lower flexible brake hose
6. Union bolt
7. Lower metal brake line

CAUTION
Cover the front wheel, fender and fuel tank with a heavy cloth or plastic tarp to protect it from accidental spilling of brake fluid. Wash off any brake fluid from any painted or plated surface or plastic parts immediately, as it will destroy the finish. Use soapy water and rinse completely.

1A. On XL600R models, remove the flexible brake line from the clamp (**Figure 44**) on the left-hand fork slider. It is not necessary to disconnect the metal brake line from the flexible brake line at this time.
1B. On all other models, remove brake hose from the clip on the fender stay (**Figure 45**).
2. Clean the top of the master cylinder of all dirt and foreign matter.
3. Loosen the screws securing the master cylinder cover (**Figure 46**). Pull up and loosen the cover, plate (models so equipped) and the diaphragm. This will allow air to enter the reservoir and allow the brake fluid to drain out more quickly in the next step.
4. Place a container under the brake line at the caliper. Remove the union bolt and sealing washers (A, **Figure 33**) securing the brake hose or metal brake line to the caliper assembly.

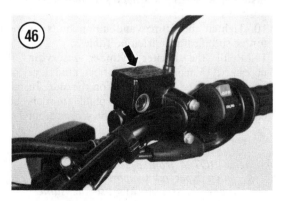

11

5. Remove the brake hose or line and let the brake fluid drain out into the container. Dispose of this brake fluid—never reuse brake fluid. To prevent the entry of moisture and dirt, cap the end of the brake line and tie the loose end up to the forks.

> **WARNING**
> *Dispose of this brake fluid—never reuse brake fluid. Contaminated brake fluid can cause brake failure.*

6A. On 1983-1984 XR500R models, perform the following:
   a. Unscrew the fitting (**Figure 47**) securing the brake hose to the master cylinder.
   b. Remove the brake hose and tie it up, then cover the end to prevent the entry of foreign matter.
6B. On XL600R models, unscrew the fitting securing the brake hose to the metal brake line at the top of the upper fork bridge (A, **Figure 22**).
6C. On XR600R models, unscrew the union bolt (**Figure 48**) and sealing washers securing the brake hose to the master cylinder. Remove the brake hose. Tie the brake hose up and cover the end to prevent the entry of foreign matter.
7. On XL600R models, to replace the upper brake hose, unscrew the hose from the master cylinder. Remove the brake hose and sealing washer.
8. On XL600R models, to replace the lower brake hose, perform the following:
   a. Unscrew the lower hose from the upper metal brake line (A, **Figure 22**).
   b. Unscrew the mounting bracket (B, **Figure 22**) securing the upper portion of the lower hose at the lower fork bridge.
   c. Unscrew the lower portion of the lower hose from the lower metal brake line (**Figure 49**) and remove the brake hose.
9. Install a new hose, sealing washers and union bolts in the reverse order of removal. Be sure to install new sealing washers and in the correct positions.
10. Tighten the fittings and union bolts to the torque specifications listed in **Table 3**.
11. Refill the master cylinder reservoir, if necessary, to maintain the correct fluid level as seen through the viewing port on the side. Install the diaphragm, diaphragm plate (models so equipped) and cover. Tighten the screws securely.

> **WARNING**
> *Use brake fluid clearly marked DOT 3 or DOT 4 from a sealed container. Other types may vaporize and cause brake failure. Always use the same brand name; do not intermix as many brands are not compatible. Do not intermix silicone-based (DOT 5) brake fluid as it can cause brake component damage leading to brake system failure.*

> **WARNING**
> *Do not ride the motorcycle until you are sure that the brakes are operating properly.*

12. Bleed the brake as described in this chapter.

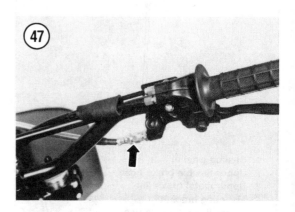

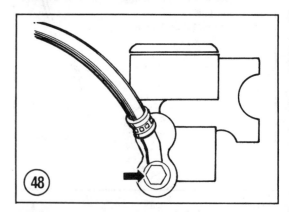

FRONT BRAKE DISC

Removal/Installation

1. Remove the front wheel as described in Chapter Nine.

> *NOTE*
> *Place a piece of wood or vinyl tube in the caliper in place of the disc. This way, if the brake lever is inadvertently squeezed the pistons will not be forced out of the cylinder. If this does happen, the caliper might have to be disassembled to reseat the pistons and the system will have to be bled.*

> *CAUTION*
> *Do not set the wheel down on the disc surface, as it may get scratched or warped. Set the wheel on 2 blocks of wood.*

2. Remove the nuts or bolts (**Figure 50**) securing the brake disc to the hub and remove the disc.

3. Install by reversing these removal steps, noting the following.
4. Tighten the disc mounting nuts or bolts to the torque specifications listed in **Table 3**.

Inspection

It is not necessary to remove the disc from the wheel to inspect it. Small marks on the disc are not important, but radial scratches deep enough to snag a fingernail reduce braking effectiveness and increase brake pad wear. If these grooves are found, the disc should be replaced.

1. Measure the thickness of the disc at several locations around the disc with a micrometer or vernier caliper (**Figure 51**). The disc must be replaced if the thickness in any area is less than that specified in **Table 2**.
2. Make sure the disc mounting nuts or bolts are tight prior to running this check. Check the disc runout with a dial indicator as shown in **Figure 52**.
3. Slowly rotate the wheel and watch the dial indicator. If the runout exceeds that listed in **Table 2** the disc must be replaced.
4. Clean the disc of any rust or corrosion and wipe clean with lacquer thinner. Never use an oil-based solvent that may leave an oil residue on the disc.

BLEEDING THE SYSTEM

This procedure is not necessary unless the brake feels spongy, there is a leak in the system, a component has been replaced or the brake fluid has been drained and replaced.

On 1988-1990 XR600R models, a bleed valve has been added to the master cylinder reservoir. This helps to remove any trapped air at the beginning of the system instead of forcing the air bubbles down to the caliper assembly.

Brake Bleeder Process

This procedure uses a brake bleeder that is available from motorcycle or automotive supply stores or from mail order outlets.

1. On 1988-1990 XR600R models, perform the following:
   a. Remove the dust cap from the bleed valve on the master cylinder reservoir.
   b. Connect the brake bleeder to the bleed valve on the master cylinder reservoir.
   c. Perform Steps 2-11 and bleed the air from the master cylinder.

11

d. After the master cylinder has been bled, perform Steps 2-11 and bleed the caliper assembly.

2. Remove the dust cap (**Figure 53**) from the bleed valve on the caliper assembly. Refer to the following:
3. Connect the brake bleeder to the bleed valve on the caliper assembly (**Figure 54**).

CAUTION
Cover the front fender and front wheel with a heavy cloth or plastic tarp to protect it from the accidental spilling of brake fluid. Wash any brake fluid off of any plastic, painted or plated surface immediately; as it will destroy the finish. Use soapy water and rinse completely.

4. Clean the top of the master cylinder of all dirt and foreign matter.
5. Remove the screws securing the reservoir cover and remove the reservoir cover, plate (models so equipped) and diaphragm.
6. Fill the reservoir almost to the top lip; insert the diaphragm, plate (models so equipped) and the cover loosely. Leave the cover in place during this procedure to prevent the entry of dirt.

WARNING
Use brake fluid from a sealed container marked DOT 3 or DOT 4 only (specified for disc brakes). Other types may vaporize and cause brake failure. Do not intermix different brands or types as they may not be compatible. Do not intermix a silicone based (DOT 5) brake fluid as it can cause brake component damage leading to brake system failure.

7. Open the bleed valve about one-half turn and pump the brake bleeder.

NOTE
If air is entering the brake bleeder hose from around the bleed valve, apply several layers of Teflon tape to the bleed valve. This should make a good seal between the bleed valve and the brake bleeder hose.

8. As the fluid enters the system and exits into the brake bleeder the level will drop in the reservoir. Maintain the level at about 3/8 inch from the top of the reservoir to prevent air from being drawn into the system.

9. Continue to pump the lever on the brake bleeder until the fluid emerging from the hose is completely free of bubbles. At this point, tighten the bleed valve.

NOTE
Do not allow the reservoir to empty during the bleeding operation or more air will enter the system. If this occurs, the entire procedure must be repeated.

10. When the brake fluid is free of bubbles, tighten the bleed valve, remove the brake bleeder tube and install the bleed valve dust cap.
11. If necessary, add fluid to correct the level in the reservoir. It should be to the upper level line.
12. Install the diaphragm, plate (models so equipped) and the reservoir cover. Tighten the screws securely.

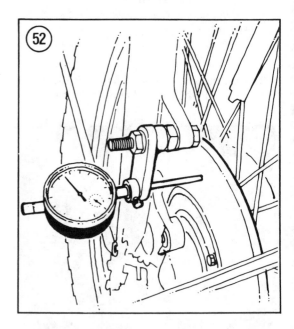

13. Test the feel of the brake lever or pedal. It should be firm and should offer the same resistance each time it's operated. If it feels spongy, it is likely that there is still air in the system and it must be bled again. When all air has been bled from the reservoir, double-check for leaks and tighten all fittings and connections.

> *WARNING*
> *Before riding the bike, make certain that the brake is operating correctly by operating the lever several times.*

14. Test ride the bike slowly at first to make sure that the brakes are operating properly.

Without a Brake Bleeder

1. On 1988-1990 XR600R models, perform the following:
   a. Remove the dust cap from the bleed valve on the master cylinder reservoir.
   b. Connect the brake bleeder to the bleed valve on the master cylinder reservoir.

c. Perform Steps 2-12 and bleed the air from the master cylinder.
   d. After the master cylinder has been bled, perform Steps 2-12 and bleed the caliper assembly.
2. Remove the dust cap from the bleed valve on the caliper assembly.
3. Connect the bleed hose to the bleed valve on the caliper assembly (**Figure 55**).
4. Place the other end of the tube into a clean container. Fill the container with enough fresh brake fluid to keep the end submerged. The tube should be long enough so that a loop can be made higher than the bleed valve to prevent air from being drawn into the caliper during bleeding.

> *CAUTION*
> *Cover the front fender and front wheel with a heavy cloth or plastic tarp to protect it from the accidental spilling of brake fluid. Wash any brake fluid off of any plastic, painted or plated surface immediately; as it will destroy the finish. Use soapy water and rinse completely.*

5. Clean the top of the master cylinder of all dirt and foreign matter.
6. Remove the screws securing the reservoir cover and remove the reservoir cover, plate (models so equipped) and diaphragm.
7. Fill the reservoir almost to the cover lip; insert the diaphragm, plate (models so equipped) and the cover loosely. Leave the cover in place during this procedure to prevent the entry of dirt.

> *WARNING*
> *Use brake fluid from a sealed container marked DOT 3 or DOT 4 only (specified for disc brakes). Other types may vaporize and cause brake failure. Do not intermix different brands or types as they may not be compatible. Do not intermix a silicone based (DOT 5) brake fluid as it can cause brake component damage leading to brake system failure.*

8. Slowly apply the brake lever several times as follows:
   a. Pull the lever in. Hold the lever in the applied position.
   b. Open the bleed valve about one-half turn. All the lever to travel to its limit.
   c. When this limit is reached, tighten the bleed screws.

11

9. As the fluid enters the system, the level will drop in the reservoir. Maintain the level at about 3/8 inch from the cover of the reservoir to prevent air from being drawn into the system.

10. Continue to pump the lever and fill the reservoir until the fluid emerging from the hose is completely free of bubbles.

NOTE
Do not allow the reservoir to empty during the bleeding operation or more air will enter the system. If this occurs, the entire procedure must be repeated.

11. Hold the lever in, tighten the bleed valve, remove the bleed tube and install the bleed valve dust cap.

12. If necessary, add fluid to correct the level in the reservoir. It should be to the upper level line.

13. Install the diaphragm, plate (models so equipped) and reservoir cover. Tighten the screws securely.

14. Test the feel of the brake lever. It should be firm and should offer the same resistance each time it's operated. If it feels spongy, it is likely that there is still air in the system and it must be bled again. When all air has been bled from the system and the fluid level is correct in the reservoir, double-check for leaks and tighten all fittings and connections.

WARNING
Before riding the bike, make certain that the brakes are operating correctly by operating the lever or pedal several times.

15. Test ride the bike slowly at first to make sure that the brakes are operating properly.

REAR DRUM BRAKE

Disassembly

1. Remove the rear wheel as described in Chapter Ten.

2. Pull the brake assembly straight up and out of the brake drum.

3. Prior to removing the brake shoes, inspect them as described under *Inspection* in this chapter.

4. Place a clean shop rag on the linings to protect them from oil and grease during removal.

5. Remove the brake shoes from the backing plate. Pull up on the center of each shoe as shown in **Figure 56**.

6. Remove the return springs and separate the brake shoes.

7. Remove the bolt and nut securing the brake arm and remove the brake arm, wear indicator and dust seal. Withdraw the camshaft from the backing plate.

Inspection

1. Thoroughly clean and dry all parts except the brake linings.

2. Check the contact surface of the drum (**Figure 57**) for scoring. If there are grooves deep enough to snag your fingernail the drum should be reground.

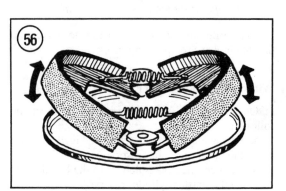

3. Measure the inside diameter of the brake drum with a vernier caliper (**Figure 58**). If the measurement is greater than the service limit listed in **Table 1** the brake drum must be replaced.

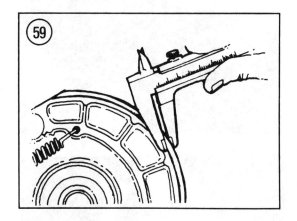

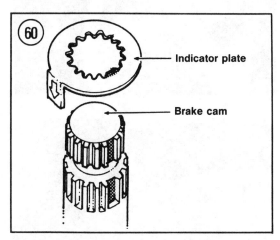

4. If the drum can be turned and still stay within the maximum service limit diameter, the linings will have to be replaced and the new ones arced to conform to the new drum contour.
5. Measure the brake linings with a vernier caliper (**Figure 59**). They should be replaced if the lining portion is worn to the service limit dimension or less. Refer to specifications listed in **Table 1**.
6. Inspect the linings for embedded foreign material. Dirt can be removed with a stiff wire brush. Check for any traces of oil or grease; if they are contaminated they must be replaced.
7. Inspect the cam lobe and pivot pin area of the backing plate for wear or corrosion. Minor roughness can be removed with fine emery cloth.
8. Inspect the brake shoe return springs for wear. If they are stretched, they will not fully retract the brake shoes. Replace as necessary.

Assembly

1. Grease the camshaft with a light coat of molybdenum disulfide grease. Install the cam into the backing plate from the backside.
2. From the outside of the backing plate install the dust seal.
3. Align the wear indicator to the camshaft as shown in **Figure 60** and push it down all the way to the backing plate.
4. When installing the brake arm onto the camshaft, be sure to align the punch marks on the two parts (**Figure 61**). Tighten the bolt and nut securely.
5. Grease the camshaft and pivot post with a light coat of molybdenum disulfide grease; avoid getting any grease on the brake backing plate where the brake linings may come in contact with it.

11

> *NOTE*
> *If new linings are being installed, file off the leading edge of each shoe a little so that the brake will not grab when applied.*

6. Hold the brake shoes in a "V" formation with the return springs attached and snap them into place on the brake backing plate. Make sure they are firmly seated on it.
7. Install the brake panel assembly into the brake drum.
8. Install the rear wheel as described in Chapter Nine.
9. Adjust the rear brake as described in Chapter Three.

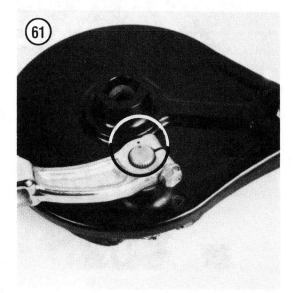

BRAKE CABLE
(DRUM BRAKE MODELS)

Front brake adjustment should be checked at the interval listed in Chapter Three as the cable stretches with use and increases brake lever free play. Free play is the distance that the brake lever travels between the released position and the point when the brake shoes come in contact with the brake drum.

If the brake adjustment described in Chapter Three can no longer be achieved, the brake cable must be replaced.

Front Cable Replacement

1. At the brake lever, loosen the locknut (A, **Figure 62**) and turn the adjuster (B, **Figure 62**) all the way into the cable sheath.
2. At the brake panel assembly, loosen the locknut (A) and loosen the adjusting nut (B). Refer to **Figure 63** or **Figure 64**.
3. Disconnect the cable from the backing plate.
4. Pull the hand lever all the way back to the grip. Remove the cable nipple holder and remove the cable from the lever.

NOTE
Prior to removing the brake cable, make a drawing (or take a Polaroid picture) of the cable routing through the frame. It is very easy to forget how it was, once the cable has been removed. Replace the cable exactly as it was, avoiding any sharp turns.

5. On models so equipped, remove the screws on cable clip and remove the cabale from the clip on the front fork (**Figure 65**) and front fork.

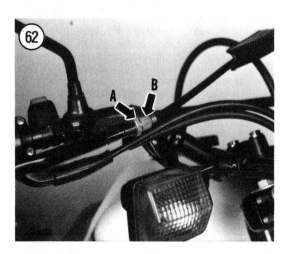

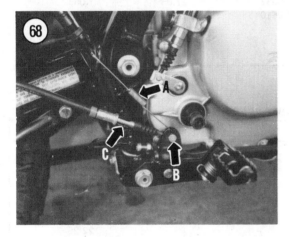

6. Remove the brake cable from the loops on the front fork (**Figure 66**).

7. Install by reversing these removal steps.

8. Adjust the front brake as described in Chapter Three.

Rear Cable Replacement (Models So Equipped)

1. At the brake panel assembly, unscrew the adjusting nut and the cable retainer (A, **Figure 67**).

2. At the brake panel, remove the brake light switch spring (A, **Figure 68**) from the cable end.

3. Remove the cable and retainer (B, **Figure 68**) from the brake pedal.

4. Pull the rear end of the cable out from the guide on the swing arm (B, **Figure 67**) and the frame guide (C, **Figure 68**).

> *NOTE*
> *Prior to removing the brake cable, make a drawing of the cable routing through the frame. It is very easy to forget how it was, once the cable has been removed. Replace the cable exactly as it was, avoiding any sharp turns.*

5. Install by reversing these removal steps.

6. Adjust the rear brake as described in Chapter Three.

11

Table 1 DRUM BRAKE SPECIFICATIONS

	Standard		Service limit	
	mm	in.	mm	in.
Front brake drum ID				
XL500S, XR500	140.0	5.51	141.0	5.55
XL500R, XR500R	130.0	5.12	131.0	5.16
Rear brake drum ID				
XR600R	110.0	4.33	111.0	4.37
All other models	130.0	5.12	131.0	5.16
Brake shoe thickness	4.0	0.16	2.0	0.08

Table 2 DISC BRAKE SPECIFICATIONS

Model	Standard		Service limit	
	mm	in.	mm	in.
Master cylinder				
1983-1984 XR500R, XL600R				
ID	12.7-12.743	0.5000-0.5017	12.755	0.5022
Piston OD	12.657-12.684	0.4983-0.4994	12.640	0.4976
XR600R				
ID	11.0-11.043	0.4330-0.4348	11.06	0.435
Piston OD	10.957-10.984	0.4314-0.4324	10.770	0.428
Caliper				
1983-1984 XR500R, XL600R				
ID	25.400-25.405	1.000-1.0002	25.45	1.002
Piston OD	25.318-25.368	0.9968-0.9987	25.30	0.9996
XR600R				
ID	27.000-27.005	1.0630-1.0632	27.05	1.065
Piston OD	26.900-26.950	1.0591-1.0610	26.85	1.057
Brake disc				
Thickness	3.5	0.14	3.0	0.12
Runout	–	–	0.30	0.012

Table 3 BRAKE TORQUE SPECIFICATIONS

Item	N•m	ft.-lb.
Drum brakes		
Brake cam and arm		
bolts and nuts	8-12	6-9
Caliper mounting bolts		
Upper and lower	20-30	15-22
Pin bolts	15-20	11-15
Caliper union bolt	30-40	22-29
Master cylinder		
Fitting	12-15	9-11
Union bolt	30-40	22-29
XL600R		
Brake hose-to-master		
cylinder	30-40	22-29
Brake disc mounting		
Bolt or nuts	14-16	10-12

INDEX

12

12

WIRING
DIAGRAMS

1979-1980 XR500

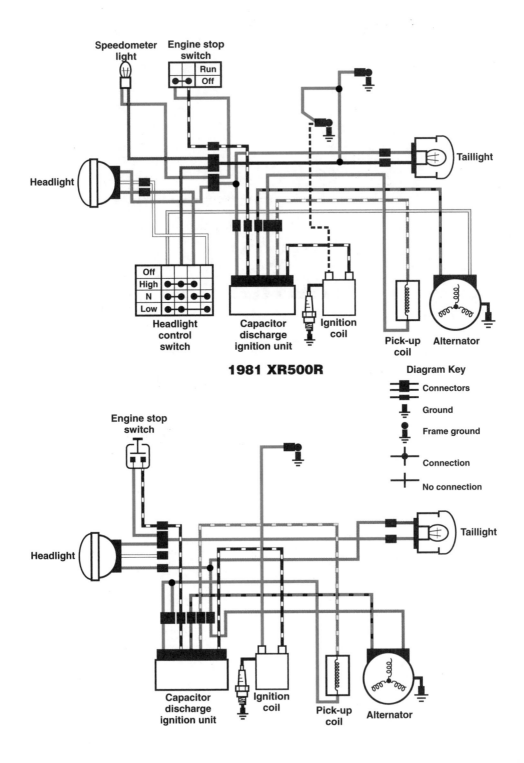

1981 XR500R

1983-1984 XR500R

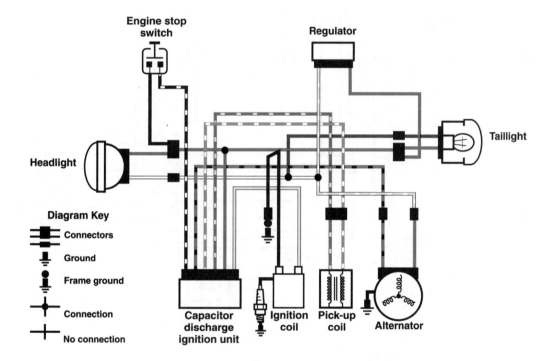

1979-1981 XL500S

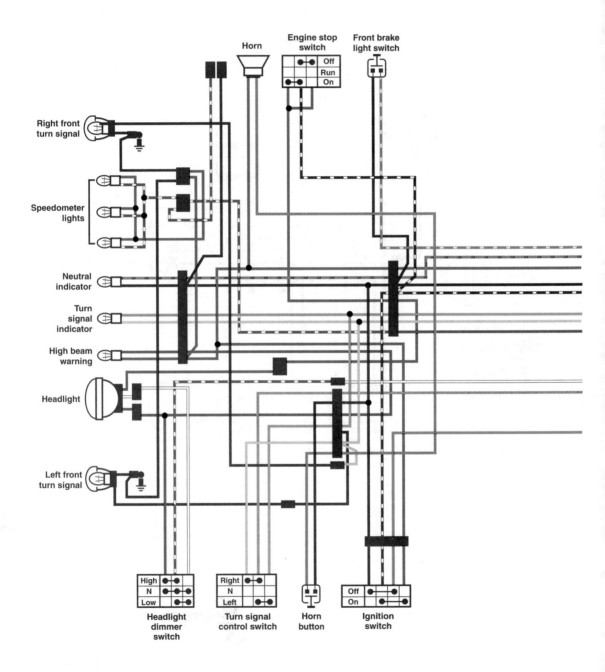

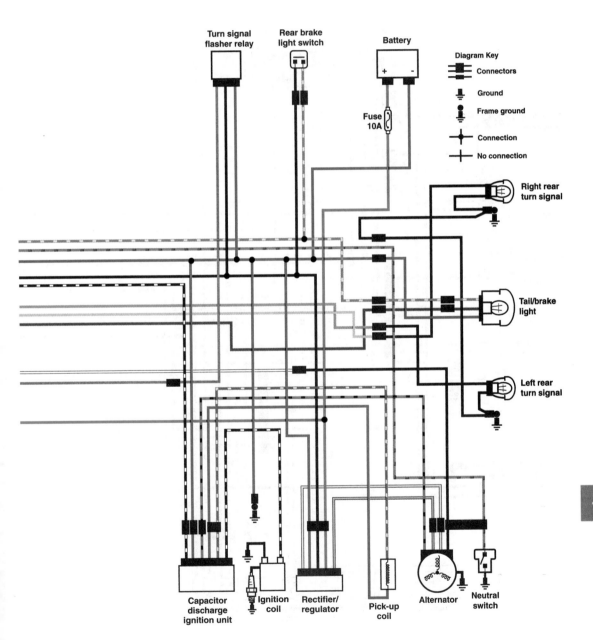

13

1982 XL500R

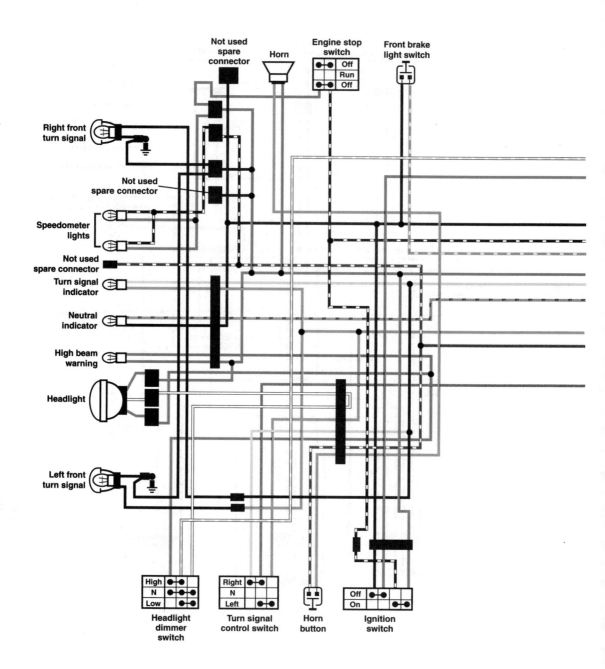

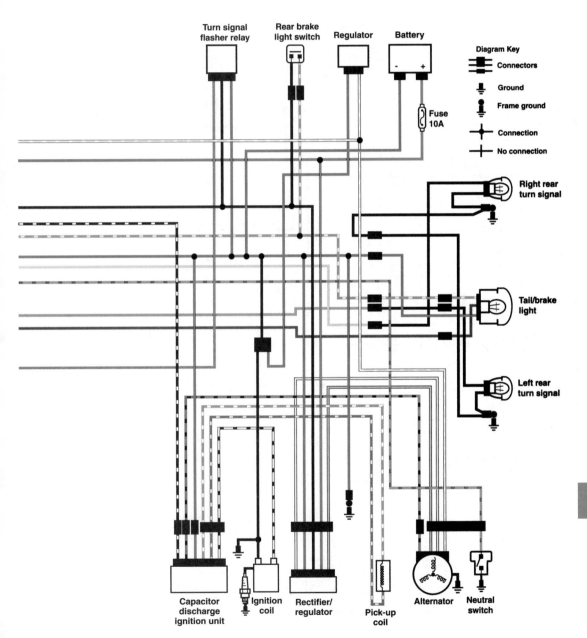

1983-1985 XL600R

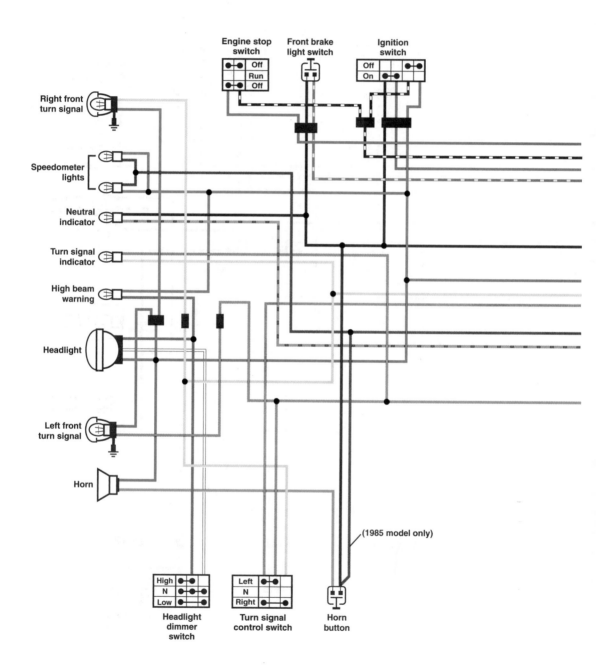

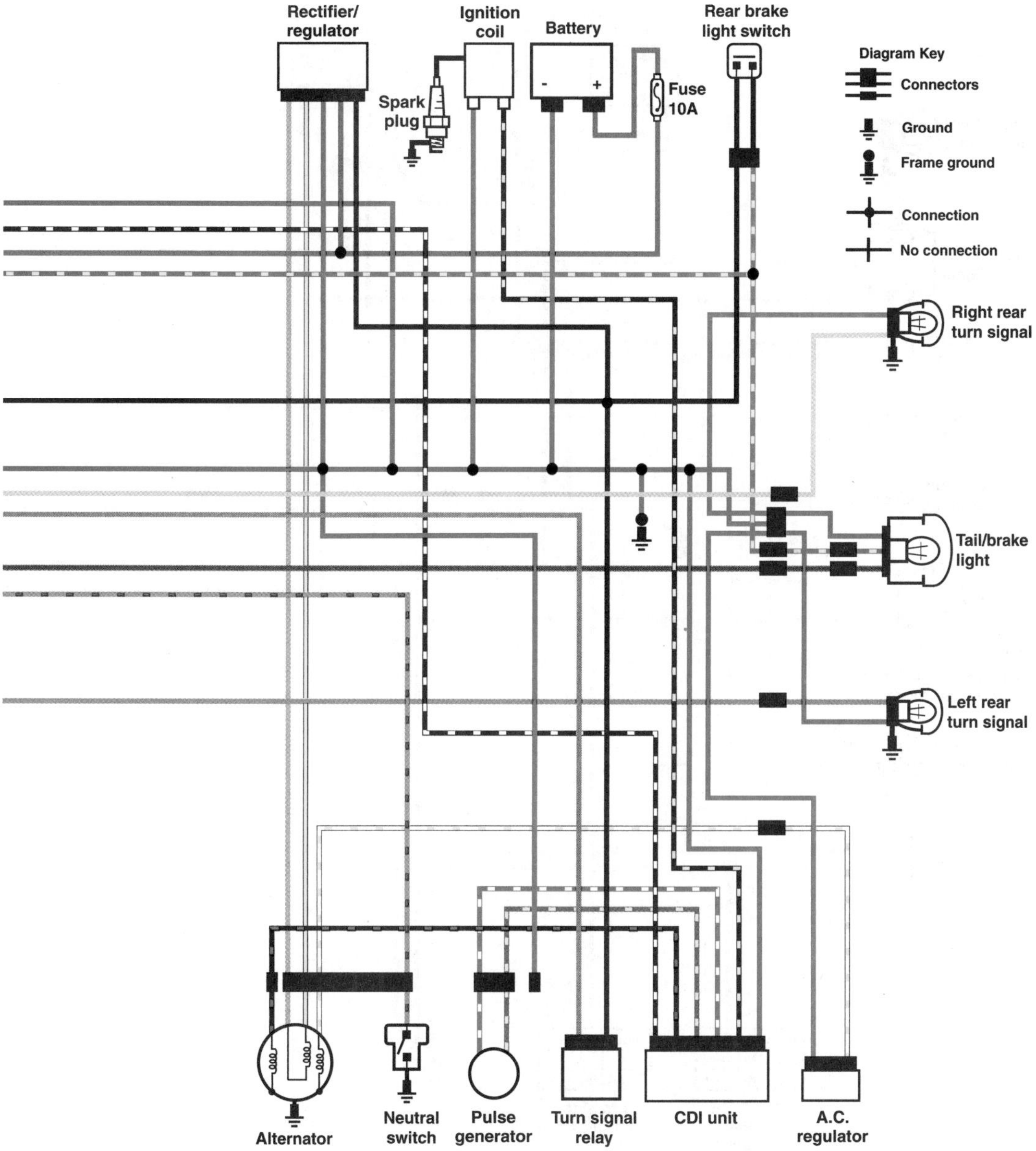

Rectifier/
regulator

Ignition
coil

Battery

Rear brake
light switch

Spark
plug

Fuse
10A

Diagram Key

Connectors

Ground

Frame ground

Connection

No connection

Right rear
turn signal

Tail/brake
light

Left rear
turn signal

Alternator

Neutral
switch

Pulse
generator

Turn signal
relay

CDI unit

A.C.
regulator

13

1986-1987 XL600R

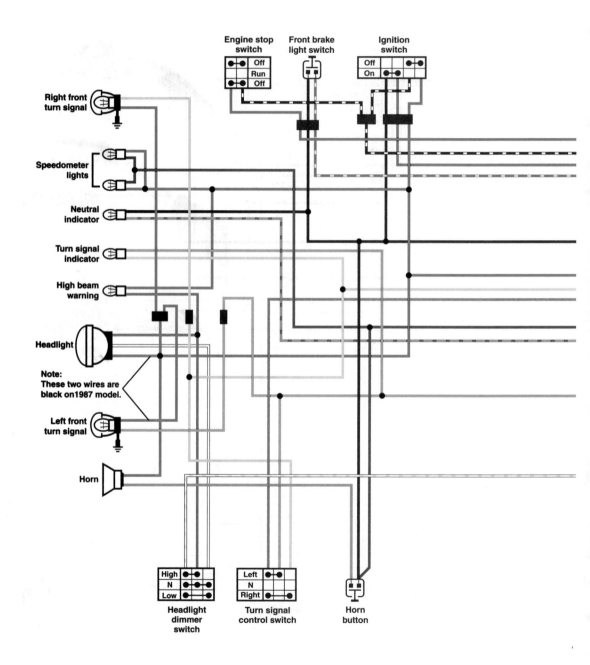

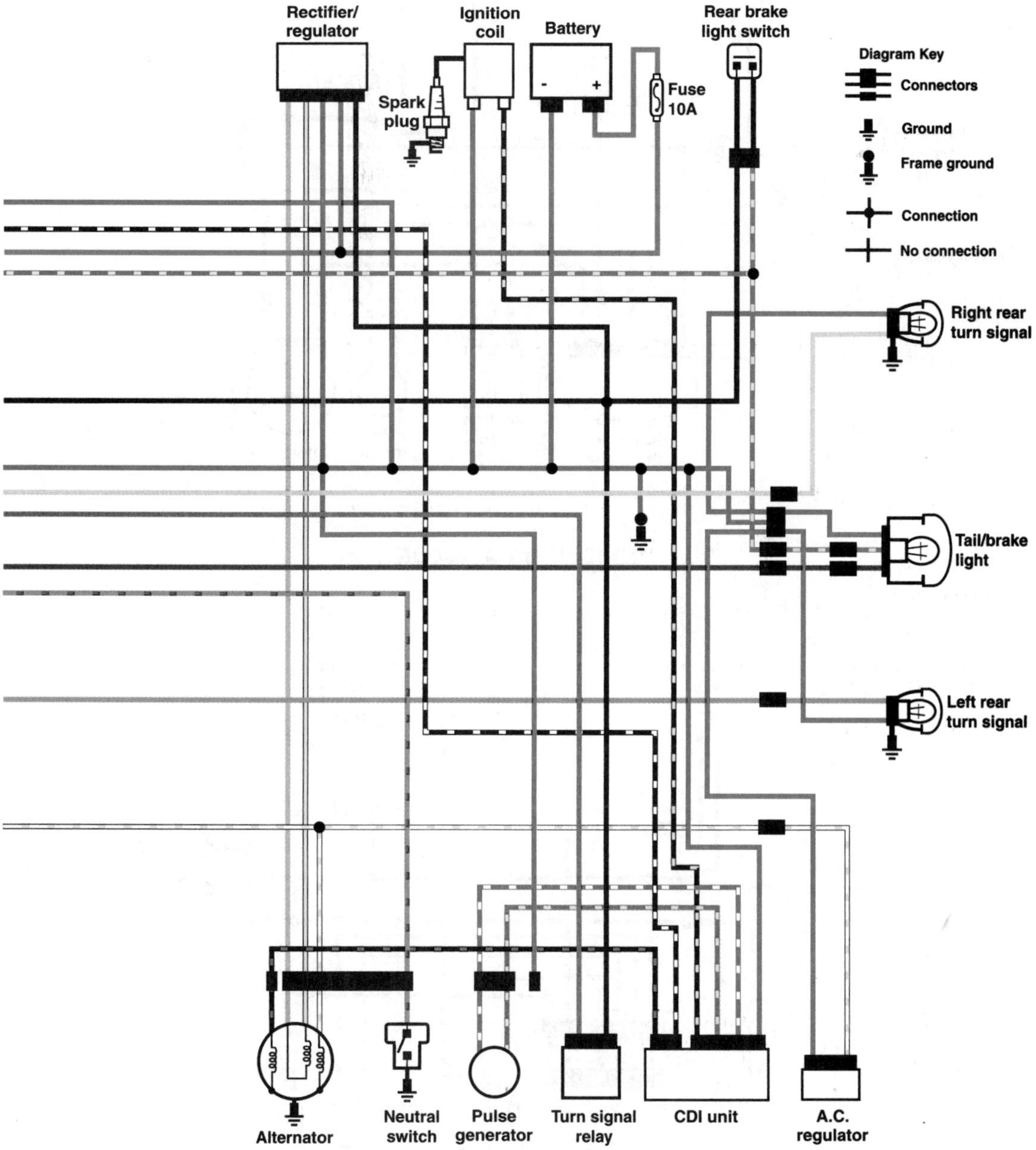

Rectifier/regulator

Ignition coil

Battery

Rear brake light switch

Spark plug

Fuse 10A

Diagram Key

Connectors

Ground

Frame ground

Connection

No connection

Right rear turn signal

Tail/brake light

Left rear turn signal

Alternator

Neutral switch

Pulse generator

Turn signal relay

CDI unit

A.C. regulator

13

1985-1987 XR600R

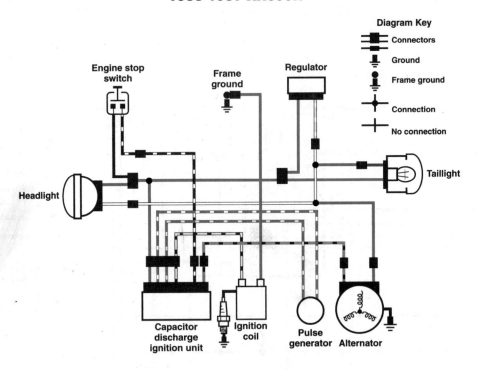

1988-1990 XR600R

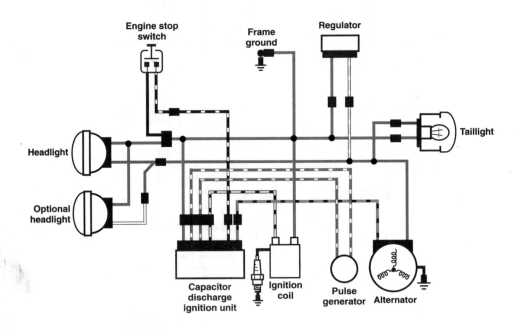